MODERN AMERICAN DIPLOMACY

MODERN

AMERICAN

DIPLOMACY

EDWARD O. GUERRANT

The University of New Mexico Press - Albuquerque

Also by Edward O. Guerrant:

ROOSEVELT'S GOOD NEIGHBOR POLICY

To My Mother and My Father

PREFACE

THIS VOLUME is designed to serve as a text or as a supplementary text in American foreign policy. I have endeavored to trace the major aspects of the foreign policy of the United States from the years just prior to the turn of the present century, when various groups of American citizens envisioned this nation as a future world power, until 1954, after the United States had attained a position of world leadership.

This book is largely a collection of documents, selected from a mass of material which could have been included except for space limitations. My purpose is to furnish the student with material written or spoken by men who formed our policy, or by those whose contemporary comments are highly relevant to a better understanding of our actions. In the opinion of the writer, no later account is an adequate substitute for original documents—if one is to capture the spirit and feeling of the times when the events themselves transpired. In conjunction with these selections I have written introductory summaries for each of the eighteen chapters. In these summaries, I have attempted to point out the major objectives of American foreign policy and the measures taken to achieve those goals. I would like to emphasize the fact, however, that these introductions are no more than that. They were included to furnish the student with the main thread in the tangled web of American diplomatic history and as an aid to a greater understanding of the documents.

Although any volume destined for use at the college and university level is obviously written for the purpose of serving the needs of the student, I intended to produce a book which would also appeal to the instructor. In deciding on the ratio of approximately one to four for textual and documentary material, I planned to produce a work which would allow the professor a maximum degree of flexibility in expanding and explaining the introductory surveys and documents in his classroom lectures.

Acknowledgments

It would be impossible to mention the names of all the persons who have in some measure been responsible for the writing of this volume. The list would include all those who by a word of encouragement or a pertinent bit of advice have had a share in the final product. There are several persons, however, who have devoted many hours and days of their time to a careful reading of certain parts or all of the manuscript; and to them I would like to express my sincere gratitude and acknowledge their most valuable assistance. Professor Thomas A. Bailey, Chairman of the Department of History at Stanford University; Professor Donald W. Rowland, Chairman of the Department of History at the University of Southern California; and Professor Richard W. Van Alstyne, Department of History at the University of Southern California each have made a number of very pertinent suggestions which have been incorporated into this volume. These men, of course, are not responsible for any errors I may have made or for any of my interpretations.

Several members of my family also rendered assistance which I gratefully acknowledge. My brother, Peter D. Guerrant, Jr., read all the introductory material for the purpose of checking clarity and style. My wife, Charlotte, and my daughter, Helen, spent many dreary hours aiding me in checking the accuracy of the manuscript copy with the original documents.

I also acknowledge the kindness of the following persons and publishers in graciously permitting the reproduction of copyrighted and other materials in this volume:

The Atlantic Monthly: for an excerpt from "The Isthmus and Sea Power," by A. T. Mahan. *Foreign Affairs:* for excerpts from "The Sources of Soviet Conduct," by X; and for excerpts from "The Challenge to Americans," by Henry L. Stimson. Harper and Brothers: for a selection from *On Active Service in Peace and War* by Henry L. Stimson and McGeorge Bundy, copyright, 1947, 1948, by Henry L. Stimson; for a selection from *The Public Papers and Addresses of Franklin D. Roosevelt,* compiled with Special Material and Explanatory Notes by Samuel I. Rosenman, copyright, 1950, by Samuel I. Rosenman; for selections from *Roosevelt and Hopkins* by Robert E. Sherwood; and for excerpts from an article, "Our 'Dollar Diplomacy' and Secretary Knox,"

by An American Diplomat, which appeared in *Harper's Weekly,*
April 23, 1910. Houghton Mifflin Company: for an excerpt from
a speech by Albert J. Beveridge in *Beveridge and the Progressive
Era* by Claude Bowers. Daniel Mebane, publisher of the *New
Republic:* for a quotation from *Willard Straight* by Herbert
Croly, published by The Macmillan Company. *The New York
Times:* for several speeches by Franklin D. Roosevelt and the
text of the Axis Pact signed by Germany, Italy, and Japan. Fleming H. Revell Company: for a quotation from *The New Era or
the Coming Kingdom,* by Josiah Strong, published by the Baker
and Taylor Company. Charles Scribner's Sons: for excerpts from
a letter from Theodore Roosevelt to Henry Cabot Lodge from
*Selections from the Correspondence of Roosevelt and Lodge
1884-1918.* Mrs. Joseph W. Stilwell: for a selection from *The
Stilwell Papers* by Joseph W. Stilwell, edited by Theodore H.
White, and published by W. Sloane Associates. *Vital Speeches:*
for excerpts from "An Appeal for Peace," by Charles A. Lindbergh; and for excerpts from "Neutrality: the Immediate Problem," by Walter Lippmann. *The Washington Post:* for excerpts
from a speech by Dwight D. Eisenhower. World Peace Foundation: for selections from Vols. I and II, *Documents on American
Foreign Relations,* edited by Shepard S. Jones and Denys P.
Myers.

EDWARD O. GUERRANT

April, 1954
Davidson College
Davidson, North Carolina

CONTENTS

MODERN AMERICAN DIPLOMACY

CHAPTER I

AMERICAN EXPANSIONISM

IN 1898, several months before he was elected to the Senate of the United States, Albert J. Beveridge told an enthusiastic Boston audience that

"American factories are making more than the American people can use; American soil is producing more than they can consume. Fate has written our policy for us; the trade of the world must and shall be ours. And we shall get it as our mother [England] has told us how. We will establish trading posts throughout the world as distributing-points for American products. We will cover the ocean with our merchant marine. We will build a navy to the measure of our greatness. Great colonies governing themselves, flying our flag and trading with us, will grow about our posts of trade. Our institutions will follow our flag on the wings of our commerce. And American law, American order, American civilization, and the American flag will plant themselves on shores hitherto bloody and benighted, but by those agencies of God to be made beautiful and bright."[1]

That anyone in the United States could have made such a statement at the turn of the century to a receptive audience was indicative of the profound change in American thinking that had taken place during the latter years of the nineteenth century. The War Hawks of 1812 and the Manifest Destiny men of the 1840's had been aggressively expansionistic, but very few of them visualized American civilization as an evangelistic faith destined to encircle the globe. And during the decades immediately preceding the 1890's many Americans were hardly conscious of the fact that this nation was even part of the world.

From the end of the Civil War until the late 1880's, the energies and interests of the American people had been devoted almost entirely to domestic matters. The South was concerned primarily with the problems created by the war and reconstruction. The North and East were becoming highly industrialized. And the West, rich in mineral and agricultural resources, was a land of

[1] Claude G. Bowers, *Beveridge and the Progressive Era,* p. 69.

opportunity for tens of thousands of those who were discontented
with their lot in the more settled regions.

Because of an ever-expanding market and the coming of the
Industrial Revolution to America, some businessmen of moderate
means in 1860 were multimillionaires by the 1890's. Statesmen
such as Webster, Calhoun, Clay, and Jackson had dominated the
American scene before the Civil War, but the history of this country after 1865 largely revolved around such figures as Rockefeller,
Carnegie, Huntington, Flagler, and Vanderbilt. The big men
were in business. They were intent on amassing fortunes from the
boundless wealth of this country, and they were not diverted from
that goal by any major foreign problems.

The Spanish-American War demonstrated to the world that
this period of intense preoccupation with domestic affairs had
ended in the United States. But for a decade prior to that conflict,
life in America had been undergoing a subtle change, and numerous voices were preaching the gospel that our destiny was to
spread our civilization and to exert our influence into the far cor-
ners of the globe. Historians, such as John Fiske, and political
scientists, like John W. Burgess, who had come under the influence
of Darwin and Gobineau, taught the superiority of Anglo-Saxon
institutions and pointed up our duty to spread this culture throughout the world. Theologians thought of our peoples as God's chosen
instrument to spread Christianity to foreign lands. Captain Alfred
T. Mahan, of the United States Navy, an authority on the role
of sea power on the course of history, clearly demonstrated the
necessity for America to become a major power by increasing the
size of its navy and expanding its trade. And men of politics like
Theodore Roosevelt and Henry Cabot Lodge, sensitive to the
vital influences of the age, were enthusiastic supporters of the new
religion of expansion. American businessmen, fearing the economic instability that might flow from unbridled expansion, lagged
behind the academicians, politicians, and journalists in pressing for
a more aggressive overseas policy. Not until the outbreak of the
war with Spain did the spokesmen for American business climb
aboard the bandwagon.

These new winds of American thought found tangible outlet
in the Spanish-American War. The American people looked on
the conflict as a crusade for "justice" in Cuba and they were eager
to enter the fray; but the problems of making peace first startled
and then divided the nation.

American statesmen were not only called upon to right the "wrongs" perpetrated against the Cuban peoples, but they were also under pressure to satisfy the desires of the expansionists who demanded the annexation of certain parts of the Spanish Empire. The disposition of Spanish possessions in the Caribbean was a relatively simple matter, but the Philippine Islands were annexed only after bitter debate. The expansionists, intoxicated by the prevailing theories concerning America's destiny and the ease of our victory over Spain, carried the day in the Senate. But the opposition, composed of many Democrats and the nonpartisan Anti-Imperialist League, pointed out the inconsistency between the war and peace aims of the nation and argued that the annexation of alien peoples would bring about the destruction of our representative form of government and was contrary to our best traditions.

The expansionists of 1898 were victorious. Possibly the majority of the American people, who before the war had no more knowledge or interest in the Philippine Archipelago than they had in Madagascar or the Celebes, were thrilled at the visible evidence of our growing importance as a world power. The United States had not come of age in 1898; but it had reached the stage of lusty adolescence. The nation was young, strong and confident. Its peoples, proud of its past accomplishments, looked enthusiastically to the future. But like an adolescent, the American people, excited by the sense of their potential power and dimly aware of great goals ahead, failed to realize the complexity of the problems and the responsibilities that come with power and influence.

1. Mahan—The Importance of Sea Power

Captain Alfred Thayer Mahan wrote extensively during the latter part of the nineteenth century on the general subject of the influence of sea power on the history of the world. Mahan's philosophy, which was respected by such men as Theodore Roosevelt, Henry Cabot Lodge, Elihu Root, and John Hay, was based on the concept that world power was predicated on economic power which in turn rested on control of the seas. Consequently he advocated the creation of a navy sufficiently powerful to allow the United States to realize its potential as a great world power.[2]

[2] A. T. Mahan, "The Isthmus and Sea Power," *The Atlantic Monthly*, LXXII (October, 1893), pp. 459-72.

"Under this increased importance of the Isthmus, we cannot safely anticipate for the future the cheap acquiescence which, under very different circumstances, has in the past been yielded to our demands. Already it is notorious that European powers are betraying symptoms of increased sensitiveness as to the importance of Caribbean positions, and strengthening their grip upon those they now hold. Moral considerations undoubtedly count for more than they did, and nations are more reluctant to enter into war; but still, the policy of states is determined by the balance of advantages, and it behooves us to know what our policy is to be, and what advantages are needed to turn in our favor the scale of negotiations and the general current of events.

"If the decision of the nation, following one school of thought, is that the weaker we are the more likely we are to have our way, there is little to be said. Drifting is perhaps as good a mode as another to reach that desirable goal. If, on the other hand, we determine that our interests and dignity require that our rights should depend upon the will of no other state, but upon our own power to enforce them, we must gird ourselves to admit that freedom of inter-oceanic transit depends upon predominance in a maritime region—the Caribbean Sea—through which pass all the approaches to the Isthmus. Control of a maritime region is insured primarily by a navy; secondarily, by positions, suitably chosen and spaced one from the other, upon which as bases the navy rests, and from which it can exert its strength. At present the positions of the Caribbean are occupied by foreign powers, nor may we, however, disposed to acquisition, obtain them by means other than righteous; but a distinct advance will have been made when public opinion is convinced that we need them, and should not exert our utmost ingenuity to dodge them when flung at our head. If the Constitution really imposed difficulties, it provides also a way by which the people, if convinced, can remove its obstructions. A protest, however, may be entered against a construction of the Constitution which is liberal, by embracing all it can be constrained to imply, and then immediately becomes strict in imposing these ingeniously contrived fetters.

"Meanwhile, no moral obligation forbids developing our navy upon lines and proportions adequate to the work it may be called upon to do. Here again the crippling force is a public impression, which limits our potential strength to the necessities of an imperfectly realized situation. A navy 'for defense only,' is a popular catchword. When, if ever, people recognize that we have three seaboards, that the communication by water of one of them with the other two will in a not remote future depend upon a strategic position hundreds of miles distant from our nearest port, at the mouth of the Mississippi, they will also see that the word 'defense' already too narrowly understood, has its application at points far away from our own coast.

"That the organization of military strength implies provocation to war is a fallacy, which the experience of each succeeding year is now refuting.

The immense armaments of Europe are onerous; but, nevertheless, by the mutual respect and caution they enforce, they present a cheap alternative, certainly in misery, probably in money, to the frequent devastating wars which preceded the era of general military preparation. Our own impunity has resulted, not from our weakness, but from the unimportance to our rivals of the points in dispute, compared with their more immediate interests at home. With the changes consequent upon the canal, this indifference will diminish. We also shall be entangled in the affairs of the great family of nations, and shall have to accept the attendant burdens. Fortunately, as regards other states, we are an island power, and can find our best precedents in the history of the people to whom the sea has been a nursing mother."

2. *The Destiny of the Anglo-Saxon Race*

Josiah Strong, a Congregational clergyman, at one time Secretary of the Evangelical Society of the United States, and a rather prolific writer during the late nineteenth century, was one of a number of persons who vigorously supported the theory that the Anglo-Saxons were God's chosen people to spread Christianity throughout the world, by force if necessary.[3]

"No nation can now become or remain a first-class power without an adequate physical basis. The time has not yet come when the nations will consent to be controlled wholly by considerations of right and reason. It is still true that the argument is on the side of the heaviest battalions; still true among nations that the weight of an opinion depends much on the fighting weight of the government which utters it. Before the machinery of war was invented the strength, skill, and bravery of the individual soldier were everything. Now they count for comparatively little. The wars of the future will be won or lost by the national treasury, the patent office, and the census department. It is devoutly to be hoped that the various branches of the Anglo-Saxon race will sustain such relations to each other in the future that their overwhelming superiority of power will be able to compel the world's peace and deliver the nations from the vampire of militarism.

"Imagine all the races of Europe transformed into one blood, their babel of sixty tongues hushed, and the custom-houses of a score of frontiers closed. Imagine these many lands occupied by 380,000,000 Anglo-Saxons, speaking one language, having common institutions and interests, and all under one government. The mightiest empire that ever existed would be but a faint suggestion of the resistless power of such a people. But this is only a picture of what the United States will be one century hence. All Europe, including the vast plains of Russia, may be laid down within our national bounds, and by a conservative estimate we shall have a population of 373,000,000 in 1990.

[3] Josiah Strong, *The New Era or the Coming Kingdom,* pp. 74-80.

'A hundred years hence,' says the late Émile de Laveleye, 'leaving China out of the question, there will be two colossal powers in the world, beside which Germany, England, France, and Italy will be as pygmies—the United States and Russia.' But Russia is scarcely worthy to be named in this connection. She will be great in numbers, but can hardly become a rival to Anglo-Saxondom in any other respect. Her civilization is Asiatic rather than European. It suppresses the individual. Such an empire can never excel in the arts of peace without which she must remain poor, and lacking wealth her military power will be insignificant when compared with that of the Anglo-Saxon race. . . .

"In other important characteristics of the Anglo-Saxon race have Americans outgrown the English. Referring to individualism the eminent author just quoted [James Bryce] says: 'Everything tended to make the United States in this respect more English than England, for the circumstances of colonial life, the process of settling the western wilderness, the feelings evoked by the struggle against George III., all went to intensify individualism, the love of enterprise, the pride in personal freedom.' Many causes have here operated to intensify Anglo-Saxon energy and aggressiveness. A stimulating climate, the undeveloped resources of a continent, our social and political institutions, have all united to produce the most forceful and tremendous energy in the world. Archdeacon Farrar said in 1885: 'In America I have been most struck with the enormous power, vivacity, and speed in every department of exertion.' Moreover the colonizing tendency of this race is here intensified. It was those in whom this tendency was strongest who settled this country, and this inherited tendency has been further developed by the westward sweep of successive generations across the continent.

"Now what is the interpretation of these facts? It seems to me that God, with infinite wisdom and skill, is here training the Anglo-Saxon race for an hour sure to come in the world's future. Heretofore in the history of mankind there has always been a comparatively unoccupied land westward into which the crowded countries of the East have poured their surplus populations. But the widening waves of migration, which milleniums ago rolled east and west from the valley of the Euphrates, meet to-day on our Pacific Coast. There are no more new worlds. The unoccupied arable lands of the earth are limited, and will soon be taken. The time is coming when the pressure of population on the means of subsistence will be felt here as it is now felt in Europe and Asia. Then will the world enter on a new stage of its history— *the final competition of races, for which the Anglo-Saxon is being schooled.* Long before the thousand millions are here, the mighty centrifugal tendency inherent in this stock and strengthened in the United States will assert itself. Then this race of unequalled energy, with all the majesty of numbers and the might of wealth behind it—the representative, let us hope, of the largest liberty, the purest Christianity, the highest civilization—having developed peculiarly aggressive traits calculated to impress its institutions upon mankind, will spread itself over the earth. And can any one doubt that the result of this competition of races will be the survival of the fittest? Is it not reasonable to believe that this race is destined to dispossess many weaker ones, assimilate others, and mould the remainder, until, in a very true and important sense, it has Anglo-Saxonized mankind?"

3. McKinley's War Message to Congress

The expansionists of 1898 did not conspire to bring on the Spanish-American War, but they aided in the creation of a public opinion which literally demanded war with Spain. It is true that Spain had misgoverned Cuba, that a bloody rebellion had ravaged the island, and that the Spanish government did not appear to have either the political wisdom or physical strength to bring order out of chaos. But war between the United States and Spain was unnecessary. President William McKinley shunned the idea of war with Spain, but in view of a population rabid for war with Spain, and the possibility that Congress might declare war without a request by him, he sent a message to Congress on April 11, 1898, asking for the power to use the armed forces to bring peace to Cuba. On April 25, Congress declared that a state of war had been in existence since April 21. The following selections are excerpts from McKinley's April 11 message to Congress:[4]

"Obedient to that precept of the Constitution which commands the President to give from time to time to the Congress information of the state of the Union and to recommend to their consideration such measures as he shall judge necessary and expedient, it becomes my duty to now address your body with regard to the grave crisis that has arisen in the relations of the United States to Spain by reason of the warfare that for more than three years has raged in the neighboring Island of Cuba. . . .

"Since the present revolution began, in February, 1895, this country has seen the fertile domain at our threshold ravaged by fire and sword in the course of a struggle unequaled in the history of the island and rarely paralleled as to the numbers of the combatants and the bitterness of the contest by any revolution of modern times where a dependent people striving to be free have been opposed by the power of the sovereign state. . . .

"The war in Cuba is of such a nature that short of subjugation or extermination a final military victory for either side seems impracticable. The alternative lies in the physical exhaustion of the one or the other party, or perhaps of both—a condition which in effect ended the ten years' war by the truce of Zanjon. The prospect of such a protraction and conclusion of the

[4] *Congressional Record*, 55th Cong., 2nd Sess., Vol. XXXI, Part IV, pp. 3699-3702.

present strife is a contingency hardly to be contemplated with equanimity by the civilized world, and least of all by the United States, affected and injured as we are, deeply and intimately, by its very existence. . . .

"The forcible intervention of the United States as a neutral to stop the war, according to the large dictates of humanity and following many historical precedents where neighboring states have interfered to check the hopeless sacrifices of life by internecine conflicts beyond their borders, is justifiable on rational grounds. It involves, however, hostile constraint upon both the parties to the contest as well to enforce a truce as to guide the eventual settlement.

"The grounds for such intervention may be briefly summarized as follows:

"First. In the cause of humanity and to put an end to the barbarities, bloodshed, starvation, and horrible miseries now existing there, and which the parties to the conflict are either unable or unwilling to stop or mitigate. It is no answer to say this is all in another country, belonging to another nation, and is therefore none of our business. It is specially our duty, for it is right at our door.

"Second. We owe it to our citizens in Cuba to afford them that protection and indemnity for life and property which no government there can or will afford, and to that end to terminate the conditions that deprive them of legal protection.

"Third. The right to intervene may be justified by the very serious injury to the commerce, trade, and business of our people by the wanton destruction of property and devastation of the island.

"Fourth, and which is of utmost importance. The present condition of affairs in Cuba is a constant menace to our peace, and entails upon this Government an enormous expense. With such a conflict waged for years in an island so near us and with which our people have such trade and business relations—when the lives and liberties of our citizens are in constant danger and their property and themselves ruined—where our trading vessels are liable to seizure and are seized at our very door by war ships of a foreign nation, the expeditions of filibustering that we are powerless to prevent altogether, and the irritating questions and entanglements thus arising—all these and others that I need not mention, with the resulting strained relations, are a constant menace to our peace, and compel us to keep on a semiwar footing with a nation with which we are at peace. . . .

"In view of these facts and of these considerations, I ask the Congress to authorize and empower the President to take measures to secure a full and final termination of hostilities between the Government of Spain and the people of Cuba, and to secure in the island the establishment of a stable government, capable of maintaining order and observing its international obligations, insuring peace and tranquillity and the security of its citizens as well as our own, and to use the military and naval forces of the United States as may be necessary for these purposes.

"And in the interest of humanity and to aid in preserving the lives of the starving people of the island I recommend that the distribution of food and supplies be continued, and that an appropriation be made out of the public Treasury to supplement the charity of our citizens.

"The issue is now with the Congress. It is a solemn responsibility. I have exhausted every effort to relieve the intolerable condition of affairs which is at our doors. Prepared to execute every obligation imposed upon me by the Constitution and the law, I await your action.

"Yesterday, and since the preparation of the foregoing message, official information was received by me that the latest decree of the Queen Regent of Spain directs General Blanco, in order to prepare and facilitate peace, to proclaim a suspension of hostilities, the duration and details of which have not yet been communicated to me.

"This fact with every other pertinent consideration will, I am sure, have your just and careful attention in the solemn deliberations upon which you are about to enter. If this measure attains a successful result, then our aspirations as a Christian, peace-loving people will be realized. If it fails, it will be only another justification for our contemplated action."

4. *Argument Against Annexation of the Philippines*

The treaty ending the Spanish-American War was signed in Paris on December 10, 1898. The article providing for the annexation of the Philippine Islands by the United States provoked long and acrimonious debate. The Democratic Party and the Anti-Imperialist League constituted the strongest opposition to the ratification of the treaty. They contended that the annexation of alien peoples was contrary to American democratic tradition which was based on government by consent, that it would lead to the creation of a large standing army and raise taxes, and that it might ultimately tend to subvert our own representative form of government at home.

On February 3, 1899, three days before the treaty was ratified, John W. Daniel, Democratic Senator from Virginia, pointed out some of the main arguments against ratification in an address before the Senate:[5]

". . . We stand to-day by the bank of a broader and a deeper Rubicon than ever Caesar meditated beside. At our feet we hear the swash of the great Pacific Ocean, and beyond lies the expansionists' dream—Caesar's

[5] *Congressional Record,* 55th Cong., 3rd. Sess., Vol. XXXII, Part II, pp. 1431-32.

Rome. Caesar never did wrong without just cause. That is the imperialistic plea. America will not do wrong without a great temptation. That to-day is the emancipationists' plea. For my country I hope that she will ne'er do wrong.

"Let no glittering temptation of trade, let no gold from the gorgeous East tempt her eye or her hand. She stands to-day the foremost nation of the world. She stands to-day the foremost nation that ever the world has seen. Let her tread with secure and steady steps along her own highways, respecting nations and respecting men, putting into the dream of every child that goes to school that vision of liberty of which the Declaration is the great figure and of which the Constitution is the rock-bound foundation. Let her to the tempter of expansion to-day say, as He said, who stood upon the mount when the glories of the earth were stretched before Him, 'Get thee behind me, Satan.'

"Mr. President, peace! peace! This treaty is not a treaty of peace except in formal ceremony with Spain. It is a declaration of war against the Philippine people, not by Congress, but in necessary and logical effect. We know that the Filipinos are in arms. We know that they have an army of from 12,000 to 30,000. We know that they are seeking to work out their own destiny. The moment that this treaty is adopted the Filipinos are made citizens, and the moment they are made citizens, if they do not instantly lay down their arms they become rebels. The tie of allegiance is created with this Government, and when the President or Commander in Chief says, 'Our sovereignty is here; lay down your arms,' they bear them no longer, under the penalty of death.

"Mr. President, my country—may she ever be right; but my country, right or wrong. That is my doctrine. If the treaty is passed, I believe it is constitutional and authoritative. I do not deny the legal or constitutional right. I accept the fate and the decree of my country, and I stand with my people and my kind. At the same time I know what it means. I would that this cup might pass from us. There is a line of battle in the Philippine Islands of a dusky race, who have reared a flag and who have asked that they might be free. The moment this treaty passes, if they do not lay down their arms, it is the duty of the American President to order it, and it is the duty of the American soldier to shoot them to death and to make them lay down their arms under the penalty of execution in battle.

"I hope that may not happen. I pray it may not happen. But, oh, if it should happen, what a conclusion is that of a holy war and a righteous war begun for humanity and for liberty, and what justification has this nation before God and man? . . . .

"Mr. President, there be those who see an American scepter in the eastern sky. It may be that that scepter is there; but if that scepter be there, it is not a scepter that sparkles by the side of the star that shone over the manger of Bethlehem when the shepherds watched their flocks at night and when the wise men, looking over the Messiah, came.

"No, Mr. President; I would rather invoke to-day that star which hovered over old Independence Hall on the morning of that 4th of July, 1776, when the world waited the deliverance of a mighty message; I would point to that star, the star of the great northern Republic, founded by the great white race of the northern nations; I would say we go on no war of conquest; I would say that we respect the weakest and the most helpless of mankind; I would say to the men who are fighting for their freedom, be they many or be they few, be they in Cuba or be they in the Philippine Islands, that to them the great American Republic gives the salute of honor and dares not condescend to put her foot upon their necks.

"I would point again, Mr. President, to that bright star that beamed over Independence Hall in the bright morning of our birthright, and I would hope that ever hereafter we might say of it that of its—

—true-fix'd and resting quality
There is no fellow in the firmament.

"[Applause in the galleries.]"

5. *Treaty of Paris*

The Spanish-American War, which was officially declared by the United States on April 25, 1898, ended on August 12. Peace negotiations, which were begun on July 26, ended with the signing of the Treaty of Paris on December 10. The treaty was ratified on February 6, 1899.[6]

"Article I

"Spain relinquishes all claim of sovereignty over and title to Cuba.

"And as the island is, upon its evacuation by Spain, to be occupied by the United States, the United States will, so long as such occupation shall last, assume and discharge the obligations that may under international law result from the fact of its occupation, for the protection of life and property.

"Article II

"Spain cedes to the United States the island of Porto Rico and other islands now under Spanish sovereignty in the West Indies, and the island of Guam in the Marianas or Ladrones.

"Article III

"Spain cedes to the United States the archipelago known as the Philippine Islands, and comprehending the islands lying within the following line: . . . .

[6] *Compilation of Treaties in Force, 1904,* pp. 722-27.

"Article VI

"Spain will, upon the signature of the present treaty, release all prisoners of war, and all persons detained or imprisoned for political offenses, in connection with the insurrections in Cuba and the Philippines and the war with the United States.

"Reciprocally, the United States will release all persons made prisoners of war by the American forces, and will undertake to obtain the release of all Spanish prisoners in the hands of the insurgents in Cuba and the Philippines. . . .

"Article VII

"The United States and Spain mutually relinquish all claims for indemnity, national and individual, of every kind, of either Government, or of its citizens or subjects, against the other Government, that may have arisen since the beginning of the late insurrection in Cuba and prior to the exchange of ratifications of the present treaty, including all claims for indemnity for the cost of the war.

"The United States will adjudicate and settle the claims of its citizens against Spain relinquished in this article. . . .

"Article IX

"Spanish subjects, natives of the Peninsula, residing in the territory over which Spain by the present treaty relinquishes or cedes her sovereignty, may remain in such territory or may remove therefrom, retaining in either event all their rights of property, including the right to sell or dispose of such property or of its proceeds; and they shall also have the right to carry on their industry, commerce and professions, being subject in respect thereof to such laws as are applicable to other foreigners. In case they remain in the territory they may preserve their allegiance to the Crown of Spain by making, before a court of record, within a year from the date of the exchange of ratifications of this treaty, a declaration of their decision to preserve such allegiance; in default of which declaration they shall be held to have renounced it and to have adopted the nationality of the territory in which they may reside.

"The civil rights and political status of the native inhabitants of the territories hereby ceded to the United States shall be determined by the Congress.

"Article X

"The inhabitants of the territories over which Spain relinquishes or cedes her sovereignty shall be secured in the free exercise of their religion.

"Article XI

"The Spaniards residing in the territories over which Spain by this treaty cedes or relinquishes her sovereignty shall be subject in matters civil as well as criminal to the jurisdiction of the courts of the country wherein they reside, pursuant to the ordinary laws governing the same; and they shall have the right to appear before such courts, and to pursue the same course as citizens of the country to which the courts belong. . . .

"Article XV

"The Government of each country will, for the term of ten years, accord to the merchant vessels of the other country the same treatment in respect of all port charges, including entrance and clearance dues, light dues, and tonnage duties, as it accords to its own merchant vessels, not engaged in the coastwise trade.

"This article may at any time be terminated on six months' notice given by either Government to the other.

"Article XVI

"It is understood that any obligations assumed in this treaty by the United States with respect to Cuba are limited to the time of its occupancy thereof; but it will upon the termination of such occupancy, advise any Government established in the island to assume the same obligations. . . ."

CHAPTER II.

THE FAR EAST, 1898—1914

THE YEAR 1898 was a milestone in America's relations with the Far East. The Spanish-American War did not bring as drastic a change in our policy toward the Far East as it did toward the Caribbean area; but the acquisition of the Philippine Islands meant that the United States was now a Far Eastern power, not merely a nation with interests in that area as had been the case prior to the war.

China, as the largest, most populous nation of the Far East as well as its geographic center, had for well over a half a century before 1898 been the center of attraction for American interests. From 1844, when our first treaty was signed with China, the major objective of American policy had been to gain and retain for our citizens the same economic privileges granted by China to other powers. By 1898, however, the Government of China had become so weak, and the designs of the foreign powers with interests in China so extensive, that the collapse of China as an independent nation appeared imminent. The problem confronting the United States following the conclusion of the war with Spain was to devise a way to maintain the principle of equality of commercial opportunity irrespective of the fate of China as an independent state.

Britain's position in China was quite different from that of the United States, but its objectives coincided quite closely with ours. Although the British had a large "sphere of influence," centered mainly in the Yangtze River valley, they opposed any division of China among the Western nations and Japan which might result in limiting their economic activities to their own "sphere." In 1898, Great Britain requested the United States to join it in a cooperative plan to preserve China from impending collapse, but President William McKinley, engrossed with the events preceding the Spanish-American War and reluctant to take any step which might appear to involve us in an "entangling alliance," declined the invitation.

The United States, however, favored the idea of expressing its objections to any plan by the major powers to alter the situation in China which would be to our disadvantage. In 1899, Secretary of State John Hay, in a unilateral action reminiscent of American policy relative to the circumstances surrounding the announcement of the Monroe Doctrine, sent notes to the various powers which had "spheres of influence" in China inviting them to subscribe to the Open Door Policy. These notes expressed the American desire that the principle of equality of trading privileges would not be altered in the event of any change in the relationship between China and the other powers. In 1900, during the Boxer Rebellion, Hay sent another note to the powers stating that in addition to a determination to guard American lives and property in China, the policy of the United States was to preserve the territorial and administrative integrity of the Chinese Empire.

Contrary to expectations, China did not disappear as an independent nation. The Boxer Rebellion shocked the Chinese Government into a realization that it would have to undertake drastic internal reforms to survive foreign penetration. And no European nation wished to take the initiative in destroying China—a move which might have upset the equilibrium of power not only in the Orient but also in Europe, thereby precipitating a general war.

Chinese reforms, coupled with the precarious balance of world power, had brought the results which the United States had desired in sending the Open Door Notes, with one exception. From 1900 to 1904 it was obvious that the Russians were rapidly closing the door in Manchuria. Not only did they fail to withdraw from Manchuria, through which they had sent troops to Peking at the time of the Boxer Rebellion, but they cast longing glances toward Korea. The United States repeatedly informed the Russians that they were violating the principle of the Open Door. The Japanese, however, who were even more concerned over Russian designs than was the United States, ended this threat by attacking Russia in 1904.

President Theodore Roosevelt sympathized with the Japanese, but he warned their diplomats assembled at the peace conference near Portsmouth, New Hampshire, against demanding such severe terms that the Russians would prefer to continue the war rather than to make an unfavorable peace. Roosevelt's method of achieving the Open Door was to protect China by creating a balance of power between Japan and Russia in the Far East. In agreeing to the establishment of a Japanese protectorate over Korea following the Russo-Japanese War and to the increase of Japanese influence in southern Manchuria, Roosevelt failed to realize that the Japanese were no more interested in keeping the door open in the areas under their dominance than the Russians had been. The Root-Takahira agreement of 1908 between the United States and Japan was yet another indication that Roosevelt was willing to accept the *status quo* in Korea and southern Manchuria despite the contradiction in that same accord whereby both powers endorsed the policy of the Open Door in the Chinese Empire.

When William Howard Taft became President in 1909 he understood that, despite verbal adherence to the Open Door, the Japanese were fast closing it in Manchuria. He and his Secretary of State, Philander C. Knox, attempted to open the door there by proposing what became known as the Knox Neutralization Plan. This project was to afford all the major powers with Far Eastern interests a share in a consortium to be subscribed to by the bankers of the various powers which was designed to develop the railroads of Manchuria and at the same time allow the Chinese government to retain the title of ownership. Taft and Knox failed, primarily because Japan and Russia, already strongly entrenched in Manchuria, had no desire to share their gains with other nations.

Although the major interest of the United States was centered on the fate of the Celestial Empire and the ambitions of the various powers in the Far East, the large scale emigration of Japanese coolies to California and other western states posed a difficult problem in United States-Japanese relations.

In 1906 the San Francisco Board of Education passed a ruling requiring segregation of the Japanese in the public schools. The Japanese Government, as might have been expected, was highly indignant at such discrimination. Theodore Roosevelt, who was opposed to this action and to passage of any such law as the Chinese Exclusion Act of 1882, arranged a compromise. San Francisco was persuaded to abrogate its segregation order, and the two nations concluded in 1907-1908 what was known as the Gentlemen's Agreement, under the terms of which the Japanese

Government agreed to issue no more passports to coolies. This solved the problem, at least temporarily.

1. Open Door Policy

Secretary of State John Hay sent notes to Great Britain, France, Germany, Russia, Italy, and Japan asking them in substance to preserve equality of commercial opportunity in their "spheres of influence." The note to Great Britain was sent on September 6, 1899.[1]

"Sir: The Government of Her Britannic Majesty has declared that its policy and its very traditions preclude it from using any privileges which might be granted it in China as a weapon for excluding commercial rivals, and that freedom of trade for Great Britain in that Empire meant freedom of trade for all the world alike. While conceding by formal agreements, first with Germany and then with Russia, the possession of 'spheres of influence or interest' in China in which they are to enjoy special rights and privileges, more especially in respect of railroads and mining enterprises, Her Britannic Majesty's Government has therefore sought to maintain at the same time what is called the 'open-door' policy, to insure to the commerce of the world in China equality of treatment within said 'spheres' for commerce and navigation. This latter policy is alike urgently demanded by the British mercantile communities and by those of the United States, as it is justly held by them to be the only one which will improve existing conditions, enable them to maintain their positions in the markets of China, and extend their operations in the future. While the Government of the United States will in no way commit itself to a recognition of exclusive rights of any power within or control over any portion of the Chinese Empire under such agreements as have within the last year been made, it can not conceal its apprehension that under existing conditions there is a possibility, even a probability, of complications arising between the treaty powers whch may imperil the rights insured to the United States under our treaties with China.

"This Government is animated by a sincere desire that the interests of our citizens may not be prejudiced through exclusive treatment by any of the controlling powers within their so-called 'spheres of interest' in China, and hopes also to retain there an open market for the commerce of the world, remove dangerous sources of international irritation, and hasten thereby united or concerted action of the powers at Pekin in favor of the administrative reforms so urgently needed for strengthening the Imperial Government and maintaining the integrity of China in which the whole western world is

[1] *United States Relations With China With Special Reference to the Period 1944-1949*, Dept. of State, Far East. Ser. 30 (Washington, 1949), pp. 414-16.

alike concerned. It believes that such a result may be greatly assisted by a declaration by the various powers claiming 'spheres of interest' in China of their intentions as regards treatment of foreign trade therein. The present moment seems a particularly opportune one for informing Her Britannic Majesty's Government of the desire of the United States to see it make a formal declaration and to lend its support in obtaining similar declarations from the various powers claiming 'spheres of influence' in China, to the effect that each in its respective spheres of interest or influence.

"First. Will in no wise interfere with any treaty port or any vested interest within any so-called 'sphere of interest' or leased territory it may have in China.

"Second. That the Chinese treaty tariff of the time being shall apply to all merchandise landed or shipped to all such ports as are within said 'sphere of interest' (unless they be 'free ports'), no matter to what nationality it may belong, and that duties so leviable shall be collected by the Chinese Government.

"Third. That it will levy no higher harbor duties on vessels of another nationality frequenting any port in such 'sphere' than shall be levied on vessels of its own nationality, and no higher railroad charges over lines built, controlled, or operated within its 'sphere' on merchandise belonging to citizens or subjects of other nationalities transported through such 'sphere' than shall be levied on similar merchandise belonging to its own nationals transported over equal distances.

"The recent ukase of His Majesty the Emperor of Russia, declaring the port of Ta-lien-wan[2] open to the merchant ships of all nations during the whole of the lease under which it is to be held by Russia, removing as it does all uncertainty as to the liberal and conciliatory policy of that power, together with the assurance given this Government by Russia, justifies the expectation that His Majesty will cooperate in such an undertaking as is here proposed, and our ambassador at the court of St. Petersburg has been instructed accordingly to submit the propositions above detailed to His Imperial Majesty, and ask their early consideration. Copy of my instruction to Mr. Tower is herewith inclosed for your confidential information.

"The action of Germany in declaring the port of Kiaochao a 'free port,' and the aid the Imperial Government has given China in the establishment there of a Chinese custom-house, coupled with the oral assurance conveyed to the United States by Germany that our interests within its 'sphere' would in no wise be affected by its occupation of this portion of the province of Shantung, tend to show that little opposition may be anticipated from that power to the desired declaration.

"The interests of Japan, the next most interested power in the trade of China, will be so clearly served by the proposed arrangement, and the decla-

[2] Dairen.

ration of its statesmen within the last year are so entirely in line with the views here expressed, that its hearty cooperation is confidently counted on.

"You will, at as early date as practicable, submit the considerations to Her Britannic Majesty's principal secretary of state for foreign affairs and request their immediate consideration.

"I inclose herewith a copy of the instructions sent to our ambassador at Berlin, bearing on the above subject.

"I have the honor to be [etc.]

John Hay"

2. *Roosevelt on Results of the Russo-Japanese War*

On June 16, 1905, President Theodore Roosevelt wrote a letter to his close personal friend, Senator Henry Cabot Lodge, explaining his efforts to bring about a peace agreement between Russia and Japan and expressing his ideas concerning the projected settlement.[3]

". . . I have treated both Takahira[4] and Cassini[5] with entire frankness, saying the same things in effect to each, except that I have of course concealed from everyone—literally everyone—that fact that I acted in the first place on Japan's suggestion. I told Russia that it was nonsense for her to stick at trifles, that if the war went on she would lose all her possessions in eastern Asia and that the blow to her would be well-nigh irreparable; that while I had not sympathized with her at the outset I should be very sorry, because of my real regard for the Russian people and because of my regard for the interests of the world generally, to see her driven out of territory which had been hers for a couple of centuries; and that I hoped that she would make up her mind that she would have to make concessions in order to obtain peace because her military position was now hopeless, and that however future wars might come out this war was assuredly a failure. To the Japanese I have said that if they made such terms that Russia would prefer to fight for another year, they would without doubt get all eastern Siberia, but that in my opinion it would be an utterly valueless possession to them, while they would make of Russia an enemy whose hostility would endure as long as the nation herself existed. . . . Japan now has Port Arthur and Korea and the dominance in Manchuria, and I should feel that the less she asked for in addition the better it would be. . . .

"It is for the real interest of Japan to make peace, if she can get suitable terms, rather than fight on for a year at a great cost of men and money and then find herself in possession of eastern Siberia . . . and much strained by

[3] *Selections from the Correspondence of Theodore Roosevelt and Henry Cabot Lodge, 1884-1918*, II, pp. 138-56.
[4] Kogoro Takahira was the Japanese Ambassador to the United States.
[5] Count Cassini was the Russian Ambassador to the United States.

the struggle. . . . While for the rest of us, while Russia's triumph would have been a blow to civilization, her destruction as an eastern Asiatic power would also in my opinion be unfortunate. It is best that she should be left face to face with Japan so that each may have a moderating action on the other. . . . I do not believe she [Japan] will look toward the Philippines until affairs are settled on the mainland of Asia in connection with China, even if she ever looks toward them, and on the mainland in China her policy is the policy to which we are already committed."

3. *Comment by Willard Straight*

In 1905, the United States and Japan concluded the Taft-Katsura agreement by which the United States recognized the dominance of Japan over Korea as one of the fruits of the Russo-Japanese War.

The following selection is taken from the writings of Willard Straight, who was stationed in Korea and Manchuria as a member of the Foreign Service of the United States. Later he resigned from the government to accept a position representing a group of New York bankers who were interested in making investments in Manchuria. Despite his youth, Straight had a profound knowledge of the Far East and his advice was respected in the highest diplomatic and business circles in the United States.[6]

"There is one thing I want to do and that is to give people some idea of what the Japanese occupation of Korea really means. . . . Japan has appealed to the great interests of human progress, has boasted of her enlightenment and the world has swallowed it all. Russia spoke of Christianizing the Chinese, of the fulfillment of her destiny, and the world laughed in scorn. Why one and not the other? Have the Japanese sent missionaries to educate and care for the Koreans? Do they encourage them to trade? Do they make ports such as Dalny?—that they may profit, it is true, but that the natives as well may reap a harvest? . . . . Who is to reap the harvest in Manchuria? Not the foreigners surely—not the exponents of the Open Door. Never. Japan. Under the guise of waging a war for the preservation of her national existence, she has carried on a war of aggression. Is there any difference in the attitude of the Japanese in Chemulpo and that of the Russians at Newchwang? Do you hear fewer complaints from British and Americans? No. Assuredly not. Were Russians flocking into Manchuria, bargaining the Chinese out of land and trade, following the army everywhere with a flock of small traders, who were preparing to take the bread from the natives' mouths? The Japanese are doing this in Manchuria today."

[6] Herbert Croly, *Willard Straight*, pp. 169-70.

4. Root-Takahira Agreement

Shortly before Roosevelt left office the United States and Japan reached an accord as to their policies in the Far East. The agreement consisted of notes exchanged between Elihu Root, the American Secretary of State, and K. Takahira, the Japanese Ambassador in Washington.[7]

"Secretary Root to the Japanese Ambassador (Takahira)
"Washington, November 30, 1908.

"EXCELLENCY: I have the honor to acknowledge the receipt of your note of to-day setting forth the results of the exchange of views between us in our recent interviews defining the understanding of the two Governments in regard to their policy in the region of the Pacific Ocean.

"It is a pleasure to inform you that this expression of mutual understanding is welcome to the Government of the United States as appropriate to the happy relations of the two countries and as the occasion for a concise mutual affirmation of that accordant policy respecting the Far East which the two Governments have so frequently declared in the past.

"I am happy to be able to confirm to your excellency, on behalf of the United States, the declaration of the two Governments embodied in the following words:

"1. It is the wish of the two Governments to encourage the free and peaceful development of their commerce on the Pacific Ocean.

"2. The policy of both Governments, uninfluenced by any aggressive tendencies, is directed to the maintenance of the existing status quo in the region above mentioned, and to the defense of the principle of equal opportunity for commerce and industry in China.

"3. They are accordingly firmly resolved reciprocally to respect the territorial possessions belonging to each other in said region.

"4. They are also determined to preserve the common interests of all powers in China by supporting by all pacific means at their disposal the independence and integrity of China and the principle of equal opportunity for commerce and industry of all nations in that Empire.

"5. Should any event occur threatening the status quo as above described or the principle of equal opportunity as above defined, it remains for the two Governments to communicate with each other in order to arrive at an understanding as to what measures they may consider it useful to make.

"Accept [etc.]

Elihu Root"

[7] *United States Relations With China, op. cit.*, p. 428.

5. Knox Neutralization Proposal

Theodore Roosevelt seemed content to allow Japan to extend its control over Korea and increase its influence in Manchuria. Although the Root-Takahira agreement pledged both nations to the principle of the Open Door, there was no clear indication that either nation intended for the agreement to include Manchuria. Taft and Knox, however, obviously interpreted the Open Door in China to cover, not only the eighteen original Chinese provinces, but also the dependent areas, of which Manchuria was one. Knox's plan to open the door in Manchuria which was being rapidly closed by Japan and Russia was to suggest that a group of bankers from Britain, France, Russia, Japan, and the United States form a syndicate designed primarily to finance and operate the major railroads in Manchuria. His idea was summarily rejected by both Japan and Russia.[8]

"*Memorandum by Secretary Knox on the Neutralization of the Manchurian Railways*

"Now that there has been signed and ratified by an unpublished imperial decree an agreement by which American and British interests are to cooperate in the financing and construction of the Chin Chou Tsitsihar Aigun Railroad, the Government of the United States is prepared cordially to cooperate with the British Government in diplomatically supporting and facilitating this, so important alike to the progress and the commercial development of China.

"The Government of the United States would be disposed to favor ultimate participation to a proper extent on the part of other interested powers whose inclusion might be agreeable to China and which are known to support the principle of equality of commercial opportunity and the maintenance of the integrity of the Chinese Empire.

"However, before the further elaboration of the actual arrangement the Government of the United States asks the British Government to give their consideration to the following alternative and more comprehensive projects:

"1. Perhaps the most effective way to preserve the undisturbed enjoyment by China of all political rights in Manchuria and to promote the development of those Provinces under a practical application of the policy of the open door and equal commercial opportunity would be to bring the Manchurian highways and railroad under an economic and scientific and impartial administration by some plan vesting in China the ownership of the railroads through funds furnished for that purpose by the interested powers willing

[8] *Ibid.*, pp. 428-30.

to participate. Such loan should be for a period ample to make it reasonably certain that it could be met within the time fixed, and should be upon such terms as would make it attractive to bankers and investors. The plan should provide that nationals of the participating powers should supervise the rail-road system during the term of the loan, and the Governments concerned should enjoy for such period the usual preferences for their nationals and materials upon an equitable basis *inter se*.

"The execution of such a plan would naturally require the cooperation of China and of Japan and Russia, the reversionary and the concessionaries, respectively, of the existing Manchurian railroads, as well as that of Great Britain and the United States, whose special interests rest upon the existing contract relative to the Chin Chou Aigun Railroad.

"The advantages of such a plan to Japan and to Russia are obvious. Both those powers, desiring in good faith to protect the policy of the open door and equal opportunity in Manchuria, and wishing to assure to China unim-paired sovereignty, might well be expected to welcome an opportunity to shift the separate duties, responsibilities, and expenses they have undertaken in the protection of their respective commercial and other interests for im-partial assumption by the combined powers, including themselves, in propor-tion to their interests. The Government of the United States has some reason to hope that such a plan might meet favorable consideration on the part of Russia, and has reason to believe that American financial participation would be forthcoming.

"2. Should this suggestion not be found feasible in its entirety, then the desired end would be approximated if not attained by Great Britain and the United States diplomatically supporting the Chin Chou Aigun arrangement and inviting interested powers friendly to the complete commercial neutrality of Manchuria to participate in the financing and construction of that line and of such additional lines as future commercial development may demand, and at the same time to supply funds for the purchase by China of such of the existing lines as might be offered for inclusion in this system.

"The Government of the United States hopes that the principle involved in the foregoing suggestions may commend itself to His Britannic Majesty's Government. That principle finds support in the additional reasons that the consummation of some such plan would avoid the irritations likely to be engendered by the uncontrolled direct negotiations of bankers with the Chinese Government, and also that it would create such community of sub-stantial interest in China as would facilitate a cooperation calculated to simplify the problem, fiscal and monetary—reforms now receiving such earnest attention by the Imperial Chinese Government."

CHAPTER III

LATIN-AMERICAN POLICY, 1898–1914

THE Spanish-American War was a decided turning point in the Latin-American policy of the United States, particularly in the Caribbean region. The annexation of Puerto Rico and the establishment of a protectorate over Cuba, in 1901, by the United States gave this nation definite responsibilities in that area. In addition to that, the American people, in viewing the forced-draft voyage of the U.S.S. *Oregon* from the Pacific Coast through the Straits of Magellan to Cuba during the war, came to the full realization of the fact that the long-projected interoceanic canal was necessary in the interest of national security.

From the end of the war in 1898 until 1903, when Panama revolted against Colombia and then signed a canal treaty with the United States, the primary aim of this nation was to clear the way diplomatically for the construction of a canal.

Before this project could be undertaken, the United States wanted a new agreement with Britain to replace the Clayton-Bulwer Treaty of 1850 which provided that neither would obtain exclusive control over any future canal. The British, hard-pressed in the Boer War, concerned over the growing might of Germany, and interested in securing the good will of the United States, signed an agreement in 1901 which met the desires of this country for exclusive control of the canal.

The next task was to secure from Colombia the right to construct a canal through the Isthmus of Panama. The two nations negotiated a treaty allowing the United States canal rights for which Colombia was to have received $10,000,000 and $250,000 a year starting nine years after the ratification of the instrument. But Colombia rejected the treaty. Many persons in the United States were convinced that the Colombian Senate was merely bargaining for a higher price. Following that action by Colombia there were discussions in the United States about the possibility of building the canal through Nicaragua, which had originally been preferred to the Panama route by certain groups. This dilemma was solved to the satisfaction of the United States, however, when Panama revolted in November 1903, and declared itself independent from Colombia. The United States recognized the new regime immediately and the two nations signed a treaty which was almost identical to that which had been rejected by Colombia.

Theodore Roosevelt, in characteristic manner, had achieved his goal. The United States had its canal route and proceeded with the construction of the great project. The circumstances of the revolution, however, were damaging to the reputation of this country. It was known that persons with a financial interest in the French company, which had the option to build the canal, were involved in the revolution. The United States Government was not only aware of the fact that a revolution was being planned, but, in ordering its forces to prevent Colombian troops from suppressing the revolution, actually guaranteed its success. And the immediate recognition of the revolutionary government in Panama was obvious proof of the pleasure of the United States at the turn of events.

From 1903 until the end of World War I, the overriding preoccupation of the United States in the Caribbean was to protect the approaches to the canal. The methods of the various administrations differed. Roosevelt used the Big Stick. Taft relied on Dollar Diplomacy. Wilson, whose policy is discussed in more detail in a later chapter, couched his policy in terms of high idealism. But their objectives were the same: the security of the United States.

The Dominican Republic, strategically located in the Caribbean adjacent to one of the ocean passages leading to the Isthmus of Panama, was the scene of the next step in the unfolding of Roosevelt's Latin American policy. In 1905, when it appeared that European nations might intervene to collect debts owed them, as Germany had done in Venezuela in 1902-03, Roosevelt forestalled any such action by establishing an American financial protectorate over the Dominican Government.

In taking this action, Roosevelt acted under a theory which became known as the Roosevelt Corollary to the Monroe Doctrine. The substance of the Corollary was: when a Latin American nation found itself in a position to invite non-American intervention, the United States would undertake the responsibility of acting, even to the point of intervention. This policy not only would uphold the Monroe Doctrine, but it would force the delinquent nation to meet its financial obligations. The Roosevelt Corollary was an eminently satisfactory solution to the President, but for obvious reasons it did not evoke any great enthusiasm from the Latin Americans.

The other American nations, in opposing the Roosevelt Corollary, strongly supported the principles of the Drago Doctrine, which held that the "public debt can not occasion armed intervention nor even the actual occupation of the territory of American nations. . . ." Not until 1930, however, did the United States officially renounce the Roosevelt Corollary of the Monroe Doctrine.

The attention of the United States was next focused on Latin America in 1907, when it appeared that José Zelaya, Nicaraguan dictator, was on the verge of precipitating a Central American war. Revolutions and wars had been almost endemic in that area, but they were of no particular concern to this nation until 1903. With the canal under construction, the United States became very sensitive to all political and economic developments in the entire Caribbean area. Instability in any Caribbean nation might lead to the growth of European influence which would be a threat to American security. With this in mind, the United States and Mexico invited the five Central American nations to send representatives to Washington to draw up a treaty designed to bring more political stability to the region.

In December, 1907, the Central American nations signed a treaty which pledged them to settle their differences amicably, created a Central American Court of Justice, and bound them to non-recognition of revolutionary regimes. From the viewpoint of the United States, these treaties were designed to prevent a situation which, if allowed to go unchecked, might force us to intervene.

The treaties were well drawn, and if they had been adhered to, the results undoubtedly would have been beneficial to the Central American nations as well as to the United States. The difficulty was that they were based on Anglo-Saxon concepts of law and experience which did not fit the historic pattern of the Central American nations. Revolution was almost as normal in that area as it was rare in the United States, and it became evident during the Taft Administration that the Central American treaties were not operating as we had hoped they would.

Revolution in Nicaragua in 1909 and hopeless financial conditions in Honduras and Haiti caused Taft to intervene with armed force in Nicaragua and to set up financial protectorates over all three nations. President Taft and Secretary of State Philander C. Knox acted toward Latin America under the principles of the Roosevelt Corollary of the Monroe Doctrine in the three above-mentioned countries. Their widely heralded Dollar Diplomacy, however, was designed to prevent a situation which might cause the United States to intervene under the Roosevelt Corollary.

The essence of Dollar Diplomacy was that the Government took the initiative in persuading American bankers to invest in Latin America to supplant European capital with American capital. Taft and Knox reasoned that this not only would benefit the Latin Americans, but it also would add to the security of the United States. If the Latin Americans defaulted, it would not concern European bankers who had in the past persuaded their governments to intervene on their behalf. Wall Street bankers would make a profit, because the repayment of the debt was virtually guaranteed by the United States Government, but the profits of American bankers were merely incidental from the viewpoint of the Government, which was primarily interested in preventing European intervention.

1. Treaty with Cuba, 1903

For almost a century before the Spanish-American War, there were many citizens of the United States who believed that the annexation of Cuba was merely a matter of time. Paradoxically enough, the reasons which motivated the American people virtually to demand war with Spain in 1898 also precluded the United States from annexing the island which had been freed of Spanish domination. Although committed to a policy of independence for Cuba, the United States Government did not believe that the peoples of Cuba were ready for self-government in 1898. The result was the establishment of a protectorate over Cuba designed to continue until the Cubans appeared to be ready for complete independence. This result was achieved by a section to the Army appropriations bill in 1901 called the Platt Amendment. The Constituent Convention in Cuba incorporated the Platt Amendment into their Constitution in June, 1901, and it was put in the form of a treaty between the United States and Cuba which was signed in 1903.

It formed the pattern of other protectorates which the United States established in the Caribbean region during the years following 1903.

"Article I.[1]

"The Government of Cuba shall never enter into any treaty or other compact with any foreign power or powers which will impair or tend to impair the independence of Cuba, nor in any manner authorize or permit any foreign power or powers to obtain by colonization or for military or naval purposes, or otherwise, lodgment in or control over any portion of said Island.

"Article II.

"The Government of Cuba shall not assume or contract any public debt to pay the interest upon which, and to make reasonable sinking-fund provisions for the ultimate discharge of which, the ordinary revenues of the Island of Cuba, after defraying the current expenses of the Government, shall be inadequate.

"Article III.

"The Government of Cuba consents that the United States may exercise the right to intervene for the preservation of Cuban independence, the maintenance of a government adequate for the protection of life, property, and individual liberty, and for discharging the obligations with respect to Cuba imposed by the Treaty of Paris on the United States, now to be assumed and undertaken by the Government of Cuba.

"Article IV.

"All acts of the United States in Cuba during its military occupancy thereof are ratified and validated, and all lawful rights acquired thereunder shall be maintained and protected.

"Article V.

"The Government of Cuba will execute, and, as far as necessary, extend the plans already devised, or other plans to be mutually agreed upon, for the sanitation of the cities of the island, to the end that a recurrence of epidemic and infectious diseases may be prevented, thereby assuring protection to the people and commerce of Cuba, as well as to the commerce of the Southern ports of the United States and the people residing therein.

"Article VI.

"The Island of Pines shall be omitted from the boundaries of Cuba specified in the Constitution, the title thereto being left to future adjustment by treaty.

"Article VII.

"To enable the United States to maintain the independence of Cuba, and to protect the people thereof, as well as for its own defense, the Government

[1] William M. Malloy (comp.), *Treaties, Conventions, International Acts, Protocols and Agreements between the United States and Other Powers 1776-1909*, Vol. 1, pp. 362-64.

of Cuba will sell or lease to the United States lands necessary for coaling or
naval stations, at certain specified points, to be agreed upon with the President of the United States.

"Article VIII.

"The present Convention shall be ratified by each party in conformity
with the respective Constitutions of the two countries. . . .

H. G. Squiers   [Seal.]

Carlos de Zaldo [Seal.]"

2. Roosevelt Corollary to the Monroe Doctrine

During the first years of the Theodore Roosevelt Administration, the United States was faced with a dilemma in Latin America. The almost chronic financial and political instability of many
Latin-American nations, particularly in the Caribbean region, was
a constant invitation to the European nations to intervene with
armed force to protect their interests.

Roosevelt believed most thoroughly in the Anglo-Saxon concept of the sanctity of contract and was of the opinion that a
nation which had borrowed money should repay it. He was not
averse to the use of force to guarantee payment, but he was opposed to the idea of European intervention, which he believed
could easily lead to a violation of the Monroe Doctrine.

The President explained his solution of the Dominican problem in his Annual Address to Congress in 1904:[2]

"It is not true that the United States feels any land hunger or entertains
any projects as regards the other nations of the Western Hemisphere save
such as are for their welfare. All this country desires is to see the neighboring
countries stable, orderly, and prosperous. Any country whose people conduct
themselves well can count upon our hearty friendship. If a nation shows
that it knows how to act with reasonable efficiency and decency in social
and political matters, if it keeps order and pays its obligations, it need fear
no interference from the United States. Chronic wrongdoing, or an impotence which results in a general loosening of the ties of civilized society,
may in America, as elsewhere, ultimately require intervention by some civilized nation, and in the Western Hemisphere the adherence of the United
States to the Monroe Doctrine may force the United States, however reluctantly, in flagrant cases of such wrongdoing or impotence, to the exercise
of an international police power. If every country washed by the Caribbean
Sea would show the progress in stable and just civilization which with the

[2] *Papers Relating to the Foreign Affairs of the United States, 1904,* pp. xli-xlii.

aid of the Platt Amendment Cuba has shown since our troops left the island, and which so many of the republics in both Americas are constantly and brilliantly showing, all question of interference by this Nation with their affairs would be at any end. Our interests and those of our southern neighbors are in reality identical. They have great natural riches, and if within their borders the reign of law and justice obtains, prosperity is sure to come to them. While they thus obey the primary laws of civilized society they may rest assured that they will be treated by us in a spirit of cordial and helpful sympathy. We would interfere with them only in the last resort, and then only if it became evident that their inability or unwillingness to do justice at home and abroad had violated the rights of the United States or had invited foreign aggression to the detriment of the entire body of American nations. It is a mere truism to say that every nation, whether in America or anywhere else, which desires to maintain its freedom, its independence, must ultimately realize that the right of such independence can not be separated from the responsibility of making good use of it."

3. *Central American Treaties, 1907*

Neither the United States nor Mexico, which called the conference of the Central American nations to meet in Washington, signed the treaties drawn up at that meeting. The United States, however, endorsed those provisions which could have applied to nations other than the five signatories and adopted the non-recognition of revolutionary regimes as its own policy until 1934, when the treaty virtually went out of existence as a result of non-compliance by the Central American nations.[3]

"General Treaty of Peace and Amity
"Article I.
"The Republics of Central America consider it as one of their first duties, in their mutual relations, the maintenance of peace; and they bind themselves to always observe the most complete harmony, and decide every difference or difficulty that may arise amongst them, of whatsoever nature it may be, by means of the Central American Court of Justice, created by the Convention which they have concluded for that purpose on this date. . . .
"Article XVI.
"Desiring to prevent one of the most frequent causes of disturbances in the Republics, the contracting Governments shall not permit the leaders or principal chiefs of political refugees, nor their agents, to reside in the departments bordering on the countries whose peace they might disturb.

[3] *Papers Relating to the Foreign Relations of the United States, 1907*, Part II, pp. 692-711.

"Those who may have established their permanent residence in a frontier department may remain in the place of their residence under the immediate surveillance of the Government affording them an asylum, but from the moment when they become a menace to public order, they shall be included in the rule of the preceding paragraph.

"Article XVII.

"Every person, no matter what his nationality, who, within the territory of one of the contracting Parties, shall initiate or foster revolutionary movements against any of the others, shall be immediately brought to the capital of the Republic, where he shall be submitted to trial according to law. . . .

"Additional convention to the general treaty

"Article I.

"The Governments of the High Contracting Parties shall not recognize any other Government which may come into power in any of the five Republics as a consequence of a *coup d'etat,* or of a revolution against the recognized Government, so long as the freely elected representatives of the people thereof have not constitutionally reorganized the country.

"Article II.

"No Government of Central America shall in case of civil war intervene in favor of or against the Government of the country where the struggle takes place.

"Article III.

"The Governments of Central America, in the first place, are recommended to endeavor to bring about, by the means at their command, a constitutional reform in the sense of prohibiting the reelection of the President of a Republic, where such prohibition does not exist, secondly to adopt all measures necessary to effect a complete guarantee of the principle of alternation in power.

"Signed at the city of Washington on the twentieth day of December, one thousand nine hundred and seven."

4. *Dollar Diplomacy*

A contemporary account of the nature and aims of Dollar Diplomacy by a person who signed his name as an "American Diplomat," appeared in *Harper's Weekly* in 1910.[4]

"The merit claimed for what is set down here is that it accurately reflects what I know to be the motives and purposes governing the State Department in one aspect, at least, of its foreign policy. An attempt is made, necessarily

[4] An American Diplomat, "Our 'Dollar Diplomacy' and Secretary Knox," *Harper's Weekly,* LIV, (April 23, 1910), p. 8.

sketchy, to outline simply and clearly what is meant by the term 'Dollar Diplomacy,' as it has come to be commonly applied to certain of the activities of Secretary Knox as manifested in Honduras, in Liberia, and in negotiations now in progress looking to the participation of American capital in railway construction in the Far East.

"Because American capital under the shadow, under the guidance and control, and, in a rough manner of speaking, under the protection of the State Department has sought an outlet in various legitimate enterprises in lands beyond the seas, the Secretary of State and his conduct of foreign affairs have been harshly criticized. The alien and foreign criticism is easily enough understood. The domestic criticism, apparently in large part, springs from a lack of understanding of the circumstances, and of what is sought to be accomplished. . . .

"The sum of much of the recent criticism directed against the Department of State has been that our Foreign Office has become an annex of Wall Street. The facts are just the other way about. Wall Street is being used as a tool of the Department of State. . . .

"The government of Honduras, some months ago, sent agents to New York to negotiate with American bankers for the refunding of the debt of Honduras, the reorganization of its finances on a sound basis and a sufficient loan, in addition, to make possible the completion of a railway line, together with some other useful improvements. These negotiations, which have had the support of the Department of State, are in a fair way toward success. The neutrality of Honduras was recognized by all Central America, as well as by Mexico and the United States in the Washington conventions, as being the greatest guarantee to peaceful progress in those naturally rich republics; and it has long been felt that a strong Honduras financially stated, would be the greatest practical contribution to peaceful conditions which no number of courts of arbitration or expressions of lofty sentiment can realize. . . .

"In each of the foregoing examples of how Secretary Knox has been using Wall Street it will be obvious that the enterprise could not succeed without the support of the Department of State, from which it follows, as a matter of course, that the Department of State is able to dictate to the bankers what must be the terms of any arrangement which can be diplomatically supported. In these circumstances, since the interest of this government can only be the extension of American commerce, directly or indirectly, the amelioration of political conditions upon which commerce, progress, and civilization depend, and the furtherance of American prestige, the advance of which is commercial as well as moral, it is, of course, impossible that the Department of State would support the bankers' enterprises, of the kind which, to be particularly profitable, must be particularly onerous. Indeed, the wonder is that our bankers are willing to go as far afield and undertake such difficult negotiations for ordinary profits when their own country affords so much easier business. . . ."

CHAPTER IV.

WILSON'S FAR EASTERN POLICY

WOODROW WILSON, like his immediate Republican predecessors, adhered to the traditional American policy of the Open Door in China, to the principle of the self-determination of peoples throughout the Far East, and to the maintenance of a stable political balance in that area. The mere statement of these general objectives, however, is almost meaningless unless related to the course of events in the Far East during those turbulent years from 1913 to 1921.

After over 250 years of rule by the Manchus, the Chinese people recovered their independence in 1911, but the revolution continued. China never had a stable government at any time during the period covered by this chapter or one which was able to extend its authority over all the Chinese people; and these facts alone made the Chinese an easy prey for any aggressor nation.

The next fact which was of vital import to the Far East was the outbreak of World War I. Until the summer of 1914, the holdings of the various major powers in the Far East had brought a certain stability to the area. The outbreak of war in Europe, however, ended the equilibrium of power in the Orient and left a vacuum. The involvement of Britain, France, Russia and Germany in war, left Japan as the only nation in the western Pacific capable of waging modern war. The Japanese were quick to realize this unparalleled opportunity and sought to acquire a stranglehold on China when the European powers were involved in a life-and-death struggle on the other side of the globe.

Japanese action took the form of Twenty-One Demands presented secretly to China in 1915, which if accepted *in toto* by the Chinese would have made that nation a virtual protectorate of Japan. Some of these Demands were incorporated into a treaty which the Chinese later claimed was signed under duress.

In addition to the almost impossible task of attempting to establish a stable government and protect themselves from the predatory Japanese at the same time, China hoped to rid itself of all the unequal treaties which they had been forced to accept during the nineteenth century. China's entry into World War I was, to a degree, based on the hope that participation in the war against Germany might cause the Allies to treat them as an equal in diplomatic and economic matters.

The entire Far Eastern situation was further complicated by the Russian Revolution of 1917, which led indirectly to Allied intervention in Siberia in the summer of 1918.

It was against this backdrop of events that the United States had to form and carry out a policy.

Woodrow Wilson had been in office only fourteen days when he issued his first statement on Far Eastern policy. On March 18, 1913, he publicly rejected Dollar Diplomacy in disapproving of the projected participation of a group of American bankers in a consortium for a reorganizational loan to the Chinese Government. In contrast to Taft, who believed that such a joint loan would strengthen the Open Door Policy, Wilson thought that it might well impair the administrative integrity of China. By 1918, however, he had changed his opinion and supported a consortium as a means of safeguarding the Open Door.

The most serious threat to the integrity of China came, of course, when Japan presented its Twenty-One Demands to the Peking government. The United States, not then at war with Germany, strongly objected to Japan's expansionistic policies. Wilson was unwilling, however, to implement strong words with deeds, and words alone did not seriously disturb the Japanese who proceeded with their plans somewhat modified to consolidate their position in China.

In November, 1917, after the United States had entered the war on the Allied side, Japan and the United States came to an understanding called the Lansing-Ishii agreement. The American Secretary of State and the Japanese Ambassador in Washington exchanged notes which expressed the policies of their governments at the time. While these notes endorsed the principle of the Open Door, they also recognized that Japan's "territorial propinquity" to China created a special relationship between those two Far Eastern powers and that Japan had "special interests in China."

The Chinese Government, fearing that the Lansing-Ishii

agreement meant a reversal of American policy, announced that it would not be bound by the accord.

The Japanese looked upon the agreement as a diplomatic victory for themselves, which indicated that they interpreted the understanding very much as the Chinese did.

The United States Government, in attempting to pacify the Chinese, stated that the terms "territorial propinquity" and "special interests" did not mean a reversal of policy but that they were merely statements of geographic and economic truths. The explanation of this shift in policy lay in the fact that both Japan and the United States were allies in the conflict against the Central Powers, and cooperation in the war against Germany was the primary objective of the United States until the Armistice was signed on November 11, 1918.

When the war ended, the situation in the Far East was more confusing and complicated than it had been at the start of the great conflict. China was in political turmoil, with several groups claiming power. Japan had been able to strengthen its hold on China by forcing the Peking regime to accept some of the Twenty-One Demands. The United States hoped that the peace conference would bring justice and peace to the Far East; but at the same time American and Japanese troops, ostensible allies, were eyeing each other suspiciously in Siberia.

The delegates to the conference which assembled in Paris in January, 1919, left the Far East much as they had found it when the war ended. The major Allied powers, bound by a number of secret war-time treaties upholding Japan's aspirations, were mainly interested in European affairs. The Allied Powers and the United States did virtually nothing to satisfy the desires of the Chinese or to bring any real stability to the Far East.

1. *Wilson's Disapproval of Loan to China, 1913*

When Wilson entered the White House on March 4, 1913, he was confronted with the problem of whether or not to continue Taft's Dollar Diplomacy. On March 18, he issued a statement to the press in which he outlined his policy toward China which included a rejection of the idea of a banking consortium.[1]

"We are informed that at the request of the last administration a certain group of American bankers undertook to participate in the loan now desired

[1] *Papers Relating to the Foreign Relations of the United States, 1913*, pp. 170-71.

by the Government of China (approximately $125,000,000). Our Government wished American bankers to participate along with the bankers of other nations, because it desired that the good will of the United States toward China should be exhibited in this practical way, that American capital should have access to that great country, and that the United States should be in a position to share with the other powers any political responsibilities that might be associated with the development of the foreign relations of China in connection with her industrial and commercial enterprises. The present administration has been asked by this group of bankers whether it would also request them to participate in the loan. The representatives of the bankers through whom the administration was approached declared that they would continue to seek their share of the loan under the proposed agreements only if expressly requested to do so by the Government. The administration has declined to make such request, because it did not approve the conditions of the loan or the implications of responsibility on its own part which it was plainly told would be involved in the request.

"The conditions of the loan seem to us to touch very nearly the administrative independence of China itself, and this administration does not feel that it ought, even by implication, to be a party to those conditions. The responsibility on its part which would be implied in requesting the bankers to undertake the loan might conceivably go the length in some unhappy contingency of forcible interference in the financial, and even the political, affairs of that great oriental State, just now awakening to a consciousness of its power and of its obligations to its people. The conditions include not only the pledging of particular taxes, some of them antiquated and burdensome, to secure the loan, but also the administration of those taxes by foreign agents. The responsibility on the part of our Government implied in the encouragement of a loan thus secured and administered is plain enough and is obnoxious to the principles upon which the government of our people rests.

"The Government of the United States is not only willing, but earnestly desirous, of aiding the great Chinese people in every way that is consistent with their untrammeled development and its own immemorial principles. The awakening of the people of China to a consciousness of their responsibilities under free government is the most significant, if not the most momentous, event of our generation. With this movement and aspiration the American people are in profound sympathy. They certainly wish to participate, and participate very generously, in the opening to the Chinese and to the use of the world the almost untouched and perhaps unrivaled resources of China.

"The Government of the United States is earnestly desirous of promoting the most extended and intimate trade relationship between this country and the Chinese Republic. The present administration will urge and support the legislative measures necessary to give American merchants, manufacturers, contractors, and engineers the banking and other financial facilities which they now lack and without which they are at a serious disadvantage as compared with their industrial and commercial rivals. This is its duty. This is the main material interest of its citizens in the development of China. Our interests are those of the open door—a door of friendship and mutual advantage. This is the only door we care to enter."

2. *The Reaction to Japan's Twenty-One Demands*

On January 18, 1915, the Japanese Minister in China handed to Yuan Shih Kai, the President of China, a document which became known as the Twenty-One Demands. This document was in the form of a proposed treaty between the two nations, and it contained provisions which would have made China a protectorate of Japan. Although the Japanese Minister pledged the Chinese to secrecy "on pain of serious consequences to China,"[2] the diplomatic corps in Peking and newsmen found out that the Japanese had made certain demands on China. Within a short time the American Minister in China, Paul S. Reinsch, obtained a copy of the original document handed to the President of China. It was obvious that if China were forced to accept this proferred treaty, Japan would control China and it would be the end of the Open Door Policy.

The United States Government, on learning the full nature of the demands, took a vigorous stand in opposing them. On March 13, 1915, Secretary of State William Jennings Bryan handed a note to the Japanese Ambassador in Washington which reviewed the various treaties to which Japan and the United States were bound to observe the Open Door in China and lodged a vigorous protest against this Japanese proposal.[3]

"EXCELLENCY: On February 8 last your excellency left with me at the Department a memorandum setting forth the demands which the Imperial Japanese Government felt obliged to make upon China, and on the 22d of the same month your excellency delivered to me an additional memorandum presenting certain 'requests' affecting the relations between the two countries which the Imperial Government has urged China to consider.

"The American Government is glad to learn from these two communications of the Imperial Government that the 'requests' were not presented to China as 'demands' but that they were but 'wishes' for which 'friendly consideration' was asked on the part of China. The American Government

[2] *Ibid., 1915*, p. 79.
[3] *Ibid.*, pp. 105-111.

understands from this distinction between the 'demands' and the 'requests' that the latter are not to be pressed if the Chinese Government should decline to consider them. . . .

"It remains to call attention to Article III [4] forbidding the alienation or lease of any port, harbor or island on the coast of China, and to Article V, paragraph 1, requiring China to employ competent Japanese subjects as advisers for conducting administrative, financial and military affairs, and paragraph 3 suggesting the joint policing of China, 'where it is deemed necessary.'

"With reference to the first of these three proposals, Baron Kato has explained to the American Ambassador at Tokyo that Japan has no desire for a naval station on the coast of China, either at Tsingtau, or south of that point, as it would be valueless to her, but that it would however object to another nation having such a station. With reference to the employment of advisers the United States believes it may be assumed that the Chinese will not discriminate unfairly in their selection, although it should be pointed out that this Government understands that Japan has six out of twenty-five advisers to the Republic representing eight nations. In respect to the proposed joint policing of certain places where there has been some friction between Japanese and Chinese, this Government feels apprehensive that this plan, instead of tending to lessen such friction might create greater difficulties than those which it is desired to remove.

"But what is more important is the fact that these proposals, if accepted by China, while not infringing the teritorial integrity of the Republic, are clearly derogatory to the political independence and administrative entity of that country. The same is in a measure true of Paragraph 4 of Article V relative to the purchase of arms. It is difficult for the United States, therefore, to reconcile these requests with the maintenance of the unimpaired sovereignty of China, which Japan, together with the United States and the Great Powers of Europe, has reaffirmed from time to time during the past decade and a half in formal declarations, treaties and exchanges of diplomatic notes. The United States, therefore, could not regard with indifference the assumption of political, military or economic domination over China by a foreign Power, and hopes that your excellency's Government will find it consonant with their interests to refrain from pressing upon China an acceptance of proposals which would, if accepted, exclude Americans from equal participation in the economic and industrial development of China and would limit the political independence of that country.

"The United States is convinced that an attempt to coerce China to submit to these proposals would result in engendering resentment on the part of the Chinese and opposition by other interested Powers, thereby creating a situation which this Government confidently believes the Imperial Government do not desire.

[4] Of the Twenty-One Demands.

"The United States Government embraces this opportunity to make known that it has viewed the aspirations of Japan in the Far East with that friendship and esteem which have characterized the relations of the two nations in the past. This Government cannot too earnestly impress upon your excellency's Government that the United States is not jealous of the prominence of Japan in the East or of the intimate cooperation of China and Japan for their mutual benefit. Nor has the United States any intention of obstructing or embarrassing Japan, or of influencing China in opposition to Japan. On the contrary the policy of the United States, as set forth in this note, is directed to the maintenance of the independence, integrity and commercial freedom of China and the preservation of legitimate American rights and interests in that Republic.

"Accept [etc.]

W. J. Bryan."

3. *Lansing-Ishii Notes and Reaction to Them*

The following is Secretary Robert Lansing's note to Ambassador K. Ishii:[5]

"The Secretary of State to
the Japanese Ambassador on Special Mission

"DEPARTMENT OF STATE

"Washington, November 2, 1917.

"EXCELLENCY: I have the honor to communicate herein my understanding of the agreement reached by us in our recent conversations touching the questions of mutual interest to our Governments relating to the Republic of China.

"In order to silence mischevious reports that have from time to time been circulated, it is believed by us that a public announcement once more of the desires and intentions shared by our two Governments with regard to China is advisable.

"The Governments of the United States and Japan recognize that territorial propinquity creates special relations between countries, and, consequently, the Government of the United States recognizes that Japan has special interests in China, particularly in the part to which her possessions are contiguous.

"The territorial sovereignty of China, nevertheless, remains unimpaired and the Government of the United States has every confidence in the repeated assurances of the Imperial Japanese Government that while geographical position gives Japan such special interests they have no desire to discriminate against the trade of other nations or to disregard the commercial rights heretofore granted by China in treaties with other powers.

[5] *Ibid.*, 1917, p. 264.

"The Government of the United States and Japan deny that they have any purpose to infringe in any way the independence or territorial integrity of China and they declare, furthermore, that they always adhere to the principles of the so-called 'open-door' or equal opportunity for commerce and industry in China.

"Moreover, they mutually declare that they are opposed to the acquisition by any Government of any special rights or privileges that would affect the independence or territorial integrity of China or that would deny to the subjects or citizens of any country the full enjoyment of equal opportunity in the commerce and industry of China.

"I shall be glad to have your excellency confirm this understanding of the agreement reached by us.

"Accept [etc.]

ROBERT LANSING"

The Japanese Ambassador did confirm this understanding on the same day by a note to the Secretary of State which contained the identical language used by Lansing.

The Chinese, who had not been apprised of these negotiations, were not overly pleased with the agreement. Although the United States had strongly championed their cause at the time of the Twenty-One Demands in 1915, the Chinese feared that this Lansing-Ishii agreement might somehow mean a rapproachment between the United States and Japan to the disadvantage of China. In an attempt to allay Chinese fears on this score, Robert Lansing had a conversation with the Chinese Minister in Washington on November 12 in which the Secretary of State explained the meaning of the agreement with Japan. The following is a report of this conversation sent to the American Ambassador in Tokyo:[6]

"On November 12 the Chinese Minister left me with a declaration of his Government concerning the American-Japanese exchange of notes of November 2, . . .[7]

"For your information I made substantially the following comment thereon to the Minister: There was no thought or intention to bind China; for that reason I had refrained from consulting him while the negotiations were pending; knowledge of negotiations pending and failure to object before completion might really have bound China; our friendship for China unchanged but the financing of the present war prevented large independent

[6] *Ibid.*, p. 273.

[7] This declaration stated that China would not allow itself to be bound by any agreement entered into by other nations.

investments in China and made inadvisable attempts to secure such investments by financial competition with Japan; China could not longer, because of those conditions, continue to play the United States against Japan in the matter of such investments; that we were still anxious to manifest friendship by aiding China financially; which, however, was possible only by some arrangement for cooperation with Japan thereby preventing Japan's sole appropriation of the Chinese investment field; I assumed China preferred us to join with Japan rather than to leave China to that country alone.

"He asked what 'special interests' meant. I said it was the statement of an axiom; that it was a statement which could not be successfully denied and could be universally applied and that, in view of declaration in last clause of note signed by Ishii, it was advantageous to China for both Governments declared themselves opposed it [sic] 'any government' infringing China's independence and territorial integrity, a declaration which applied to the parties of the understanding as well as to others; that such a bargain seemed decidedly in China's favor; further in reply to his inquiry I stated I believed phrase 'territorial propinquity' applied alike to Japan, Russia, France and England and that China might also apply it.

"Further, that I believed Chinese Government had acted wisely in presenting memorandum above but that no reservation or caveat could change the natural consequences of propinquity.

"Repeat to Peking.

LANSING"

CHAPTER V.

LATIN-AMERICAN POLICY
OF WOODROW WILSON

WOODROW WILSON was an unusual man and an unusual President. The son of a Presbyterian minister, Wilson was a former university professor and president who carried out his policies with the zeal of a reformer and the coolness of an academician. Wilson had the idealism as well as the sternness of a Puritan disciplinarian, and his personality and character puzzled the Latin Americans to the same degree that he misunderstood the volatile Latins. The peoples of the other American Republics understood but disliked the blunt, straightforward Big Stick policy of Theodore Roosevelt and the Dollar Diplomacy of William Howard Taft; yet they neither understood nor liked Wilson's idealistic approach which also brought marines to their shores.

When Wilson entered the White House, he repudiated the policies of his predecessors and talked to the Latin Americans in terms of friendship, understanding, and good-neighborliness. But he intervened in their affairs more times than either Roosevelt or Taft had done. He castigated Wall Street bankers for using dollars to control Latin America, and yet he lifted an arms embargo to allow the opponents of the Mexican general, Victoriano Huerta, to secure munitions from this country. A former professor of political science, he disliked the political instability which was almost endemic in Latin America; and he once said that he would teach the Latin Americans how to elect good governments. Revolutions displeased him, and he decided not to recognize regimes which had come into power illegally. A sharp critic of American protectorates which had been established by his Repubican predecessors, he used American forces to institute military protectorates over Haiti and the Dominican Republic.

Wilson pleased neither the American businessman with investments in Latin America nor the peoples in that area. As far as anyone can discover, he did not teach the Latin Americans how to elect good governments, nor did he prevent revolutions. However, given Wilson's character and personality and training, he probably could not have acted differently. His object—like Jonathan Edwards—was not to please, but to do his duty as he saw it.

1. Statement of Mexican Policy

Wilson delivered an address to a joint session of the Congress of the United States on August 27, 1913.[1]

"GENTLEMEN OF THE CONGRESS:

"It is clearly my duty to lay before you, very fully and without reservation, the facts concerning our present relations with the Republic of Mexico. The deplorable posture of affairs in Mexico I need not describe, but I deem it my duty to speak very frankly of what this Government has done and should seek to do in fulfillment of its obligation to Mexico herself, as a friend and neighbor, and to American citizens whose lives and vital interests are daily affected by the distressing conditions which now obtain beyond our southern border. . . .

"The present circumstances of the Republic, I deeply regret to say, do not seem to promise even the foundations of such a peace. We have waited many months, months full of peril and anxiety, for the conditions there to improve, and they have not improved. They have grown worse, rather. The territory in some sort controlled by the provisional authorities at Mexico City has grown smaller, not larger. The prospect of the pacification of the country, even by arms, has seemed to grow more and more remote; and its pacification by the authorities at the capital is evidently impossible by any other means than force. Difficulties more and more entangle those who claim to constitute the legitimate government of the Republic. They have not made good their claim in fact. Their successes in the field have proved only temporary. War and disorder, devastation and confusion, seem to threaten to become the settled fortune of the distracted country. As friends we could wait no longer for a solution which every week seemed further away. It was our duty at least to volunteer our good offices—to offer to assist, if we might, in effecting some arrangement which would bring relief and peace and set up a universally acknowledged political authority there.

"Accordingly, I took the liberty of sending the Honorable John Lind, former governor of Minnesota, as my personal spokesman and representative, to the City of Mexico, with the following instructions: . . . .

[1] *Congressional Record,* 63rd Cong., 1st Sess., Vol. 50, Part 4, pp. 3803-04.

'A satisfactory settlement seems to us to be conditioned on—

'(a) An immediate cessation of fighting throughout Mexico, a definite armistice solemnly entered into and scrupulously observed.

'(b) Security given for an early and free election in which all agree to take part.

'(c) The consent of Gen. Huerta to bind himself not to be a candidate for election as President of the Republic at this election.

'(d) The agreement of all parties to abide by the results of the election and cooperate in the most loyal way in organizing and supporting the new administration. . . .'

"Mr. Lind executed his delicate and difficult mission with singular tact, firmness, and good judgment, and made clear to the authorities at the City of Mexico not only the purpose of his visit but also the spirit in which it had been undertaken. But the proposals he submitted were rejected, in a note the full text of which I take the liberty of laying before you. . . .

"Meanwhile, what is it our duty to do? Clearly, everything that we do must be rooted in patience and done with calm and disinterested deliberation. . . . It is now our duty to show what true neutrality will do to enable the people of Mexico to set their affairs in order again and wait for a further opportunity to offer our friendly counsels. The door is not closed against the resumption, either upon the initiative of Mexico or upon our own, of the effort to bring order out of the confusion by friendly cooperative action, should fortunate occasion offer. . . .

"For the rest, I deem it my duty to exercise the authority conferred upon me by the law of March 14, 1912, to see to it that neither side to the struggle now going on in Mexico receive any assistance from this side of the border. I shall follow the best practice of nations in the matter of neutrality by forbidding the exportation of arms or munitions of war of any kind from the United States to any part of the Republic of Mexico—a policy suggested by several interesting precedents and certainly dictated by many manifest considerations of practical expediency. We can-not in the circumstances be the partisans of either party to the contest that now distracts Mexico or constitute ourselves the virtual umpire between them. . . ."

2. *Wilson's New Policy toward Mexico*

Although Wilson told a joint session of the Congress in August, 1913, that our true policy toward Mexico was one of neutrality and that we should not become an "umpire" in their civil war, his policy had obviously changed by November of that same year, as indicated by an instruction sent to American Embassies by the Secretary of State.[2]

[2] *Papers Relating to the Foreign Relations of the United States, 1914*, pp. 443-44.

"Department of State
"Washington, November 24, 1913.
"Our Purposes in Mexico

"The purpose of the United States is solely to secure peace and order in Central America by seeing to it that the processes of self-government there are not interrupted or set aside.

"Usurpations like that of General Huerta[3] menace the peace and development of America as nothing else could. They not only render the development of ordered self government impossible; they also tend to set law entirely aside, to put the lives and fortunes of citizens and foreigners alike in constant jeopardy, to invalidate contracts and concessions in any way the usurper may devise for his own profit and to impair both the national credit and all the foundations of business, domestic or foreign.

"It is the purpose of the United States therefore to discredit and defeat such usurpations whenever they occur. The present policy of the Government of the United States is to isolate General Huerta entirely; to cut him off from foreign sympathy and aid and from domestic credit, whether moral or material, and to force him out.

"It hopes and believes that isolation will accomplish this end and shall await the results without irritation or impatience. If General Huerta does not retire by force of circumstances it will become the duty of the United States to use less peaceful means to put him out. It will give other Governments notice in advance of each affirmative or aggressive step it has in contemplation should it unhappily become necessary to move actively against the usurper; but no such step seems immediately necessary.

"Its fixed resolve is that no such interruptions of civil order shall be tolerated in so far as it is concerned. Each conspicuous instance in which usurpations of this kind are prevented will render their recurrence less and in the end a state of affairs will be secured in Mexico and elsewhere upon this continent which will assure the peace of America and the untrammeled development of its economic and social relations with the rest of the world.

"Beyond this fixed purpose the Government of the United States will not go. It will not permit itself to seek any special or exclusive advantages in Mexico or elsewhere for its own citizens but will seek, here as elsewhere, to show itself the consistent champion of the open door. In the meantime it is making every effort that the circumstances permit to safeguard foreign lives and property in Mexico and is making the lives and fortunes of the subjects of other Governments as much its concern as the lives and fortunes of its own citizens.

"You will communicate this to the foreign office.

[Signed] Bryan."

[3] Huerta had come into power following the assassination of President Francisco Madero. Wilson steadfastly refused to recognize the Huerta regime because of strong suspicions that he had been at least indirectly responsible for Madero's murder.

3. Mexican Protest of Bombing of Vera Cruz

American isolation of General Huerta did not force him to resign "by force of circumstances" as Wilson had hoped. Instead, the revolution in Mexico continued and relations between the two nations became steadily worse. Wilson removed the arms embargo to allow munitions to cross the border to Huerta's opponents which increased the intensity of the war; but Huerta remained in power.

In April, 1914, two incidents occurred which almost brought full scale war between the United States and the forces of General Huerta. The first was the arrest of American sailors in Tampico by Mexican officers under Huerta's authority and the failure of the General to make appropriate apologies to this Government. The second was the bombardment of Vera Cruz by American naval vessels in order to prevent a German merchant ship from unloading arms and munitions destined for Huerta's forces. Possibly war would have resulted if Argentina, Brazil, and Chile had not offered to mediate the dispute. Wilson quickly accepted the offer, which finally led to the overthrow of Huerta and an easing of the tension between the two nations, although it did not bring an end to civil strife in Mexico.

Huerta's chief opponent in Mexico was Venustiano Carranza, later President of Mexico, who was receiving American arms in the spring of 1914. Carranza, who was grateful for American aid, was bitter over the shelling of Vera Cruz as indicated in the document quoted below:[4]

"*Special Agent Carothers to the Secretary of State*

"[Telegram]

"El Paso, Texas, *April 22, 1914.*

"Department's April 21, 9:50 p.m.

"Following is translation of text of reply from Carranza:

"In answer to the message of Secretary of State Bryan, which was communicated to me through you, please transmit to Mr. Bryan the following note addressed to President Wilson:

'Pending the action of the American Senate on Your Excellency's message directed to that body, caused by the lamentable incident which occurred between the crew of a whaleboat of the cruiser *Dolphin* and the

[4] *Papers Relating to the Foreign Relations of the United States, 1914,* pp. 483-84.

soldiers of the usurper Huerta, certain acts of hostility have been executed by the naval forces under the command of Admiral Fletcher at the port of Vera Cruz. In view of this violation of the national sovereignty, which the Constitutionalist Government did not expect from a Government which had reiterated its desire to maintain peace with the Mexican people, I comply with a duty of high patriotism in directing this note to you with a view of exhausting all honorable means before two friendly powers sever the pacific relations that still unite them.

'The Mexican nation—the real people of Mexico—have not recognized as their executive a man who has sought to blemish the national integrity, drowning in blood its free institutions. Consequently the acts of the usurper Huerta and his accomplices do not signify legitimate acts of sovereignty, they do not constitute real public functions of domestic and foreign relations, and much less do they represent the sentiments of the Mexican nation, which are of confraternity towards the American people. The lack of representative character in General Victoriano Huerta as concerns the relations of Mexico with the United States as well as with Argentina, Brazil, Chile and Cuba has been clearly established by the justifiable attitude of these nations, who have refused to recognize the usurper, thus lending a valuable moral support to the noble cause that I represent. . . .

'The individual acts of Victoriano Huerta will never be sufficient to involve the Mexican nation in a disastrous war with the United States, because there is no solidarity whatever between the so-called Government of Victoriano Huerta and the Mexican nation, for the fundamental reason that he is not the legitimate organ of our national sovereignty.

'But the invasion of our territory and the stay of your forces in the port of Vera Cruz, violating the rights that constitute our existence as a free and independent sovereign entity, may indeed drag us into an unequal war, with dignity but which until today we have desired to avoid.

'In the fact of the real situation of Mexico—weak in comparison with the formidable power of the American nation and weaker than ever after three years of bloody strife—and considering the acts committed at Vera Cruz to be highly offensive to the dignity and independence of Mexico, contrary to your repeated declarations of not desiring to disturb the state of peace and friendship with the Mexican nation, and contrary also to the resolution of the American Senate, which has just declared that the United States does not assume any attitude inimical to the Mexican people and does not purpose to levy war against them; . . . I interpret the sentiment of the great majority of the Mexican people, so jealous of its rights and so respectful of the rights of foreigners, and invite you only to suspend the hostile acts already begun, to order your forces to evacuate all places that they hold in the port of Vera Cruz and to present to the Constitutionalist Government, which I as Constitutional Governor of the State of Coahuila and First Chief of the Constitutionalist Army represent, and demand on the part of the United States in regard to acts recently committed at the port of Tampico, in the security that the demand will be considered in a spirit of elevated justice and conciliation.

V. Carranza' "

4. United States' Protectorate over Haiti

In 1915, following the murder of President Guillaume Sam of Haiti when it appeared that the chaos in that small nation located approximately 600 miles from the Panama Canal might bring European intervention, Wilson sent American marines to restore order. On September 16, 1915, the United States and Haiti signed a treaty which gave this nation military, political, and economic control of Haiti:[5]

"Article I

"The Government of the United States will, by its good offices, aid the Haitian Government in the proper and efficient development of its agricultural, mineral and commercial resources and in the establishment of the finances of Haiti on a firm and solid basis.

"Article II

"The President of Haiti shall appoint, upon nomination by the President of the United States, a General Receiver and such aids and employees as may be necessary, who shall collect, receive and apply all customs duties on imports and exports accruing at the several custom houses and ports of entry of the Republic of Haiti.

"The President of Haiti shall appoint, upon nomination by the President of the United States, a Financial Adviser, who shall be an officer attached to the Ministry of Finance, to give effect to whose proposals and labors the Minister will lend efficient aid. The Financial Adviser shall devise an adequate system of public accounting, aid in increasing the revenues and adjusting them to the expenses, inquire into the validity of the debts of the Republic, enlighten both Governments with reference to all eventual debts, recommend improved methods of collecting and applying the revenues, and make such other recommendations as the Minister of Finance may be deemed necessary for the welfare and prosperity of Haiti....

"Article V

"All sums collected and received by the General Receiver shall be applied, first, to the payment of the salaries and allowances of the General Receiver, his assistants and employees and the expenses of the Receivership, including the salary and expenses of the Financial Adviser, which salaries

---

[5] *Treaties, Conventions, International Acts, Protocols, and Agreements between the United States of America and Other Powers, 1910-1923,* Vol. III, pp. 2673-77.

will be determined by previous agreement; second, to the interest and sinking fund of the public debt of the Republic of Haiti; and, third, to the maintenance of the constabulary referred to in Article X, and then the remainder to the Haitian Government for purposes of current expenses. . . .

"Article VIII

"The Republic of Haiti shall not increase its public debt except by previous agreement with the President of the United States, and shall not contract any debt or assume any financial obligation unless the ordinary revenue of the Republic available for that purpose, after defraying the expenses of the Government, shall be adequate to pay the interest and provide a sinking fund for the final discharge of such debt. . . .

"Article X

"The Haitian Government obligates itself, for the preservation of domestic peace, the security of individual rights and full observance of the provisions of this treaty, to create without delay an efficient constabulary, urban and rural, composed of native Haitians. This constabulary shall be organized and officered by Americans, appointed by the President of Haiti, upon nomination by the President of the United States. The Haitian Government shall clothe these officers with the proper and necessary authority and uphold them in the performance of their functions. These officers will be replaced by Haitians as they, by examination, conducted under direction of a board to be selected by the senior American officer of this constabulary and in the presence of a representative of the Haitian Government, are found to be qualified to assume such duties. The constabulary herein provided for, shall, under the direction of the Haitian Government, have supervision and control of arms and ammunition, military supplies, and traffic therein, throughout the country. The high contracting parties agree that the stipulations in this Article are necessary to prevent factional strife and disturbances. . . .

"Article XIV

"The high contracting parties shall have authority to take such steps as may be necessary to insure the complete attainment of any of the objects comprehended in this treaty; and, should the necessity occur, the United States will lend an efficient aid for the preservation of Haitian Independence and the maintenance of a government adequate for the protection of life, property and individual liberty. . . .

"Article XVI

"The present treaty shall remain in full force and virtue for the term of ten years, to be counted from the day of exchange of ratifications, and further for another term of ten years if, for specific reasons presented by either of the high contracting parties, the purpose of this treaty has not been fully accomplished. . . ."

CHAPTER VI

NEUTRALITY, 1914–1917

NEITHER the Government nor the people of the United States were thoroughly familiar with the intricate pattern of European politics and deep-seated rivalries which led to the outbreak of the great war in 1914. Whereas this Government had demonstrated great interest in Latin America and the Far East, especially after 1898, it did not have quite the same interest or influence in European politics.

Shortly after the outbreak of the war, Woodrow Wilson called on the American people to be neutral in mind as well as in deed. He realized that since most Americans were of European origin there was the possibility, even probability, that partisan discussion would seriously divide the population.

Laudable as was this objective of absolute neutrality, even of thought, in August 1914, the course of the war soon demonstrated the impossibility for either the people or the Government of this country to be completely impartial. America was the most powerful neutral nation in the world. Its commercial and cultural ties with Europe proved stronger than most people had realized, and the course of the war affected the United States as profoundly as the Napoleonic wars had a century earlier.

At the outset, the United States hoped and possibly expected that as a neutral it would be allowed to carry on trade with the belligerent nations with a minimum of interference. This soon proved to be a vain hope. The British, by virtue of their control of the seas, used their historic policy of blockade on the high seas in an attempt to bring Germany to its knees. In carrying out this policy, however, the British and also the French continually interfered with American and other neutral shipping. They issued a more comprehensive list of contraband than we thought justifiable. They stopped American ships wherever they happened to be beyond our own three-mile limit, conducted searches at sea, and often detoured them to English ports for adjudication by prize courts. They limited the amount of merchandise which could be shipped to European neutral nations. They searched American mail for contraband. Repeated protests over these actions were sent to London and Paris from Washington, but the Allies continued those practices so irritating to the United States.

Our troubles with the Germans were even more serious than those with the Allies, because they involved the loss of American lives. The problem confronting Germany was almost identical to that which Napoleon had faced: how to break the British blockade. Napoleon had issued a series of decrees to prevent neutrals from trading with England, but had lacked really effective means to enforce his orders. The Germans, possessing the submarine, had a much more effective weapon than any available to Napoleon, and they came closer to achieving their goal.

The submarine was a deadly weapon, and if it had been used solely against belligerent warships it would not have raised problems which affected all nations with a merchant marine. The submarine, however, was most effective against merchant ships which in most cases were not equipped to defend themselves against this weapon. Consequently, when the Germans started using their submarines, first against belligerent merchant ships, and then against those belonging to the neutrals, they not only violated international law but in doing so they killed and injured non-combatant citizens of the belligerent nations as well as citizens of neutral countries.

The first real German-American crisis over submarine warfare came with the sinking of the British passenger ship *Lusitania* in May 1915. More than one hundred American lives were lost, and the United States lodged severe protests with Germany. In the correspondence and discussions which followed, it became clear that the United States believed that Germany should abandon the use of the submarine unless it could be used in such a way as to comply with international law. The Germans argued that they had been forced to use the submarine to offset the effect of the illegal, long-range British blockade and stated that they could not abandon this weapon. After lengthy discussions the Germans did agree, with certain limitations, in May 1916, to the principle of visit and search, and they promised that unresisting merchant ships would not be sunk without warning and without attempting to save the lives of the crew and passengers.

Before the end of the year, however, the Germans had decided that the surest and quickest means of ending the war was to use its large fleet of submarines in an effort to isolate the Allies, particularly Britain, from the rest of the world. The German Government was fully aware of the probable action of the United States, but in making this decision they took a calculated risk: they were willing to chance bringing the United States into the war in the belief that the policy which forced us into war—unrestricted use of the submarine—would also prevent us from playing an effective part in the conflict.

On January 31, 1917, Germany announced its intent to sink all ships irrespective of nationality which entered the war zone starting February 1—the next day. The United States severed diplomatic relations with Germany two days later, and declared war on April 6, 1917, after the Germans had implemented their January 31 declaration by deeds.

The United States had moved a long way from strict impartiality in 1914 to war in 1917. Countless volumes have been written about those years, and American historians are by no means agreed today as to all the causes for our entry into that conflict. The largest number of historians who have studied that era are agreed that Germany's decision to use unrestricted submarine warfare was the main cause for American involvement. It is true that most Americans sympathized with the Allied cause almost from the very beginning; British propaganda prior to the outbreak of the conflict and after it probably influenced many Americans. No one now doubts that J. P. Morgan and other bankers, the munition makers and American business men in general, made huge profits before and after 1917, but war has always brought profits to some individuals. No evidence has yet been produced, however, to substantiate the assertion heard so often during the two decades following World War I, that American business men used their influence to force the United States into the war for the sake of profits.

To Wilson and to most other Americans in April, 1917, the submarine in the hands of the Germans was a menace to humanity and had no place in modern warfare. As Wilson saw it, the contest between the United States and Germany was one between right and wrong, between morality and immorality. Wilson's concept was unquestionably over-simplified; but the fact remains that after the United States had entered the war against Germany, Wilson was supported by the overwhelming majority of the people of this country, who agreed with the President in viewing our participation in the war as a Great Crusade for freedom, liberty, democracy, and justice. The results of the war which brought such disillusionment to the American people merely demonstrated how naïve they and their President had been in anticipating Utopia following the conflict.

1. Wilson's Appeal for Neutrality

On August 4, 1914, a few days after the outbreak of the European War, Wilson issued an official statement on the neutrality of the United States as required by American as well as international law. Fifteen days later he issued an appeal to the American people urging them to adopt an attitude of true neutrality.[1]

"MY FELLOW COUNTRYMEN: I suppose that every thoughtful man in America has asked himself, during these last troubled weeks, what influence the European war may exert upon the United States, and I take the liberty of addressing a few words to you in order to point out that it is entirely within our choice what its effects upon us will be and to urge very earnestly upon you the sort of speech and conduct which will best safeguard the nation against distress and disaster.

"The effect of the war upon the United States will depend upon what American citizens say and do. Every man who really loves America will act and speak in the true spirit of neutrality, which is the spirit of impartiality and fairness and friendliness to all concerned. The spirit of the nation in this critical matter will be determined largely by what individuals and society and those gathered at public meetings do and say, upon what newspapers and magazines contain, upon what ministers utter in their pulpits, and men proclaim as their opinions on the street.

"The people of the United States are drawn from many nations, and chiefly from the nations now at war. It is natural and inevitable that there should be the utmost variety of sympathy and desire among them with regard to the issues and circumstances of the conflict. Some will wish one nation, others another, to succeed in the momentous struggle. It will be easy to excite passion and difficult to allay it. Those responsible for exciting it will assume a heavy responsibility, responsibility for no less a thing than that the people of the United States, whose love of their country and whose loyalty to its Government should unite them as Americans all, bound in

[1] *Papers Relating to the Foreign Relations of the United States, 1914, Supplement, The World War*, pp. 551-52.

honor and affection to think first of her and her interests, may be divided in camps of hostile opinion, hot against each other, involved in war itself in impulse and opinion if not in action.

"Such divisions among us would be fatal to our peace of mind and might seriously stand in the way of the proper performance of our duty as the one great nation at peace, the one people holding itself ready to play a part of impartial mediation and speak the counsels of peace and accommodation, not as a partisan, but as a friend.

"I venture, therefore, my fellow countrymen, to speak a solemn word of warning to you against that deepest, most subtle, most essential breach of neutrality which may spring out of partisanship, out of passionately taking sides. The United States must be neutral in fact as well as in name during these days that are to try men's souls. We must be impartial in thought as well as in action, must put a curb upon our sentiments as well as upon every transaction that might be construed as a preference of one party to the struggle before another.

"My thought is of America. I am speaking, I feel sure, the earnest wish and purpose of every thoughtful American that this great country of ours, which is, of course, the first in our thoughts and in our hearts, should show herself in this time of peculiar trial a nation fit beyond others to exhibit the fine poise of undisturbed judgment, the dignity of self-control, the efficiency of dispassionate action; a nation that neither sits in judgment upon others nor is disturbed in her own counsels and which keeps herself fit and free to do what is honest and disinterested and truly serviceable for the peace of the world.

"Shall we not resolve to put upon ourselves the restraints which will bring to our people the happiness and the great and lasting influence for peace we covet for them?"

2. *Bryan on American Neutrality*

Despite Wilson's lofty appeal for neutrality and impartiality, there were many in the United States who thought that the Administration was more partial to England and France than to Germany and Austria-Hungary. On January 8, 1915, William J. Stone, Chairman of the Senate Foreign Relations Committee, sent a letter to Secretary of State Bryan noting these charges and asking for an explanation of American policy. Bryan answered this note on January 20 as follows:[2]

"DEAR MR. STONE: I have received your letter of the 8th instant, referring to frequent complaints or charges made in one form or another

2 *Ibid.,* pp. vii-xiv.

through the press that this Government has shown partiality to Great Britain, France, and Russia against Germany and Austria during the present war. . . . You summarize the various grounds of these complaints and ask that you be furnished with whatever information the Department may have touching these points. . . .

"In order that you may have such information as the Department has on the subjects referred to in your letter, I will take them up *seriatim*.

"(1) *Freedom of communication by submarine cable versus censored communication by wireless.*

"The reason that wireless messages and cable messages require different treatment by a neutral government is as follows:

"Communications by wireless can not be interrupted by a belligerent. With a submarine cable it is otherwise. The possibility of cutting the cable exists, and if a belligerent possesses naval superiority the cable is cut, as was the German cable near the Azores by one of Germany's enemies and as was the British cable near Fanning Island by a German naval force. Since a cable is subject to hostile attack, the responsibility falls upon the belligerent and not upon the neutral to prevent cable communication.

"A more important reason, however, at least from the point of view of a neutral government, is that messages sent out from a wireless station in neutral territory may be received by belligerent warships on the high seas. If these messages, whether plain or in cipher, direct the movements of warships or convey to them information as to the location of any enemy's public or private vessels, the neutral territory becomes a base of naval operations, to permit which would be essentially unneutral. . . .

"(2) *Censorship of mails and in some cases repeated destruction of American letters on neutral vessels.*

"As to the censorship of mails, Germany as well as Great Britain has pursued this course in regard to private letters falling into their hands. The unquestioned right to adopt a measure of this sort makes objection to it inadvisable. . . . Complaints have come to the Department that mail on board neutral steamers has been opened and detained, but there seem to be but few cases where the mail from neutral countries has not been finally delivered. When mail is sent to belligerent countries open and is of a neutral and private character, it has not been molested, so far as the Department is advised. . . .

"(4) *Submission without protest to British violations of the rules regarding absolute and conditional contraband as laid down in the Hague conventions, the Declaration of London, and international law.*

"There is no Hague convention which deals with absolute or conditional contraband, and, as the Declaration of London is not in force, the rules of international law only apply. As to the articles to be regarded as contraband, there is no general agreement between nations. It is the practice for a country, either in time of peace or after the outbreak of war, to declare the articles which it will consider as absolute or conditional contraband. It is true that a neutral government is seriously affected by this declaration, as the rights of its subjects or citizens may be impaired. But the rights and interests of belligerents and neutrals are opposed in respect to contraband articles and trade and there is no tribunal to which questions of difference may be readily submitted.

"The record of the United States in the past is not free from criticism. When neutral, this Government has stood for a restricted list of absolute and conditional contraband. As a belligerent, we have contended for a liberal list, according to our conception of the necessities of the case.[3]

"The United States has made earnest representations to Great Britain in regard to the seizure and detention by the British authorities of all American ships or cargoes *bona fide* destined to neutral ports, on the ground that such seizures and detentions were contrary to the existing rules of international law. It will be recalled, however, that American courts have established various rules bearing on these matters. The rule of 'continuous voyage' has been not only asserted by American tribunals but extended by them. They have exercised the right to determine from the circumstances whether the ostensible was the real destination. . . .

"(5) *Acquiescence without protest to the inclusion of copper and other articles in the British lists of absolute contraband.*

"The United States now has under consideration the question of the right of a belligerent to include 'copper unwrought' in its list of absolute contraband instead of in its list of conditional contraband. As the Government of the United States has in the past placed 'all articles from which ammunition is manufactured' in its contraband list, and has declared copper to be among such materials, it necessarily finds some embarrassment in dealing with the subject.

"Moreover, there is no instance of the United States acquiescing in Great Britain's seizure of copper shipments. In every case in which it has been done vigorous representations have been made to the British Government, and the representatives of the United States have pressed for the release of the shipments.

"(6) *Submission without protest to interference with American trade to neutral countries in conditional and absolute contraband.*

"The fact that the commerce of the United States is interrupted by Great Britain is consequent upon the superiority of her Navy on the high seas. History shows that whenever a country has possessed that superiority our trade has been interrupted and that few articles essential to the prosecution of the war have been allowed to reach its enemy from this country. The

[3] Bryan was obviously referring to our policy toward Britain and France before the War of 1812 when the United States was in favor of a restricted contraband list, and to the attitude of this country during the Civil War in adopting a more liberal list.

Department's recent note to the British Government, which has been made public, in regard to detentions and seizures of American vessels and cargoes, is a complete answer to this complaint. . . .

"(8) *Submission to British interference with trade in petroleum, rubber, leather, wool, etc.*

"Petrol and other petroleum products have been proclaimed by Great Britain as contraband of war. In view of the absolute necessity of such products to the use of submarines, aeroplanes, and motors, the United States Government has not yet reached the conclusion that they are improperly included in a list of contraband. . . .

"(9) *The United States has not interfered with the sale to Great Britain and her allies of arms, ammunition, horses, uniforms, and other munitions of war, although such sales prolong the conflict.*

"There is no power in the Executive to prevent the sale of ammunition to the belligerents.

"The duty of a neutral to restrict trade in munitions of war has never been imposed by international law or by municipal statute. It has never been the policy of this Government to prevent the shipment of arms or ammunition into belligerent territory, except in the case of neighboring American Republics, and then only when civil strife prevailed . . . the United States has itself[4] taken no part in contraband traffic, and has, so far as possible, lent its influence toward equal treatment for all belligerents in the matter of purchasing arms and ammunition of private persons in the United States. . . .

"(11) *British warships are permitted to lie off American ports and intercept neutral vessels.*

"The complaint is unjustified from the fact that representations were made to the British Government that the presence of war vessels in the vicinity of New York Harbor was offensive to this Government, and a similar complaint was made to the Japanese Government as to one of its cruisers in the vicinity of the port of Honolulu. In both cases the warships were withdrawn. . . .

"(13) *Change of policy in regard to loans to belligerents.*

"War loans in this country were disapproved because inconsistent with the spirit of neutrality. There is a clearly defined difference between a war loan and the purchase of arms and ammunition. *The policy of disapproving of war loans affects all governments alike, so that the disapproval is not an unneutral act.* The case is entirely different in the matter of arms and ammunition, because prohibition of export not only might not, but in this case would not, operate equally upon the nations at war. . . . The taking of money out of the United States during such a war as this might seriously embarrass the Government in case it needed to borrow money. . . .

---

[4] Bryan is here making a distinction between the Government and private citizens of the United States.

"(14) *Submission to arrest of native-born Americans on neutral vessels and in British ports and their imprisonment.*

"The general charge as to the arrest of American-born citizens on board neutral vessels and in British ports, the ignoring of their passports, and their confinement in jails, requires evidence to support it. That there have been cases of injustice of this sort is unquestionably true, but Americans in Germany have suffered in this way as Americans have in Great Britain. This Government has considered that the majority of these cases resulted from overzealousness on the part of subordinate officials in both countries. Every case which has been brought to the attention of the Department of State has been promptly investigated and, if the facts warranted, a demand for release has been made. . . .

"(20) *General unfriendly attitude of Government toward Germany and Austria.*

"If any American citizens, partisans of Germany and Austria-Hungary, feel that this administration is acting in a way injurious to the cause of those countries, this feeling results from the fact that on the high seas the German and Austro-Hungarian naval power is thus far inferior to the British. It is the business of a belligerent operating on the high seas, not the duty of a neutral, to prevent contraband from reaching an enemy. Those in this country who sympathize with Germany and Austria-Hungary appear to assume that some obligation rests upon this Government in the performance of its neutral duty to prevent all trade in contraband, and thus to equalize the difference due to the relative naval strength of the belligerents. No such obligation exists; it would be an unneutral act, an act of partiality on the part of this Government, to adopt such a policy if the Executive had the power to do so. If Germany and Austria-Hungary can not import contraband from this country, it is not, because of that fact, the duty of the United States to close its markets to the Allies. The markets of this country are open upon equal terms to all the world, to every nation, belligerent or neutral.

"The foregoing categorical replies to specific complaints are sufficient to answer the charge of unfriendliness to Germany and Austria-Hungary.

"I am [etc.]

W. J. Bryan."

3. *American and German Views on Submarine Warfare*

Undoubtedly Wilson and Bryan made a sincere attempt at impartiality during the first year of the war. After the sinking of the *Lusitania* on May 7, 1915, however, relations between Germany and the United States became very strained; and at no time after that incident were there any doubts that American sentiment

favored the Allies. On May 13, Secretary Bryan sent a protest to
the German Government over the sinking of the *Lusitania* which
led to a diplomatic exchange that lasted for approximately a year.[5]

"*The Secretary of State to the Ambassador in Germany (Gerard)*

"[Telegram]

"Washington, *May 13, 1915.*

"1664. Please call on the Minister of Foreign Affairs and, after reading
to him this communication, leave him with a copy:

"In view of the recent acts of the German authorities in violation of
American rights on the high seas which culminated in the torpedoing and
sinking of the British steamship *Lusitania* on May 7, 1915, by which over
100 American citizens lost their lives, it is clearly wise and desirable that the
Government of the United States and the Imperial German Government
should come to a clear and full understanding as to the grave situation which
has resulted. . . .

"The Government of the United States has been apprised that the Imperial German Government considered themselves to be obliged by the
extraordinary circumstances of the present war and the measures adopted
by their adversaries in seeking to cut Germany off from all commerce, to
adopt methods of retaliation which go much beyond the ordinary methods of
warfare at sea, in the proclamation of a war zone from which they have
warned neutral ships to keep away. This Government has already taken
occasion to inform the Imperial German Government that it can not admit
the adoption of such measures or such a warning of danger to operate as in
any degree an abbreviation of the rights of American shipmasters or of
American citizens bound on lawful errands as passengers on merchant ships
of belligerent nationality; and that it must hold the Imperial German Government to a strict accountability for any infringement of those rights, in-
tentional or incidental. It does not understand the Imperial German Government to question those rights. It assumes, on the contrary, that the
Imperial Government accept, as of course, the rule that the lives of noncombatants, whether they be of neutral citizenship or citizens of one of the
nations at war, can not lawfully or rightfully be put in jeopardy by the capture or destruction of an unarmed merchantman, and recognize also, as all
other nations do, the obligation to take the usual precaution of visit and
search to ascertain whether a suspected merchantman is in fact of belligerent
nationality or is in fact carrying contraband of war under a neutral flag.

"The Government of the United States, therefore, desires to call attention of the Imperial German Government with the utmost earnestness to
the fact that the objection to their present method of attack against the trade
of their enemies lies in the practical impossibility of employing submarines

[5] *Papers Relating to the Foreign Relations of the United States, 1915, Supplement, The World War,* pp. 393-96.

in the destruction of commerce without disregarding those rules of fairness, reason, justice, and humanity, which all modern opinion regards as imperative. . . . Manifestly submarines can not be used against merchantmen, as the last few weeks have shown, without an inevitable violation of many sacred principles of justice and humanity. . . .

"The Imperial German Government will not expect the Government of the United States to omit any word or any act necessary to the performance of its sacred duty of maintaining the rights of the United States and its citizens and of safeguarding their free exercise and enjoyment.

BRYAN"

After delivering the above message to Gottlieb E. G. von Jagow, the German Foreign Minister, James W. Gerard, the American Ambassador in Berlin, reported the following to Bryan :[6]

"2234. Your 1664, May 13, 11 a.m., did not arrive until 10 p.m. last night. It was sent from Rome 4 p.m. yesterday. I presented it at 10:30 this morning to Von Jagow personally; he asked that he might read it himself as he understands written better than spoken English. While reading it he laughed and said, 'Rights of free travel on the seas, why not the right of free travel on land in war territory?'

"In confidential conversation he said that there would have to be a sitting of the authorities and no answer should be expected before Monday or Tuesday, but that he was sure Germany would never give up this method of submarine warfare. . . ."

On July 8, 1915, the German Government sent a note to the United States explaining its position on submarine warfare.[7]

"The undersigned has the honor to make the following reply to the note of his excellency, Mr. James W. Gerard, Ambassador of the United States of America. . . .

"The Imperial Government has learned with satisfaction from the note how earnestly the Government of the United States is concerned in seeing the principles of humanity realized in the present war. Also, this appeal meets with full sympathy in Germany, and the Imperial Government is quite willing to permit its statements and decisions in the case under consideration to be governed by the principles of humanity just as it has done always. . . .

"It is known to the American Government how Germany's adversaries, by completely paralyzing peaceable traffic between Germany and the neutral countries, have aimed from the very beginning, and with increasing lack of consideration, at the destruction not so much of the armed forces, as the life

6 *Ibid.*, p. 396.
7 *Ibid.*, pp. 463-66.

of the German nation. . . . Thus Germany was driven to submarine war on trade. . . .

"In the spirit of friendship with which the German nation has been imbued toward the Union and its inhabitants since the earliest days of its existence, the Imperial Government will always be ready to do all it can, during the present war, to prevent the jeopardizing of the lives of American citizens.

"The Imperial Government therefore repeats the assurances that American ships will not be hindered in the prosecution of legitimate shipping, and the lives of American citizens on neutral vessels shall not be placed in jeopardy. . . .

". . . the Imperial Government is unable to admit that American citizens can protect an enemy ship through the mere fact of their presence on board. . . . Consequently accidents suffered by neutrals on enemy ships in this area of war can not well be judged differently from accidents to which neutrals are at all times exposed at the seat of war on land when they betake themselves into dangerous localities in spite of previous warning. . . .

Von Jagow"

Even before the United States and Germany had come to any agreement over the sinking of the *Lusitania,* the Germans sank another British liner, the *Arabic,* which resulted in the death of two American citizens. The Secretary of State and many Americans favored severance of diplomatic relations then, but on September 1, 1915, the German Government assured the United States that in the future passenger ships would not be sunk without warning and without an attempt to save the passengers unless the ship attempted to escape. This appeared to be a satisfactory solution from the viewpoint of the United States until the French vessel, the *Sussex,* was sunk without warning in March 1916. Germany had clearly violated its pledge to Wilson and for well over a month following the sinking it appeared that the United States was on the verge of a diplomatic break. The following is a conversation held between Secretary of State Lansing and the German Ambassador in Washington, Count Johann H. von Bernstorff, on April 20, 1916, relative to the crisis:[8]

"L [Lansing] Good morning.

"B [Bernstorff] Good morning, Sir. You handed me a copy of the note yesterday, and in the present state of affairs of course my chief object is to find a way how this break can be avoided, because I hope it can be avoided.

[8] *Papers Relating to the Foreign Relations of the United States, The Lansing Papers, 1914-1920,* Vol. I, pp. 555-59.

My idea is to find a way out of it, but of course I had to telegraph my Government that this Government seemed to offer little opportunity for settlement. If it means the entire stoppage of the use of the submarines, I am afraid that it cannot be arranged.

"L You will recall that we said in the first *Lusitania* note that we thought it was impossible to use submarines in a really humane way and that later, in our note of July 21, we said that the way submarine warfare had been conducted for the past two months showed that it was possible and therefore we hoped that course would be pursued. Then we had the sinking of the *Arabic* right on top of that, which was another great disaster. Our position is that, if submarine warfare had been conducted in that way, that possibly there would have been no further question raised. But it was not. It has been conducted in the most indiscriminate way and we cannot help but believe that it is ruthless. In those conditions submarine warfare should stop against commercial vessels, unless visit and search is observed.

"B That, of course, is impossible. Germany cannot abandon submarine warfare. No government could come out and say—'We give up the use of submarines.' They would have to resign.

"L What possible methods in the use of submarines, that are effective from a belligerent standpoint, can be suggested which will comply with the law?

"B I had always supposed that warning was to be given.

"L We do not consider that the people on board—the noncombatants on board the vessels—are in a place of safety when put into an open boat a hundred miles from land. It might be calm there, but in the two days it would take them to reach land there might be a severe storm. This is one of the grounds of complaint.

"B That, of course, speaking of neutral vessels—

"L The fact that we do not have Americans on these vessels does not remove the menace to American lives. The sinking of neutral vessels shows that Americans cannot travel with safety on neutral vessels even. That is the serious part of it and I do not know how your Government can modify submarine warfare and make it effective and at the same time obey the law and dictates of humanity.

"B Humanity. Of course war is never humane.

"L 'Humanity' is a relative expression when used with 'war' but the whole tendency in the growth of international law in regard to warfare in the past 125 years has been to relieve noncombatants of needless suffering.

"B Of course I think it would be an ideal state of affairs, but our enemies violate all the rules and you insist on their being applied to Germany.

"L One deals with life; the other with property.

"B Yes.

"L The German method seems reckless to me. It is as if a man who had a very dim vision should go out on the street with a revolver in search of an enemy and should see the outline of a figure and should immediately fire on him and injure him seriously and then go up and apologize and say he made a mistake. I do not think that would excuse him. That seems to be the course pursued by your submarine commanders—they fire first and inquire afterwards.

"B I myself cannot at all explain how it comes that so many neutral vessels have been attacked. I have not the slightest evidence. I do not know anything about it from our communications. . . .

"B . . . Your idea is that the submarine cannot be used if it does not comply with the rules.

"L That is true. My view is that certain instruments of war are not proper to use under certain conditions, and that is the viewpoint that has largely been held in regard to the submarine as a commerce destroyer. . . . It attacks without being seen and so avoid[s] responsibility. It gives every opportunity to kill indiscriminately and recklessly.

"B I perfectly agree with you that sinking without warning would have to stop entirely, sinking without warning is an international offense, and that is why I thought possibly my Government might give up the retaliation, but I do not think it would be possible to say we would give up submarine warfare. I do not think we would do it.

"L And if they should now sink another vessel it would be very serious —that is the way I look at the situation.

"B And if they continue submarine warfare and an instance should happen directly after the break of diplomatic relations, if that should come, it would be still more serious.

"L That is logical.

"B That is why I look at it so seriously.

"L I do not feel that breaking off of diplomatic relations necessarily means war.

"B I do not say it myself but I do not see how it can be avoided. If we refuse it will be because we are to continue submarine warfare and then something might happen which would mean war. I came to see if something could not be done.

"L I am very much obliged to you for coming in, Sir.

"B Good bye, Mr. Secretary.

"L Good bye."

4. *Wilson's War Message to Congress*

In December, 1916, the German Government decided that the most effective way to win the war, which was virtually stalemated on the Western Front, was to engage in unrestricted submarine warfare. On January 31, 1917, the German Ambassador in Washington handed a note to the State Department which announced that beginning February 1 "all sea traffic will be stopped with every available weapon and without further notice in the . . . blockaded zones around Great Britain, France, Italy, and in the Eastern Mediterranean."[9] The United States broke diplomatic relations with Germany on February 3, and on April 2, following the destruction of several American vessels and the publication of the Zimmerman note which revealed Germany's hope to enlist the support of Mexico's aid against the United States in the event of war, Woodrow Wilson asked Congress for a declaration of war. This was done on April 6, 1917.[10]

"GENTLEMEN OF THE CONGRESS: I have called the Congress into extraordinary session because there are serious, very serious, choices of policy to be made, and made immediately, which it was neither right nor constitutionally permissible that I should assume the responsibility of making.

"On the 3rd of February last I officially laid before you the extraordinary announcement of the Imperial German Government that on and after the 1st day of February it was its purpose to put aside all restraints of law or of humanity and use its submarines to sink every vessel that sought to approach either the ports of Great Britain and Ireland or the western coasts of Europe or any of the ports controlled by the enemies of Germany within the Mediterranean. That has seemed to be the object of the German submarine warfare earlier in the war, but since April of last year the Imperial Government had somewhat restrained the commanders of its undersea craft in conformity with its promise then given to us that passenger boats should not be sunk and that due warning would be given to all other vessels which its submarines might seek to destroy, when no resistance was offered or escape attempted, and care taken that their crews were given at least a fair chance to save their lives in their open boats. . . . The new policy has swept every restriction aside. Vessels of every kind, whatever their flag, their character, their cargo, their destination, their errand, have been ruthlessly sent to the bottom without warning and without thought of help or mercy for those on board, the vessels of friendly neutrals along with those of belligerents. . . .

"It is a war against all nations. American ships have been sunk, American lives taken, in ways which it has stirred us very deeply to learn of, but the ships and people of other neutral and friendly nations have been sunk and overwhelmed in the waters in the same way. There has been no discrimination. The challenge is to all mankind. . . .

[9] *Papers Relating to the Foreign Relations of the United States, 1917, Supplement 1, The World War*, p. 101.
[10] *Ibid.,* pp. 195-203.

"With a profound sense of the solemn and even tragical character of the step I am taking and of the grave responsibilities which it involves, but in unhesitating obedience to what I deem my constitutional duty, I advise that the Congress declare the recent course of the Imperial German Government to be in fact nothing less than war against the Government and the people of the United States; that it formally accept the status of belligerent which has thus been thrust upon it; and that it take immediate steps not only to put the country in a more thorough state of defense but also to exert all its power and employ all its resources to bring the Government of the German Empire to terms and end the war. . . .

"We have no quarrel with the German people. We have no feeling towards them but one of sympathy and friendship. It was not upon their impulse that their Government acted in entering this war. . . . It was a war determined upon as wars used to be determined upon in the old, unhappy days when peoples were nowhere consulted by their rulers and wars were provoked and waged in the interest of dynasties or of little groups of ambitious men who were accustomed to use their fellow men as pawns and tools. . . .

"It is a distressing and oppressive duty, gentlemen of the Congress, which I have performed in thus addressing you. There are, it may be, many months of fiery trial and sacrifice ahead of us. It is a fearful thing to lead this great peaceful people into war, into the most terrible and most disastrous of all wars, civilization itself seeming to be in the balance. But the right is more precious than peace, and we shall fight for the things which we have always carried nearest our hearts—for democracy, for the right of those who submit to authority to have a voice in their own government, for the rights and liberties of small nations, for a universal dominion of right by such a concert of free peoples as shall bring peace and safety to all nations and make the world itself at last free. To such a task we can dedicate our lives and our fortunes, everything that we are and everything that we have, with the pride of those who know that the day has come when America is privileged to spend her blood and her might for the principles that gave her birth and happiness and the peace which she has treasured. God helping her, she can do no other."

CHAPTER VII.

THE FIRST WORLD WAR

WOODROW WILSON'S war objectives were two-fold: that German militarism should be crushed on the field of battle and that the United States should assume a position of moral leadership which would lead to a lasting peace based on justice. In many respects the problems confronting the military leaders were simpler than those facing the diplomats, although this did not become evident until after the end of the war.

The most serious military threat to the United States immediately after our entry into war was the submarine. Our great potential strength would be of no avail to the Allies or to ourselves if the Germans could carry out their avowed purpose to isolate Great Britain and France from the rest of the world. When the United States declared war, the Germans were destroying British ships much faster than these could be replaced. It was only after the might of the American Navy had been added to that of the British and French, plus the use of the convoy system, that the tide of the battle in the Atlantic was finally turned against Germany.

Although the United States had a navy which was immediately used against the enemy, it had no army large enough or well enough equipped to send against the German legions in April, 1917. Consequently the first year was spent largely in raising, training, and equipping an army and increasing the size of the navy. By the summer of 1918 this force had become so formidable that the more than one million men in the American Expeditionary Force in France were able to give the added strength needed to turn the tide against the Kaiser's forces and bring the war to a rapid conclusion in November.

Although America's main military effort on land was on the Western Front, a small number of troops were sent to North Russia and Siberia in 1918, largely as a result of almost constant prodding by the British and French who made a desperate effort to reform an Eastern Front following Russia's withdrawal from the war. Although Wilson finally agreed to send American troops to Russia, they were not sent there, as the Allies had hoped, to reform the Eastern Front, but to guard military stores from falling into the hands of the Germans at Archangel and in Siberia and to aid in the evacuation of Czechoslovak troops to Vladivostok.

That the directives given our commanding generals in Russia were not clear, was indicated by the fact that in North Russia, American troops had occasional skirmishes with the Bolsheviks; and in Siberia, where the situation was even more chaotic, the chief worry of the American commander was that our ostensible allies, the Japanese, would annex all Russian territory east of Lake Baikal.

If our position in Russia was confusing before the Armistice, it was worse after that event. With the Germans still at war it could be argued that Allied troops should be on Russian soil, but Germany was no menace after November 11, 1918. However, American troops remained in North Russia until late 1919 and in Siberia until the early part of 1920. At no time did the military commanders in the field or the American people ever have any adequate explanation as to what they were supposed to be doing there.

The British and French had clear objectives after the defeat of Germany: they hoped to overthrow the Bolshevik Government, but the United States never announced this as its goal, although it did furnish a very limited amount of aid to the White Russians then at war with the Reds.

American intervention in Russia from 1918 to 1920 was a fiasco. We sent too few troops to accomplish anything from a military viewpoint but enough to make it appear that we were intervening in Russian affairs. This policy pleased neither the British nor French who wanted to overthrow the Lenin regime, nor the Japanese whose ambitions in Siberia were somewhat thwarted by the presence of American troops, nor the White Russians who wanted real aid, nor the Red Russians who accused us of intervening in their affairs, nor American citizens who did not know what our troops were doing there in the first place.

During the war the military effort naturally took precedence over American diplomacy. We had no relations with our enemies except on the field of battle; and since cooperation was of para-

mount importance on the fighting front, the United States chose
to postpone the discussion of any serious differences with our
Allies until the end of the war. Wilson made it clear, however, in
a number of addresses as to type of peace settlement he desired;
and he was fully aware of the fact that our vast military and economic strength would give us a powerful voice at the peace conference. His most comprehensive statement of America's war and
peace goals was in an address to Congress on January 8, 1918,
which contained his famous Fourteen Points. These objectives,
Wilson believed, not only constituted the basis of a just peace settlement but they would also prevent the occurrence of any future
world war.

When the war ended President Wilson and the American
people believed that our sacrifices had been justified by the results.
Germany had been utterly defeated and Americans were confident
that the world had been made "safe for democracy."

1. *Wilson's Fourteen Points*

President Wilson delivered an address to a joint session of
Congress on January 8, 1918, which dealt largely with the peace
conference then in progress at Brest-Litovsk between the Germans and the Bolsheviks who had seized power in Russia in November, 1917. Although the United States had not recognized
this newly established regime, Wilson spoke of their leaders in
laudatory terms, believing at the time that they were committed
to the same democratic objectives as he. In this address he presented his Fourteen Points.[1]

"I. Open covenants of peace, openly arrived at, after which there shall
be no private international understandings of any kind but diplomacy shall
proceed always frankly and in the public view.

"II. Absolute freedom of navigation upon the seas, outside territorial
waters, alike in peace and in war, except as the seas may be closed in whole
or in part by international action for the enforcement of international
covenants.

"III. The removal, so far as possible, of all economic barriers and the
establishment of an equality of trade conditions among all the nations con-
senting to the peace and associating themselves for its maintenance.

"IV. Adequate guarantees given and taken that national armaments
will be reduced to the lowest point consistent with domestic safety.

[1] *Papers Relating to the Foreign Relations of the United States, 1918, Supplement 1, The World War*, Vol. I, pp. 12-17.

"V. A free, open-minded, and absolutely impartial adjustment of all colonial claims, based upon a strict observance of the principle that in determining all such questions of sovereignty the interests of the populations concerned must have equal weight with the equitable claims of the government whose title is to be determined.

"VI. The evacuation of all Russian territory and such a settlement of all questions affecting Russia as will secure the best and freest cooperation of the other nations of the world in obtaining for her an unhampered and unembarrassed opportunity for the independent determination of her own political development and national policy and assure her of a sincere welcome into the society of free nations under institutions of her own choosing; and, more than a welcome, assistance also of every kind that she may herself need and may herself desire. The treatment accorded Russia by her sister nations in the months to come will be the acid test of their good will, of their comprehension of her needs as distinguished from their own interests, and of their intelligent and unselfish sympathy.

"VII. Belgium, the whole world will agree, must be evacuated and restored, without any attempt to limit the sovereignty which she enjoys in common with other free nations. No other single act will serve as this will serve to restore confidence among the nations in the laws which they have themselves set and determined for the government of their relations with one another. Without this healing act the whole structure and validity of international law is forever impaired.

"VIII. All French territory should be freed and the invaded portions restored, and the wrong done to France by Prussia in 1871 in the matter of Alsace-Lorraine, which has unsettled the peace of the world for nearly fifty years, should be righted, in order that peace may once more be made secure in the interest of all.

"IX. A readjustment of the frontiers of Italy should be effected along clearly recognizable lines of nationality.

"X. The peoples of Austria-Hungary, whose place among the nations we wish to see safeguarded and assured, should be accorded the freest opportunity of autonomous development.

"XI. Rumania, Serbia, and Montenegro should be evacuated; occupied territories restored; Serbia accorded free and secure access to the sea; and the relations of the several Balkan states to one another determined by friendly counsel along historically established lines of allegiance and nationality; and international guarantees of the political and economic independence and territorial integrity of the several Balkan states should be entered into.

"XII. The Turkish portions of the present Ottoman Empire should be assured a secure sovereignty, but the other nationalities which are now under Turkish rule should be assured an undoubted security of life and an absolutely unmolested opportunity of autonomous development, and the Dardanelles should be permanently opened as a free passage to the ships and commerce of all nations under international guarantee.

"XIII. An independent Polish state should be erected which should include the territories inhabited by indisputably Polish populations, which should be assured a free and secure access to the sea, and whose political and economic independence and territorial integrity should be guaranteed by international covenant.

"XIV. A general association of nations must be formed under specific covenants for the purpose of affording mutual guarantees of political independence and territorial integrity to great and small nations alike."

2. The Military Situation in December, 1917

Following the entry of the United States into the war, it became very evident that close collaboration among all the nations joined in the struggle against Germany was necessary to bring victory. The disastrous defeat of the Italian army at Caporetto convinced the British, French, and Italian Governments that a close liaison was mandatory to fend off defeat. At a conference held at Rapallo on November 7, 1917, a Supreme War council was created. Ten days later, the United States joined this group, and Wilson sent his close friend Colonel Edward M. House to represent him on the Council as the political member, and General Tasker H. Bliss was chosen as our military representative.

On December 18, 1917, General Bliss sent a long memorandum to the Secretary of War, outlining the general military situation as described to him by the other members of the Supreme War Council, and containing his recommendations to our Government.[2]

"1. A military crisis is to be apprehended, culminating not later than the end of the next spring, in which, without great assistance from the United States, the advantage will probably lie with the Central Powers.[3]

"2. This crisis is largely due to the collapse of Russia as a military factor and to the recent disaster in Italy. But it is also largely due to lack of military coordination, lack of unity of control on the part of the Allied forces in the field.

"3. The lack of unity of control results from military jealousy and suspicion as to ultimate national aims.

[2] Papers Relating to the Foreign Relations of the United States, The Lansing Papers, 1914-1920, Vol. II, pp. 212-15.

[3] This prediction was correct. The Germans launched their "victory" drive in March, 1918, in an effort to end the war before large numbers of American troops could reach France.

"4. Our Allies urge us to profit by their experience in three and a half years of war; to adopt the organization, the types of artillery, tanks, etc. that the test of war has proved to be satisfactory. We should go further. In making the great military effort now demanded of us we should demand as a prior condition that our Allies also profit by the experience of three and a half years of war in the matter of absolute unity of military control. National jealousies and suspicions and susceptibilities of national temperament must be put aside in favor of this unified control; even going if necessary (as I believe it is) to the limit of unified command. Otherwise, our dead and theirs may have died in vain.[4]

.   .   .   .

"6. To meet a probable military crisis we must meet the unanimous demand of our Allies to send to France the maximum number of troops that we can send as early in the year 1918 as possible. There may be no campaign of 1919 unless we do our best to make the campaign of 1918 the last.

"7. To properly equip these troops, so that we may face the enemy with soldiers and not merely men, we should accept every proffer of assistance from our Allies, continuing our own program of construction for later needs, but accepting everything from them which most quickly meets the immediate purposes of the war and which will most quickly enable us to play a decisive part in it. This should be the only test.

"8. To transport these troops before it is too late we should take every ton of shipping that can possibly be taken from trade. Especially should every ton be utilized that is now lying idle, engaged neither in trade nor in war. The Allies and the neutrals must tighten their belts and go without luxuries and many things which they think of as necessities must be cut to the limit. Every branch of construction which can be devoted to an extension of our ship-building program, and which is not vitally necessary for other purposes, should be so devoted in order to meet the rapidly growing demand for ships during 1918. The one all-absorbing necessity now is soldiers with which to beat the enemy in the field, and ships to carry them. . . .

Tasker H. Bliss,
General, Chief of Staff, U. S. Army."

3. Intervention in Russia

Undoubtedly the most confusing aspect of American foreign policy from 1918 to 1920 was our relationship to Russia.

The salient facts are these: Shortly after the overthrow of the Czarist Government in March, 1917, the United States enthusiastically recognized the new regime, believing it to be demo-

[4] This was finally achieved on April 3, 1918, when Marshal Ferdinand Foch was named Commander in Chief of the Allied Armies on the Western Front.

cratic. The Bolshevik Revolution which came in November, 1917, was obviously of a different character. While it would have been difficult if not impossible for anyone to have completely analyzed the nature of Communism in Russia immediately after this revolution, much less to have correctly presaged the future, there were serious doubts in the United States as to the nature of the new regime of Lenin and Trotsky. Although Wilson praised this group in his January 8, 1918, address to Congress, the United States did not recognize this new government which had devoted itself to the program of world-wide revolution.

Russia became an important factor in the military picture in 1918 because of its peace treaty with Germany at Brest-Litovsk which released German troops for use on the Western Front in the spring offensive. Britain and France first wanted Allied troops sent to Russia to reform an Eastern Front, then to overthrow the Soviet regime. America finally agreed to send a limited number of troops to Russia. The results have already been noted.

General Tasker H. Bliss's concept of this operation was contained in his 1920 report of his activities as a member of the Supreme War Council to the Secretary of State.[5]

"*4. Siberia and North Russia*

   "(a)   Siberia

"At the close of the year 1917 and beginning of the year 1918 the Allies watched day by day the Germans withdrawing an increasing number of divisions from their Russian front and adding them to the forces which it was evident that they intended to employ in a tremendous effort early in the latter year. The situation was such as to cause the Allies the gravest apprehension. They were ready to clutch at every straw which seemed to afford the slightest chance of supporting their sinking weight.

"In the month of February, 1918, the American Military Representative was informed that one of the Allies was strongly pressing the Government of the United States to participate in an Allied expedition to Siberia by way of Vladivostok. . . .

"It was represented that enormous stores of military supplies of all kinds had been brought to Vladivostok during the régime of the Czar and that the general collapse of the transportation system, both before and after the revolution, had prevented their being brought into European Russia. There was reason to believe that the new government might dispose of these stores to the advantage of Germany and to the detriment of the Allies. . . .

   [5] *Papers Relating to the Foreign Relations of the United States, The Lansing Papers, 1914-1920*, Vol. II, pp. 199-303.

"This situation gave a valid reason for the military occupation of Vladivostok and the railway as far as Harbin, as a similar one gave a military reason for the subsequent project to occupy the ports of Murmansk and Archangel. But, as far as these considerations alone were concerned, neither of them gave a reason for a further advance into the interior.

"With reference to Siberia, the studies showed that no other Allied troops than those of Japan (except, possibly, in very small numbers) could be made available for this expedition. . . .

"At that time there was, in the mind of many, a misconception as to the extent of the revolutionary feeling in Russia, whether Bolshevik or otherwise, and the American Military Representative always held that the plans for the intervention in that country and the ultimate objects were too largely based on that misconception. The others[6] believed that the great mass of the people in European Russia and, especially, in Siberia wanted nothing but a leader and some support from the outside to overthrow a government whose local iniquities were then beginning to appal the world. Too little weight was given to the fact that the great mass of the 180,000,000 people living in Russia knew little of these iniquities and suffered little or nothing from them; while they attributed all of the evils from which they suffered to war in the abstract. People who believed that were not likely to rally to the support of anyone who proposed further war.[7] Whether the basic idea was incorrect or not, it was assumed that, after getting possession of the military stores at Vladivostok and Archangel, an Allied force of only a few divisions could work its way along the trans-Siberian railway as far as Cheliabinsk, occupying the important centers of population on or near that railway, and thus furnishing nuclei about which the orderly elements would rally and thence, by a process of peaceful penetration, their influence would be carried into European Russia. The occupation of the Siberian railway, it was believed, would first of all deprive the Germans of any possible hope of the grain supply of that great province. Furthermore, it was believed that the influence permeating the rest of the empire from the restoration of orderly government in Siberia would lead to a rehabilitation of a Russian Army to operate on the Eastern frontier of Germany. Could this be realized in time, it would prevent further withdrawals of German divisions from that front and might possibly force the return of some that had already been withdrawn.

"Thus, it will be seen that the original idea was not primarily to initiate a war against Bolshevism as such but was merely to bring about a renewal of a Russian thrust against Eastern Germany. . . .

"However, on April 9, 1918, at a full meeting of the Military Representatives, there was presented the draft of Joint Note No. 20 for discussion.

[6] British, French, and Italian members of the Supreme War Council.

[7] General Bliss's analysis was very accurate in this regard. Such Allied-supported White Russians as Kolchak and Denikin aroused very little enthusiasm among the people of Russia.

The subject of this note was 'The Situation in the Eastern Theatre.' It emphasized the necessity of an immediate Allied intervention in Russia as the only course that would insure any 'serious military resistance to Germany' from that direction. Here, again, was an evidence of the frequent tendency to divert efforts from measures to attain a common end, for the purpose of guarding some threatened national interest. In Joint Note No. 20 appeared very clearly the British fear of influences that might seriously threaten India. . . .

"I explained to my colleagues that the instructions which I had received from my Government were to the effect that the whole question of intervention in Siberia was the subject of diplomatic negotiation; that I, therefore, could not join with them in signing the note but that, as it was a clear exposition of the situation from their point of view, I would transmit it, unsigned by me, for the information of my Government. . . .

"(b) The Archangel and Murmansk Expeditions

". . . At this time[8] the attitude of the United States Government with regard to its participation in the occupation of the northern ports of Russia was perfectly clear. It recognized that, at the best, only a limited force was available. It was not contemplated by it nor (so far as was known to it) by any other government to conduct operations into the interior of the country,—certainly not except with the cordial consent of the Russian people. It agreed to the occupation of the ports for the purpose of getting possession of valuable military material and of preventing, as long as possible with the available force, access by the Germans to them and the establishment by them there of bases. . . .

"From time to time after the dispatch of the above force to Murmansk,[9] and in one way or another, efforts were made to convince me that I should urge my government to further augment the forces in Northern Russia. The expressed purpose for the increase in forces urged was offensive Allied action by the Northern Russian Expedition and I consistently held to the view that the Murmansk and Archangel Expeditions were intended for a specific defensive purpose, namely: the retention of those ports and for that purpose should not be augmented. Further I made it clear that the Government of the United States had definitely declined to take part in organized intervention in the interior of Russia in adequate force from Murmansk or Archangel."

4. *The Armistice*

In October, 1918, the Germans, staggering under continuing blows on the Western Front from the Allied armies increasingly

[8] March 23, 1918.
[9] In July, 1918, Wilson decided to allow three companies of infantry and three companies of engineers to participate in an expedition to Murmansk.

augmented by fresh American troops, asked Wilson for an armistice based on his Fourteen Points. The Germans believed that they might receive more lenient treatment from Wilson, the idealist, than from their more realistic foes nearer at hand. Wilson made it clear, however, that any armistice allowed Germany would be the result of joint action of the Allied Powers, not just the United States. In the period prior to the signing of the Armistice it became evident that the major Allied Powers were not fully satisfied to grant an armistice based on the Fourteen Points without qualifications. The statement finally agreed upon was as follows:[10]

"The Allied Governments have given careful consideration to the correspondence which has passed between the President of the United States and the German Government. Subject to the qualifications which follow they declare their willingness to make peace with the Government of Germany on the terms of peace laid down in the President's address to Congress of January, 1918, and the principles of the settlement enunciated in his subsequent addresses. They must point out, however, that clause 2, relating to what is usually described as the freedom of the seas, is open to various interpretations, some of which they could not accept. They must, therefore, reserve to themselves complete freedom on this subject when they enter the peace conference.

"Further, in the conditions of peace laid down in his address to Congress of January 8, 1918, the President declared that invaded territories must be restored as well as evacuated and freed, the Allied Governments feel that no doubt ought to be allowed to exist as to what this provision implies. By it they understand that compensation will be made by Germany for all damage done to the civilian population of the Allies and their property by the aggression of Germany by land, by sea and from the air."

[10] *Papers Relating to the Foreign Relations of the United States 1918, Supplement 1, The World War*, Vol. I, pp. 468-69.

CHAPTER VIII.

LIQUIDATION OF WORLD WAR I

AMERICA'S foreign policy was Woodrow Wilson's policy in a very real sense during and immediately after the first World War. This was true not only because of the great powers which any American President has in war-time, but because Wilson chose to exert all the powers that were legally his in a manner reminiscent of Abraham Lincoln.

To Wilson the war was a great crusade for human freedom. In asking Congress to declare war on Germany on April 2, 1917, Wilson indicated one of his desires in saying that the "world must be made safe for democracy." A few days after the Armistice, Wilson's hopes for the future were illustrated in his Thanksgiving Proclamation, when he told the nation that "Complete victory has brought us, not peace alone, but the confident promise of a new day as well in which justice shall replace force and jealous intrigue among the nations."

The President was aware of the conflicting interests of certain of the Allied powers during the war, and he probably was not so naive as to expect a Utopian world after the war. But he was confident that a better day had emerged; and he believed that the supreme mission of his life was to create a League of Nations based on the concept of a concert of nations to supplant the old balance of power which would guarantee peace, justice, and freedom for all nations.

President Wilson went to the Paris Peace Conference fully aware of his prestige throughout the Allied world. He was conscious of the fact that of the major Allied and Associated powers, the United States alone, had not committed itself by secret or open treaties to any postwar plan. To Wilson this meant that he, of all the major delegates at the conference, was the only one who had absolute freedom of negotiation; and he intended to use his power and position to see that a just settlement was reached.

Wilson's high hopes of January, 1919, were largely shattered before the end of that year. Upon arriving in Paris, he found that despite his great prestige, he was unable to force the other great powers to adopt all of his ideas. Clemenceau, Lloyd George, Orlando, Baron Makino, and others were not nearly as interested in idealism as Wilson was. He learned that in some cases it was physically impossible to arrive at a particular settlement without violating at least one of his Fourteen Points. The Polish settlement will serve as an illustration. If the Poles were given access to the sea (as was done), it would violate the principle of the self-determination of peoples (as was done with respect to the Germans). If they were denied an outlet to the Baltic, then the principle of access to the sea would have been violated.

He was never able to persuade the British to include the principle of absolute freedom of the seas in the Treaty of Versailles. The Japanese, supported by the British and French, were allowed to retain a foothold on the Shantung Peninsula of China, contrary to Wilson's idea of self-determination of peoples. The Italians were bitterly disappointed in their failure to receive all the benefits promised them in 1915 by the British and French in the secret Treaty of London. Wilson compromised enough to allow the Italians to gain some territory which included over 250,000 Austrians, yet he did not yield enough to satisfy all of Italy's desires. And the mandate system did not jibe with his statement in the Fourteen Points.

His growing dismay over the compromises he was forced to accept in the treaty convinced him more firmly that world justice would have to emerge from the League of Nations. By the time he had returned from Paris to present the completed treaty to the Senate for ratification, he was firm in the belief that the League would atone for any sins committed in the main body of the treaty itself.

Wilson's defeats in Paris, however, were mild in comparison to the bitterness and humiliation he suffered when the Senate rejected the treaty. Few men in history with such power and prestige have experienced such a severe defeat for so little reason. He had alienated the Republicans in calling for a Democratic victory in Congress in 1918 and irritated them still further in failing to take at least one prominent Republican leader with him to Paris. His lack of political acumen plus his stubbornness in rejecting all Senate reservations to the treaty made it easy for

Wilson's political foes to thwart the fulfillment of his fondest dream.

In considering the period from the signing of the Armistice to the end of the Washington Conference in 1922, it is apparent that the United States attained more of its immediate objectives than seems to be the case when American success is judged solely by Wilson's efforts at Versailles and by his battle with the Senate. It is true that Wilson failed in a very personal sense. On the other hand the League was created, even if the United States did not join it. The war was ended by a joint resolution of Congress in 1921, and the United States accepted most of the provisions except those relating to the Covenant of the League; and the treaty did bring about a settlement, if not a solution, to all areas affected by the war, except Russia and the Far East.

No Russian delegation was invited to the Paris Conference. The Russians who had been driven from their homeland did not constitute a government; and the Reds, who had disavowed all international obligations to the Czarist Government, did not meet the requirements of international law for recognition as a government.

The men at Versailles, who had a blurred picture of the course of events in Russia in 1918 and 1919 were, in effect, waiting for the dust to settle. No one in Paris in the spring of 1919 thought that the Bolsheviks could maintain control of Russia for long. Allied troops were on Russian soil until well after the end of the Paris Conference, but, with the possible exception of Japan, none had any well defined objectives toward that vast area over which the Bolsheviks were gradually extending their grip.

The Shantung settlement at Paris did not please the United States, or Japan, or China; and as American and Japanese troops were still in Siberia when the conference ended—with no agreement as to the disposition of these forces—the situation in the Far East was far from settled.

After the election of Warren G. Harding to the presidency in 1920, the United States took the initiative in calling a conference of all the powers with Far Eastern interests to meet in Washington in November, 1921. The delegates of the nine powers which came to the United States concluded a series of treaties which provided for a settlement in the Far East that lasted for a decade.

All nine powers, including China and Japan, signed an agreement which recognized the principle of the Open Door. The five major powers signed a naval limitation treaty; and four powers—the United States, Britain, France, and Japan—signed an innocuous accord which was a polite way for Britain to end its twenty-year-old military alliance with Japan.

No treaty dealt with the question of Japanese troops on Russian soil (American troops had been withdrawn from Siberia early in 1920), but the problem was discussed in Washington; and Japan withdrew its forces from the mainland in 1922 and from Sakhalin in 1925.

1. Wilson's Peace Objectives

Less than a month after the Armistice, Wilson, in a mood of high confidence, addressed Congress on December 2, 1918, as to his plans for the peace.[1]

". . . now we are sure of the great triumph for which every sacrifice was made. It has come, come in its completeness, and with the pride and inspiration of these days of achievement quick within us we turn to the tasks of peace again, —a peace secure against the violence of irresponsible monarchs and ambitious military coteries and made ready for a new order, for new foundations of justice and fair dealing.

"We are about to give order and organization to this peace not only for ourselves but for the other peoples of the world as well, so far as they will suffer us to serve them. It is international justice that we seek, not domestic safety merely. . . .

"The allied Governments have accepted the bases of peace which I outlined to the Congress on the eighth of January last,[2] as the Central Empires also have, and very reasonably desire my personal counsel in their interpretations and application, and it is highly desirable that I should give it in order that the sincere desire of our Government to contribute without selfish purpose of any kind to settlements that will be of common benefit to all the nations concerned may be made fully manifest. . . . The gallant men of our armed forces on land and sea have consciously fought for the ideals which they knew to be the ideals of their country; I have sought to express those ideals; they have accepted my statements of them as the substance of their own thought and purpose, as the associated Governments have accepted them; I owe it to them to see to it, so far as in me lies, that no false or mistaken interpretation is put upon them, and no possible effort

[1] *Congressional Record,* 65th Cong., 3rd Sess., Vol. LVII, Pt. 1, pp. 5-8.
[2] They were accepted with reservations already noted.

omitted to realize them. It is now my duty to play my full part in making good what they offered their life's blood to obtain. I can think of no call to service which could transcend this. . . ."

2. *Dispute over the Shantung Peninsula*

One of the major disputes at the Paris Peace Conference concerned the disposition of the former German leasehold at Kiaochow on the Shantung Peninsula in China. Japan had seized this area in 1914 and had virtually forced the Chinese to sign a treaty in 1915 recognizing Japan's rights to this area. In 1917 the British and French had signed a secret treaty with Japan whereby they agreed to back up Japan's demands on China at the end of the war. The United States had signed no such agreement, and the crux of the dispute in Paris was whether or not Japan should stay in China in violation of Wilson's principle of the self-determination of peoples. The following are excerpts of a discussion held in Paris on April 22, 1919, with Wilson, Clemenceau, Lloyd George, Baron Makino, and Viscount Chinda (Japanese delegates) as the main participants.[3]

"(1) BARON MAKINO read the following statement:—

'In January last I had the privilege to present and explain before the Supreme Council Japan's claims which we deemed as just and fair in the light of the circumstances which led Japan to take part in the war and of the actual situations created or found in the regions to which the claims related. . . .

'The German stronghold at Kiaochow was captured on the 7th of November, 1914, and has, together with the Shantung Railway, remained to this day under Japanese occupation.

'Looking to the eventual termination of the war, Japan approached China in January, 1915,[4] with a view to reaching beforehand an agreement as to the basis of the restitution to China of the leased territory of Kiaochow, and of disposing other German rights in relation to Shantung, so that Germany might find no pretext to refuse acquiescence in Japan's demands at the final peace conference and that she might not find it possible to recover her influence in China, thereby becoming again a grave menace to the peace of the Far East.

'As a result of the negotiations that ensued, a treaty respecting the Province of Shantung, accompanied by an exchange of notes, was signed on the 25th of May, 1915. In that treaty China engaged to recognise all

---

[3] *Papers Relating to the Foreign Relations of the United States, The Paris Peace Conference, 1919,* Vol. V, pp. 123-33.

[4] The Twenty-One Demands.

matters that might be agreed upon between the Japanese Government and the German Government respecting the disposition of all the rights, interests and concessions, which Germany possessed, vis-a-vis China in relation to the Province of Shantung. . . .'

"MR. LLOYD GEORGE said that so far as Great Britain was concerned they were in the same position towards Japan as towards Italy. They had a definite engagement with Japan, as recorded in the Note of the British Ambassador at Tokio, dated 16th February, 1917. . . .

"PRESIDENT WILSON pointed out that, as had happened in many instances, he was the only one present whose judgment was entirely independent. His colleagues were both bound by Treaties, although perhaps he might be entitled to question whether Great Britain and Japan had been justified in handing around the islands in the Pacific. This, however, was a private opinion.

"MR. LLOYD GEORGE pointed out that there were only the German islands.

"PRESIDENT WILSON pointed out that in the circumstances he was the only independent party present. He would like to repeat the point of view which he had urged on the Japanese Delegation a few days before. He was so firmly convinced that the Peace of the Far East centered upon China and Japan that he was more interested from this point of view than any other. He did not wish to see complex engagements that fettered free determination. He was anxious that Japan should show to the world as well as China that she wanted to give the same independence to China as other nations possessed; that she did not want China to be held in manacles. . . . He did not wish to interfere with treaties. As Mr. Lloyd George had remarked earlier, the war had been partly undertaken in order to establish the sanctity of treaties. Although he yielded to no-one in this sentiment there were cases he felt where treaties ought not be have been entered into. . . .' "

Later that same day, April 22, 1919, the Chinese delegation was invited to discuss the Shantung matter with Wilson, Lloyd George, and Clemenceau. The chief Chinese delegates were Lou Tseng-Tsiang and V. K. Wellington Koo. Excerpts from the conversation follow:[5]

". . . MR. KOO said that the Treaties of 1915 and the subsequent exchange of Notes were the outcome of the 21 demands which Japan had made on China and were all part and parcel of one transaction. He hoped he had made this clear before the Council of Ten. He felt that the Treaties and Notes which had been exchanged after Japan had delivered an ultimatum stood outside of the regular procedure and course of Treaties. They dealt with matters arising out of the war.

"MR. LLOYD GEORGE asked what ultimatum he referred to.

[5] *Ibid.,* pp. 138-48.

"PRESIDENT WILSON asked if Mr. Lloyd George had never heard of the twenty-one points.

"MR. LLOYD GEORGE said he had not.

"MR. KOO said that in January, 1915 after the capture of Kiau Chau that port had been opened up to trade; China then asked Japan to withdraw her troops from the interior of the province. The Japanese took occasion to treat this note as though it were an unfriendly act and shortly after sprung on China twenty-one demands divided into five groups for example, that China should accept Japanese advisers; that they should give up railway concessions in which Western Powers were concerned, and he would draw Mr. Lloyd George's attention to the fact that Great Britain was concerned. China was put in an extremely embarrassing position. She resisted and resisted and only gave up when she was absolutely compelled to. On the 7th. May the Japanese sent China an ultimatum in regard to the majority of demands giving China only 48 hours within which to accept; otherwise Japan would consider herself free to take such steps as she thought fit to enforce them. This caused absolute consternation to the Chinese Government which eventually had to submit to *force majeure*.

"MR. LLOYD GEORGE asked if they had not appealed to the United States of America.

"PRESIDENT WILSON said they had and the United States had intervened in regard to the infringement of sovereignty and political independence. The whole transaction however, had been kept extremely secret and the United States only learnt of it in a roundabout way.

"MR. KOO said that secrecy had been imposed upon China by Japan under severe penalties. . . .

"MR. KOO said that he could not lay too much emphasis on the fact that the Chinese people were now at the parting of the ways. The policy of the Chinese Government was cooperation with Europe and the United States as well as with Japan. If, however, they did not get justice, China might be driven into the arms of Japan. There was a small section in China which believed in Asia for the Asiatics and wanted the closest co-operation with Japan. . . .

"PRESIDENT WILSON said that these were serious considerations, but he would not like Mr. Koo even personally to entertain the idea that there was an injustice in an arrangement that was based on treaties which Japan had entered into. The sacredness of treaties had been one of the motives of the war. It had been necessary to show that treaties were not mere scraps of paper. If treaties were inconsistent with the principles on which the peace was being formed, nevertheless, we could not undo past obligations. . . .

"MR. KOO said he believed prevention to be better than cure. He thought that it would be better to undo unfortunate engagements now, if they endangered the permanence of the future peace. . . ."

3. Dispute at Versailles over Italian Claims

Italy entered the war on the side of the Allies in 1915 partially as a result of the Secret Treaty of London, which promised the Italians certain portions of Austrian territory in the Alps and along the eastern shore of the Adriatic Sea among other things. The United States was not a party to this agreement, and when it became evident to Wilson that full compliance with this treaty would violate his principle of self-determination, he opposed it on the same grounds that he opposed the Japanese demands on China.

The following selection is taken from notes of a meeting held in Paris on May 3, 1919, in which the main participants were Wilson, Lloyd George, and Clemenceau.[6]

". . . MR. LLOYD GEORGE said it was necessary to speak very frankly in the intimacy of these conversations. It must not be forgotten that there was a growing feeling that Europe was being bullied by the United States of America. In London this feeling was very strong and that matter had to be handled with the greatest care. Any such rift would be the saddest possible ending of the present Conference. It would put an end to the League of Nations. He understood that the London press had behaved extremely well and had not gone as far as British public opinion. The position was one of real danger and wanted to be handled with the greatest care, otherwise we might have the worst catastrophe since 1914.

"PRESIDENT WILSON said he did not speak with authority [in] regard to British public opinion. Nevertheless, he was sure that the so-called bullying was recognized by the common man as based on the principles which inspired the Peace. In his view, it was indispensable clearly to show Italy that in all essentials Great Britain, France, and the United States were united, otherwise the Italians would continue to be troublesome.

"MR. LLOYD GEORGE said that in fact they were not completely united. In regard to Fiume they were united. M. Clemenceau and he, however, were not in the same position as President Wilson, owing to the fact they were bound by the Treaty of London.

"PRESIDENT WILSON pointed out that Mr. Lloyd George and M. Clemenceau had both signed the memorandum to M. Orlando. This showed that they were united with him in judgment even though not in position.

"MR. LLOYD GEORGE said that it was no use being united in judgment when a decision was wanted. France and Great Britain were bound by the Treaty of London. If Italy insisted he was bound to stand by

[6] *Ibid.,* pp. 426-34.

the Treaty. He could not possibly help that. This was the bottom fact of the whole situation.

"PRESIDENT WILSON thought that this was a position which could not be got out of. Moreover, it was an indefensible position. The Treaty had been entered into when only a little group of nations was at war. Since then half the World had joined in. There could be no right in coercing other Parties to this Treaty which were just as much bound by conscience as Great Britain and France were by the Treaty. It was neither good morals nor good statesmanship.

"MR. LLOYD GEORGE said that Great Britain had been brought into the war largely in protest against the breach of a Treaty. She could not contemplate herself breaking a Treaty at the end of the war when the other partner to the Treaty had lost half a million lives in giving effect to it. This had been worrying him for several days past. . . ."

4. Wilson's Message in Presenting the Treaty of Versailles to the Senate

The proceedings of the Paris Peace Conference began on January 12, 1919, and the final treaty with Germany was signed at Versailles on June 28, 1919. The major nations at the Conference, designated as the "Principal Allied and Associated Powers," were the United States, the United Kingdom, France, Italy, and Japan. The Treaty of Versailles was virtually written by these nations, in fact almost by Lloyd George, Clemenceau, Wilson, and Orlando. The other eighteen powers which had declared war on Germany and the four which had merely broken relations attended certain sessions of the Conference in which they had a special interest. The essential features of the treaty were presented to the Germans on May 7. The German reply, which was a sharp condemnation of the treaty, was returned to the Allies on May 29. After a cabinet crisis in Germany and an ultimatum by the Allied powers a new German delegation finally signed the treaty.

The treaties with Austria, Bulgaria, Hungary, and Turkey were negotiated and signed after the Germans had accepted the Treaty of Versailles.

After the conclusion of the treaty with Germany, Wilson returned to the United States and on July 10, 1919, presented this document to the Senate of the United States for ratification.[7]

---

[7] *Congressional Record,* 66th Cong., 1st Sess., Vol. LVIII, Pt. 3, pp. 2336-39.

"GENTLEMEN OF THE SENATE:

"The treaty of peace with Germany was signed at Versailles on the twenty-eighth of June. I avail myself of the earliest opportunity to lay the treaty before you for ratification and to inform you with regard to the work of the Conference by which that treaty was formulated.

"The treaty constitutes nothing less than a world settlement. It would not be possible for me either to summarize or to construe its manifold provisions in an address which must of necessity be something less than a treatise. My services and all the information I possess will be at your disposal and at the disposal of your Committee on Foreign Relations at any time, either informally or in session, as you may prefer; and I hope that you will not hesitate to make use of them. I shall at this time, prior to your own study of the document, attempt only a general characterization of its scope and purpose. . . .

"The atmosphere in which the Conference worked seemed created, not by the ambitions of strong governments, but by the hopes and aspirations of small nations and of peoples hitherto under bondage to the power that victory had shattered and destroyed. Two great empires had been forced into political bankruptcy, and we were the receivers. Our task was not only to make peace with the Central Empires and remedy the wrongs their armies had done. The Central Empires had lived in open violation of many of the very rights for which the war had been fought, dominating alien peoples over whom they had no natural right to rule, enforcing, not obedience, but veritable bondage, exploiting those who were weak for the benefit of those who were masters and overlords only by force of arms. There could be no peace until the whole order of Central Europe was set right.

"That meant that new nations were to be created,—Poland, Czecho-Slovakia, Hungary itself. No part of ancient Poland had ever in any true sense become a part of Germany, or of Austria, or of Russia. Bohemia was alien in every thought and hope to the monarchy of which she had so long been an artificial part; and the uneasy partnership between Austria and Hungary had been one rather of interest than of kinship or sympathy. The Slavs whom Austria had chosen to force into her empire on the south were kept to their obedience by nothing but fear. Their hearts were with their kinsmen in the Balkans. These were all arrangements of power, not arrangements of natural union or association. It was the imperative task of those who would make peace and make it intelligently to establish a new order which would rest upon the free choice of peoples rather than upon the arbitrary authority of Hapsburgs or Hohenzollerns.

"More than that, great populations bound by sympathy and actual kin to Rumania were also linked against their will to the conglomerate Austro-Hungarian monarchy or to other alien sovereignties, and it was part of the task of peace to make a new Rumania as well as a new slavic state clustering about Serbia.

"And no natural frontiers could be found to these new fields of adjustment and redemption. It was necessary to look constantly forward to other related tasks. The German colonies were to be disposed of. They had not been governed; they had been exploited merely, without thought of the interests or even the ordinary human rights of their inhabitants.

"The Turkish Empire, moreover, had fallen apart, as the Austro-Hungarian had. It had never had any real unity. It had been held together only by pitiless, inhuman force. Its peoples cried aloud for release, for succor from unspeakable distress, for all that the new day of hope seemed at last to bring within its dawn. Peoples hitherto in utter darkness were to be led out into the same light and given at last a helping hand. Undeveloped peoples and peoples ready for recognition but not yet ready to assume the full responsibilities of statehood were to be given adequate guarantees of friendly protection, guidance and assistance.

"And out of the execution of these gerat enterprises of liberty sprang opportunities to attempt what statesmen had never found the way before to do; an opportunity to throw safeguards about the rights of racial, national and religious minorities by solemn international covenant; an opportunity to limit and regulate military establishments where they were most likely to be mischevious; an opportunity to effect a complete and systematic internationalization of waterways and railways which were necessary to the free economic life of more than one nation and to clear many of the normal channels of commerce of unfair obstructions of law or of privilege; and the very welcome opportunity to secure for labor the concerted protection of definite international pledges of principle and practice.

"These were not tasks which the Conference looked about it to find and went out of its way to perform. They were inseparable from the settlements of peace. They were thrust upon it by circumstances which could not be overlooked. . . .

"That there should be a League of Nations to steady the counsels and maintain the peaceful understandings of the world, to make, not treaties alone, but the accepted principles of international law as well, the actual rule of conduct among the governments of the world, had been one of the agreements accepted from the first as the basis of peace with the Central Powers. The statesmen of all the belligerent countries were agreed that such a league must be created to sustain the settlements that were to be effected. But at first I think there was a feeling among some of them that, while it must be attempted, the formation of such a league was perhaps a counsel of perfection which practical men, long experienced in the world of affairs, must agree to very cautiously and with many misgivings. It was only as the difficult work of arranging an all but universal adjustment of the world's affairs advanced from day to day from one stage of conference to another that it became evident to them that what they were seeking would be little more than something written on paper, to be interpreted and applied by such methods as the chances of politics might make available if they did not provide a means of common counsel which all were obliged to accept, a common authority whose decisions would be recognized as decisions which all must respect. . . .

"The fact that the Covenant of the League was the first substantive part of the Treaty to be worked out and agreed upon, while all else was in solution, helped to make the formulation of the rest easier. The Conference was, after all, not to be ephemeral. The concert of nations was to continue, under a definite Covenant which had been agreed upon and which all were convinced was workable. They could go forward with confidence to make arrangements intended to be permanent. The most practical of the conferees were at last the most ready to refer to the League of Nations the superintendence of all interests which did not admit of immediate determination, of all administrative problems which were to require a continuing oversight. What had seemed a counsel of perfection had come to seem a plain counsel of necessity. The League of Nations was the practical statesman's hope of success in many of the most difficult things he was attempting. . . .

"And so the result of the Conference of Peace, so far as Germany is concerned, stands complete. The difficulties encountered were very many. Sometimes they seemed insuperable. It was impossible to accommodate the interests of so great a body of nations,—interests which directly or indirectly affected almost every nation in the world,—without many minor compromises. The treaty, as a result, is not exactly what we would have written. It is probably not what any one of the national delegations would have written. But results were worked out which on the whole bear test. I think that it will be found that the compromises which were accepted as inevitable nowhere cut to the heart of any principle. The work of the Conference squares, as a whole, with the principles agreed upon as the basis of the peace as well as with the practical possibilities of the international situations which had to be faced and dealt with as facts. . . .

"America may be said to have just reached her majority as a world power. . . .

". . . There can be no question of our ceasing to be a world power. The only question is whether we can refuse the moral leadership that is offered us, whether we shall accept or reject the confidence of the world. . . .

"The stage is set, the destiny disclosed. It has come about by no plan of our conceiving, but by the hand of God who led us into this way. We cannot turn back. We can only go forward, with lifted eyes and freshened spirit, to follow the vision. It was of this that we dreamed at our birth. America shall in truth show the way. The light streams upon the path ahead, and nowhere else."

5. *Senate Debate on Treaty of Versailles*

From July 10, 1919, when Wilson presented the Treaty of Versailles to the Senate for its consideration, until the Treaty was defeated both with and without reservations on November 19, the Senate of the United States was the scene of one of the most bitterly fought and vicious contests in the long history of that body. Senators William E. Borah of Idaho and Hiram Johnson of California were the chief spokesmen of a group of isolationists called "Bitter-Enders." They were opposed not only to the Covenant of the League but also to the Treaty altogether as an evil instrument which would involve us in the troubles of the world that should not concern us. The "Irreconcilables," led by Senator Henry Cabot Lodge of Massachusetts, were by no means isolationists. Lodge's objections were aimed at the League of Nations and at Woodrow Wilson rather than at the main body of the Treaty ending the war with Germany. His strategy was to draft reservations, which in themselves, did little damage to the Treaty. Lodge knew that Wilson was opposed to any reservation, and that the Treaty with reservations would probably be voted down by administration Democrats. Lodge's tactics proved successful. The Treaty without reservations was defeated by a combination of "Bitter-Enders" and "Irreconcilables"; and the Treaty with reservations was defeated by the Democrats and the "Bitter-Enders." Wilson, who had seen the handwriting on the wall, took the issue to the nation, collapsed physically in September—two months before the Treaty was finally defeated. The only victors in this deadly struggle were the "Bitter-Enders" and Henry Cabot Lodge.

The following selection is taken from a debate in the Senate on November 4, 1919:[8]

"Mr. BORAH . . . We went to Paris pledged to a renunciation of the dominancy of the sea and to a declaration in favor of the freedom of the sea. England decided before we got there that we must abandon our position, and we accommodated her. We could not help it. Having sat down at their table in their own house, and in their game, being practically their guest, we could not help accommodating them in such matters.

"The next thing they decided was that all the secret treaties, however unconscionable and vicious they were, should be written into this treaty. I have no doubt that all the representatives of the United States who sat in that conference felt just as bitter and just as thoroughly humiliated over that situation as any of the rest of us. Does anybody doubt that the representative of the United States would have rejected the Shantung infamy if he had felt he could do so? But we were there, intermingling in their affairs, subject to their intrigue and their manipulation, and, under the threat of another

[8] *Congressional Record,* 66th Cong., 1st Sess., Vol. LVIII, Part 8, pp. 7947-48.

World War and enternal chaos, we yielded to their suggestion. When we sit in the council at Geneva, with their power to manipulate and to control, with the things near at hand which they better understand than do we, the mere question of sending 100,000 men for the purpose of preserving peace will be but a bagatelle, indeed, compared with the sacrifice which we have already made.

"Mr. President I do not criticize the President of the United States for not withholding the rapacious power of the imperial systems of Europe, for it was an impossible task; but we are entering into a conclave of nations where our representatives will do that every time that a European situation arises. The reason, sir, why I am against this league and against all leagues and combinations and conclaves is because I know that instead of Americanizing Europe, Europe will Europeanize America. That is what is being done now, and that is what will continue to happen.

"You may appeal to your Constitution; you may say that technically we have not the power to take the action proposed, but if you do that and any European representative insists that we act, as a matter of moral obligation we will do so, or else tear down and destroy the league at once.

"Mr. President, it has been asked here how could the President send troops? I ask again, as I asked a moment ago, why are our troops being kept in Russia? Under what authority are they there, and what Member of Congress is proposing to challenge that authority in any legal way? I have on my desk a news item of yesterday afternoon to the effect that 60,000 rifles have been sent from America to Kolchak. Who is Kolchak?[9] What are our relations with him? Under what authority do we send him 60,000 rifles? Well, I will tell you by what authority, Mr. President.

"As a matter of fact, a league of nations was formed in Versailles while the peace conference was sitting there; and this Covenant is like an election in Mississippi; it is simply a ratification of the primary proceedings. Troops and rifles were sent to Russia because the five men sitting at Versailles decided to send them. They are being sent there from day to day, and munitions are sent there from day to day, not by any action of Congress, not by any authority of ours, not by any constitutional authority, but because those with whom we are associated thought that a wise thing to do. So, Mr. President, it is not the technical power with which I am concerned. If we had some supreme court like that of the United States or some other supreme judicial tribunal by which we could call every act into question, by which we could ask the cancellation of orders, or by which we could test delegated authority, the men who talk of technicalities would have their day of hearing. We have, however, no such tribunal. These men are their own umpires; there is no appeal from them. The jurisdiction given them is of the world, their au-

[9] Aleksandr V. Kolchak, an Admiral in the Czarist Navy, was at the time of Borah's speech the leader of an army of White Russians engaged in civil war with the Reds.

thority the peace of the world; and whether it is technically authorized or not we are granting it to them. What right have we to say that they shall not exercise it? . . . ."

6. *Policy toward the Soviets, December, 1919*

The United States really had no policy in 1918 toward the regime set up by Lenin and Trotsky, unless doing nothing but await developments can be considered a policy. Even during the early part of 1919, Wilson had not made up his mind precisely as to what our policy should be. In March, 1919, when the Peace Conference was in session in Paris, Wilson sent William C. Bullitt on a special mission to Russia to make an on-the-spot report of conditions there. Bullitt's reports, sent from Russia to Wilson at Versailles, presented a much more favorable picture of conditions there under Bolshevik rule than other reports which had emanated from Russia. He even advocated making peace with the revolution,[10] but his recommendations were not adopted by Wilson. By the latter part of 1919, the United States, after having observed the theory and practice of the Bolsheviks for two years, had reached the conclusion that the Communists were hostile to all non-Communist governments. This American policy is revealed in the following instruction sent by the Secretary of State to the American Ambassador in London on December 4, 1919:[11]

"For your information and guidance the following comments are submitted with respect to the oral statements made on November 24 by Lloyd George to Polk.[12] At your discretion you may inform appropriate members of the British Government concerning the substance of these observations as occasion may make it desirable to do so.

"The uselessness of reaching a satisfactory understanding with the Bolsheviki has been demonstrated by past experience. The ultimate aims of the Bolsheviki are hostile to all existing governments and any apparent compromise which they may make with these governments is vitiated by their avowed opportunism.

"There is the possibility, however, that the Bolsheviki faction never will be forcibly driven from Russia, but will gradually yield to new leaders and

[10] The Bullitt reports are found in *Papers Relating to the Foreign Relations of the United States, 1919, Russia*, p. 76 ff.

[11] *Ibid.*, pp. 129-130.

[12] Frank Lyon Polk was an American delegate at the peace conference from July 28 to December 9, 1919. Lloyd George had spoken to him of the possible advantages of having Russia divided into several parts and of reaching some agreement with the Soviets.

change into a régime with which it will be possible to establish relations. It will be necessary to use the greatest care in this eventuality to determine the exact time at which the process of change has so far developed that countenance or recognition of the resulting government by foreign states will help to quicken rather than retard its evolution along rational lines. To grant premature recognition would check such development, it is believed, by giving aid and encouragement to ultra-radical and uncompromising elements which still remained.

"It is my conviction that neither Lenin nor his immediate followers will ever give up permanently the dream of a world-wide revolution and loyally enter into friendly relations with governments which are not communistic.

"Clearly even if evolution of the nature suggested has begun it is not sufficiently advanced to render it desirable or possible to try to reach an understanding with those now in control of the Soviet régime. . . . It is my belief that if Lloyd George seeks to reach such an understanding he will incur serious moral responsibility as well as make a great tactical mistake.

"The American Government will give no support to the view that the dismemberment of Russia should be encouraged because a united Russia will be a menace to Europe. To take advantage of the present misfortune of the Russian people to interfere intentionally in the manner suggested with their future political rehabilitation would be a moral wrong and would pave the way for conflicts in the future. Granting that it is permissible to revert to such pre-war diplomatic methods, it is believed that a divided Russia not able to cope with existing Japanese territorial ambition or a possible revival of German imperialism would be by far a greater menace to the British Empire than would be a united, democratic Russia, well able to defend itself, but not disposed to attack.

"Repeat confidentially to Ambassador in France.

Lansing"

7. *Washington Conference, 1921-1922*

The Treaty of Versailles and the treaties with the other Central Powers settled, at least for a time, the most pressing problems which faced the Allies at the end of the war. The peace treaties, however, did not solve all world problems, or even all problems confronting the United States.

The economy-minded Republican Administration which came into power in 1921 was interested in the limitation of naval construction, but any such move on the part of the United States necessarily depended, not only on a settlement of Far Eastern affairs, but also on agreement by the other major powers to limit the size of their navies.

The Washington Conference, which was in session from November 12, 1921, to February 6, 1922, achieved both these objectives, or so it seemed in 1922.

The following excerpts are from the Five Power Naval Limitation Treaty signed by the United States, the United Kingdom, France, Italy, and Japan:[13]

"Article IV.

"The total capital ship replacement tonnage of each of the Contracting Powers shall not exceed in standard displacement, for the United States 525,000 tons (533,400 metric tons); for the British Empire 525,000 tons (533,400 metric tons); for France 175,000 tons (177,800 metric tons); for Italy 175,000 (177,800 metric tons); for Japan 315,000 tons (320,040 metric tons).

"Article V.

"No capital ship exceeding 35,000 tons (35,560 metric tons) standard displacement shall be acquired by, or constructed by, for, or within the jurisdiction of, any of the Contracting Powers.

"Article VI.

"No capital ship of any of the Contracting Powers shall carry a gun with a calibre in excess of 16 inches (406 millimetres).

"Article VII.

"The total tonnage for aircraft carriers of each of the Contracting Powers shall not exceed in standard displacement, for the United States 135,000 tons. . . ; for the British Empire 135,000 tons. . . ; for France 60,000 tons. . . ; for Italy 60,000 tons. . . ; for Japan 81,000 tons. . . .

"Article XI.

"No vessel of war exceeding 10,000 tons . . . standard displacement, other than a capital ship or aircraft carrier, shall be acquired by, or constructed by, for, or within the jurisdiction of, any of the Contracting Powers. . . .

"Article XII.

"No vessel of war of any of the Contracting Powers, hereafter laid down, other than a capital ship, shall carry a gun with calibre in excess of 8 inches. . . .

"Article XIX.

"The United States, the British Empire and Japan agree that the status quo at the time of the signing of the present Treaty, with regard to fortifications and naval bases, shall be maintained in their respective territories and possessions specified hereunder:

"(1) The insular possessions which the United States now holds or may hereafter acquire in the Pacific Ocean, except (a) those adjacent to the coast

[13] *U. S. Statutes at Large,* 1923-24, Vol. XLIII, Part 2., pp. 35-65.

of the United States, Alaska and the Panama Canal Zone, not including the Aleutian Islands, and (b) the Hawaiian Islands;

"(2) Hongkong and the insular possessions which the British Empire now holds or may hereafter acquire in the Pacific Ocean, east of the meridian of 110 east longitude, except (a) those adjacent to the coast of Canada, (b) the Commonwealth of Australia and its Territories, and (c) New Zealand;

"(3) The following insular territories and possessions of Japan in the Pacific Ocean, to wit: the Kurile Islands, the Bonin Islands, Amami-Oshima, the Loochoo Islands, Formosa and the Pescadores, and any insular territories or possessions in the Pacific Ocean which Japan may hereafter acquire.

"The maintenance of the status quo under the foregoing provisions implies that no new fortification or naval bases shall be established in the territories and possessions specified; that no measures shall be taken to increase the existing naval facilities for the repair and maintenance of naval forces, and that no increase shall be made in the coast defenses of the territories and possessions above specified. This restriction, however, does not preclude such repair and replacement of worn-out weapons and equipment as is customary in naval and military establishments in time of peace."

The Nine Power Treaty signed at the Washington Conference by the United States, Belgium, the British Empire, China, France, Italy, Japan, the Netherlands and Portugal on February 6, 1922, was designed to preserve the sovereignty of China. Although this agreement fell far short of the Chinese demands for complete equality with other world powers, it did contain the essence of the Open Door Policy which had long been advocated by the United States.

Selections from the Nine Power Pact [14]

"Article I

"The Contracting Powers, other than China, agree:

"(1) To respect the sovereignty, the independence, and the territorial and administrative integrity of China;

"(2) To provide the fullest and most unembarrassed opportunity to China to develop and maintain for herself an effective and stable government;

"(3) To use their influence for the purpose of effectually establishing and maintaining the principle of equal opportunity for the commerce and industry of all nations throughout the territory of China;

"(4) To refrain from taking advantage of conditions in China in order to seek special rights or privileges which would abridge the rights of subjects

[14] *U. S. Statutes at Large,* 1925-26, Vol. XLIV, Part 2, pp. 121-39.

or citizens of friendly States, and from countenancing action inimical to the security of such States. . . .

"Article III

"With a view to applying more effectually the principles of the Open Door or equality of opportunity in China for the trade and industry of all nations, the Contracting Powers, other than China, agree that they will not seek, nor support their respective nationals in seeking—

"(a) any arrangement which might purport to establish in favour of their interests any general superiority of rights with respect to commercial or economic development in any designated region of China;

"(b) any such monopoly or preference as would deprive the nationals of any other Power of the right of undertaking any legitimate trade or industry in China, or of participating with the Chinese Government, or with any local authority, in any category of public enterprise, or which by reason of its scope, duration or geographical extent is calculated to frustrate the practical application of the principle of equal opportunity.

"It is understood that the foregoing stipulations of this Article are not to be so construed as to prohibit the acquisition of such properties or rights as may be necessary to the conduct of a particular commercial, industrial, or financial undertaking or to the encouragement of invention and research.

"China undertakes to be guided by the principles stated in the foregoing stipulations of this Article in dealing with applications for economic rights and privileges from Governments and nationals of all foreign countries, whether parties to the present Treaty or not.

"Article IV

"The Contracting Powers agree not to support any agreements by their respective nationals with each other designed to create Spheres of Influence or to provide for the enjoyment of mutually exclusive opportunities in designated parts of Chinese territory. . . .

"Article VII

"The Contracting Powers agree that, whenever a situation arises which in the opinion of any one of them involves the application of the stipulations of the present Treaty, and renders desirable discussion of such application, there shall be full and frank communication between the Contracting Powers concerned. . . ."

CHAPTER IX.

POSTWAR DIPLOMACY

THERE have been few periods in the history of the American people when the nation was as united in its objectives, both domestic and foreign, as in the decade following World War I. Warren G. Harding, in campaigning for the presidency in 1920, promised to lead the nation back to "normalcy." The American people, tired of war and disillusioned by the fact that the brave new world had not emerged from the great crusade, looked upon "normalcy" as a fine objective. No one ever defined "normalcy" or attempted to find out if there ever had been such a state of existence, but to most of the American people it meant getting back to business and letting the rest of the world solve the problems which we thought they had created. The escapism of Americans in the 1920's was as unrealistic as was their unbounded confidence in 1917-1918 that Utopia was just around the corner.

Fortunately for America, the events in the decade following the war did not constitute a threat to the security of this nation. Germany had been crushed. The Washington Conference appeared to have settled Far Eastern problems; and the hegemony of the United States within the Western Hemisphere was almost complete.

Our main troubles were with our former Allies. During and after the war the United States had loaned over $10,000,000,000 to Great Britain, France, Italy, and to seventeen other nations which had fought against the Central Powers or had been created since the war. Our Government consistently held to the view that the loans had been made on a business basis and that they should be repaid on that basis. Most of the debtor nations came to the conclusion following the war that these loans should be considered part of the over-all war effort to defeat Germany. They argued that from 1914 to 1917 they were fighting our war as well as theirs. Another contention was that the inter-Allied loans should be directly related to the reparations due from Germany. The United States, which had not received German reparations, refused to see any connection between the two transactions.

There was never any basic agreement concerning the inter-Allied loans during the decade of the twenties. Germany paid reparations during that period, mainly with capital invested there by British and American citizens. The Allies made payments on the inter-Allied loans while they were receiving reparations from Germany, although their bitterness toward the United States increased with each payment. The United States remained firm in its position, refusing to see that the outflow of American capital had any connection with the payment of reparations and the inter-Allied loans until the coming of the world-wide depression of 1929.

During this same decade, the United States not only remained out of the League of Nations but also continued to take pride in having steered clear of the web of European politics into which Wilson would have plunged the nation. America was willing to participate in any disarmament conference, especially since it would reduce expenditures. In fact, President Coolidge called for a naval disarmament conference in 1927 which ended in complete failure. In 1928 the United States enthusiastically signed the Pact of Paris which renounced war as an instrument of national policy, and Coolidge's Secretary of State, Frank B. Kellogg, took the initiative in persuading a number of nations to sign bilateral arbitration treaties.

Herbert Hoover, who entered the White House in 1929, was faced with a far different world from that of his predecessors. Whereas Harding and Coolidge enjoyed peace and prosperity, Hoover had to cope with the worst economic depression during the twentieth century. One measure adopted by the Hoover Administration to alleviate the depression in the United States (which also had results throughout the world) was the passage of the Smoot-Hawley tariff in 1930—the highest tariff in the history of the nation. Hoover signed this bill despite the protest of over one thousand American economists who believed that the enactment of that legislation would hinder rather than encourage economic recovery. With economic conditions in this country and abroad worse in 1931 than they had been in 1930, Hoover proposed a one-year moratorium on all intergovernmental debts—reparations as well as the inter-Allied debts. In December, 1932, when the moratorium ended with the world still in depression, six debtor nations defaulted on their payments to the United States, but the problem now lay with Franklin D. Roosevelt, the president-elect.

Possibly no generation can accurately appraise the significance of its own times. Unquestionably hindsight is better than foresight, but the generation following World War I lived in a fool's paradise. The United States had become a major world power as a result of the first World War. There were many in the nation who realized the great potential of this country, but very few were able to understand that great power carries commensurate responsibilities. The United States attempted to isolate itself from the world, and for a while, until the fall of 1929, the experiment seemed to be a great success. Before Hoover left office, however, the great depression had demonstrated in a most tragic manner the fact that the economic life of this nation was most intimately connected with the economic welfare of the entire world. And the Japanese seizure of Manchuria in 1931 proved that treaties renouncing war as an instrument of national policy were just words unless those nations which truly wanted peace were willing to back up their words with deeds. The American people did not fully learn this lesson until the Pearl Harbor attack—a decade later.

1. American Economic Policies Following World War I

World War I brought a profound change in the economy of the United States, but our post-war policy did not indicate that the Government or the people who supported it fully understood the significance of the altered situation. The war accelerated the transition of the United States from a debtor to a creditor nation. When the war ended the Allied nations owed the United States over $10,000,000,000 and American bankers and businessmen had a surplus of capital, much of which was invested abroad during the 1920's.

By 1919 the United States had arrived at a point in its economic development similar to that reached by Britain almost a century earlier. After Great Britain had started exporting capital as a result of its rapid industrialization, its Government relaxed tariff barriers to encourage imports from the nations where its capital was invested as a means of receiving a return from the investments. Following World War I, however, the United States, which as a debtor nation had been committed to a high tariff policy, continued to maintain a high tariff wall which tended to prevent the nations which had received American capital from being able to return the profits by exporting goods to the United States.

American export trade would have suffered more heavily than it did during the 1920's as a direct result of the high tariff policy if American businessmen had not continued to make large scale loans abroad. As long as the loans from America were forthcoming, the foreign nations could continue to buy American products; but with the coming of the depression in 1929, American loans abroad fell off sharply—this led to a curtailment of American exports. Not until the 1930's did it become apparent to a larger number of our citizens that the prosperity of the United States as a capital-exporting nation was intimately connected with our willingness to create a tariff policy which would stimulate rather than throttle world trade.

The following statement relative to American economic policy during the 1920's was taken from a study by the United States Department of Commerce, entitled *The United States in the World Economy*, published in 1943.[1]

"A Period of Uncertain Balance, 1922-29

"Despite initial currency disorders, controversies over reparations and war debts, and some growth in tariff barriers, the years from 1922 to 1929 were marked, on the whole, by world-wide economic expansion and rising incomes, with a corresponding increase in international transactions. The supply of dollars was expanded not merely by a rise in United States imports but also by increasing American tourist expenditures and other service remittances, and by a strong flow of loans and other investments abroad. These sources provided ample funds out of which foreign countries bought our goods, made war-debt payments, and serviced the growing volume of private American investments.

"The relatively close correspondence between the supply and use of dollars and their common upward movements from 1922 to 1929 suggest the existence and successful operation of a balancing mechanism relating the various items through forces inherent in the economic system of the period. Our imports, loans, and other payments undoubtedly helped to sustain and promote economic growth and the rise in incomes abroad and thus supported foreign demand for our goods and services during the period as a whole.

[1] Hal B. Lary, *The United States in the World Economy*, (Dept. of Commerce), Econ. Ser., No. 23, pp. 3-7.

There is also some evidence of year-to-year adjustments of a compensating nature between the various transactions. Maintenance of approximate balance between the total supply and use of dollars in these years must be largely attributed, however, to the absence of any undue and prolonged disturbance in any of the major items—a situation that was abruptly and violently changed toward the end of the period.

"It is commonplace to point out various maladjustments and weaknesses in the world economic structure of the twenties which led to its eventual undoing. While the mere enumeration of such factors scarcely constitutes convincing evidence of the inevitability of collapse, they undeniably represented points of vulnerability susceptible of breaking under pressure. Among the most prominent was the general weakness of prices. The failure of manufactured goods to rise appreciably in price during a period of economic expansion may have resulted merely from the increasing efficiency of industry. There was also striking technical progress in agriculture, but the declining tendency in primary prices must be largely attributed to war-time and postwar expansion of production in the face of relatively inelastic demand. This maladjustment was aggrevated by numerous ill-conceived schemes for maintaining artificially high prices, leading to an accumulation of surplus stocks and a generally vulnerable position for many key commodities.

"Another serious weakness in the world economy of the twenties was what is now generally recognized as the overvaluation of the pound sterling, along with various satellite currencies, and the undervaluation of the French franc in the return to the gold standard. Restoration of the pound to its old gold parity with the dollar, undertaken despite the relatively higher cost and price structure in the United Kingdom, contributed to that country's generally weak position in the world economy and to its excessive and vulnerable dependence on foreign short-term capital as a means of balancing its international accounts.

"On the other hand, stabilization of the franc at one-fifth its pre-war parity did not reflect its true equilibrium level but rather a depreciation due largely to flight of capital. The French balance-of-payments position was thus excessively 'strong' and, together with the reflux of private capital, resulted in an accumulation of large French balances in other countries subject to sudden withdrawal. The French action intensified the weakness in the British position, and both made for a generally unstable international situation.

"One of the most critical features in this country's international transactions was the behavior of capital. To regard the United States' position as a lending country as artificial or improper would be totally unwarranted. There was no inherent reason why there should have been an immediate adjustment in foreign trade to the newly acquired creditor status at the end of the war period (although the higher tariffs of 1921 and 1922 could only increase the difficulty of the eventual adaptation). Foreign countries needed and demanded American goods and American capital, and it was natural that the United States should have supplied both. The mistakes were rather in the particular behavior of our lending operations—not so much in our investment policy as in the lack of one.

"Under the high-pressure salesmanship methods by which foreign issues were solicited and sold, our loans proved to be their own undoing. The flotation of one loan frequently came to be regarded as adequate justification for further issues to the same borrower or the same country without adequate regard to the growing burden of indebtedness. In some instances, notably in loans to Germany, new lending was vigorously prosecuted long after warnings from high places were sounded. The very operations that expanded the incomes and consumption of foreign countries and made them increasingly dependent on an unfailing source of exchange thus helped to ensure the inevitability of a change and the probability that it would be disastrously abrupt and complete.

"Another weakness in American investment activity was that our issuing houses never really regarded foreign issues as more than a side line, which they exploited for a time but felt free to drop when more attractive opportunities presented themselves at home. In these circumstances it is not surprising that, under the intense competition of the stock-market boom, new flotations for foreign countries were suddenly curtailed in the middle of 1928 and, aside from a brief upturn in the first half of 1930, failed to recover thereafter."

2. *Foreign Policy Objectives, 1923*

After the death of Warren G. Harding, Calvin Coolidge assumed the Presidency. In his first annual message to Congress on December 6, 1923, Coolidge presented his views on foreign policy. In a statement which was frank, simple, and straightforward, Coolidge revealed not only a great deal of his own philosophy, but also reflected quite accurately the American spirit of the 1920's concerning foreign affairs.[2]

"Foreign Affairs

"For us peace reigns everywhere. We desire to perpetuate it always by granting full justice to others and requiring of others full justice to ourselves.

"Our country has one cardinal principle to maintain in its foreign policy. It is an American principle. It must be an American policy. We attend to our own affairs, conserve our own strength, and protect the interests of our own citizens; but we recognize thoroughly our obligation to help others, reserving to the decision of our own judgment the time, the place, and the method. We realize the common bond of humanity. We know the inescapable law of service.

[2] *Papers Relating to the Foreign Relations of the United States, 1923*, Vol. 1, pp. vii-ix.

"Our country has definitely refused to adopt and ratify the covenant of the League of Nations. We have not felt warranted in assuring the responsibilities which its members have assumed. I am not proposing any change in this policy; neither is the Senate. The incident, so far as we are concerned, is closed. The League exists as a foreign agency. We hope it will be helpful. But the United States sees no reason to limit its own freedom and independence of action by joining it. We shall do well to recognize this basic fact in all national affairs and govern ourselves accordingly.

"World Court

"Our foreign policy has always been guided by two principles. The one is the avoidance of permanent political alliances which would sacrifice our proper independence. The other is the peaceful settlement of controversies between nations. By example and by treaty we have advocated arbitration. For nearly 25 years we have been a member of The Hague Tribunal, and have long sought the creation of a permanent World Court of Justice. I am in full accord with both of these policies. I favor the establishment of such a court intended to include the whole world. That is, and has long been, an American policy.

"Pending before the Senate is a proposal that this Government give its support to the Permanent Court of International Justice, which is a new and somewhat different plan. This is not a partisan question. It should not assume an artificial importance. The court is merely a convenient instrument of adjustment to which we could go, but to which we could not be brought. It should be discussed with entire candor, not by a political but by a judicial method, without pressure and without prejudice. Partisanship has no place in our foreign relations. As I wish to see a court established, and as the proposal presents the only practical plan on which many nations have ever agreed, though it may not meet every desire, I therefore commend it to the favorable consideration of the Senate, with the proposed reservations clearly indicating our refusal to adhere to the League of Nations.

"Russia

"Our diplomatic relations, lately so largely interrupted, are now being resumed, but Russia presents notable difficulties. We have every desire to see that great people, who are our traditional friends, restored to their position among the nations of the earth. We have relieved their pitiable destitution with an enormous charity. Our Government offers no objection to the carrying on of commerce by our citizens with the people of Russia. Our Government does not propose, however, to enter into relations with another régime which refuses to recognize the sanctity of international obligations. I do not propose to barter away for the privilege of trade any of the cherished rights of humanity. I do not propose to make merchandise of any American principles. These rights and principles must go wherever the sanctions of our Government go.

"But while the favor of America is not for sale, I am willing to make very large concessions for the purpose of rescuing the people of Russia. Already encouraging evidences of returning to the ancient ways of society can be detected. But more are needed. Whenever there appears any disposition to compensate our citizens who were despoiled, and to recognize that debt contracted wth our Government, not by the Czar, but by the newly formed Republic of Russia; whenever the active spirit of enmity to our institutions is abated; whenever there appear works mete for repentance; our country ought to be the first to go to the economic and moral rescue of Russia. We have every desire to help and no desire to injure. We hope the time is near at hand when we can act.

"Debts

"The current debt and interest due from foreign Governments, exclusive of the British debt of $4,600,000,000, is about $7,200,000,000. I do not favor the cancellation of this debt, but I see no objection to adjusting it in accordance wth the principle adopted for the British debt. Our country would not wish to assume the rôle of an oppressive creditor, but would maintain the principle that financial obligations between nations are likewise moral obligations which international faith and honor require should be discharged.

"Our Government has a liquidated claim against Germany for the expense of the army of occupation of over $255,000,000. Besides this, the Mixed Claims Commission have before them about 12,500 claims of American citizens, aggregating about $1,225,000,000. These claims have already been reduced by a recent decision, but there are valid claims reaching well toward $500,000,000. Our thousands of citizens with credits due them of hundreds of millions of dollars have no redress save in the action of our Government. These are very substantial interests, which it is the duty of our Government to protect as best it can. That course I propose to pursue.

"It is for these reasons that we have a direct interest in the economic recovery of Europe. They are enlarged by our desire for the stability of civilization and the welfare of humanity. That we are making sacrifices to that end none can deny. Our deferred interest alone amounts to a million dollars every day. But recently we offered to aid with our advice and counsel. We have reiterated our desire to see France paid and Germany revived. We have proposed disarmament. We have earnestly sought to compose differences and restore peace. We shall persevere in well-doing, not by force, but by reason."

3. Kellogg-Briand Pact

Although the American people adopted a negative attitude about joining the League of Nations or taking any part in solving world problems, they gave enthusiastic support to a suggestion by the French Foreign Minister, Aristide Briand, that the United States and France conclude a pact outlawing war as an instrument of national policy. Probably neither government considered the idea, when first broached, as having any great significance, but the American people backed it so vigorously that when the Kellogg-Briand Pact was signed in Paris on August 27, 1928, many in this country looked upon it as a milestone in world history. Originally conceived as an agreement between the United States and France, the pact was ultimately adhered to by a majority of the nations of the world. The following selections are the text of the agreement and the commentary on the treaty by President Coolidge in his Annual Message to Congress in 1928.[3]

"Article I

"The High Contracting Parties solemnly declare in the names of their respective peoples that they condemn recourse to war for the solution of international controversies, and renounce it as an instrument of national policy in their relations with one another.

"Article II

"The High Contracting Parties agree that the settlement or solution of all disputes or conflicts of whatever nature or of whatever origin they may be, which may arise among them, shall never be sought except by pacific means. . . ."

Calvin Coolidge's Address[4]

"No Congress of the United States ever assembled, on surveying the state of the Union, has met with a more pleasing prospect than that which appears at the present time. In the domestic field there is tranquillity and contentment, harmonious relations between management and wage earner, freedom from industrial strife, and the highest record of years of prosperity. In the foreign field there is peace, the good will which comes from mutual understanding, and the knowledge that the problems which a short time ago appeared so ominous are yielding to the touch of manifest friendship. The great wealth created by our enterprise and industry, and saved by our economy, has had the widest distribution among our own people, and has gone out in a steady stream to serve the charity and the business of the world. The requirements of existence have passed beyond the standard of necessity into the region of luxury. Enlarging production is consumed by an increasing demand at home and an expanding commerce abroad. The country can regard the present with satisfaction and anticipate the future with optimism. . . .

[3] *Papers Relating to the Foreign Relations of the United States, 1928,* Vol. 1, p. 155.
[4] *Ibid.,* pp. vii-xi.

"Peace Treaty

"One of the most important treaties ever laid before the Senate of the United States will be that which the 15 nations recently signed at Paris, and to which 44 other nations have declared their intention to adhere, renouncing war as a national policy and agreeing to resort only to peaceful means for the adjustment of international differences. It is the most solemn declaration against war, the most positive adherence to peace, that it is possible for sovereign nations to make. It does not supersede our inalienable sovereign right and duty of national defense or undertake to commit us before the event to any mode of action which the Congress might decide to be wise if ever the treaty should be broken. But it is a new standard in the world around which can rally the informed and enlightened opinion of nations to prevent their governments from being forced into hostile action by the temporary outbreak of international animosities. The observance of this covenant, so simple and so straightforward, promises more for the peace of the world than any other agreement ever negotiated among the nations."

4. *Hoover's Moratorium Proposal, 1931*

Less than a year after Coolidge's confident statement to Congress concerning the essential soundness of America's economy, the stock market crash in October, 1929, precipitated the most disastrous depression in the history of the nation. By mid-1931, the entire world faced such a severe crisis that Herbert Hoover, who had tried various remedies to stem the tide in the United States without any visible success, decided to call for a year's moratorium on the payment of all intergovernmental obligations. The statement which the President gave to the press on June 21, 1931, was as follows:[5]

"The American Government proposes the postponement during one year of all payments on intergovernmental debts, reparations and relief debts, both principal and interest, of course, not including obligations of governments held by private parties. Subject to confirmation by Congress, the American Government will postpone all payments upon the debts of foreign governments to the American Government payable during the fiscal year beginning July 1 next, conditional on a like postponement for one year of all payments on intergovernmental debts owing the important creditor powers.

"This course of action has been approved by the following Senators: Henry F. Ashurst, Hiram Bingham, Wm. E. Borah, James F. Byrnes, Arthur Capper, Simeon D. Fess, Duncan U. Fletcher, Carter Glass, William

[5] *Ibid., 1931,* Vol. 1, pp. 33-35.

J. Harris, Pat Harrison, Cordell Hull, William H. King, Dwight D. Morrow, George H. Moses, David A. Reed, Claude A. Swanson, Arthur Vandenberg, Robert F. Wagner, David I. Walsh, Thomas J. Walsh, James E. Watson; and by the following Representatives: Isaac Bacharach, Joseph W. Byrns, Carl R. Chindbloom, Frank Crowther, James W. Collier, Charles R. Crisp, Thomas H. Cullen, George P. Darrow, Harry A. Estep, Willis C. Hawley, Carl E. Mapes, J. C. McLaughlin, Earl C. Michener, C. William Ramseyer, Bertrand H. Snell, John Q. Tilson, Allen T. Treadway and Will R. Wood. It has been approved by Ambassador Charles G. Dawes and by Mr. Owen D. Young.

"The purpose of this action is to give the forthcoming year to the economic recovery of the world and to help free the recuperative forces already in motion in the United States from retarding influences from abroad.

"The world-wide depression has affected the countries of Europe more severely than our own. Some of these countries are feeling to a serious extent the drain of this depression on national economy. The fabric of intergovernmental debts, supportable in normal times, weighs heavily in the midst of this depression.

"From a variety of causes arising out of the depression such as the fall in the price of foreign commodities and the lack of confidence in economic and political stability abroad there is an abnormal movement of gold into the United States which is lowering the credit stability of many foreign countries. These and the other difficulties abroad diminish buying power for our exports and in a measure are the cause of our continued unemployment and continued lower price to our farmers.

"Wise and timely action should contribute to relieve the pressure of these adverse forces in foreign countries and should assist in the reestablishment of confidence, thus forwarding political peace and economic stability in the world.

"Authority of the President to deal with this problem is limited as this action must be supported by the Congress. It has been assured the cordial support of leading members of both parties in the Senate and the House. The essence of this proposition is to give time to permit debtor governments to recover their national prosperity. I am suggesting to the American people that they be wise creditors in their own interest and be good neighbors.

"I wish to take this occasion also to frankly state my views upon our relations to German reparations and the debts owed to us by the Allied Governments of Europe. Our government has not been a party to, or exerted any voice in determination of reparation obligations. We purposely did not participate in either general reparations or the divison of colonies or property. The repayment of debts due to us from the Allies for the advance for war and reconstruction were settled upon a basis not contingent upon German reparations or related thereto. Therefore, reparations is necessarily wholly a European problem with which we have no relation.

"I do not approve in any remote sense of the cancellation of the debts to us. World confidence would not be enhanced by such action. None of our debtor nations has ever suggested it. But as the basis of the settlement of these debts was the capacity under normal conditions of the debtor to pay, we should be consistent with our own policies and principles if we take into account the abnormal situation now existing in the world. I am sure the American people have no desire to attempt to extract any sum beyond the capacity of any debtor to pay and it is our view that broad vision requires that our government should recognize the situation as it exists.

"This course of action is entirely consistent with the policy which we have hitherto pursued. We are not involved in the discussion of strictly European problems, of which the payment of German reparations is one. It represents our willingness to make a contribution to the early restoration of world prosperity in which our own people have so deep an interest.

"I wish further to add that while this action has no bearing on the conference for limitation of land armaments to be held next February, inasmuch as the burden of competitive armaments has contributed to bring about this depression, we trust that by this evidence of our desire to assist we shall have contributed to the good will which is so necessary in the solution of this major question."

CHAPTER X.

AMERICA'S HEGEMONY
IN THE WESTERN WORLD

THE END of the first World War brought a significant change in the policy of the United States toward Latin America. Prior to that conflict the security of the Panama Canal and its approaches was of primary importance to this country. Powerful European nations were a potential threat to American control of the Caribbean area, which Mahan had pointed out earlier was vital to our security.

The outcome of the war brought no change in our basic objectives: control of the approaches to the Canal. But because of the increase in American strength relative to any potential threat to that area from overseas, the means of implementing our policy were somewhat altered. Whereas the United States had thought it was necessary to intervene a number of times prior to and during World War I, the results of that war removed the basic reason for additional interventions.

This altered power situation within the Western Hemisphere prompted the United States to begin a process of gradual liquidation of controls over the Caribbean and Central American nations. American marines were withdrawn from the Dominican Republic in 1924, although financial controls were retained. Troops finally left Nicaragua shortly before the end of Hoover's term in office; and arrangements had been made for the ending of military intervention in Haiti before Franklin D. Roosevelt became President.

In spite of this trend, however, the United States maintained controls over Cuba, Panama, the Dominican Republic, Haiti, and Nicaragua throughout the twenties and into the thirties. America's post-war policy of maintaining a measure of control in Latin America was primarily to fulfill obligations assumed at an earlier date. Although the real or fancied menaces that had prompted earlier interventions had been removed after 1918, the responsibilities undertaken by the United States remained. In most instances the American bankers who had loaned funds to the Latin Americans were assured by our Government that financial supervision would be maintained until the bonds were liquidated.

Although the United States Government felt a legal and a moral responsibility to retain its controls over various Latin-American nations, the peoples in the other American nations were not impressed with such arguments. The Latin Americans gave vigorous support to the Drago Doctrine which would outlaw armed intervention for the purpose of collecting a public debt. The United States consistently rejected this doctrine on the grounds that it did not constitute a part of international law. The resentment of the Latins reached a boiling point at the Havana Conference in 1928 when a number of their delegations virtually demanded a showdown on the question of intervention. Charles Evans Hughes, the American delegate, pointed up our policy of gradual withdrawal and said this nation planned no new interventions; but he resolutely refused to abandon our right to intervene. Hughes's statement probably marked the low point in inter-American cooperation during this century.

Harding and Coolidge went to great lengths to insist that our rights be respected in Latin America to the letter of the law. Herbert Hoover, however, adopted a policy of cultivating more friendly relations with those nations—a policy which was expanded into broader vistas by Franklin D. Roosevelt.

1. American Objectives in Mexico, 1923

The United States' relations with Mexico had not been amicable from the time of the Huerta regime in 1913. Wilson had spoken in lofty terms of good will toward the Mexican people, but he intervened in their affairs too often to win their affections. Then in 1917 the revelation of the Zimmerman note, which was a German attempt to enlist Mexico's aid against the United States, aroused a certain amount of hostility toward Mexico in the southwestern part of this country. The promulgation of a new Mexican Constitution in May, 1917, added to the tension between the two nations. The main point at issue was whether Article 27 of the Constitution would be applied retroactively—

which would deprive American citizens of property rights acquired before 1917. The following is an excerpt from an instruction sent by Secretary of State Charles Evans Hughes to the American Commission to negotiate a settlement with Mexico on May 8, 1923.[1]

"SIR: I have the honor to transmit herewith, for your information and guidance, in accordance with your mission to Mexico, a dossier of the principal correspondence between the Department of State and the administration now functioning in Mexico, in regard to the questions at issue between the United States and Mexico, together with other related papers and documents.

"In order that you may appreciate the spirit and purpose of this Government in its policy toward Mexico, I may refer to the following statement which I made in an address upon this subject at Boston in October, 1922:

" 'Our feelings towards the Mexican people is one of entire friendliness and we deeply regret the necessity for the absence of diplomatic relations. We have had no desire to interfere in the internal concerns of Mexico. It is not for us to suggest what laws she shall have relating to the future, for Mexico, like ourselves, must be the judge of her domestic policy. We do, however, maintain one clear principle which lies at the foundation of international intercourse. When a nation has invited intercourse with other nations, has established laws under which investments have been lawfully made, contracts entered into and property rights acquired by citizens of other jurisdictions, it is an essential condition of international intercourse that international obligations shall be met and that there shall be no resort to confiscation and repudiation. We are not insistent on the form of any particular assurance to American citizens against confiscation, but we desire in the light of the experience of recent years the substance of such protection, and this is manifestly in the interest of permanently friendly relations. I have no desire to review the history of the past. The problem is a very simple one and its solution is wholly within Mexico's keeping.'

"It will be observed that the fundamental question at issue has been the safeguarding of American property rights in Mexico, especially as against a confiscatory application of the provisions of the Mexican Constitution of 1917. In view of the fact that the recognition of the government of General Carranza had been based upon his explicit assurances that there would be no confiscation of American properties, and of the subsequent confiscatory measures actually taken, it was deemed important, in order to avoid a serious crisis, that there should be a clear understanding of the policy of General Obregon's regime before it was recognized and diplomatic relations

[1] *Papers Relating to the Foreign Relations of the United States, 1923*, Vol. II, pp. 536-38.

were resumed.[2] In answer to the objection that General Obregon could not enter into an agreement prior to recognition, I proposed, soon after the present Administration took office, that a treaty should be made between the United States and Mexico, containing appropriate provisions protecting valid titles of American citizens, which had been obtained prior to the Constitution of 1917. It was explained that the signing of this treaty between the President of the United States and the President of Mexico would in itself constitute recognition and thus the act of recognition would be coincident with the formal assurances of protection against confiscation."

2. *Protection of American Rights*

Probably no American President was more determined to uphold the rights of American citizens in Latin America, by intervention if necessary, than Calvin Coolidge. American marines were first sent to Nicaragua in 1912 and they were kept there until 1925 for the protection of American lives and property. They were withdrawn for a short time in 1925 and returned when new disturbances threatened the stability of that nation. As Coolidge was severely criticized in the United States and elsewhere for continuing the intervention, he defended his policy in an address to Congress on January 10, 1927.[3]

"TO THE CONGRESS OF THE UNITED STATES: While conditions in Nicaragua and the action of this Government pertaining thereto have in general been made public, I think the time has arrived for me officially to inform the Congress more in detail of the events leading up to the present disturbances and conditions which seriously threaten American lives and property, endangering the stability of all Central America, and put in jeopardy the rights granted by Nicaragua to the United States for the construction of a canal. It is well known that in 1912 the United States intervened in Nicaragua with a large force and put down a revolution, and that from that time to 1925 a legation guard of American marines was, with the consent of the Nicaraguan Government, kept in Managua to protect American lives and property. In 1923 representatives of the five Central American countries, namely, Costa Rica, Guatemala, Honduras, Nicaragua, and Salvador, at the invitation of the United States, met in

[2] General Obregon's regime was recognized on August 31, 1923, after an agreement had been reached at the Bucareli Conference that the Constitution would not be applied retroactively. After Obregon had left office, the Mexican Congress passed legislation which the United States claimed invalidated the Bucareli agreement.

[3] *Papers Relating to the Foreign Relations of the United States, 1927,* Vol. III, pp. 288-98.

Washington and entered into a series of treaties. These treaties dealt with limitation of armament, a Central American tribunal for arbitration, and the general subject of peace and amity. The treaty last referred to specifically provides . . . that the Governments of the contracting powers will not recognize any other government which may come into power in any of the five Republics through a *coup d'etat* or revolution and disqualifies the leaders of such coup d'etat or revolution from assuming the presidency or vice-presidency. . . .

"The United States was not a party to this treaty, but it was made in Washington under the auspices of the Secretary of State, and this Government has felt a moral obligation to apply its principles in order to encourage the Central American States in their efforts to prevent revolution and disorder. The treaty, it may be noted in passing, was signed on behalf of Nicaragua by Emiliano Chamorro himself, who afterwards assumed the presidency in violation thereof and thereby contributed to the creation of the present difficulty. . . .

"There is no question that if the revolution continues American investments and business interests in Nicaragua will be very seriously affected, if not destroyed. The currency, which is now at par, will be inflated. American as well as foreign bondholders will undoubtedly look to the United States for the protection of their interests.

"It is true that the United States did not establish the financial plan by any treaty, but it nevertheless did aid through diplomatic channels and advise in the negotiation and establishment of this plan for the financial rehabilitation of Nicaragua.

"Manifestly the relation of this Government to the Nicaraguan situation, and its policy in the existing emergency, are determined by the facts which I have described. The proprietary rights of the United States in the Nicaraguan canal route, with the necessary implications growing out of it affecting the Panama Canal, together with the obligations flowing from the investments of all classes of our citizens in Nicaragua, place us in a position of peculiar responsibility. I am sure it is not the desire of the United States to intervene in the internal affairs of Nicaragua or of any other Central American Republic. Nevertheless it must be said that we have a very definite and special interest in the maintenance of order and good government in Nicaragua at the present time, and that the stability, prosperity, and independence of all Central American countries can never be a matter of indifference to us. The United States can not, therefore, fail to view with deep concern any serious threat to stability and constitutional government in Nicaragua tending toward anarchy and jeopardizing American interests, especially if such state of affairs is contributed to or brought about by outside influences or by any foreign power. It has always been and remains the policy of the United States in such circumstances to take the steps that may be necessary for the preservation and protection of the lives, the property, and the interests of its citizens and of this Government itself. In this respect I propose to follow the path of my predecessors.

"Consequently, I have deemed it my duty to use the powers committed to me to insure the adequate protection of all American interests in Nicaragua, whether they be endangered by internal strife or by outside interference in the affairs of that Republic."

3. Havana Conference, 1928

At the Sixth International Conference of American States, held in Havana in 1928, a group of Latin-American states introduced a proposal which would have outlawed the intervention by one state in the affairs of another. Charles Evans Hughes, the chairman of the American delegation, attempted to avoid discussion of this highly controversial subject, but when that proved impossible, he replied that while the United States did not plan any new interventions it could not abandon the right to intervene which was allowed under international law in some circumstances. The following selection was taken from the instructions furnished by Secretary of State Frank B. Kellogg to the American delegation on January 5, 1928.[4]

"SIRS: The International Conference of American States to which you have been designated as representatives of our country is the sixth conference of this type to be held in the Western Hemisphere, covering a period of approximately forty years. It is an established principle of our international policy that: 'Among the Foreign Relations of the United States as they fall into categories, the Pan American policy takes first place in our diplomacy.'

"In this regard I wish to express your Government's appreciation of the importance of the occasion and its sense of the responsibility you have undertaken in accepting appointment to represent it as a gathering where there will be present delegates from all the American Republics.

"Our country has occupied a unique position with regard to the nations of Latin America. Our national individuality and independence were acquired before theirs, and when they achieved independence, they turned to us for moral guidance and support. But today and for many years past, they have stood alone, free, independent, self-reliant. The United States does not desire and in no sense can it be contemplated that any of the American peoples should be in a state of tutelage. We wish the fullest possible development of the national life of the republics of America in complete accord with

[4] *Papers Relating to the Foreign Relations of the United States, 1928,* Vol. 1, pp. 534-85.

their own national characteristics and aptitudes. If it is possible for us to assist them in any way, through our development and our achievements in science and industry, we shall be glad to extend such assistance in the most friendly manner, but we shall not proffer it unless it is desired. The policy of the Government of the United States toward the Republics of Latin America is one of mutually beneficial cooperation, and it is of paramount importance that the spirit of this policy be manifested in your attitude and action at the Conference.

"To the task of these conferences, which in the first instance were consultative and recommendatory only, has been added that of approval. The programs of the various conferences, which dealt primarily with political, commercial and social matters included subjects concerning which an element of controversy was notably absent. Only those topics were inserted about which the American States held similar opinions and where a complete accord might be looked for through a friendly and frank exchange of views. In this connection, and as stated in the instructions to the American delegates to the Fifth Pan American Conference: 'It should be borne in mind that the function of these Pan American Conferences is to deal so far as possible with non-controversial subjects of general interest, upon which free and full discussion may be had with the purpose and probability of arriving at agreement and cooperation. International questions which cause prolonged, and even bitter controversial debates, are not infrequently, in their important aspects, of actual interest only to a small group of nations. It is believed that in this Conference the most fruitful results will be obtained if discussion is confined to those aspects of the various topics which are of interest to all the Republics. In this connection, you will bear in mind that the present Conference has not been called to sit in judgment on the conduct of any nation, or to attempt to redress alleged wrongs.'

"It nevertheless is possible that attempts may be made to introduce for discussion subjects not incorporated in the program. For your guidance in such a contingency, there have been prepared a brief analysis of the political affairs of the several American Republics and an analysis of economic affairs, which are attached hereto as appendices Nos. 1 and 2. . . .

"[Appendix 1]

"*Special Political Memorandum*

"The past year has seen the development of a vigorous anti-American propaganda throughout Latin America based on charges of 'imperialism' and characterized by violent criticism of the relations existing between the United States and Mexico and the American policy in Nicaragua. . . . Every effort should be made to have the topics discussed at the Conference confined to those on the pre-arranged agenda, or such additional topics as do not involve any discussion or criticisms of the foreign policy of this or any other country. . . .

"AN AGREEMENT TO RESPECT THE TERRITORIAL AND POLITICAL INTEGRITY OF THE LATIN AMERICAN NATIONS

"Such an obligation would be quite acceptable to this Government, which has frequently given public and emphatic assurances that it does not covet the territory of any other nation. (Any obligation, however, not to intervene under any circumstances in the internal affairs of another country or not to go to war until after the pronouncement of an arbitral award, while commendable so far as the general purpose in view is concerned, would be likely to encounter opposition in this country as inconsistent with the constitutional authority of the Congress and thus would give rise to unnecessary controversy. . . .)

"This Government could not, of course, undertake to limit or bind its action in future unknown contingencies regarding the measure of protection which it might deem it incumbent upon it to exert on behalf of American citizens and property endangered by revolution or other civil turmoil in a foreign country.

"You will of course understand that should this Government be obliged thus to afford protection to its nationals abroad its action would, as in the past, be limited to this object alone. When this object has been obtained and the danger is removed, the forces of the United States would of course be withdrawn. This has been the traditional policy of the United States."

4. Restatement of Monroe Doctrine, 1930

The Monroe Doctrine had never been overly popular in Latin America, but after Theodore Roosevelt added his corollary to the Doctrine in 1904, it was looked upon as an instrument of oppression. Frank B. Kellogg, Coolidge's Secretary of State, asked J. Reuben Clark, a prominent international lawyer, to make a thorough study of the Monroe Doctrine. Clark submitted to Kellogg his conclusions—which were not entirely to the liking of Calvin Coolidge. After Hoover became President, he had Clark's work printed under the title, *Memorandum on the Monroe Doctrine* and issued as a public document in 1930. The most important aspect of this document was its repudiation of the Roosevelt Corollary.[5]

"The so-called 'Roosevelt corollary' was to the effect, as generally understood, that in case of financial or other difficulties in weak Latin American countries, the United States should attempt an adjustment thereof lest

[5] J. Reuben Clark, *Memorandum on the Monroe Doctrine*, Dept. of State, Pub. 37. (Washington, 1930), pp. XXIII-XXV.

European Governments should intervene, and intervening should occupy territory—an act which would be contrary to the principles of the Monroe Doctrine. . . .

"As has already been indicated above, it is not believed that this corollary is justified by the terms of the Monroe Doctrine, however much it may be justified by the application of the doctrine of self-preservation. . . .

"The Doctrine does not concern itself with purely inter-American relations; it has nothing to do with the relationship between the United States and other American nations, except where other American nations shall become involved with European governments in arrangements which threaten the security of the United States, and even in such cases, the Doctrine runs against the European country, not the American nation, and the United States would primarily deal thereunder with the European country and not with the American nation concerned. The Doctrine states a case of the United States *vs.* Europe, and not of the United States *vs.* Latin America. Furthermore, the fact should never be lost to view that in applying this Doctrine during the period of one hundred years since it was announced, our Government has over and over again driven it in as a shield between Europe and the Americas to protect Latin America from the political and territorial thrusts of Europe; and this was done at times when the American nations were weak and struggling for the establishment of stable, permanent governments; when the political morality of Europe sanctioned, indeed encouraged, the acquisition of territory by force; and when many of the great powers of Europe looked with eager, covetous eyes to the rich, undeveloped areas of the American hemisphere. Nor should another equally vital fact be lost sight of, that the United States has only been able to give this protection against designing European powers because of its known willingness and determination, if and whenever necessary, to expend its treasure and to sacrifice American life to maintain the principles of the Doctrine. So far as Latin America is concerned, the Doctrine is now, and always has been, not an instrument of violence and oppression, but an unbought, freely bestowed, and wholly effective guaranty of their freedom, independence, and territorial integrity against the imperialistic designs of Europe."

5. *The Protection of Americans under Hoover*

Realizing that the prestige of the United States was at low ebb when he became President, Herbert Hoover made a number of moves to improve relations with our neighbors to the south. Shortly after his election he made a good will tour of Latin America. In adopting the Clark *Memorandum on the Monroe Doctrine* as his official policy, he mitigated some of the hostility felt throughout Latin America toward this nation. Probably the most important step taken by Hoover was his reversal of the Coolidge policy, which had been to protect American property rights in Latin America without reservations. This policy change was indicated in an instruction sent to the American Minister in Managua, Nicaragua on April 16, 1931.[6]

"In view of the outbreak of banditry in portions of Nicaragua hitherto free from such violence you will advise American citizens that this Government cannot undertake general protection of Americans throughout that country with American forces. To do so would lead to difficulties and commitments which this Government does not propose to undertake. Therefore, the Department recommends to all Americans who do not feel secure under the protection afforded them by the Nicaraguan Government through the Nicaraguan National Guard to withdraw from the country, or at least to the coast towns whence they can be protected or evacuated in case of necessity. Those who remain do so at their own risk and must not expect American forces to be sent inland to their aid. A similar message has been sent to the Consulate at Bluefields."

[6] *Papers Relating to the Foreign Relations of the United States, 1931,* Vol. II, p. 808.

CHAPTER XI.

ISOLATIONISM

THE LIFE of every nation is marked by certain days of high exultation. Armistice Day, November 11, 1918, was one of those occasions. The "war to end all wars" and the "war to make the world safe for democracy" had ended in a smashing victory for the United States and the other Allied powers. The Great Crusade was over and the people of America, viewing their past with understandable pride, looked to the future with supreme confidence.

Unfortunately the people of the United States were not to remain in this joyous mood for long. President Wilson, "the saviour of mankind," went to Paris to participate in the drawing up of the treaties of peace, but before the conference had ended Wilson was disappointed to find that his wartime allies did not share all of his hopes and plans for the postwar world. The American President hoped, however, that while the treaty contained some compromises with his principles, the League of Nations would serve as the instrument to bring peace with justice to the world. To Wilson, the war had been fought for certain moral principles which were to have been implemented by the League; consequently, when the Senate refused to approve the treaty, Wilson felt that the war had been fought in vain.

The fight over the Treaty of Versailles, the wars and revolutions which followed as an aftermath of the war, the bitterness which developed between the United States and the Allies over the war debts, all brought disillusionment to the people of the United States. Scholars and journalists who became intensely interested in looking into the causes of the war concluded that Germany was not solely responsible for the war. The intrigues, rivalries, and secret alliances which were revealed by the publication of the documents of the major European powers following the war, "proved" to many Americans that we had been duped into believing that there was anything noble about the war.

Although space prohibits any real analysis of this radical change in thinking on the part of the American public from the war to the postwar years, one thing is certain: they were probably no nearer the truth after the war than they had been during the conflict. A person or a nation cannot be disillusioned unless it has first been illusioned. The American people undoubtedly were illusioned during the war both as to its causes and the objectives of the major Allied powers. Consequently, when they learned that all nobility and justice and humanity had not been on their side, they became disillusioned.

Most Americans were willing to believe that we had been drawn into the war by scheming, selfish European rulers and politicians and by a few American international bankers and munition makers who had made fantastic profits from the venture. They became convinced that the United States had made a tragic mistake in interfering in the quarrels of Europe which was composed of peoples congenitally destined to constant warfare. Washington, Monroe and other American great men were quoted freely by statesmen and writers who claimed that we had ignored the wisdom of our distinguished forefathers who had warned the American people against such pitfalls.

This sentiment in the twenties led to self-incrimination and holy vows to remain out of the League of Nations. Nothing happened in the decade following the end of World War I to cause Americans even to suggest that we should interfere with the course of events outside this hemisphere. The coming of the 1930's, however, brought a significant change in the international situation.

In 1931, the Japanese seized Manchuria in an obvious act of aggression, and it was so labeled by a League of Nations commission. Hitler came to power in 1933 and promptly started to build Germany into the dominant military power it had been in 1914. Mussolini, pointing to the glories of ancient Rome, told the Italian people that they were a people of destiny; and in 1935 the Italian invasion of poorly-defended Ethiopia was Mussolini's method of proving this "fact" not only to his own people but to the world. These and the other aggressions by the Japanese, Germans, and Italians in the 1930's had a profound effect in the United States.

Many Americans, probably the vast majority, were deeply disturbed over these events. Americans sympathized with the

Chinese, Manchurians, Ethiopians, and other victims of aggression; but Americans were firm in their determination not to allow their sympathy to extend to the point where they might become involved. They had allowed their sentiments full sway before and during World War I. This time they decided to follow their minds and not their hearts.

This intense desire to stay out of war, irrespective of the issues involved, resulted in the Neutrality Acts passed by Congress in 1935, 1936, and 1937. Among other things these acts prohibited Americans from traveling on belligerent vessels except by Presidential permission, prohibited the export of arms and ammunition from the United States for the use of a belligerent nation, prohibited the arming of American merchant vessels, provided that all merchandise shipped to belligerent nations be paid for in cash before leaving this country, and forbade American citizens from purchasing the bonds or securities of any belligerent nation.

The theory behind this legislation was that insistence on our neutral rights from 1914 to 1917 had led us into the war; consequently the obvious thing to do would be for us to renounce these rights since we wanted to remain at peace. Peace at all costs was the main objective. Americans adopted the attitude that there was no morality in war, or even if one side might have more justice on its side than the other, it was not clear-cut; and the difficulty of arriving at any moral judgment was too difficult. Many other Americans were convinced that all wars were purely economic in their origins, and that we would have no difficulty staying neutral if we could prevent greedy Americans from having any economic interest in any of the belligerents. Such arch-isolationists as Senators Gerald P. Nye, Hiram Johnson, William E. Borah, Burton K. Wheeler, and Arthur H. Vandenberg were convinced that they were the realists in not only understanding the true nature of international politics, but in fashioning legislation to prevent the United States from ever again engaging in a foreign war.

Not everyone was an isolationist and not everyone favored the Neutrality Acts, but the voices of those who opposed them were drowned in the din of the shouts of those who favored this legislation. Opponents of this legislation were either considered fuzzy-minded idealists, like Woodrow Wilson, or profit-seeking "merchants of death."

The 1930's can be conveniently divided by the period before and after October 5, 1937, when Roosevelt delivered his "quarantine the aggressor nation" speech in Chicago. Before that address, few raised their voices against absolute neutrality irrespective of the outcome of any struggle abroad. After that date the isolationists who were very influential until the very moment of the Pearl Harbor attack had to contend with an ever-growing number of persons who wanted this nation to exert its influence, one way or another, to check the international anarchy brought about by the continued aggressions of the Axis nations.

The arguments of the isolationists remained the same, except that they became more vociferous in direct ratio to the degree that the Administration veered away from a position of strict impartiality. They pointed out that Americans were being subjected to propaganda by European as well as American warmongers, that only munition makers and international bankers profited by war, that war itself was the worst evil that could befall man, that America was so secure behind its two oceans that invasion by any enemy was a physical impossibility, that in any case the outcome of any struggle overseas was not really important to the security or the welfare of the United States.

President Franklin D. Roosevelt was the undoubted leader of the group of those who were branded internationalists, interventionists, or in some cases, warmongers. Very few in this group ever denounced neutrality by name or advocated our entrance into the war. However, after Japan began its full scale invasion of China in 1937, and after the outbreak of the European war in 1939, Roosevelt and a large group of citizens took the position that a total victory in Europe and Asia and possibly Africa by the Axis powers would be a serious threat to the security of the United States. They never denied that peace was preferable to war; but they argued that the Fascist nations were following policies which would destroy the basis upon which Western Christian civilization was founded, and that the more area the Fascists occupied, the less chance the remaining nations would have to defend themselves. The conclusion of this argument was that the United States for reasons of national security should take whatever action it could short of war to uphold those nations battling against the Axis powers.

Roosevelt spearheaded the drive to aid the victims of Axis aggression and was largely successful in his efforts. The arms embargo was removed in November, 1939, following the German invasion of Poland. The destroyer-bases deal was announced in September, 1940, whereby the United States transferred fifty overage destroyers to the British in return for the use of certain British bases in the Western Hemisphere. In March, 1941, Congress passed the lend-lease act, which authorized the President to extend aid to any nation the defense of which in his opinion was essential to the United States. Later in the year, Roosevelt authorized American naval vessels to patrol the Atlantic in order to insure the safe delivery of those goods to the British and later on to the Russians. Shortly before Pearl Harbor, Congress authorized the arming of American merchant vessels. This nation, under the guidance of Roosevelt, had gone as far as it could go without actually sending troops to assist Britain, Russia, and China.

The isolationists, however, were still strong and articulate. Their denunciations of the Administration became increasingly bitter during the summer and fall of 1941 when it was obvious that our relations with the Axis powers were very near the breaking point. On the eve of the Pearl Harbor attack, "America Firsters" and the isolationists in general said that we were being lured into a war merely to pull British, Russian, or Chinese chestnuts out of the fire.

The Japanese attack on December 7, 1941, ended the great debate. Isolationism was not killed, but the isolationists were silenced. In striking at our great naval base in the Pacific the Japanese not only dealt our forces a staggering blow, but they probably were guilty of the greatest psychological error of the entire war. No lesser act than a direct attack on the United States could have so unified the American people and galvanized their determination to wage war against the Axis until total victory.

1. *Argument for Neutrality — Gerald P. Nye*

Senator Gerald P. Nye of North Dakota, one of the most outspoken isolationists in the period prior to the outbreak of World War II, made an address at Carnegie Hall on May 27, 1935, in which he argued for the passage of a neutrality act which would keep this nation out of war.[1]

[1] *Congressional Record*, 74th Cong., 1st Sess., vol. 79, part 8, pp. 8338-41.

"If Europe is to again blow up in our very face, America can avoid being dragged into a repetition of other days if America but possesses the intelligence to permit experience to be its light.

"Do we have that intelligence? Sometimes I wonder. I cannot forget that it was only 17 years ago that found us giving thanks for the end of that conflict which had left on every hand wreckage, wastage, debt, despair, heartache. We found our consolation and compensation quite alone in the thought that ours had been a successful effort to make the world safe for democracy, and in the further thought that we had engaged with success in a 'war to end war'. We swore then with greatest fervor that we would never, never again let that experience be visited upon this earth again.

"But look upon ourselves today, so shortly after that engagement to save democracy and end war! Democracy has never been upon thinner ice than since then! There is more actual threat and danger of more war now than was true a few days before the World War came!

"This past year has witnessed the most intensive inquiry into the questions of arms traffic, munitions, war profits, and profits from preparedness for war that the world ever saw undertaken. It has been my privilege to work with six other Members of the United States Senate in this study. I am happy to say that it grows increasingly evident that our labors have not been in vain and that truly worth-while legislation will be forthcoming to meet the frightful challenge which the inquiry disclosures have been. Largely because the people have shown tremendous interest in the subject, I am sure that substantial legislation is on the way to restrain those racketeers who find large profit in breeding hate, fear, and suspicion as a base for large preparedness programs, and who have learned that while there is large profit in preparing for war, there is larger profit for them in war itself. . . .

"I think we will do well to give some thought to causes behind our entry into the Great War. Those causes as well as the results which have since followed are an experience we should not soon forget.

"Nineteen hundred and fourteen found America just as determined, just as anxious for peace as it is now. But less than 3 years later we were in the greatest of all wars, creating obligations and burdens which even to this day bend our backs. What was it that took us into that war in spite of our high contrary resolve?

"To me there is something sinister involved in using the language of 1914 in this present pre-war year of 1935. There is, I fear, danger that the soft, evasive, unrealistic, untrue language of 21 years ago will again take root and then rise up and slay its millions as it did then, both during and after a war.

"Let me make this clear. If the people of the world are told again that the next war is a political war for the noblest possible ideals, those same people will be the ones to suffer not only during the war, but also when the war is over and the peace signed on the basis of the crude, economic struggle.

"It was only after the war that President Wilson confessed that he knew what it was all about. He said at St. Louis in 1919:

" 'Why, my fellow citizens, is there any man here or any woman, let me say is there any child here, who does not know that the seed of war in the modern world is industrial and commercial rivalry? The real reason that the war that we have just finished took place was that Germany was afraid her commercial rivals were going to get the better of her, and the reason why some nations went into the war against Germany was that they thought Germany would get the commercial advantage of them. The seed of the jealousy, the seed of deep-seated hatred was hot, successful commercial and industrial rivalry.

" 'This was in its inception a commercial and industrial war. It was not a political war.'

"Ah, the rulers of the world, the foreign offices, the state departments, the presidents and kings and czars and kaisers, knew what the war was about all the time. It was only afterwards that the people were informed why they had been fighting. There was fraud perpetrated by the governments of the world in hiding from their people the economic causes for which they were fighting.

"That fraud was paid for after the war was over. The spokesmen of the world looked at the peace with cold, calculating eyes which took little account of idealistic slogans. The French could only see that America had to get into the war because American bankers had advanced $2,000,000,000 worth of credits, which would have been worthless if we had not gotten into the war. But the American people did not know this at the time.

"The fraud of pretending that wars are political—involve national honor—when they are essentially for economic causes—leads to friction when the wars are over. Fraud and friction go hand in hand.

"Let us be as frank before the next war as Wilson was frank after the last war was over. Let us know that it is sales and shipments of munitions and contraband, and the lure of the profits in them, that will get us into another war, and that when the proper time comes and we talk about national honor, let us know that simply means the right to go on making money out of a war.

"Let us have done with all the fraud, and we will have done with all the post-war friction.

"There are many who have tried to keep us from being involved in entangling foreign political alliances. But since wars are for economic causes basically, it is as important to avoid becoming involved in entangling foreign economic alliances. That is the crux of the matter. It is useless to pretend that our isolation from foreign political entanglements means anything if we open wide the gates to foreign loans and credits for munitions and spread out a network of munition ships that will be ignition points of another war.

"Senate Joint Resolution 120, which Senator Clark[2] and I have proposed and introduced, forbids the export of arms and ammunition to any belligerent country or to anyone acting on behalf of a belligerent in time of war. This provision is mandatory. It recognizes that tremendous pressure will be brought to bear on the President should he seek to curb a profitable trade in war materials after war has broken out. The embargo on arms and ammunition, therefore, becomes effective automatically on the declaration of war by any foreign government. It applies to all arms, ammunition, and implements exclusively designed and intended for land, sea, or aerial warfare.

"This does not cover all war materials. It is virtually impossible, however, to impose a mandatory embargo on all war materials because of the practical difficulties of defining articles which have a commercial use as well as a military use in war time. Many commodities, such as fuel oil, nitrates, manganese, cotton liners, and metals of all kinds, are regarded as essential war materials in time of war. In the case of a major war it might be advisable to forbid the export of some of these commodities, in a limited war between two small states such an embargo might not be necessary. Section 1, therefore, gives the President some discretion in this matter by authorizing an embargo on 'any other article or articles which the United States declares to be war materials.'

"In the case of armed conflicts or international disputes short of war, the President is given full discretion by section 2 as to when the embargo shall be put in force. If he decides to impose an embargo on arms and munitions of war, however, this term shall in any case include the full list of articles attached to this section. The President may add, at his discretion, such other war material as he deems essential to the conduct of war or armed conflict.

"Section 4 recognizes the fact that the United States has not been able to bring about an understanding between the principal maritime powers on freedom of the seas or the definition of contraband. It recognizes, further, that the shipment of contraband may involve the United States in the danger of being forced to defend such shipments at the risk of American lives and with the other economic and social losses involved in the conduct of war. It provides that, in the absence of any treaty or agreement between the principal maritime powers, the President shall proclaim that the export of any article declared to be contraband by any belligerent government shall be solely at the risk of the American shipper or the foreign government or national.

"This proposition is simply to let other nations make their own poison gases. If we sell them any contraband that will help them make those gases, it will be transported at their own risk. Let them wrap their own flags around their own poison gas. Let us be determined to be on a cash-and-carry basis as respects this kind of business.

[2] Senator Bennett Champ Clark of Missouri.

"Senate Joint Resolution 100 provides for an embargo on all loans and credits to belligerents during the war. The proposition here is simple: Let them pay for their own wars. If Morgans[3] and other bankers must get into another war, let them do it by enlisting in the Foreign Legion. That's always open.

"We must not overlook the importance of another famous neutral right in any chain of causes leading to war. Just as trade with belligerents became a matter of national honor—so called—which was to be defended without question by the national suicide of war, so the right of a few individuals to travel into war zones in pursuit of that trade was made the cause of our whole nation plunging into terrible and costly war.

"Modern war finds whole nations desperately struggling for existence. The commerce of any enemy is an artery that must be severed. On the very day that the *Lusitania* left New York Harbor the daily papers printed an official warning from the German Embassy that British vessels were 'liable to destruction' and that 'travelers sailing in the war zone on ships of Great Britain and her allies do so at their own risk.' But our Government issued no such statement. It did not even warn our people that the *Lusitania* carried contraband and actual munitions.

"Senate Joint Resolution 99 empowers the President to withhold passports from Americans traveling in war zones or upon vessels of belligerent nations, and gives fair warning that Americans who risk their lives in war trade can expect no greater support from their fellow countrymen than those other adventurous Americans who risk their lives by joining the foreign legions of Europe.

"Here then, it seems to me, is a well-rounded out program to give life and endurance to our intended neutrality in the event sanity breaks loose from its moorings somewhere upon this earth. Senate Joint Resolution 99, 100 and 120 constitute a studied effort to make American peace more secure. They may not alone keep us out of war, but experience dictates that this added strength to our neutrality policies in those years leading up to our entry into the World War, would probably have saved us from the frightful consequences which have since followed."

2. *Argument Against Neutrality Legislation — Walter Lippmann*

Walter Lippmann, noted American journalist, delivered a radio address on January 18, 1936, in which he argued against the proposal that additional neutrality legislation be passed which would still further limit the right of the Executive to act

[3] Nye was referring here to J. Pierpont Morgan, who was quizzed at length before the Senate Committee headed by himself.

with that freedom granted under the Constitution when a state of belligerency exists between two or more foreign powers. Although Lippmann was concerned with a particular piece of legislation, his arguments are pertinent for any legislation which is designed to set policy for a future event whose consequences cannot be foreseen.[4]

"In the course of the next four or five weeks Congress will have to pass some kind of law dealing with the subject of neutrality. I think you will agree that that is a very short time in which to deal with a very big subject. . . .

". . . There is now on the statute books a law passed last August which governs American neutrality in the war that is being fought between Italy and Ethiopia. This law is working well enough. It has not involved the United States in any serious controversies with Italy or with Ethiopia. . . . There is only one trouble with the present law. It expires automatically on the 29th of February. So far as this particular war goes all that is needed, therefore, is for Congress to extend the present law for another year or so. That could be easily done.

"If there were no other war in sight that would be all that any one would wish to do. But, of course, there are other wars, much greater wars, in sight, and it is these greater wars that Congress and the Administration are worried about. . . . The plain fact is that all the great powers of Europe and of Asia are arming feverishly and preparing for war. There is the war in Africa. There is something very much like a war in China. There are gigantic armaments being prepared. There are alliances being formed. There is powerful propaganda in several nations to implant in the minds of the people the conviction that there is no solution for their difficulties except by a resort to force and violence. In short, there exists the real danger of a very great war that might easily involve almost all the nations of Europe, Africa and Asia.

"Clearly, it is our duty to take every precaution we can take to see to it, if such a great war breaks out, that it does not involve the United States.

"The practical question now before the country, the question that has to be decided at once, is whether Congress can, before the 29th of February, determine exactly how the United States shall act in the event of a great European and Asiatic war.

"This is the fundamental question on which the American people have to make up their minds. It should be clearly grasped. Can Congress in the next four weeks decide how the United States shall act in the event of another great war? This is the real question on which Congress is divided. This is the real issue between the Administration and those who think as

---

[4] Walter Lippmann, "Neutrality: The Immediate Problem," *Vital Speeches,* II (January 27, 1936), pp. 262-63.

Senator Nye thinks. It is no use arguing about loans, and munitions and cotton and oil and steel and ships and submarines until we make up our minds on this basic question: Are we going to decide now, in the next month, what must be done about all these things? Senator Nye wishes to say what must be done. He wishes to go as far as he can in laying down a rigid policy which the government must follow.

"Those who are opposed to him say that it is in the highest degree dangerous to attempt to say now exactly what the policy of the government must be. Their contention is that while Congress should give the government all the powers it might need in order to preserve American neutrality, it is wrong, it is unwise, it is dangerous, for Senator Nye or any one else to attempt to say precisely what must be done. No one has any objections, on the contrary, every one agrees, that it may be necessary to do all the things that Senator Nye and his friends wish to do. No one has any objections to giving the government the power to do them. But there is the most serious objection to saying now, to deciding in a hurry before February 29, that any or all of these things must be done no matter what the circumstances, no matter what the conditions, no matter what the crisis may be, which may at some future time confront the American people.

"The attempt to write a binding, cast-iron law today to fix American neutrality policy in another great war is like saying: I may have to play a game of bridge next week and I have decided to lead the eight of diamonds. It is like saying: I may play football next autumn and on the second play I am going to call for a forward pass. It is like saying: I have decided that my grandchild is to be a prize fighter without knowing whether your grandchild is to be a boy or a girl.

"In the case of a possible great war in the future nobody knows today, nobody in the Senate, nobody in any country anywhere, when it will break out. Nobody knows where it will break out. Nobody knows who will be fighting. Nobody knows who will be neutral. Nobody knows who will be allied with whom. Nobody knows whether it will be fought on the sea, in the air, or on land. Nobody can look into the future and predict the character of the war which Congress is to make laws about. How, under these circumstances, can any Senator pretend that he knows enough, that he is sufficiently a prophet, to write a law which fixes in advance the correct policy of the United States?

"The best proof that this is impossible is to be found in the fact that seventeen years after the end of the World War a Senate Committee has just spent a hundred thousand dollars trying to find out how and why the United States entered it. That war is over. Yet here we are still arguing and quarreling, still writing books, still making speeches, still holding investigations, and still uncertain as to why we entered the war. If we do not know yet why we entered the last war, how on earth can Congress write a law in four weeks telling us exactly how to behave in the next war? . . .

"As a matter of fact, if it were possible today to describe the character of the next war, if it were known who is going to fight, and where, and what the military plan of the next war is to be, the next war would almost certainly not take place. If it were known who is going to attack, when he is going to attack, where he is going to attack, who is going to oppose him, there would be no great difficulty in preventing the attack. The very essence of the war danger, however, lies in the inability of the governments and the people to foresee the future. The essence of the danger is that the time, the military strategy, the purposes, cannot be foreseen—that the war, if it comes, will come as a surprise and at a moment when the world is not ready for it.

"The moral I draw from this is that for the United States to tie its hands today is to increase the danger to the United States, not to diminish it. The only way to be prepared for an unpredictable emergency is to be able to move, to have your hands free, to be alert, resourceful, powerful, and unentangled. These proposals to settle American policy in advance are an attempt to say that we know better today what the emergency will require, though we do not know what the emergency will be, than the President and Congress who actually see what the emergency is.

"It is a pretty good rule in human affairs that men should solve the problems of their own day and not try to tell their descendants and their successors how to settle their problems.

"The policy of the United States Government is to remain unentangled and free. Let us follow that policy. Let us remain unentangled and free. Let us make no alliances. Let us make no commitments. By the same token let us pass no laws which will bind the future, tie the hands of the government, deprive it of its freedom, cause it to be entangled in a statute based on what somebody at this moment thinks the government ought to do in the future.

"The simple truth is that we are not wise enough to tell a future Congress and a future President what they must do. We shall be very fortunate if we are wise enough to decide what we must do in the situation that is right before our eyes. We shall need all the wisdom we can find to cross the bridge that we are now trying to cross without deciding also how our successors shall cross the bridges that they will have to cross."

3. An Appeal for Peace — Lindbergh

On August 4, 1940, one of the foremost isolationists, Charles A. Lindbergh, delivered an address at the Keep-America-Out-of-War Rally in Chicago.[5]

[5] Charles A. Lindbergh, "An Appeal for Peace," *Vital Speeches*, VI (August 15, 1940), pp. 644-46.

"Several weeks have passed since I received the honor of your invitation to speak in Chicago. At that time it was essential to create strong and immediate opposition to the trend towards war which was taking place in this country.

"The agitation for our entry into the war was increasing with alarming rapidity. Hysteria had mounted to the point where antiparachute corps were being formed to defend American cities against air attacks from Europe. Greenland, with its Arctic climate, its mountainous terrain and its ice-filled seas, was called an easy stepping-stone for German bombing planes invading America.[6]

"Cartoons showed the Atlantic Ocean reduced the width of the English Channel. American safety was said to depend upon the success of European armies. Foreign propaganda was in full swing and it seemed in many ways that we were approaching the greatest crisis in the history of our country.

"But events move swiftly in this modern world and the true character of a nation lies beneath such surface foam. When the danger of foreign war was fully realized by our people the underlying tradition of American independence arose and in recent weeks its voice has thundered through the weaker cries of war.

"We have by no means escaped the foreign entanglements and favoritisms that Washington warned us against when he passed the guidance of our nation's destiny to the hands of future generations. We have participated deeply in the intrigues of Europe and not always in an open 'democratic' way.

"There are still interests in this country and abroad who will do their utmost to draw us into the war. Against these interests we must be continuously on our guard. But American opinion is now definitely and overwhelmingly against our involvement.

"Both political parties have declared against our entry into the war. People are beginning to realize that the problems of Europe cannot be solved by the interference of America. We have at last started to build and plan for the defense of our own continent. By these acts our eyes are turned once more in the direction of security and peace, for if our own military forces are strong, no foreign nation can invade us and if we do not interfere with their affairs none will desire to. . . .

"I have a different outlook toward Europe than most people in America. I am advised to speak guardedly on the subject of war. I am told that one must not stand too strongly against the trend of the times and that to be effective what one says must meet with general approval.

"There is much to be said for this argument, yet, right or wrong, it is contrary to the values that I hold highest in life. I prefer to say what I believe or not speak at all. . . .

[6] He referred to a speech made by Franklin D. Roosevelt following the surrender of France in June, 1940.

"I found conditions in Europe to be very different from our concept of them here in the United States. Any one who takes the trouble to read through back issues of our newspapers cannot fail to realize what a false impression we had of the belligerent nations.

"We were told that Germany was ripe for revolution, that her re-armament was a bluff, that she lacked officers, that she flew her airplanes from one field to another so they would be counted again and again by foreign observers.

"We were informed that Russia had the most powerful air fleet in the world, that the French Army was superior to any in Europe, that the British Navy was more than a match for the German Air Force, that Germany lacked enough fuel, food and raw material to wage war, that the Maginot Line was impregnable, that Italy would never enter the war against England. Statements of this sort have issued forth in an endless stream from Europe and any one who questioned their accuracy was called a Nazi agent.

"These examples show how greatly we have been misled about military conditions in Europe. If one goes still farther back, he will find that we have also been misled about political conditions. It has seemed obvious to me for many years that conditions in Europe would have to change, either by agreement or by war. I hoped that we had reached a degree of civilization where a change might come by agreement. Living in Europe made me fear that it would come only through war.

"There is a proverb in China which says that 'when the rich become too rich and the poor too poor, something happens.' This applies to nations as well as to men.

"When I saw the wealth of the British Empire I felt that the rich had become too rich. When I saw the poverty of Central Europe I felt that the poor had become too poor. That something would happen was blazoned even on the skies of Europe by mounting thousands of fighting aircraft.

"From 1936 to 1939, as I traveled through European countries, I saw the phenomenal military strength of Germany growing like a giant at the side of an aged and complacent England. France was awake to her danger, but far too occupied with personal ambitions, industrial troubles and internal politics to make more than a feeble effort to rearm. In England there was organization without spirit; in France there was spirit without organization; in Germany there were both.

"I realized that I was witnessing a clash between the heirs of another war. A generation had passed since the Treaty of Versailles. The sons of victory and the sons of defeat were about to meet on the battlefields of their fathers.

"As I traveled first among those who had won and then among those who had lost, the words of a French philosopher kept running through my mind: 'Many thrive on adversity.'

"The underlying issue was clear. It was not the support of 'democracy,' or the so-called democratic nations would have given more assistance to the struggling republic of post-war Germany.

"It was not a crusade for Christianity, or the Christian nations of the West would have carried their battle flags to the confiscated churches of Russia.

"It was not the preservation of small and hopeless nations, or sanctions would have been followed by troops in Abyssinia and England would not have refused to cooperate with the United States in Manchuria.

"The issue was one of the oldest and best known among men. It concerned the division of territory and wealth between nations. It has caused conflict in Europe since European history began.

"The longer I lived in Europe the more I felt that no outside influence could solve the problems of European nations or bring them lasting peace; they must work out their destiny, as we must work out ours. I am convinced that the better acquainted we in America become with the background of European conflicts the less we will desire to take part in them.

"But here I would like to make this point clear: While I advocate the non-interference by America in the internal affairs of Europe, I believe it is of the utmost importance for us to cooperate with Europe in our relationships with other peoples of the earth. It is only by cooperation that we can maintain the supremacy of our Western civilization and the right of our commerce to proceed unmolested throughout the world. Neither they nor we are strong enough to police the opposition of the other.

"In the past we have dealt with a Europe dominated by England and France. In the future we may have to deal with a Europe dominated by Germany. But, whether England or Germany wins this war, Western civilization will still depend upon two great centers, one in each hemisphere.

"With all the aids of modern science, neither of these centers is in a position to attack the other successfully as long as the defenses of both are reasonably strong. A war between us could easily last for generations and bring all civilization tumbling down, as has happened more than once before. An agreement between us could maintain civilization and peace throughout the world as far into the future as we can see.

"But we are often told that if Germany wins this war cooperation will be impossible and treaties no more than scraps of paper. I reply that cooperation is never impossible when there is sufficient gain on both sides and that treaties are seldom torn apart when they do not cover a weak nation.

"I would be among the last to advocate depending upon treaties for our national safety. I believe that we should rearm fully for the defense of America and that we should never make the type of treaty that would lay us open to invasion if it were broken. But, if we refuse to consider treaties with the dominant nation of Europe, regardless of who that may be, we remove all possibility of peace.

"Nothing is to be gained by shouting names and pointing the finger of blame across the ocean. Our grandstand advice to England and our criticism of her campaign has been neither wanted nor helpful.

"Our accusations of aggression and barbarism on the part of Germany simply bring back echoes of hypocrisy and Versailles. Our hasty condemnation of the French Government, struggling desperately to save a defeated nation from collapse, can do nothing but add to famine, hatred and chaos.

"If we desire to keep America out of war, we must take the lead in offering a plan of peace. That plan should be based upon the welfare of America. It should be backed by an impregnable system of defense. It should incorporate terms of mutual advantage but it should not involve the internal affairs of Europe; they never were and never will be carried on according to our desires.

"Let us offer Europe a plan for the progress and protection of the Western civilization of which they and we each form a part. But, whatever their reply may be, let us carry on the American destiny of which our forefathers dreamed as they cut their farm lands from the virgin forests. What would they think if they could hear the claim that our frontiers lie in Europe?

"Let us guard the independence that the soldiers of our Revolution won against overwhelming odds. What, I ask you, would those soldiers say if they could hear this nation, grown 130 million strong, being told that only the British Fleet protects us from invasion?

"Our nation was born of courage and hardship. It grew on the fearless spirit of the pioneers. Now that it has become one of the greatest powers on earth, ours must not be the generation that kneels in fear of future hardships or of invasion by a Europe already torn by war.

"I do not believe that we will ever accept a philosophy of calamity, weakness and fear. I have faith in an American Army, an American Navy, an American Air Force and, most important of all, the American character, which, in normal times, lies quietly beneath the surface of this nation."

CHAPTER XII.

"THE GATHERING STORM"

THE 1920's might be described as the decade when the American people believed that they could live in the world but not be an integral part of it. During the 1930's, they attempted to guarantee their isolation from the rest of the world by legislation, but before the end of that decade the United States had come slowly and painfully to the realization that events in Asia, Europe, and Africa did have an effect on our welfare and security.

When Franklin D. Roosevelt delivered his first inaugural address on March 4, 1933, both he and the American people were concerned with the economic crisis facing the nation virtually to the exclusion of all other problems. The Japanese had seized Manchuria in 1931, but no one then understood that this event was the first in a series of aggressions which finally exploded into the second World War. Hitler had come into power just prior to Roosevelt's accession to office, but again, no one in the United States or elsewhere could foresee that this hitherto inconspicuous and somewhat ludicrous ex-corporal would weld Germany into a more powerful and aggressive nation than it had been under the imperial rule of Kaiser William II.

Domestic problems continued to occupy the attention of the American people for several years, but, in 1935, Mussolini's legion's overran Ethiopia. In 1936, Hitler remilitarized the Rhineland in open violation of the Treaty of Versailles, and during the summer the Spanish Civil War started. The major powers looked the other way and pretended not to see that Germany and Italy were intervening on behalf of Generalissimo Francisco Franco and that the Soviet Union was aiding the Loyalists. In July, 1937, the peace of the Far East was again shattered by the Japanese attack on China.

The American people were disturbed by these events, but clung the more firmly to strict neutrality. The first indication given publicly that Franklin D. Roosevelt had some doubts about our neutrality by legislation came on October 5, 1937, when he condemned aggression and spoke of the need for the peace-loving nations of the world to "quarantine the aggressor." This speech aroused a storm of criticism from those who looked upon it as a departure, at least in spirit, from our avowed policy of strict impartiality.

The President never clarified the meaning of the word "quarantine," but his Chicago speech left no doubt in anyone's mind that he was not entirely satisfied with our existing legislation. If the advantages of neutrality were to avoid war, the disadvantages were that the neutral must be willing to abide by the results of any war. In October, 1937, Roosevelt must have believed that the long-range results of continued and unopposed aggression by Germany, Italy, and Japan would be more dangerous to the security of the United States than for this nation to act to restrain that aggression, even at the risk of incurring the wrath of those countries.

One speech, and especially one which was as widely condemned in this country as was Roosevelt's Chicago address, was not enough to restrain the ambitions of the Axis powers. As the Japanese pushed deeper into China, Hitler took Austria in the spring of 1938 and the Sudeten region of Czechoslovakia in the fall of that year, following the Munich agreement.

In view of the decisive actions taken by the Axis powers in 1938 to enlarge their influence and domains, the policy of the United States to counteract these aggressions seemed puny indeed. In June, Roosevelt proclaimed a moral embargo on the sale of airplanes to Japan. Later in the year, the President recalled Ambassador Hugh Wilson from Berlin as a protest against the brutal pogrom Hitler had launched against the Jews. In December, Cordell Hull pointed out the grave danger to world peace at the Lima Conference, and the American nations responded by reaffirming their solidarity and determination to resist any foreign intervention.

Roosevelt's annual message to Congress in January, 1939, indicated that a turning point had come in his thinking. For the first time since his inauguration, the President stated that foreign affairs were more important than domestic matters. For Franklin D. Roosevelt, who for six years had fought so aggressively to bring about a New Deal in the economic life of America, this was a remarkable change. He pointed to the grave danger which threatened the security of the entire free world, and suggested that the United States would have to use "methods short of war" to protect itself. In addition to recommending an increase of the armed forces of the nation, Roosevelt clearly indicated his skepticism of our neutrality acts in stating that they "may operate unevenly and unfairly—may actually give aid to an aggressor and deny it to the victim. The instinct of self-preservation should warn us that we ought not to let that happen any more."[1]

In March, Hitler violated the Munich agreement—which Neville Chamberlain had thought would bring "peace in our time"—by seizing most of what remained of Czechoslovakia. The fall of Czechoslovakia had a profound effect on opinion in Britain and France. Until the German armies actually seized Bohemia on March 15, 1939, there were arguments, some quite plausible, that Hitler's objectives were limited—that appeasement might prevent war. But appeasement died on the day that Hitler's troops marched into Prague. The Munich agreement, which guaranteed Czech sovereignty, was too fresh in the minds of everyone. By no stretch of the imagination could the Germans claim any right to Bohemia, or that they were righting any "wrong" done to them at Versailles. This was naked aggression in violation of a pledge signed five months before, and it was recognized as such throughout the world.

This action not only convinced the British and French that appeasement had failed, but it spurred Roosevelt to seek an immediate revision of the neutrality laws. During the spring and summer of 1939, the President worked unceasingly to persuade Congressional leaders to remove the arms embargo. Roosevelt's main argument was that, in view of the possibility of a war in Europe, the repeal of our embargo on arms would tend to restrain the Axis Powers. Consequently, this would lessen the chance of a major conflict in Europe and thereby add to the security of the United States.

Senator Borah's answer was that his information, which he claimed was more accurate than that available to the Administration, did not indicate the imminence of war in Europe. Congress adjourned in the summer of 1939 without repealing the arms embargo. The German armies launched an all-out attack on Poland on September 1, 1939.

[1] *Congressional Record*, 76th Cong., 1st Sess., Vol. 84, Pt. 1, p. 75.

1. Roosevelt Warns of Dangers to World Order, 1936

On January 3, 1936, the President devoted part of his annual message to Congress to the increasing disorder throughout the world and the consequent menace to world peace.[2]

"You will remember that on that fourth of March, 1933, the world picture was an image of substantial peace. International consultation and widespread hope for the bettering of relations between the Nations gave to all of us a reasonable expectation that the barriers to mutual confidence, to increased trade, and to the peaceful settlement of disputes could be progressively removed. In fact, my only reference to the field of world policy in that address was in these words: 'I would dedicate this Nation to the policy of the good neighbor—the neighbor who resolutely respects himself and, because he does so, respects the rights of others—a neighbor who respects his obligations and respects the sanctity of his agreements in and with a world of neighbors. . . .'

"Were I today to deliver an Inaugural Address to the people of the United States, I could not limit my comments on world affairs to one paragraph. With much regret I should be compelled to devote the greater part to world affairs. Since the summer of that same year of 1933, the temper and the purposes of the rulers of many of the great populations in Europe and in Asia have not pointed the way either to peace or to good-will among men. Not only have peace and good-will among men grown more remote in those areas of the earth during this period, but a point has been reached where the people of America must take cognizance of growing ill-will, of marked trends toward aggression, of increasing armaments, of shortening tempers—a situation which has in it many of the elements that lead to the tragedy of general war.

"On those other continents many Nations, principally the smaller peoples, if left to themselves, would be content with their boundaries and willing to solve within themselves and in cooperation with their neighbors their individual problems, both economic and social. The rulers of those Nations, deep in their hearts, follow these peaceful and reasonable aspirations of their peoples. These rulers must remain ever vigilant against the possibility today or tomorrow of invasion or attack by the rulers of other peoples who fail to subscribe to the principles of bettering the human race by peaceful means.

"Within those other Nations—those which today must bear the primary, definite responsibility for jeopardizing world peace—what hope lies? To say the least, there are grounds for pessimism. It is idle for us or for others to preach that the masses of the people who constitute those Nations which are dominated by the twin spirits of autocracy and aggression, are

[2] *Congressional Record,* 74th Cong., 2nd Sess., Vol. 80, Pt. 1, pp. 27-30.

out of sympathy with their rulers, that they are allowed no opportunity to express themselves, that they would change things if they could.

"That, unfortunately, is not so clear. It might be true that the masses of the people in those Nations would change the policies of their Governments if they could be allowed full freedom and full access to the processes of democratic government as we understand them. But they do not have that access; lacking it they follow blindly and fervently the lead of those who seek autocratic power.

"Nations seeking expansion, seeking the rectification of injustices springing from former wars, or seeking outlets for trade, for population or even for their own peaceful contributions to the progress of civilization, fail to demonstrate that patience necessary to attain reasonable and legitimate objectives by peaceful negotiation or by an appeal to the finer instincts of world justice.

"They have therefore impatiently reverted to the old belief in the law of the sword, or to the fantastic conception that they, and they alone, are chosen to fulfill a mission and that all the others among the billion and a half human beings in the world must and shall learn from and be subject to them.

"I recognize and you will recognize that these words which I have chosen with deliberation will not prove popular in any Nation that chooses to fit this shoe to its foot. Such sentiments, however, will find sympathy and understanding in those Nations where the people themselves are honestly desirous of peace but must constantly align themselves on one side or the other in the kaleidoscopic jockeying for position which is characteristic of European and Asiatic relations today. For the peace-loving Nations, and there are many of them, find that their very identity depends on their moving and moving again on the chess board of international politics. . . .

"We have sought by every legitimate means to exert our moral influence against repression, against intolerance, against autocracy and in favor of freedom of expression, equality before the law, religious tolerance and popular rule. . . ."

2. *Quarantine the Aggressor Nations, 1937*

The address given by President Roosevelt in Chicago on October 5, 1937, was the first public indication that he was not entirely satisfied with our existing neutrality legislation, and was in favor of doing something to restrain aggression.[3]

"Without a declaration of war and without warning or justification of any kind, civilians, including vast numbers of women and children, are being ruthlessly murdered with bombs from the air. In times of so-called

[3] *New York Times,* October 6, 1937.

peace, ships are being attacked and sunk by submarines without cause or notice. Nations are fomenting and taking sides in civil warfare in nations that have never done them any harm. Nations claiming freedom for themselves deny it to others.

"Innocent peoples, innocent nations, are being cruelly sacrificed to a greed for power and supremacy which is devoid of all sense of justice and humane considerations. . . .

"If those things come to pass in other parts of the world, let no one imagine that America will escape, that America may expect mercy, that this Western Hemisphere will not be attacked and that it will continue tranquilly and peacefully to carry on the ethics and the arts of civilization. . . .

"The peace-loving nations must make a concerted effort in opposition to these violations of treaties and those ignoring of humane instincts which today are creating a state of international anarchy and instability from which there is no escape through mere isolation or neutrality. . . .

"I am compelled and you are compelled, nevertheless, to look ahead. The peace, the freedom and the security of ninety percent of the population of the world is being jeopardized by the remaining ten percent who are threatening a breakdown of all international order and law. Surely the ninety percent who want to live in peace and order under law in accordance with moral standards that have received almost universal acceptance through the centuries, can and must find some way to make their will prevail.

"The situation is definitely of universal concern. The questions involved relate not merely to violations of specific provisions of particular treaties; they are questions of war and of peace, of international law and especially of principles of humanity. It is true that they involve definite violations of agreements, and especially of the Covenant of the League of Nations, the Briand-Kellogg Pact and the Nine Power Treaty. But they also involve problems of world economy, world security and world humanity.

"It is true that the moral consciousness of the world must recognize the importance of removing injustices and well-founded grievances; but at the same time it must be aroused to the cardinal necessity of honoring sanctity of treaties, of respecting the rights and liberties of others and of putting an end to acts of international aggression.

"It seems to be unfortunately true that the epidemic of world lawlessness is spreading.

"When an epidemic of physical disease starts to spread, the community approves and joins in a quarantine of the patients in order to protect the health of the community against the spread of the disease. . . .

"War is a contagion, whether it be declared or undeclared. It can engulf states and peoples remote from the original scene of hostilities. We are determined to keep out of war, yet we cannot insure ourselves against the disastrous effects of war and the dangers of involvement. We are adopting such measures as will minimize our risk of involvement, but we cannot have complete protection in a world of disorder in which confidence and security have broken down.

"If civilization is to survive the principles of the Prince of Peace must be restored. Trust between nations must be revived.

"Most important of all, the will for peace on the part of the peace-loving nations must express itself to the end that nations that may be tempted to violate their agreements and the rights of others will desist from such a course. There must be positive endeavors to preserve peace. . . ."

3. *We Will Not Stand Idly By*

On August 18, 1938, Franklin D. Roosevelt, in an address at Queen's University, Kingston, Ontario, made an important policy announcement: that the United States in effect considered the Monroe Doctrine to cover the Dominion of Canada as well as the nations of Latin America and that we would not remain passive if the soil of Canada were threatened by any aggressor.[4]

"Civilization, after all, is not national—it is international—even though that observation, trite as it is to most of us, seems to be challenged in some parts of the world today. Ideas are not limited by territorial borders; they are the common inheritance of all free people. Thought is not anchored in any land; and the profit of education redounds to the equal benefit of the whole world. This is one form of free trade to which the leaders of every opposing political party can subscribe.

"In a large sense we in the Americas stand charged with the maintaining of that tradition. When, speaking a little over a year ago in a similar vein in the Republic of Brazil, I included the Dominion of Canada in the fellowship of the Americas, our South American neighbors gave hearty acclaim. We in all the Americas know the sorrow and the wreckage which may follow if the ability of men to understand each other is rooted out from among the nations. . . .

"We in the Americas are no longer a far away continent, to which the eddies of controversies beyond the seas could bring no interest or no harm. Instead, we in the Americas have become a consideration to every propaganda office and to every general staff beyond the seas. The vast amount of our resources, the vigor of our commerce and the strength of our men have made us vital factors in world peace whether we choose it or not.

"Happily, you and we, in friendship and in entire understanding, can look clear-eyed at these possibilities, resolving to leave no pathway unexplored, no technique undeveloped which may, if our hopes are realized, contribute to the peace of the world. Even if those hopes are disappointed, we

[4] *New York Times,* August 19, 1938.

can assure each other that this hemisphere at least shall remain a strong citadel wherein civilization can flourish unimpaired.

"The Dominion of Canada is part of the sisterhood of the British Empire. I give to you the assurance that the people of the United States will not stand idly by if domination of Canadian soil is threatened by any other Empire. . . ."

4. *Roosevelt's Appeal to Hitler, September, 1938*

In March, 1938, Austria was annexed to Germany. Shortly after that, the Nazis turned their attention to the Sudeten region of Czechoslovakia. Using propaganda techniques which by 1938 had become quite familiar, Hitler demonstrated that the incorporation of the Sudetenland into Germany was his next objective. By the latter part of September an invasion of Czechoslovakia seemed inevitable, unless the German demands for the cession of the Sudeten area were met. The entire fabric of European peace appeared to be threatened, since Czechoslovakia had mutual defense pacts with France and the Soviet Union, and no one doubted that England would aid France in the event of war. On September 26 and 27, Roosevelt sent messages to Hitler appealing for a peaceful settlement of the dispute. The following is from the President's second communication to the German leader.[5]

"The question before the world today, Mr. Chancellor, is not the question of errors of judgment or of injustices committed in the past. It is the question of the fate of the world today and tomorrow. The world asks of us who at this moment are heads of nations the supreme capacity to achieve the destinies of nations without forcing upon them, as a price, the mutilation and death of millions of citizens.

"Resort to force in the Great War failed to bring tranquillity. Victory and defeat were alike sterile. That lesson the world should have learned. For that reason above all others I addressed on September 26 my appeal to Your Excellency and to the President of Czechoslovakia and to the Prime Ministers of Great Britain and of France.

"The two points I sought to emphasize were, first, that all matters of difference between the German Government and the Czechoslovak Government could and should be settled by pacific methods; and, second, that the threatened alternative of the use of force on a scale likely to result in a general war is as unnecessary as it is unjustifiable. It is, therefore, supremely

[5] *Documents on German Foreign Policy, 1918-1945,* Series D (1937-1945), Vol. II, Germany and Czechoslovakia, 1937-1938, Dept. of State, Pub. 3548, (Washington, 1949), pp. 983-85.

important that negotiations should continue without interruption until a fair and constructive solution is reached.

"My conviction of these two points is deepened because responsible statesmen have officially stated that an agreement in principle has already been reached between the Government of the German Reich and the Government of Czechoslovakia, although the precise time, method and detail of carrying out that agreement remain at issue.

"Whatever existing differences may be, and whatever their merits may be—and upon them I do not and need not undertake to pass—my appeal was solely that negotiations be continued until a peaceful settlement is found, and that thereby a resort to force be avoided.

"Present negotiations still stand open. They can be continued if you will give the word. Should the need for supplementing them become evident, nothing stands in the way of widening their scope into a conference of all the nations directly interested in the present controversy. Such a meeting to be held immediately—in some neutral spot in Europe—would offer the opportunity for this and correlated questions to be solved in a spirit of justice, of fair dealing, and, in all human probability, with greater permanence.

"In my considered judgment, and in the light of the experience of this century, continued negotiations remain the only way by which the immediate problem can be disposed of upon any lasting basis.

"Should you agree to a solution in this peaceful manner I am convinced that hundreds of millions throughout the world would recognize your action as an outstanding historic service to all humanity.

"Allow me to state my unqualified conviction that history, and the souls of every man, woman and child whose lives will be lost in the threatened war, will hold us and all of us accountable should we omit any appeal for its prevention.

"The Government of the United States has no political involvements in Europe, and will assume no obligations in the conduct of the present negotiations. Yet in our own right we recognize our responsibilities as a part of a world of neighbors.

"The conscience and the impelling desire of the people of my country demand that the voice of their Government be raised again and yet again to avert and to avoid war."

5. *Hitler's Policies — Before and After Munich*

The futility of Roosevelt's appeals to Hitler for a peaceful solution of European difficulties is revealed in an excerpt from the memorandum of the conversation held between Neville Chamberlain, British Prime Minister, and Adolph Hitler, at Berchtesgaden on September 15, 1938. The German leader gave his assurance that the Sudetenland was his last territorial demand in Europe,[6] but on October 21, slightly more than a month after that conversation, Hitler gave the order for the final liquidation of Czechoslovakia.[7]

"Mr. Chamberlain thanked the Führer for his clear and frank exposition of the German attitude. He believed he had rightly understood the Führer to say that he had made the demand for the return of 10 million Germans to the German Reich for racial reasons. Seven million Germans had returned to the Reich through the incorporation of Austria. Three million Sudeten Germans must in any circumstance be restored to the Reich. But the Führer had given the assurance that thereafter no territorial demands could exist any longer in other regions, which might give rise to conflicts between Germany and other countries. He (the British Prime Minister) had also understood the Führer to say that he was prepared even to run the risk of a world war in order to secure the return of these 3 million Germans to the Reich. At the moment he did not wish to make any further observation on this than that it ought to be possible for the Führer and himself to prevent a world war on account of these 3 million Sudeten Germans.

"He had, furthermore, understood the Führer to say that Czechoslovakia could not continue to exist as a sort of spearpoint aimed at Germany's flank. If the Sudeten Germans were once restored to the German Reich, would the part of Czechoslovakia still remaining also be regarded as a dangerous spearpoint in Germany's flank?

"The Führer replied that this would be the case as long as the Czechoslovak State had alliances with other countries, which made it a menace to Germany. Moreover, Czechoslovakia had hitherto been a source of great expense to Germany, since she had made it necessary for her to expand her Air Force twice as strong as she had originally intended.

"The British Prime Minister asked whether German misgivings regarding this role of Czechoslovakia's would be overcome if one succeeded in changing the relations between this country and Russia in such a way that, on the one hand, Czechoslovakia would be released from her obligations toward Russia in the event of an attack on that country and, on the other hand, she (Czechoslovakia), like Belgium, would be deprived of the possibility of assistance from Russia or another country. . . .

". . . It was, therefore, a matter of knowing whether Britain was now prepared to assent to the detachment of the Sudeten German districts on the basis of the right of national self-determination, and in this connection he (the Führer) was obliged to observe that this right of self-determination had

[6] *Ibid.,* pp. 786-98.
[7] *Ibid.,* Vol. IV, The Aftermath of Munich, October 1938–March 1939, Dept. of State, Pub. 3883, (Washington, 1951), pp. 99-100.

not just been invented by him in 1938 specially for the Czechoslovak question, but that it had already been brought into being in 1918 in order to
create a moral basis for the changes made under the Treaty of Versailles.
The conversations could continue on these lines, but the British Prime Minister must first of all state whether he could accept this basis or not, namely,
the secession of the Sudeten German region by virtue of the right of self-
determination.

"The British Prime Minister expressed his satisfaction that they had
now got down to the crux of the matter at last. He was not in a position to
make categorical statements for the whole of the British Government. Be-
sides, he was obliged, of course, to consult France and Lord Runciman also.
. . . He could state personally that he recognized the principle of the detachment of the Sudeten areas. . . ."

Hitler's Order to Liquidate Czechoslovakia

"Directive by the Führer for the Wehrmacht

"TOP SECRET   "BERLIN, October 21, 1938.
"OKW L Ia. No. 236/38

"The future tasks of the Wehrmacht and the preparations for the conduct of war resulting from these tasks will be laid down by me in a later
directive.

"Until this directive comes into force, the Wehrmacht must at all times
be prepared for the following eventualities:

"1. Securing the frontiers of the German Reich and protection against
surprise air attacks.

"2. Liquidation of the remainder of the Czech State.

"3. The occupation of Memelland. . . .

ADOLF HITLER

Certified correct: KEITEL"

6. *Appeal for Assurances of Nonaggression*

In March, 1939, German troops marched into Czechoslovakia and ended its existence as a free nation. On Easter Sunday,
April 7, 1939, Italian troops launched an attack on the small
nation of Albania, just across the narrow waters of the Straits of
Otranto which separate the heel of Italy from the Balkan peninsula. On April 14, Roosevelt sent an appeal to Hitler and Mussolini for peace and requested them to give assurances that they
would not attack a specified list of nations in Europe, Africa, and
the Near East.[8]

[8] S. Shepard Jones, and Denys P. Myers, (eds.), *Documents on American Foreign Relations, January 1938-June 1939*, Vol. i, pp. 306-09.

"You realize I am sure that throughout the world hundreds of millions of human beings are living today in constant fear of a new war or even a series of wars.

"The existence of this fear—and the possibility of such a conflict—is of definite concern to the peoples of the United States for whom I speak, as it must also be to the peoples of the other nations of the entire Western Hemisphere. All of them know that any major war, even if it were to be confined to other continents, must bear heavily on them during its continuance and also for generations to come.

"Because of the fact that after the acute tension in which the world has been living during the past few weeks there would seem to be at least a momentary relaxation—because no troops are at this moment on the march—this may be an opportune moment for me to send you this message. . . .

"Three nations in Europe and one in Africa have seen their independent existence terminated. A vast territory in another independent nation of the Far East has been occupied by a neighboring state. Reports, which we trust are not true, insist that further acts of aggression are contemplated against still other independent nations. Plainly the world is moving toward the moment when this situation must end in catastrophe unless a more rational way of guiding events is found.

"You have repeatedly asserted that you and the German people have no desire for war. If this is true there need be no war.

"Nothing can persuade the peoples of the earth that any governing power has any right or need to inflict the consequences of war on its own or any other people save in the case of self-evident home defense. . . .

"I am convinced that the cause of world peace would be greatly advanced if the nations of the world were to obtain a frank statement relating to the present and future policies of governments.

"Because the United States, as one of the nations of the Western Hemisphere, is not involved in the immediate controversies which have arisen in Europe, I trust that you may be willing to make such a statement of policy to me as the head of a nation far removed from Europe in order that I, acting only with the responsibility and obligation of a friendly intermediary, may communicate such declaration to other nations now apprehensive as to the course which the policy of your Government may take.

"Are you willing to give assurance that your armed forces will not attack or invade the territory of the following independent nations: Finland, Estonia, Latvia, Lithuania, Sweden, Norway, Denmark, The Netherlands, Belgium, Great Britain and Ireland, France, Portugal, Spain, Switzerland, Liechtenstein, Luxemburg, Poland, Hungary, Rumania, Yugoslavia, Russia, Bulgaria, Greece, Turkey, Iraq, the Arabias, Syria, Palestine, Egypt and Iran.

"Such an assurance clearly must apply not only to the present day but also to a future sufficiently long to give every opportunity to work by peaceful methods for a more permanent peace. I therefore suggest that you construe the word 'future' to apply to a minimum period of assured non-aggression—ten years at the least—a quarter of a century—if we dare look that far ahead. . . ."

7. *Hull's Appeal to End the Arms Embargo, May, 1939*

By the late spring of 1939, the Roosevelt Administration had reached the conclusion that diplomatic notes to the Axis leaders would not stop aggression, and that the United States should adopt a more realistic policy in view of the obvious fact that a major war was imminent. On May 27, Cordell Hull sent a proposal to Congressional leaders asking for a repeal of the arms embargo. Roosevelt and Hull reasoned that the Axis nations, particularly Germany, were more likely to continue their aggressions because of the preponderance of their armaments in 1939; consequently the repeal of the embargo on arms would allow the British and French to build up their might to a point where the Nazis might be restrained. Such a policy obviously favored Britain and France, but the argument of the Administration, which was not always expressed in these terms, was that the only way to stop Hitler was to prove to him that war would be too costly to Germany. Congress still preferred absolute impartiality, and Hitler's legions invaded Poland when the United States was still bound to a rigid neutrality by its own legislation.

"The Secretary of State (Hull) to the Chairman of the Senate Committee on Foreign Relations (Pittman) and of the House of Representatives Committee on Foreign Affairs (Bloom, Acting), May 27, 1939.[9]

"May 27, 1939.

"In harmony with the conversations I have had during recent weeks with you and other members of the appropriating committees of the two houses of Congress with regard to pending legislative proposals for modifying existing peace and neutrality legislation, I wish to offer the following comments.

"These proposals are intended to aid in keeping the United States from becoming involved in war. They contemplate, primarily a state of affairs in which relations in the world have ceased to be peaceful. . . .

"In considering the present proposals for legislation, we must keep in mind that, no matter how we may wish or may try to disassociate ourselves from world events, we cannot achieve disassociation. The simple fact of our

[9] *Ibid.,* pp. 536-39.

existence as a great nation in a world of nations cannot be denied; and the substance of the legislation adopted in this country inevitably influences not only this country, but also other countries. The problem for us is not whether we shall help any foreign country or any group of foreign countries. Nor is it that of passing judgment upon or interfering in other people's controversies. Rather, it is that of so conducting our affairs and our relations with other peoples, both before and after the outbreak of war elsewhere, that we shall be more, and not less, secure; so that we shall not become parties to controversies; and so that our attitude and actions will encourage other peoples to avoid, rather than to become engaged in, controversy.

"Because of troubled conditions with which we are all familiar, the Congress is rightly now considering the situation which might obtain were a state of war to develop between other nations. In such case the first concern of the United States is to its own safety as well as the desire and intent, which all of us resolutely follow, to remain at peace.

"In the event of a foreign war, we would be immediately faced with the problem of maintaining that neutrality.

"When a war begins, that body of rules for the regulation of international relations which applies in time of peace becomes impaired. Under international law the belligerent States then acquire certain rights which do not appertain to States at peace; and at the same time States which remain at peace become affected by a body of rules under which they have the rights and obligations of neutrals.

"In considering whether legislative restrictions upon our freedom of action can advantageously be maintained or adopted to insure against our being drawn into war, we should, in my opinion, avoid the error of assuming that provisions which are at the same time rigid and of universal application will serve our interests satisfactorily in every situation which may arise. The course of world affairs is unpredictable. What we should try to do for the purpose of keeping this country out of war is to enact measures adapted to the safeguarding of our interests in all situations of which we can conceive and at the same time imposing a minimum of abnormal and unnecessary burdens upon our nationals and a minimum of disruption of our peaceful economic life.

"I believe it is important that the legislation which may be enacted should conform, so far as possible, to traditional concepts of international law adhered to by this Government. International law requires that the domestic measures adopted by a neutral shall be impartially applied to the contending parties in conflict. It does not require that a neutral nation shall embargo any articles destined for belligerents.

"If we go in for embargoes on exports, for the purpose of keeping ourselves out of war, the logical thing to do would be to make our embargo all-inclusive. Modern warfare is no longer warfare between armed forces only: it is warfare between nations in every phase of their national life. Lists of contraband are no longer limited to arms and ammunition and closely related commodities. They include not only those items which contribute toward making warfare possible, but almost every item useful in the life of the enemy nation. A nation at war is no less anxious to keep cotton or petroleum, or, indeed, any useful product, from reaching an enemy nation than it is to keep guns and airplanes from reaching the enemy's armed forces. I doubt whether we can help ourselves to keep out of war by an attempt on our part to distinguish between categories of exports. Yet a complete embargo upon all exports would obviously be ruinous to our economic life. It therefore seems clear that we should have no general and automatic embargo inflexibly and rigidly imposed on any class or groups of exports. . . .

"Our involvement in controversies is more likely to arise from destruction of American lives. In this regard we can effectively diminish our risks by keeping our nationals and ships out of areas in which there is special danger. The rights of our nationals under international law may properly be restricted by our own legislation along certain lines for the purpose of avoiding incidents which might involve us in a conflict. In indicating certain restrictions upon the exercise of our rights as a neutral I do not wish to be considered as advocating the abandonment of these, or indeed of any, neutral rights; but there is reasonable ground for restricting at this time the exercise of these rights.

"For the reasons theretofore stated, it is my firm conviction that the arms embargo provision of the existing law should be eliminated. I furthermore believe that the most effective legislative contribution at this time toward keeping this country out of war, if war occurs, would be made by enacting or reenacting provisions on lines as follows:

"To prohibit American ships, irrespective of what they may be carrying, from entering combat areas;

"To restrict travel by American citizens in combat areas;

"To provide that the export of goods destined for belligerents shall be preceded by transfer of title to the foreign purchaser;

"To continue the existing legislation respecting loans and credits to nations at war;

"To regulate the solicitation and collection in this country of funds for belligerents;

"To continue the National Munitions Control Board and the system of arms export and import licenses.

"Provisions on the suggested lines would, I think, help to keep this country out of war and facilitate our adherence to a position of neutrality. They would make easier our twofold task of keeping this country at peace and avoiding imposition of unnecessary and abnormal burdens upon our citizens.

"Sincerely yours,

Cordell Hull"

CHAPTER XIII.

POLAND TO PEARL HARBOR

W HEN the German armies crossed the Polish border on the first day of September, 1939, the American people were more aware of the dreadful significance of the event than had been the case when the Kaiser's armies invaded Belgium in 1914. The Roosevelt Administration and the people of this country were firmly convinced that our true course was to remain at peace. The Neutrality Acts were in force, but in contrast to Wilson's attitude of strict impartiality in 1914, Roosevelt had made it clear long before the outbreak of the European war that his sympathies lay with the democracies.

On September 3, Roosevelt told the nation in a radio address that while the United States would be neutral, he could not ask American citizens to be neutral in thought. Ten days later the President called Congress into special session to consider the repeal of the arms embargo. Despite the bitter opposition of the isolationists, Congress repealed the embargo on arms, and Roosevelt signed the act on November 4, 1939.

Following the rapid conquest of Poland, the European war entered a peculiar phase called the "phony war," which lasted until April, 1940. Instead of immediately launching an offensive against France, the Wehrmacht remained safely behind the Siegfried Line; and the French waited for the Germans to assault their Maginot Line which they believed to be impregnable. There were minor sorties by the French and Germans in no man's land between the lines. There were token air raids, but there was no all out war.

In the east, the Germans consolidated their positions in the western half of Poland while the Russians moved into the eastern half. The Soviets moved to the Baltic by forcing Estonia, Latvia, and Lithuania to sign "mutual assistance" pacts in October, 1939. When Finland refused to sign a similar pact with the Russians, Stalin's forces opened an attack on that small nation late in November. The United States clearly indicated its disapproval of this aggression but took no action to alienate the Russians. Roosevelt still considered the Germans the major threat to our security.

During this "phony war," probably the most significant step taken by Roosevelt was to send Undersecretary of State Sumner Welles to Europe for consultation with the heads of the British, French, German, and Italian Governments. Welles did not go on a peace mission in the strict sense of the term. He had no plan to offer any of the belligerents; but Roosevelt sent him to get firsthand information and to find out whether there was any possibility that the war could be ended by negotiation. Welles's mission ended in failure, insofar as it was intended to bring an end to hostilities, and the "phony war" ended on April 9, when the Nazis struck at Denmark and Norway.

The lightninglike advance of the Germans during the spring of 1940 through Denmark, Norway, Belgium, the Netherlands, and France, changed the nature of the war completely. During the winter of 1939-40, the failure of the Germans to attack in the west had convinced most observers that the Maginot Line furnished a sure protection to the western allies. The fall of France, however, not only stunned the entire world, but it left Britain alone to face the Nazi onslaught. Although the Germans did not attempt an invasion of England during the Summer of 1940 when the British were virtually defenseless, they did start an all-out aerial bombardment of the British Isles, in September, which was designed to bring the British to their knees without an invasion.

As the course of the war in Europe changed, so did American policy. Although some of the President's advisers urged him to write Britain off as already lost after Dunquerque, Roosevelt decided to support the British in their hour of need. He sent them virtually all the arms and ammunition that could be found in our arsenals. In September, 1940, Roosevelt informed the nation of the Destroyer-Bases deal whereby we agreed to transfer fifty overage destroyers to the British in return for the use of potential bases stretching from Newfoundland to British Guiana. In the same month Congress passed the Selective Service Act—the first time that the United States had ever had a conscript army in time of peace.

The arms sent to Britain after the evacuation from Dunquerque and the fifty destroyers transferred later were a godsend to that nation, but at best they were merely stopgap measures.

The British were inadequately armed at the outbreak of the war, and to defend themselves singlehandedly against the vast military machine built up by the Germans, they needed not only all that they could produce but also all that could be procured in the United States.

The repeal of the arms embargo in November, 1939, had allowed the British to purchase military supplies in the United States, but under the provisions of the law all transactions had to be in cash. At the start of the war the British had assets in the United States amounting to over five billion dollars. By the end of 1940 their holdings had dwindled to approximately two billion dollars, and that amount would have been exhausted in a very short time.

Since the United States had fully committed itself to the defense of Britain, it was necessary that the flow of American munitions be continued irrespective of the amount of dollars available to the British in 1941. After correspondence between Churchill and Roosevelt on the subject of continuing aid to Britain, Roosevelt conceived the idea of the lend-lease program which was enacted into law on March 11, 1941. Under the authority of this act the President was empowered to "sell, transfer title to, exchange, lease, lend, or otherwise dispose of. . . ." materials to those nations he deemed essential to the defense of the United States.

The lend-lease program solved Britain's financial problem, but it pointed up the next difficulty—that of transferring American materiél safely to the British Isles. In the spring of 1941, German submarines were sinking British merchant ships two or three times faster than they could be replaced by Britain. If the Germans could win the Battle of the Atlantic by preventing American supplies from reaching Britain, not only would it have meant disaster for Britain but it would have posed a serious threat to the security of the United States.

At that critical juncture, the United States moved to acquire bases in the Atlantic. Less than a month after the passage of the lend-lease act, the United States Government and the Danish Minister in Washington signed an agreement under which the United States was given the right to establish military bases in Greenland. This was done not only to protect that area from a possible German invasion, but also to allow the United States better to protect the approaches to this hemisphere. A similar agreement was signed on July 1 with the Iceland Government, which was nominally under Danish sovereignty. These moves also allowed the United States Navy to establish bases from which they could afford better protection to transatlantic shipping.

In addition to establishing bases in these islands, the United States also extended its naval operations far into the North and South Atlantic, in what Roosevelt called a "patrol" action. His opponents continually charged that these patrols were synonymous with convoys and that the United States was actively engaged in war with Germany without a declaration of war by Congress. Irrespective of what word should have been used to describe the activity of the American Navy, the important point is that our vessels were being used to aid the British in their battle to secure American supplies.

From late spring 1941 until the Pearl Harbor attack, relations between the United States and Germany became increasingly strained. In May, Roosevelt proclaimed an unlimited national emergency. This was followed in June by an order freezing the assets within the United States held by persons or institutions in Europe. Roosevelt and Churchill indicated the close degree of harmony between their two nations as to wartime and postwar objectives by issuing the Atlantic Charter in August. On September 11, Roosevelt addressed the nation by radio following an attack on a destroyer, the U.S.S. *Greer,* by a German submarine. The President informed his listeners that this unrestricted submarine warfare, which had already resulted in the sinking of two American merchant marine ships, would not be tolerated by this nation and that German and Italian war vessels which entered waters deemed necessary for the defense of America would do so at their own peril. Over a month later, after the U.S.S. *Kearny* had been attacked, the President warned the Germans that he had given order to the United States Navy to shoot on sight.

The determination of the United States to see that the British were supplied with materiél necessary to combat Hitler irrespective of the consequences, and the equal determination of the Germans to prevent supplies from reaching the British Isles, created a situation in which an undeclared war was imminent. On November 17, Congress passed a joint resolution allowing American merchant vessels to be armed; and while the attention of the nation was concentrated chiefly on the growing crisis with Germany, the Japanese attacked Pearl Harbor and plunged the United States into war. Four days later, Germany and Italy declared war on the United States, and on that same day, December 11, Congress accepted the challenge. The United States was now at war with all three Axis powers, and while no one who had followed the course of events from the summer of 1941 could have been taken by surprise at this result, the war had come, as Roosevelt had told Congress in his 1941 annual message, "when the dictators are ready to make war upon us. . . ."[1]

1. German Invasion of Poland

On September 3, 1939, Roosevelt addressed the American people by radio pointing out the nature of our relationship to the European war.[2]

"Tonight my single duty is to speak to the whole of America.

"Until 4:30 this morning I had hoped against hope that some miracle would prevent a devastating war in Europe and bring to an end the invasion of Poland by Germany.

"For four long years a succession of actual wars and constant crises have shaken the entire world and have threatened in each case to bring on the gigantic conflict which is today unhappily a fact.

"It is right that I should recall to your minds the consistent and at times successful efforts of your Government in these crises to throw the full weight of the United States into the cause of peace. In spite of spreading wars I think that we have every right and every reason to maintain as a national policy the fundamental moralities, the teachings of religion, and the continuation of efforts to restore peace—for some day, though the time may be distant, we can be of even greater help to a crippled humanity.

"It is right, too, to point out that the unfortunate events of these recent years have been based on the use of force or the threat of force. And it seems to me clear, even at the outbreak of this great war, that the influence of America should be consistent in seeking for humanity a final peace which will eliminate, as far as it is possible to do so, the continued use of force between nations. . . .

"You are, I believe, the most enlightened and the best informed people in all the world at this moment. You are subjected to no censorship of news; and I want to add that your Government had no information which it has any thought of withholding from you.

"At the same time, as I told my press conference on Friday, it is of the highest importance that the press and the radio use the utmost caution to dis-

[1] *Congressional Record,* 77th Cong., 1st Sess., Vol. 87, Pt. 1, pp. 44-47.
[2] *New York Times,* September 4, 1939.

criminate between actual verified fact on the one hand and mere rumor on the other. . . .

"You must master at the outset the simple but unalterable fact in modern foreign relations. When peace has been broken anywhere, peace of all countries everywhere is in danger.

"It is easy for you and me to shrug our shoulders and say that conflicts taking place thousands of miles from the continental United States, and, indeed, the whole American hemisphere, do not seriously affect the Americas —and that all the United States has to do is to ignore them and go about our own business. Passionately though we may desire detachment, we are forced to realize that every word that comes through the air, every ship that sails the sea, every battle that is fought does affect the American future.

"Let no man or woman thoughtlessly or falsely talk of America sending its armies to European fields. At this moment there is being prepared a proclamation of American neutrality. This would have been done even if there had been no neutrality statute on the books, for this proclamation is in accordance with international law and with American policy.

"This will be followed by a proclamation required by the existing Neutrality Act. I trust that in the days to come our neutrality can be made a true neutrality. . . .

"This Nation will remain a neutral nation, but I cannot ask that every American remain neutral in thought as well. Even a neutral has a right to take account of the facts. Even a neutral cannot be asked to close his mind or his conscience.

"I have said not once but many times that I have seen war and that I hate war. I say that again and again.

"I hope the United States will keep out of this war. I believe that it will. And I give you assurances that every effort of your Government will be directed toward that end.

"As long as it remains within my power to prevent, there will be no blackout of peace in the United States."

2. *French Appeal for American Aid, 1940*

The Nazi blitzkrieg which ended the "phony war," shocked the world into a realization of the vast might of the German armies. The unchecked advance of the Germans toward Paris during the first ten days of June found most of the world, and particularly France, unprepared for such stupendous events. On June 10 Paul Reynaud, the French Premier, made a desperate appeal to Roosevelt for all-out material aid.[3]

[3] S. Shepard Jones, and Denys P. Myers, (eds.), *Documents on American Foreign Relations*, Vol. II, pp. 424-26.

"MR. PRESIDENT: I wish first to express to you my gratitude for the generous aid that you have decided to give us in aviation and armament.

"For six days and six nights our divisions have been fighting without one hour of rest against an army which has a crushing superiority in numbers and material. Today the enemy is almost at the gates of Paris.

"We shall fight in front of Paris; we shall fight behind Paris; we shall close ourselves in one of our provinces to fight and if we should be driven out of it we shall establish ourselves in North Africa to continue the fight and if necessary in our American possessions.

"A portion of the government has already left Paris. I am making ready to leave for the front. That will be to intensify the struggle with all the forces which we still have and not to abandon the struggle.

"May I ask you, Mr. President, to explain all this yourself to your people to all the citizens of the United States saying to them that we are determined to sacrifice ourselves in the struggle that we are carrying on for all free men.

"This very hour another dictatorship has stabbed France in the back.[4] Another frontier is threatened. A naval war will begin.

"You have replied generously to the appeal which I made to you a few days ago across the Atlantic. Today this 10th day of June 1940 it is my duty to ask you for new and even larger assistance.

"At the same time that you explain this situation to the men and women of America, I beseech you to declare publicly that the United States will give the Allies aid and material support by all means 'short of an expeditionary force.' I beseech you to do this before it is too late. I know the gravity of such a gesture. Its very gravity demands that it should not be made too late.

"You said to us yourself on the 5th day of October 1937: 'I am compelled and you are compelled to look ahead. The peace, the freedom and the security of 90% of the population of the world is being jeopardized by the remaining 10% who are threatening a breakdown of all international order and law.

" 'Surely the 90% who want to live in peace under law and in accordance with moral standards that have received almost trusty acceptance throughout the centuries, can and must find some way to make their will prevail.'

"The hour has now come for these.

PAUL REYNAUD"

3. *Roosevelt's Reply to Reynaud*[5]

". . . First of all, let me reiterate the ever-increasing admiration with which the American people and their Government are viewing the resplend-

[4] Italy declared war on France on June 10.
[5] *Loc. cit.*

ent courage with which the French armies are resisting the invaders on French soil.

"I wish also to reiterate in the most emphatic terms that, making every possible effort under present conditions, the Government of the United States has made it possible for the Allied armies to obtain during the weeks that have just passed airplanes, artillery and munitions of many kinds and that this Government so long as the Allied governments continue to resist will redouble its efforts in this direction. I believe it is possible to say that every week that goes by will see additional material on its way to the Allied nations. . . .

"In these hours which are so heart-rending for the French people and yourself, I send you the assurances of my utmost sympathy and I can further assure you that so long as the French people continue in defense of their liberty which constitutes the cause of popular institutions throughout the world, so long will they rest assured that matériel and supplies will be sent to them from the United States in ever-increasing quantities and kinds.

"I know that you will understand that these statements carry with them no implication of military commitments. Only the Congress can give such commitments."

4. *Three Power Pact*

In 1936, Germany and Italy reached a working agreement which Mussolini first referred to as the Rome-Berlin Axis. Germany and Japan also came to an agreement in 1936 as to their common hostility toward Communism. From that date, these three nations often were referred to as the Axis Powers. Not until September 27, 1940, however, did these nations sign a military alliance. The text is quoted below.[6]

"The Governments of Germany, Italy and Japan consider it the prerequisite of a lasting peace that every nation in the world shall receive the space to which it is entitled. They have, therefore, decided to stand by and cooperate with one another in their efforts in Greater Asia and the regions of Europe respectively. In doing this it is their prime purpose to establish and maintain a new order of things, calculated to promote the mutual prosperity and welfare of the peoples concerned.

"It is, furthermore, the desire of the three Governments to extend cooperation to nations in other spheres of the world who are inclined to direct their efforts along lines similar to their own for the purpose of realizing their ultimate object, world peace.

"Accordingly, the Governments of Germany, Italy and Japan have agreed as follows:

[6] *New York Times,* September 28, 1940.

"ARTICLE 1. Japan recognizes and respects the leadership of Germany and Italy in the establishment of a new order in Europe.

"ARTICLE 2. Germany and Italy recognize and respect the leadership of Japan in the establishment of a new order in Greater East Asia.

"ARTICLE 3. Germany, Italy and Japan agree to cooperate in their efforts of aforesaid lines. They further undertake to assist one another with all political, economic and military means if one of the three Contracting Powers is attacked by a Power at present not involved in the European War or in the Chinese-Japanese conflict.

"ARTICLE 4. With the view to implementing the present pact, joint technical commissions, to be appointed by the respective Governments of Germany, Italy and Japan, will meet without delay.

"ARTICLE 5. Germany, Italy and Japan affirm that the above agreement affects in no way the political status existing at present between each of the three Contracting Parties and Soviet Russia.[7]

"ARTICLE 6. The present pact shall become valid immediately upon signature and shall remain in force ten years from the date on which it becomes effective.

"In due time, before the expiration of said term, the High Contracting Parties shall, at the request of any one of them, enter into negotiations for its renewal.

"In recognition thereof, the undersigned, duly authorized by their respective governments, have signed this pact and have affixed their seals thereto.

"Done in triplicate at Berlin, the 27th day of September, 1940, in the eighteenth year of the Fascist era, corresponding to the 27th day of the ninth month of the fifteenth year of Showa."

5. *Argument against Lend-Lease*

The isolationists opposed the repeal of the arms embargo, the destroyer-bases deal, and virtually every move of the Administration to strengthen Britain, claiming that they brought the United States closer to war. The Lend-Lease bill, however, stimulated some of their most savage attacks. It was bad enough for the United States to allow belligerent nations to buy munitions for cash; but for this nation to virtually give away munitions to one or more of the belligerents was almost more than they could bear. The following was an editorial inserted in the *Congressional Record* by Senator Burton K. Wheeler, an isolationist leader.[8]

[7] The most important agreement referred to was the German-Soviet nonaggression treaty of 1939.

[8] *Congressional Record*, 77th Cong., 1st Sess., Appendix, pp. A616-21.

"Thursday, February 13, 1941

"Mr. WHEELER. Mr. President, I ask unanimous consent to have printed in the RECORD editorials from several leading newspapers and journals, all of which discuss present American foreign policy.

"There being no objection, the editorials were ordered to be printed in the RECORD as follows: . . . .

"From the Michigan Tradesman of January 15, 1941

" 'THE PRESIDENT'S FOREIGN POLICY

" '. . . Recently the President hasn't emphasized the words "measures short of war." His evident intention now is to plunge this country into the wars in Europe, Africa, and Asia.

" 'We can't be an arsenal for the so-called democracies everywhere on earth without being their allies. We can't be half way into any war. Under the lend-lease bill the President could give away a whole Navy and all of the Army supplies and strip us stark naked, as Democratic Congressman Andrew J. May, of Kentucky, says.

" 'We can't tell the democracies we are giving them the strength to regain and maintain a free world, and send them for that purpose ships, planes, tanks, and guns in ever-increasing numbers without alining ourselves as fighting with them.

" 'And how can we never permit ourselves to acquiesce in a peace dictated by aggressors and sponsored by appeasers unless we are a belligerent?

" 'Our whole foreign policy is a mess, meaningless—except that it has led us directly into war. We are behaving like cowards—hiding behind Great Britain. We call England our first line of defense, stake our all on her victory over Germany, in order to keep Hitler from sending his soldiers to swarm over America. Never before in our history have we hidden behind the skirts of any country. We helped Britain to beat Germany in the World War, yet Britain permitted Hitler to rearm and now has another World War on her hands. Even if England wins this war, too, we do not know what kind of a peace she will make, nor what kind of an England will emerge from this second world conflict.

" 'Hopes for defeat of the lend-lease bill rest mainly with the Senate, whose powers in treaty making would be destroyed if the measure should be passed.

" 'The Senate may write into the bill a provision that the President shall not have authority to give away arms and other war supplies, and another provision requiring Great Britain to put up security for loans of war munitions and supplies. Types of collateral suggested include shares in the vast British rubber and tin holdings in the Far East, and British investments in the United States, which are estimated by the Board of Governors of the Federal Reserve System at more than $5,000,000,000 worth of uncommitted assets in the country, including bank balances and gold. . . .[9]

" 'Ever since the days of George Washington, our wisest statesmen have warned us to stay out of European entanglements. Now, suddenly, we find ourselves being plunged knee-deep into the quarrels of the Old World.

" 'The people of the United States don't want to go to war to settle Europe's interminable troubles. The President knows that, every Member of Congress knows it. We have bent over backwards to stay out of this war, which will end like all the others, settling nothing and only planting the seeds for still others.

" 'What is being proposed now is nothing less than destruction of our own form of government in order to save other governments at present classified as democracies but which at any moment may become dictatorial, socialistic, anarchistic, or anything but a democracy. That would be the tragedy of the ages. . . .' "

6. Argument for Lend-Lease

In his annual message to Congress on January 6, 1941, Franklin D. Roosevelt outlined his reasons for the United States to continue furnishing munitions and other materials to those nations at war with the aggressor powers.[10]

". . . As long as the aggressor nations maintain the offensive, they—not we—will choose the time and the place and the method of their attack. . . .

"That is why this annual message to the Congress is unique in our history.

"That is why every member of the Executive Branch of the government and every member of the Congress face great responsibility—and great accountability. . . .

"I also ask this Congress for authority and for funds sufficient to manufacture additional munitions and war supplies of many kinds, to be turned over to those nations which are now in actual war with aggressor nations.

"Our most useful and immediate role is to act as an arsenal for them as well as for ourselves. They do not need manpower.

"They do need billions of dollars' worth of the weapons of defense.

"The time is near when they will not be able to pay for them in ready cash. We cannot, and will not, tell them they must surrender, merely because of present inability to pay for the weapons which we know they must have.

[9] On January 21, 1941, the Secretary of the Treasury sent a letter to Mr. Sol Bloom, chairman of the Foreign Affairs Committee of the House of Representatives, in which he quoted a British estimate that their holdings totaled only $2,316,000,000.
[10] *Congressional Record,* 77th Cong., 1st Sess., Vol. 87, Pt. 1, pp. 44-47.

"I do not recommend that we make them a loan of dollars with which to pay for these weapons—a loan to be repaid in dollars.

"I recommend that we make it possible for those nations to continue to obtain war materials in the United States, fitting their orders into our own program. Nearly all of their matériel would, if the time ever came, be useful for our own defense.

"Taking counsel of expert military and naval authorities, considering what is best for our own security, we are free to decide how much should be kept here and how much should be sent abroad to our friends who by their determination and heroic resistance are giving us time in which to make ready our own defense.

"For what we send abroad, we shall be repaid, within a reasonable time following the close of hostilities, in similar materials, or, at our option, in other goods of many kinds which they can produce and which we need. . . ."

7. *Freezing of Continental European Assets*

On May 27, 1941, the President proclaimed that an unlimited national emergency confronted the United States. On June 14, he issued an order freezing the financial assets held by the nations on the continent of Europe or their citizens, as well as those of China and Japan.[11]

"By virtue of and pursuant to the authority vested in me by Section 5 (b) of the Act of October 6, 1917 (40 Stat. 415), as amended, by virtue of all other authority vested in me, and by virtue of the existence of a period of unlimited national emergency, and finding that this order is in the public interest and is necessary in the interest of national defense and security, I, FRANKLIN D. ROOSEVELT, PRESIDENT of the UNITED STATES OF AMERICA, do prescribe the following:

"Executive Order No. 8389 of April 10, 1940, as amended, is amended to read as follows:

"SEC. 1. All of the following transactions are prohibited, except as specifically authorized by the Secretary of the Treasury by means of regulations, rulings, instructions, licenses, or otherwise, if (1) such transactions are by, or on behalf of, or pursuant to the direction of, any foreign country designated in this order, or any national thereof, of (2) such transactions involve property in which any foreign country designated in this order, or any national thereof, has at any time on or since the effective date of this order had any interest of any nature whatsoever, direct or indirect:

"A. All transfers of credit between any banking institution within

11 *New York Times*, June 15, 1941.

the United States and all transfers of credit between any banking institution within the United States and any banking institution outside the United States (including any principal, agent, home office, branch, or correspondent outside the United States, or a banking institution within the United States) ;

"B.   All payments by or to any banking institution within the United States;

"C.   All transactions in foreign exchange by any person within the United States;

"D.   The export or withdrawal from the United States, or the ear-marking of gold or silver coin or bullion or currency by any person within the United States;

"E.   All transfers, withdrawals or exportation of, or dealings in, any evidences of indebtedness or evidences of ownership of property by any person within the United States; and

"F.   Any transaction for the purpose of which has the effect of evading or avoiding the foregoing prohibitions.

"SEC. 2.   A.   All of the following transactions are prohibited, except as specifically authorized by the Secretary of the Treasury by means of regulations, rulings, instructions, licenses, or otherwise:

"(1) The acquisition, disposition or transfer of, or other dealing in, or with respect to, any security or evidence thereof on which there is stamped or imprinted, or to which there is affixed or otherwise attached, a tax stamp or other stamp of a foreign country designated in this order or a notarial or similar seal which by its contents indicates that it was stamped, imprinted, affixed or attached within such foreign country designated in this order or a notarial or similar seal which by its contents indicates that it was stamped, imprinted, affixed or attached within such foreign country, or where the attendant circumstances disclose or indicate that such stamp or seal may, at any time, have been stamped, imprinted, affixed or attached thereto; and

"(2) The acquisition by, or transfer to, any person within the United States of any interest in any security or evidence thereof if the attendant circumstances disclose or indicate that the security or evidence thereof is not physically situated within the United States.

"B.   The Secretary of the Treasury may investigate, regulate, or prohibit under such regulations, rulings, or instructions as he may prescribe, by means of licenses or otherwise, the sending, mailing, importing or otherwise bringing, directly or indirectly, into the United States, from any foreign country, of any securities or evidences thereof or the receiving or holding in the United States of any securities or evidences thereof, so brought into the United States.

"SEC. 3.   The term 'foreign country designated in this order' means a foreign country included in the following schedule, and the term 'effective date of this Order' means with respect to any such foreign country, or any national thereof, the date specified in the following schedule:

    (a) April 8, 1940—Norway and Denmark;
    (b) May 10, 1940—The Netherlands, Belgium and Luxemburg;
    (c) June 17, 1940—France (including Monaco);
    (d) July 10, 1940—Latvia, Estonia and Lithuania;
    (e) October 9, 1940—Rumania;
    (f) March 4, 1941—Bulgaria;
    (g) March 13, 1941—Hungary;
    (h) March 24, 1941—Yugoslavia;
    (i) April 28, 1941—Greece; and
    (j) June 14, 1941—Albania, Andorra, Austria, Czechoslovakia, Danzig, Finland, Germany, Italy, Liechtenstein, Poland, Portugal, San Marino, Spain, Sweden, Switzerland, and Union of Soviet Socialist Republics.
    (k) June 14, 1941—China and Japan."

8. Landing of American Troops in Iceland, Trinidad and British Guiana, July, 1941

The President sent a message to Congress on July 7, 1941, informing it that American troops had landed in various bases in the Atlantic and explaining the necessity of the move.[12]

"To the Congress:

"I am transmitting herewith for the information of the Congress a message I received from the Prime Minister of Iceland of July first and the reply I addressed on the same day to the Prime Minister of Iceland in response to this message.

"In accordance with the understanding so reached, forces of the United States Navy have arrived in Iceland in order to supplement, and eventually to replace, the British forces which have until now been stationed in Iceland in order to insure the adequate defense of that country.

"As I stated in my message to Congress of September third last regarding the acquisition of certain naval and air bases from Great Britain in exchange for certain over-age destroyers, considerations of safety from overseas attack are fundamental.

"The United States cannot permit the occupation by Germany of strategic outposts in the Atlantic to be used as air or naval bases for eventual attack against the Western Hemisphere. We have no desire to see any change in the present sovereignty of those regions. Assurance that such outposts in our defense frontier remain in friendly hands is the very foundation of our

[12] *Congressional Record,* 77th Cong., 1st Sess., Vol. 87, Pt. 6, pp. 5841-42.

national security and of the national security of every one of the independent Nations of the New World.

"For the same reason substantial forces of the United States have now been sent to the bases acquired last year from Great Britain in Trinidad and in British Guiana in the south in order to forestall any pincers movement undertaken by Germany against the Western Hemisphere. It is essential that Germany should not be able to successfully employ such tactics through sudden seizure of strategic points in the South Atlantic and in the North Atlantic.

"The occupation of Iceland by Germany would constitute a serious threat in three dimensions:

"The threat against Greenland and the northern portion of the North American Continent, including the islands which lie off it.

"The threat against all shipping in the North Atlantic.

"The threat against the steady flow of munitions to Britain—which is a matter of broad policy clearly approved by the Congress.

"It is, therefore, imperative that the approaches between the Americas and those strategic outposts, the safety of which this country regards as essential to its national security, and which it must therefore defend, shall remain open and free from all hostile activity or threat thereof.

"As Commander in Chief I have consequently issued orders to the Navy that all necessary steps be taken to insure the safety of communications in the approaches between Iceland and the United States, as well as on the seas between the United States and all other strategic outposts.

"This Government will insure the adequate defense of Iceland with full recognition of the independence of Iceland as a sovereign state.

"In my message to the Prime Minister of Iceland I have given the people of Iceland the assurance that the American forces sent there would in no way interfere with the internal and domestic affairs of that country, and that immediately upon the termination of the present international emergency all American forces will be at once withdrawn, leaving the people of Iceland and their Government in full sovereign control of their own territory."

9. *We Have Taken Our Battle Stations*

The subtitle of the 1941 volume of *The Public Papers and Addresses of Franklin D. Roosevelt* is "The Call to Battle Stations," a phrase taken from an address made by the President on Navy and Total Defense Day, October 27, 1941. This phrase and this speech accurately represented our foreign policy throughout most of the year. Neither Roosevelt nor anyone else knew for certain that we would eventually be at war with the Axis nations; but by the fall of the year almost everyone in the country knew that our relations with Germany and Japan had reached a critical state. The President's October speech well illustrated the crisis.[13]

"Five months ago tonight I proclaimed to the American people the existence of a state of unlimited national emergency.

"Since then much has happened. Our Army and Navy are temporarily in Iceland in the defense of the Western Hemisphere.

"Hitler has attacked shipping in areas close to the Americas in the North and South Atlantic.

"Many American-owned merchant ships have been sunk on the high seas. One American destroyer was attacked on September fourth. Another destroyer was attacked and hit on October seventeenth. Eleven brave and loyal men of our Navy were killed by the Nazis.

"We have wished to avoid shooting. But the shooting has started. And history has recorded who fired the first shot. In the long run, however, all that will matter is who fired the last shot.

"America has been attacked. The U.S.S. *Kearny* is not just a Navy ship. She belongs to every man, woman, and child in this Nation.

"Illinois, Alabama, California, North Carolina, Ohio, Louisiana, Texas, Pennsylvania, Georgia, Arkansas, New York, and Virginia—those are the home states of the honored dead and wounded of the *Kearny*. Hitler's torpedo was directed at every American, whether he lives on our sea coasts or in the innermost part of the country, far from the seas and far from the guns and tanks of the marching hordes of would-be conquerors of the world.

"The purpose of Hitler's attack was to frighten the American people off the high seas—to force us to make a trembling retreat. This is not the first time that he has misjudged the American spirit. That spirit is now aroused.

"If our national policy were to be dominated by the fear of shooting, then all of our ships and those of our sister Republics would have to be tied up in home harbors. Our Navy would have to remain respectfully—abjectly—behind any line which Hitler might decree on any ocean as his own dictated version of his own war zone.

"Naturally we reject that absurd and insulting suggestion. We reject it because of our own self-interest, because of our own self-respect, and because, most of all, of our own good faith. Freedom of the seas is now, as it has always been, a fundamental policy of your Government and mine. . . .

"Our American merchant ships must be armed to defend themselves against the rattlesnakes of the sea.

"Our American merchant ships must be free to carry our American goods into the harbors of our friends.

[13] *New York Times,* October 28, 1941.

"Our American merchant ships must be protected by our American Navy.

"In the light of a good many years of personal experience, I think that it can be said that it can never be doubted that the goods will be delivered by this Nation, whose Navy believes in the tradition of 'Damn the torpedoes; full speed ahead!' . . .

"Upon our American production falls the colossal task of equipping our own armed forces, and helping to supply the British, the Russians, and the Chinese. In the performance of that task we dare not fail. And we will not fail. . . .

"There are those who say that our great good fortune has betrayed us— that we are now no match for the regimented masses who have been trained in the Spartan ways of ruthless brutality. They say that we have grown fat, and flabby, and lazy—and that we are doomed.

"But those who say that know nothing of America or American life.

"They do not know that this land is great because it is a land of endless challenge. Our country was first populated, and it has been steadily developed, by men and women in whom there burned the spirit of adventure and restlessness and individual independence which will not tolerate oppression.

"Ours has been a story of vigorous challenges which have been accepted and overcome—challenges of uncharted seas, of wild forests and desert plains, of raging floods and withering droughts, of foreign tyrants and domestic strife, of staggering problems—social, economic, and physical; and we have come out of them the most powerful Nation—and the freest—in all of history.

"Today in the face of this newest and greatest challenge of them all, we Americans have cleared our decks and taken our battle stations. We stand ready in the defense of our Nation and in the faith of our fathers to do what God has given us the power to see as our full duty."

CHAPTER XIV.

THE UNITED STATES AND
THE FAR EAST, 1931–1941

THE Washington Conference of 1921-22 marked the opening of the most tranquil decade in the Far East during this century. The expansionist, army-dominated government which had controlled Japan during the first World War was replaced by one composed of businessmen and politicians. On the surface, at least, it appeared that Japan had come of age politically. The newly-established Soviet government posed no immediate threat in the Far East. China was torn with civil strife until late in the decade when Chiang Kai-shek emerged as the strongest leader the Chinese people had produced since the beginning of the revolution in 1911.

This relative calm in the Far East was ended by Japan's seizure of Manchuria in 1931; and the next decade which ended with the Japanese attack on Pearl Harbor was as crisis-filled as the previous one had been devoid of them.

The "Mukden Incident" of September 18, 1931, and the events following it were important because this action by Japan was the first in a series of major aggressions which led directly to the outbreak of the second World War. No one knows whether this war could have been prevented if the Japanese had been stopped in 1931. However, in allowing Japan to violate treaties with no more protest than regrets and verbal blasts, the democracies undoubtedly encouraged Japan, Germany, and Italy to believe that they could use their armed forces as they saw fit without running the risk of serious retaliation.

When the Japanese army moved to annex Manchuria, the United States Government assumed correctly that the Kwantung Army had acted without the full support of the Japanese Government; and for a time our Government did nothing to embarrass the Shidehara regime. Within several months it became evident that the military men had the balance of power in Japan, and the

United States took the lead in attempting to restrain the Japanese. In January, 1932, Secreary of State Henry L. Stimson sent notes to Japan and China proclaiming nonrecognition of any situation brought about by means of force. The Stimson doctrine of nonrecognition did not restrain the Japanese; but the British, French, and the League of Nations were not willing at that time to go even that far in offending Japan.

Early in 1932, the Japanese, possibly encouraged by the success of their Manchurian adventure, launched an attack on Shanghai ostensibly to "protect" their national interests. Again Secretary Stimson took the lead in denouncing the Japanese. The British were more concerned with this aggression because of their vast interests in the Yangtze Valley, and the Assembly of the League of Nations called upon both parties to end hostilities. Japan denounced this Assembly action but withdrew from Shanghai.

From 1932 to 1937, the Japanese transformed Manchuria into a puppet state called Manchukuo, launched an aggressive drive to increase their influence in North China, and finally in December, 1934, they denounced the naval limitation clauses of the Washington treaty due to expire in 1936. Although the Japanese used those years to build up their position in the Far East, this period was not as violent as the years that followed. During the same time, Chiang Kai-shek, who had gained control of the Kuomintang, solidified his position as the leader of a China that was being slowly united.

In July, 1937, when it appeared that Generalissimo Chiang might achieve his objective of unifying all of China under his authority, the Japanese struck a blow at Chinese troops near Peking and then opened a full-scale offensive against China. Not until after the Pearl Harbor attack was there a declaration of war by either participant, but from mid-1937 until August, 1945, the Chinese and the Japanese were engaged in full scale hostilities.

The United States took no immediate action against Japan following the July 7, 1937, "incident" at the Marco Polo Bridge. On October 5, 1937, however, Roosevelt, without mentioning Japan by name, delivered his famous "quarantine the aggressor nation" speech in which he indicated very clearly his opposition to growing lawlessness throughout the world.

Not until 1939, after Japan had continued its unremitting warfare against China, did the United States take any positive steps to halt the Japanese. In July of that year, this Government informed Japan that within six months the 1911 Treaty of Amity and Commerce would be abrogated. Although the ending of this agreement in January, 1940, did not damage Japan's economy, it was a warning and a harbinger of the more severe actions that followed it.

In July, 1940, Roosevelt placed an embargo on aviation gasoline, tetraethyllead, iron, and scrap steel destined for Japan. In signing the Axis pact with Germany and Italy in September, 1940, Japan drew closer to those nations engaged in deadly war with Britain and adopted a policy diametrically opposed to that of the United States. And in July, 1941, after Japanese forces had moved into southern Indochina, the United States clamped a full-scale embargo on Japan by freezing all of their assets in this country. The English and Dutch followed with similar action.

From July until December 7, 1941, it became evident that a crisis between the United States and Japan was imminent. After an endless series of discussions in Washington and Tokyo during the late summer and fall of 1941, the Japanese decided to send Saburo Kurusu to the United States to assist Admiral Kichisaburu Nomura, Japanese Ambassador, in what was ostensibly the final Japanese attempt to arrive at some amicable agreement with the United States. The Japanese proposals of November 20 and the United States' memorandum handed to the Japanese on November 26 represented the policies of the two Governments on the eve of Pearl Harbor.

A brief glance at the two documents well illustrates the impossibility of any basic agreement. In brief, the Japanese demanded that the United States recognize the *status quo* in the Far East in return for a promise that they would not institute any further aggressions. The conditions upon which America was willing to restore normal relations with Japan were virtually that the clock should be turned back to July, 1937. The inevitable result was war, which came on December 7, 1941, at Pearl Harbor.

American historians are by no means agreed in their interpretation of the events leading up to the outbreak of war with Japan. Charles A. Beard and others have argued that President Roosevelt not only did not try to prevent the outbreak of war but actually planned to maneuver the Japanese into a position where they would fire the first shot and thereby bear the onus of having started the war. The gist of this argument is that the United States, in placing severe economic restrictions on the Japanese in 1940 and 1941, virtually forced them into war.

Probably the majority of historians who have studied this period would admit that the policy of this Government, especially after July, 1941, was one which almost inevitably would have led to conflict. But they point out that it was adopted very belatedly in an effort to stem the Japanese who had been carrying out an aggressive policy for ten years prior to July, 1941.

The United States had the choice of opposing the Japanese by diplomatic and economic pressure, as it did, or of agreeing to the thesis that Japan or any other nation could seize whatever it needed or thought it needed without comment or interference. The United States could not have accepted this latter position without abandoning its professed belief that the morality of our Western Christian civilization should apply to the actions of nations as well as to individuals.

1. Stimson Nonrecognition Doctrine

After having tried in vain to dissuade Japan from its course of action in Manchuria by calling attention to its violation of the Nine-Power Treaty of 1922 and the Kellogg-Briand Pact of 1928, Secretary Henry L. Stimson sent a note to the Japanese and Chinese Governments on January 7, 1932, outlining our policy.[1]

"Please deliver to the Foreign Office on behalf of your Government as soon as possible the following note:

" 'With the recent military operations about Chinchow, the last remaining administrative authority of the Government of the Chinese Republic in South Manchuria, as it existed prior to September 18th, 1931, has been destroyed. The American Government continues confident that the work of the neutral commission recently authorized by the Council of the League of Nations will facilitate an ultimate solution of the difficulties now existing between China and Japan. But in view of the present situation and of its own rights and obligations therein, the American Government deems it to be its duty to notify both the Imperial Japanese Government and the Government of the Chinese Republic that it cannot admit the legality of any situation *de facto* nor does it intend to recognize any treaty

[1] Dept. of State, *Peace and War, United States Foreign Policy, 1931-1941,* pp. 159-60.

or agreement entered into between those Governments, or agents thereof, which may impair the treaty rights of the United States or its citizens in China, including those which relate to the sovereignty, the independence, or the territorial and administrative integrity of the Republic of China, or to the international policy relative to China, commonly known as the open door policy; and that it does not intend to recognize any situation, treaty or agreement which may be brought about by means contrary to the covenants and obligations of the Pact of Paris of August 27, 1928, to which Treaty both China and Japan, as well as the United States, are parties.'

"State that an identical note is being sent to the Chinese Government.

Stimson."

2. *Statement of American Policy, September, 1937* [2]

"The Secretary of State to the Ambassador in Japan (Grew)

"[Telegram: Paraphrase]

"WASHINGTON, September 2, 1937—2 p.m.

". . . The United States Government's course, as pursued during recent years in regard to the Far East, has been animated partly by the thought of the advantageousness of encouraging Japanese and Chinese efforts at developing toward each other and toward the world attitudes of real cooperativeness. A situation has been produced by the hostilities that have been and are now going on between Japan and China which permits scant hope of any such attitude or practice being reciprocally developed by and between those two countries in the near future. . . .

"In the current crisis the United States Government has endeavored to follow an absolutely impartial course. It is realized in Washington that hostilities are not likely to be brought to an end by manifestations of disapprobation on moral or legal grounds. It is necessary, however, in shaping the American course, to keep in mind constantly not only the possible serving of that object, not only the possible effects upon Japan, or upon China, or upon both of them, of possible steps, but also the wishes and attitude of the American people, the principles in which the United States believes, the courses which other countries pursue, and various objectives, general and ultimate as well as immediate and particular. . . .

"Your view is shared by me that fundamental American objectives should include (1) the avoidance of involvement and (2) the protection of lives, property, and rights of American citizens. . . .

"The Roosevelt Administration has not repudiated anything in the record of the efforts made on behalf of the principles and of peace by the United States Government at the time of the Manchurian affair. We have in the present crisis endeavored to dissuade Japan and China from entering

[2] *Ibid.*, pp. 377-80.

upon and from continuing hostilities; but mediation has not been offered. I am by no means certain that we wish to assume the responsibilities and role of a mediator. I would not desire, at least for the present, to encourage either side to believe or to expect that, after currently rejecting many American suggestions to exercise restraint, they may rely upon the United States Government serving them as a friendly broker whenever it suits their convenience. I want both sides to feel that should they desire good will and any form of impartial assistance from the United States, now is the time for evidence by them of appreciation of American policies and methods through being considerate of American legitimate interests and essential solicitudes.

Hull"

3. *Brussels Conference Declaration*

The United States met in conference with eighteen other nations at Brussels to consider methods of ending the Sino-Japanese conflict. This assembly, which was convened under the terms of the Nine-Power Treaty, condemned the Japanese, but there were no visible results of this action. The results of this conference well illustrated the futility of the policy of the democracies in relying solely on declarations of moral principles, international law, and treaties to stop aggression. Selections from the Declaration adopted at Brussels on November 15, 1937, follow:[3]

". . . It is clear that the Japanese concept of the issues and interests involved in the conflict under reference is utterly different from the concepts of most of the other nations and governments of the world. The Japanese Government insists that as the conflict [is] between Japan and China it concerns those two countries only. Against this the representatives of the states now met at Brussels consider this conflict of concern in fact to all countries party to the Nine Power Treaty of Washington of 1922 and to all countries party to the Pact of Paris of 1928, and of concern in fact to all countries members of the family of nations. . . .

"6. The Japanese Government has affirmed in its note of October 27 to which it refers in its note of November 12 that in employing armed force against China it was anxious to 'make China renounce her present policy'. The representatives met at Brussels are moved to point out that there exists no warrant in law for the use of armed force by any country for the purpose of intervening in the internal regime of another country and that general recognition of such a right would avoid a permanent cause of conflict.

[3] *Ibid.,* pp. 390-92.

"7. The Japanese Government contends that it should be left to Japan and China to proceed to a settlement by and between them alone. But, that a just and lasting settlement could be achieved by such a method cannot be believed.

"Japanese armed forces are present in enormous numbers on Chinese soil and have occupied large and important areas thereof. Japanese authorities have decided in substance that it is Japan's objective to destroy the will and the ability of China to resist the will and demands of Japan. The Japanese Government affirms that it is China whose actions and attitudes are in contravention of the Nine Power Treaty; yet, whereas, China is engaged in full and frank discussion of the matter with the other parties to that treaty, Japan refuses to discuss it with any of them. Chinese authorities have repeatedly declared that they will not, in fact that they cannot, negotiate with Japan alone for a settlement by agreement. In these circumstances there is no ground for any belief that, if left to themselves, Japan and China would arrive in the appreciably near future at any solution which would give promise of peace between those two countries, security for the rights and interests of other countries, and political and economic stability in the Far East. . . ."

4. *Joseph Grew's Analysis of United States— Japanese Relations*

On September 12, 1940, the American Ambassador in Japan sent a dispatch to the Secretary of State reviewing in detail the attitude of the Japanese Government on that date and giving his opinion as to the possible results of various policies which our Government might adopt. This message was sent shortly after the destroyer-bases deal with the British had been announced, several months after the surrender of France, and shortly before Japan, Germany, and Italy signed a tripartite military alliance.[4]

"3. Whatever the intentions of the present Japanese Government may be there cannot be any doubt that the military and other elements in Japan see in the present world situation a 'golden opportunity' to carry their dreams of expansion into effect; the German victories, like strong wine, have gone to their heads; they have believed implicitly until recently in Great Britain's defeat; they have argued that the war will probably be ended in a quick German victory and that Japan's position in Greater East Asia should be consolidated while Germany is still agreeable and before Japan might be robbed of her far-flung control in the Far East by the eventual hypothetical strengthening of the German naval power; although care-

[4] *Ibid.*, pp. 569-72.

fully watching the attitude of the United States they have discounted effective opposition on our part. It has been and is doubtful that the saner heads in and out of the government will be able to control these elements.

"4. However, now a gradual change can be sensed in the outburst of exhiliration which greeted the inception of the new government. It is beginning to be seen by the Japanese Government, the army, the navy, and the public, that Germany may not defeat Great Britain after all, a possibility which I have constantly emphasized in the plainest language to my Japanese contacts and now, in addition to that dawning realization, they see that Britain and the United States are steadily drawing closer together in mutual defense measures with the American support of the British fleet by the transfer of fifty destroyers and with our acquisition of naval bases in British Atlantic possessions. Reports are being heard of our rapid construction of a two-ocean Navy and of our consideration of strengthening our Pacific naval bases and they even hear rumors that we will eventually use Singapore. Japanese consciousness is logically being affected by these rumors and developments. They tend on the one hand to emphasize the potential danger facing Japan from the United States and Great Britain eventually acting together in positive action (Japan has long appreciated the danger of combined Anglo-American measures as evidenced by the efforts to avoid the simultaneous irritation of these two countries) or from the United States acting alone. They furnish cogent arguments on the other hand for those Japanese elements who seek political and economic security by securing raw material sources and markets entirely within Japanese control. In regard to Germany, it is beginning to be questioned by the Japanese whether even a victorious Germany would not furnish a new hazard to their program of expansion both in China and in their advance to the south. Meanwhile, an uncertain factor in their calculations is always the future attitude and position of Russia. They are beginning to be concerned by these various considerations. High-powered diplomacy, particularly in the Dutch East Indies, will continue. But the fact that the Japanese military forces could be restrained even temporarily by the government from their plans for a head-long invasion of Indo-China denotes a degree of caution which I have no doubt was influenced partly at least by the American attitude. Until the world situation, particularly the position of the United States, becomes clearer, the 'nibbling policy' appears likely to continue.

"5. I have expressed the opinion in previous communications that American-Japanese relations would be set on a downward curve if sanctions were applied by the United States. It is true that measures are now justified by our new program of national preparedness which need not fall within the category of outright sanctions. On the other hand, the probability must be contemplated that drastic embargoes on such important products as oil, of which a super-abundance is known to be possessed by the United States, would be interpreted by the people and government of Japan as actual sanctions and some form of retaliation might and probably would follow. The risks would depend not so much upon the careful calculations of the Japanese Government as upon the uncalculating "do or die" temper of the army and navy should they impute to the United States the responsibility for the failure of their plans for expansion. It may be that such retaliation would take the form of counter-measures by the government but it would be more likely that it would be some sudden stroke by the navy or army without the prior authorization or knowledge of the government. These dangers constitute an imponderable element which cannot be weighed with assurance at any given moment. However, it would be short sighted to deny their existence or to formulate policy and adopt measures without fully considering these potential risks and determining the wisdom of facing them squarely.

"6. In the following observations I am giving careful consideration to both fundamental purposes of my mission, namely the advancement and protection of American interests and the maintenance of good relations between Japan and the United States. Should these two fundamental purposes conflict the preponderant emphasis to be placed on either one is a matter of high policy which is not within my competency. My object is only to set before the Washington administration the outstanding factors in the situation as viewed from the standpoint of this embassy. Since I have set forth carefully the inevitable hazards which a strong policy involves, I will now turn respectfully to the hazards involved in the policy of *laissez faire*.

"7. It is impossible in a discussion of the specific question of relations between Japan and the United States to view that problem in its proper perspective unless it is considered part and parcel of the world problem which presents in brief the following aspects: (a) Britain and America are the leaders of a large world-wide group of English-speaking peoples which stand for a 'way of life' which today is being threatened appallingly by Italy, Germany, and Japan. . . . The avowed purposes of these powers is the imposition of their will upon conquered peoples by force of arms. In general, the uses of diplomacy are bankrupt in attempting to deal with such powers. Occasionally diplomacy may retard, but it cannot stem the tide effectively. Only by force or the display of force can these powers be prevented from attaining their objectives. Japan is today one of the predatory powers; having submerged all ethical and moral sense she has become unashamedly and frankly opportunist, at every turn seeking to profit through the weakness of others. American interests in the Pacific are definitely threatened by her policy of southward expansion, which is a thrust at the British Empire in the east. (b) Admittedly America's security has depended in a measure on the British fleet, which has been in turn and could only have been supported by the British Empire. (c) If the support of the British Empire in this her hour of travail is conceived to be in our interest, and most emphatically do I so conceive it, we must strive by every means to preserve the status quo in the Pacific, at least until the war in Europe has been won or lost. This cannot be done, in my opinion, nor can we further protect our interests properly and adequately merely by the expression of disapproval and carefully keeping a record thereof. Clearly Japan has been deterred from the taking of greater liberties with American interests only because she respects our potential power; equally is it [clear] that she has trampled upon our rights to an extent in exact ratio to the strength of her conviction that the people of the United States would not permit that power to be used. It is possible that once that conviction is shaken the uses of diplomacy may again become accepted. (d) Therefore, if by firmness we can preserve the status quo in the Pacific until and if Great Britain is successful in the European war, a situation will be faced by Japan which will render it impossible for the present opportunist philosophy to keep the upper hand. Then it might be possible at a moment to undertake a readjustment of the whole problem of the Pacific on a frank, fair, and equitable basis which will be to the lasting benefit of both Japan and America. Until there is in Japan a complete regeneration of thought, a show of force, coupled with the determination that it will be used if necessary, alone can effectively contribute to such an outcome and to our own future security.

"8. . . . I believe that in the present outlook and situation we have come to the time when the continuance of restraint and patience by the United States may and will probably lead to developments which will make progressively precarious relations between the United States and Japan. I hope that if the people and the Government of Japan can be led to believe that they are overplaying their hand, eventually there will come about a reverse swing of the pendulum in which it will be possible to reconstruct good relations between the United States and Japan. I consider the alternative to be hopeless. . . .

Grew"

5. *Rumor of the Attack on Pearl Harbor*

In January, 1941, Ambassador Grew reported that he had heard a rumor that in the event of war the Japanese would attack the Pearl Harbor base. Authorities in Washington obviously must not have put too much credence in this report.[5]

"125. A member of the Embassy was told by my ————— colleague that from many quarters, including a Japanese one, he had heard that a surprise mass attack on Pearl Harbor was planned by the Japanese military forces, in case of 'trouble' between Japan and the United States;

[5] *Ibid.*, pp. 618-19.

that the attack would involve the use of all the Japanese military facilities. My colleague said that he was prompted to pass this on because it had come to him from many sources, although the plan seemed fantastic.

Grew"

6. Roosevelt's Order Freezing Japanese Assets

German troops invaded the Soviet Union on June 22, 1941, amid Nazi predictions that their armies would shortly liquidate Russian resistance. As the Germans were advancing into Russia, the Japanese moved into southern Indochina in the latter part of July. The Vichy Government, under German domination, had no choice in granting the Japanese the right to station troops and to maintain air and naval bases in French Indochina. This new aggression by Japan into an area which not only threatened the Philippine Islands but also posed a threat to our lines of communication with Malaya and the East Indies, prompted the United States to freeze all Japanese assets in this country.[6]

"Statement Issued by the White House on July 26, 1941

"In view of the unlimited national emergency declared by the President, he issued, on July 26, an Executive order freezing Japanese assets in the United States in the same manner in which assets of various European countries were frozen on June 14, 1941. This measure, in effect, brings all financial and import and export trade transactions in which Japanese interests are involved under the control of the Government and imposes criminal penalties for violation of the order.

"This Executive order, just as the order of June 14, 1941, is designed among other things to prevent the use of the financial facilities of the United States and trade between Japan and the United States in ways harmful to national defense and American interests, to prevent the liquidation in the United States of assets obtained by duress or conquest, and to curb subversive activities in the United States.

"At the specific request of Generalissimo Chiang Kai-shek, and for the purpose of helping the Chinese Government, the President has, at the same time, extended the freezing control to Chinese assets in the United States. The administration of the licensing system with respect to Chinese assets will be conducted with a view to strengthening the foreign trade and exchange position of the Chinese Government. The inclusion of China in the Executive Order, in accordance with the wishes of the Chinese Government, is a continuation of this Government's policy of assisting China."

[6] *Ibid.*, pp. 704-05.

7. Conversation Between Hull, Nomura, and Kurusu

From the time of the order freezing Japanese assets in the United States until the outbreak of war on December 7, relations between the United States and Japan deteriorated rapidly. Conversations were continued during the entire period both in Washington and Tokyo. Late in the summer and during the early fall, the Japanese Prime Minister, Prince Fumimaro Konoye, repeatedly urged President Roosevelt to meet him for high level conversations to solve the rapidly developing crisis. Roosevelt expressed his willingness for such a conference, but insisted that there be an agreement on basic principles before the meeting in order to forestall the possibility of failure which might increase the danger of conflict. There was never any meeting of the minds on essential points, which included Japan's relationship with Germany and Japan's objectives in China.

In November, the Japanese Government sent Saburo Kurusu to Washington to assist Admiral Nomura in negotiating with Roosevelt and Hull. These conversations only served to point up the basic differences in policies being pursued by the two governments. Selections from the December 1, 1941, talk between Hull, Nomura, and Kurusu are quoted as follows:[7]

"The Japanese Ambassador and Mr. Kurusu called at their request at the Department. Mr. Kurusu said that he noted that the President was returning to Washington in advance of his schedule and inquired what the reason for this was. The Secretary indicated that one of the factors in the present situation was the loud talk of the Japanese Prime Minister. The Secretary added that the Prime Minister seemed to be in need of advice which would deter him from indulging in such talk at a time when the Ambassador was here talking about good relations. . . .

"The Ambassador expressed the view that as a matter of fact there is not much difference between Japan's idea of a co-prosperity sphere and Pan-Americanism, except that Japanese methods may be more primitive. He denied that it was Japan's purpose to use force. The Secretary asked whether, when the Japanese Government was moving on the territory of other countries, inch by inch by force, the Ambassador thought that this was a part of our policy. The Ambassador replied that Japan was motivated by self-defense in the same way as Britain had been motivated by her acts,

[7] *Ibid.*, pp. 817-22.

for example, in Syria; that Japan needed rice and other materials at a time when she was being shut off by the United States and other countries and she had no alternative but to endeavor to obtain access to these materials. . . .

"The Ambassador commented that today war is being conducted through the agency of economic weapons, that Japan was being squeezed, and Japan must expand to obtain raw materials. The Secretary pointed out that we were selling Japan oil until Japan moved suddenly into Indochina; that he could not defend such a situation indefinitely; and that the United States would give Japan all she wanted in the way of materials if Japan's military leaders would only show that Japan intended to pursue a peaceful course. The Secretary emphasized that we do not propose to go into partnership with Japan's military leaders; that he has not heard one whisper of peace from the Japanese military, only bluster and blood-curdling threats. . . .

"The Secretary went on to enumerate various points in the Japanese proposal of November 20. He reminded the Ambassador that on November 22 he had promptly told the Ambassador that we could not sell oil to the Japanese Navy, although we might be prepared to consider the release of some oil for civilian purposes. He made it clear that this Government was anxious to help settle the China affair if the Japanese could reach a settlement in accordance with the basic principles which we had discussed in our conversations, and that under such circumstances we would be glad to offer our good offices. The Secretary went on to say that under existing circumstances, when Japan was tied in with the Tripartite Pact, Japan might just as well ask us to cease aiding Britain as to cease aiding China. He emphasized again that we can't overlook Japan's digging herself into Indochina, the effect of which is to create an increasing menace to America and her friends; that we can't continue to take chances on the situation; and that we will not allow ourselves to be kicked out of the Pacific. . . . Mr. Kurusu said that he felt it was a shame that nothing should come out of the efforts which the conversations of several months had represented. He said he felt that the two sides had once been near an agreement except for two or three points, but that our latest proposals seem to carry the two sides further away than before.

"The Secretary pointed out that every time we get started in the direction of progress the Japanese military does something to overturn us. The Secretary expressed grave doubts whether we could now get ahead in view of all the threats that had been made. . . . He [Hull] pointed out that the Japanese had been telling us that if something quick is not done something awful was about to happen; that they kept urging upon the Secretary the danger of delay, and kept pressing the Secretary to do something. He said that in view of all the confusion, threats and pressure, he had been brought to the stage where he felt that something must be done to clear the foggy atmosphere; that his conclusion was that he must bring us back to fundamentals; and that these fundamentals were embodied in the proposal which we had offered the Japanese on November 26. He said that we have stood from the first on the points involved in this proposal. He pointed out that everything that Japan was doing and saying was in precisely the opposite direction from the course we have been talking about in our conversations, and that these should be reversed by his government before we can further seriously talk peace. . . .

"Mr. Kurusu disclaimed on the part of Japan any similarity between Japan's purposes and Hitler's purposes. The Ambassador pointed out that wars never settle anything and that war in the Pacific would be a tragedy, but he added that the Japanese people believe that the United States wants to keep Japan fighting China and to keep Japan strangled. He said that the Japanese people feel that they are faced with the alternative of surrendering to the United States or of fighting. The Ambassador said that he was still trying to save the situation. The Secretary said that he was practically exhausted himself here, that the American people are going to assume that there is real danger to this country in the situation, and that there is nothing he can do to prevent it.

"The Ambassadors said that they understood the Secretary's position in the light of his statements and they would report the matter to the Japanese Government with a view to seeing what could be done."

CHAPTER XV.

LATIN-AMERICAN POLICY, 1933–1954

THE Latin-American policy of the United States from 1933 to 1954 falls into three distinct periods: (1) the development of the Good Neighbor Policy to 1939, (2) the culmination of the Good Neighbor Policy from 1939 to 1945, and (3) the postwar period.

The widely-heralded Good Neighbor Policy of Franklin D. Roosevelt was not a complete break with the immediate past. Herbert Hoover fully realized that the interventionist policies of the United States had aroused deep resentment among the Latin-American peoples; and in contrast to some of his predecessors he made a genuine effort to improve relations within this Hemisphere. However, it was not until the administration of Franklin D. Roosevelt that the United States committed itself fully to absolute nonintervention in the affairs of its American neighbors—which was the keystone of the Good Neighbor Policy.

In 1933, at the Seventh International Conference of American States held in Montevideo, this country signed a nonintervention treaty with certain reservations, but at Buenos Aires in 1936 the United States agreed to a more definitive nonintervention agreement without reservations. In addition to committing itself legally to this doctrine so important to the Latin Americans, the United States abrogated the Platt Amendment in 1934 which had allowed us to intervene in Cuba, ended the intervention treaty with Panama in 1936, withdrew American marines from Haiti in 1934, and refused to use armed force against Mexico in 1938 at the time of the expropriation of American oil properties.

The Roosevelt Administration also made significant changes in our economic policy. We abandoned the practice of using force to protect American capital invested abroad just because it was American capital. The State Department made it clear to investors that they could not expect their Government to guarantee that their capital would have the same protection that it would have at home. In other words, this Government argued that if an American citizen decided to risk his capital in Latin America, he was probably doing it because he thought he would make greater profits than he could make on funds invested in this country. If the results proved otherwise, because of political instability or other factors, he would have to assume that responsibility.

Another major change in the economic relationship between the United States and the Latin American nations was the creation of the Export-Import Bank. This government agency, created in 1934, was empowered to operate in all areas of the world except with the Soviet Union, but most of its operations were in Latin America. The Export-Import Bank functioned chiefly to facilitate trade, to lend money for various purposes, and to stabilize foreign currencies.

The Reciprocal Trade Agreement program, also initiated in 1934, was an important part of our economic policy toward Latin America. Although trade agreements were by no means restricted to Latin America, as a matter of fact the great majority of the agreements concluded were with the other American nations. The Trade Agreement program operated to bring about a general reduction of tariff barriers among all the nations that entered into agreements with this country.

While the most important aim of the United States in the years immediately following 1933 was to overcome the resentment felt throughout Latin America as a result of our past policies, a second objective, which became of great importance after 1936, was to create a spirit of continental solidarity because of the rising tide of lawlessness throughout the world. At the Buenos Aires Conference in December, 1936, the United States advocated the establishment of the machinery of consultation among the American nations for use in the event of a major crisis. Two years later the delegates to the Lima Conference voted to create the foreign ministers meeting as the instrumentality of consultation.

Less than a year after the Lima Conference the Nazis invaded Poland, and the American nations immediately made use of machinery of consultation by calling the first Foreign Ministers Meeting at Panama. The American nations proclaimed a neutrality zone of three hundred miles around themselves as a measure of security. After the sinking of the *Admiral Graf von Spee* in December, 1939, this Declaration of Panama became almost a dead letter.

Following the German invasion of Scandinavia, the Low Countries, and France, the American foreign ministers met again—this time at Havana in July, 1940, to declare that no non-American territory in the Western Hemisphere could be transferred to another non-American nation. The object of this Act of Havana was to prevent Germany from assuming control of French or Dutch or even British possessions in the New World.

The third meeting of the foreign ministers was held in January, 1942, at Rio de Janeiro, after the Pearl Harbor attack. The delegates decided to recommend to their governments a break with the Axis powers. All but two nations, Argentina and Chile, followed the recommendation of the Rio Conference and severed relations with the Axis nations almost immediately. Chile broke with the Axis in January, 1943, and Argentina followed suit belatedly in January, 1944.

There was a remarkable degree of collaboration among all the American nations during World War II, with the marked exception of Argentina. Brazil and Mexico sent expeditionary forces to the fighting fronts; a number of nations granted army, navy, and air bases to the United States; most of the Latin-American countries adopted measures to stamp out Axis subversive activity; and there was a high degree of economic cooperation among the nations of the Hemisphere.

The Roosevelt Administration did not adopt the Good Neighbor Policy merely to gain continental solidarity during the war; but there would have been very little wartime cooperation without an earlier adherence to nonintervention by the United States.

The death of Franklin D. Roosevelt and the end of the war in 1945, brought no conscious change in American policy toward Latin America. In fact, President Truman and various State Department officials virtually went out of their way to stress their acceptance of the Good Neighbor Policy. However, the altered international situation which emerged with the defeat of the Axis powers, and the rise of the Soviet Union as a menace to the peace of the world, tended to center the attention of the United States on Europe and the Far East and away from Latin America.

Despite the fact that the United States remains fully committed to the policy of strict nonintervention, the Latin-American nations have felt neglected since 1945. Perhaps this was inevitable in view of changed circumstances and in view of the assiduous efforts made by the Roosevelt Administration to cultivate good-will in the New World.

In June, 1952, Secretary of State Dean Acheson made a special trip to Brazil to stem this feeling and to assure all Latin Americans that they had not been forgotten. In 1953, the newly elected President, recognizing this problem, sent his brother Milton Eisenhower on a good will tour to Latin America.

That the American nations would still cooperate in the face of danger was illustrated, however, by the results of the Inter-American Conference held in Caracas, Venezuela in March, 1954. By an overwhelming vote, the Conference, with the Communist threat in Guatemala in mind, adopted a resolution presented by Secretary John Foster Dulles condemning international Communism and calling for joint action should any American nation fall under Communist domination. Also at Caracas, a Latin-American resolution was approved, calling for a special conference to consider the economic problems of the Western World.

1. Buenos Aires Conference, 1936

The Inter-American Conference for the Maintenance of Peace held in Buenos Aires in December, 1936, was a milestone in the development of the Good Neighbor Policy. At Buenos Aires, with Roosevelt in attendance, the United States pledged itself without reservations to absolute nonintervention in the internal or external affairs of any American nation. Sumner Welles, an Assistant Secretary of State, explained some of the accomplishments of the conference in a speech delivered in New York on February 4, 1937.[1]

"During the 3 weeks of its sessions, the Conference unanimously adopted 11 treaties and conventions and 62 resolutions and declarations. I can, of course, tonight refer even very briefly to only the most significant of these instruments, but I should like to read to you in full the text of the declaration of principles of inter-American solidarity and cooperation, adopted by the Conference upon the initiative of the 5 republics of Central

[1] Sumner Welles, "The Accomplishments of the Inter-American Conference for the Maintenance of Peace," Dept. of State, Conf. Ser., No. 26, (Washington, 1937), pp. 6-9.

America, because I believe it to be, as a declaration of the national policy of each of our 21 nations, of the utmost significance. . . .

" 'The Inter-American Conference for the Maintenance of Peace

" 'DECLARES:

" '1. That the American Nations, true to their republican institutions, proclaim their absolute juridical liberty, their unrestricted respect for their several sovereignty and the existence of a common democracy throughout America;

" '2. That every act susceptible of disturbing the peace of America affects each and every one of them, and justifies the initiation of the procedure of consultation provided for in the Convention for the Maintenance, Preservation and Reestablishment of Peace, executed at this Conference; and

" '3. That the following principles are accepted by the international American community:

" '(a) Proscription of territorial conquest and that, in consequence, no acquisition made through violence shall be recognized;

" '(b) Intervention by one State in the internal or external affairs of another State is condemned;

" '(c) Forcible collection of pecuniary debts is illegal; and

" '(d) Any difference or dispute between the American nations, whatever its nature or origin, shall be settled by the methods of conciliation, or full arbitration, or through operation of international justice.' . . . .

"In that same spirit the Conference adopted the convention for the maintenance, preservation, and reestablishment of peace. This convention is very brief but it marks a great step forward in inter-American relationships. It establishes in contractual form the obligation on the part of the American republics to consult together for the purpose of finding and adopting methods of peaceful cooperation in certain contingencies. These contingencies are the following: Whenever the peace of the American republics is menaced, whether that menace arises through the threat of war between American states, or whether it be of any other nature whatsoever; and second, this consultation shall also take place 'in the event of an international war outside America which might menace the peace of the American republics,' in order to 'determine the proper time and manner in which the signatory states, if they so desire, may eventually cooperate in some pacific action tending to preserve the peace of the continent.' "

2. Declaration of Lima

After the Buenos Aires Conference, Sumner Welles referred to the cloud of war as being no bigger than the "palm of a man's hand." By the time of the Lima Conference in December,

1938, the cloud of war had turned into an ominous thunderhead. The Japanese now occupied most of the coastline and the major river valleys of China. Hitler had seized Austria and the Munich Agreement had given him the Sudeten region of Czechoslovakia. The Spanish Civil War was still in progress, but Franco's forces—aided by Germany and Italy—were not far from victory. Nazi agents were waging an effective campaign in Latin America, and all signs pointed to continued aggression in Europe.

Probably the most important action taken by the delegates assembled at the Eighth International Conference of American States was the adoption of the Declaration of Lima.[2]

"The Governments of the American States

"DECLARE:

"First, That they reaffirm their continental solidarity and their purpose to collaborate in the maintenance of the principles upon which the said solidarity is based.

"Second. That faithful to the above-mentioned principles and to their absolute sovereignty, they reaffirm their decision to maintain them and to defend them against all foreign intervention or activity that may threaten them.

"Third. And in case the peace, security or territorial integrity of any American Republic is thus threatened by acts of any nature that may impair them, they proclaim their common concern and their determination to make effective their solidarity, coordinating their respective sovereign wills by means of the procedure of consultation, established by conventions in force and by declarations of the Inter-American Conferences, using the measures which in each case the circumstances may make advisable. It is understood that the Governments of the American Republics will act independently in their individual capacity, recognizing fully their juridical equality as sovereign states.

"Fourth. That in order to facilitate the consultations established in this and other American peace instruments, the Ministers for Foreign Affairs of the American Republics, when deemed desirable and at the initiative of any one of them, will meet in their several capitals by rotation and without protocolary character. Each Government may, under special circumstances or for special reasons, designate a representative as a substitute for its Minister for Foreign Affairs.

"Fifth. This Declaration shall be known as the 'Declaration of Lima'

"(Approved December 24, 1938.)"

[2] *Report of the Delegation of the United States of America to the Eighth International Conference of American States,* Dept. of State, Conf. Ser., No. 50, (Washington, 1941), p. 190.

3. Declaration of Panama

Approximately three weeks after German troops marched into Poland, the American nations, using the machinery of consultation provided for at Buenos Aires and Lima, sent their foreign ministers to Panama to study the situation created by the outbreak of a major war in Europe. The delegates at Panama were unanimous in their desire to remain neutral and to bolster their economies against the anticipated shock of war. The Declaration of Panama, which proclaimed a three hundred mile safety zone around the Hemisphere, was a somewhat novel attempt to keep war from the New World.[3]

"Declaration of Panamá

"The governments of the American republics meeting at Panamá, have solemnly ratified their neutral status in the conflict which is disrupting the peace of Europe, but the present war may lead to unexpected results which may affect the fundamental interests of America and there can be no justification for the interests of the belligerents to prevail over the rights of neutrals causing disturbances and suffering to nations which by their neutrality in the conflict and their distance from the scene of events, should not be burdened with its fatal and painful consequences. . . .

"There is no doubt that the governments of the American republics must foresee those dangers and as a measure of self-protection insist that the waters to a reasonable distance from their coasts shall remain free from the commission of hostile acts or from the undertaking of belligerent activities by nations engaged in a war in which the said governments are not involved.

"For these reasons the governments of the American republics

RESOLVE AND HEREBY DECLARE:

"1. As a measure of continental self-protection, the American republics, so long as they maintain their neutrality, are as of inherent right entitled to have those waters adjacent to the American Continent, which they regard as of primary concern and direct utility in their relations, free from the commission of any hostile act by any non-American belligerent nation, whether such hostile act be attempted or made from land, sea, or air.

"Such waters shall be defined as follows. All waters comprised within the limits set forth hereafter except the territorial waters of Canada and of the undisputed colonies and possessions of European countries within these limits:

[3] *Report of the Delegate of the United States of America to the Meeting of the Foreign Ministers of the American Republics*, Dept. of State, Conf. Ser., 44, (Washington, 1940), pp. 62-64.

[An exact description in terms of longitude and latitude of the three hundred mile limit which extended around the Hemisphere from the U.S.-Canadian boundary in the east to the same boundary in the west was given.]

"2. The governments of the American republics agree that they will endeavor, through joint representation to such belligerents as may now or in the future be engaged in hostilities, to secure the compliance by them with the provisions of this declaration, without prejudice to the exercise of the individual rights of each state inherent in their sovereignty.

"3. The governments of the American republics further declare that whenever they consider it necessary they will consult together to determine upon the measures which they may individually or collectively undertake in order to secure the observance of the provisions of this declaration.

"4. The American republics, during the existence of a state of war in which they themselves are not involved, may undertake, whenever they may determine that the need therefor exists, to patrol, either individually or collectively, as may be agreed upon by common consent, and in so far as the means and resources of each may permit, the waters adjacent to their coasts within the area above defined.

"(Approved October 3, 1939.)"

4. The Havana Conference, 1940

The end of the "phony war" and the German blitzkrieg which brought Denmark, Norway, the Netherlands, Belgium, and France to their knees in rapid succession in the spring and early summer of 1940, forced the American foreign ministers to meet again. The major threat to the Western Hemisphere in July, 1940, appeared to be the possibility that Germany might assume the administration of French and Dutch possessions in the Caribbean area. The Act of Havana, which was designed to prevent this transfer of sovereignty, undoubtedly was looked upon by the delegates themselves as the most important work of the conference. However, as the Germans did not move to seize these areas, possibly because of the Act of Havana, the machinery of administration instituted to govern those colonies in the event of aggression never was used. Of greater significance since the conference than the Act of Havana, was the declaration of Reciprocal Assistance and Cooperation for the Defense of the Nations of the Americas. The idea contained in this statement—that an attack on one nation was to be considered an attack against all the nations—was later incorporated into the Act of Chapultepec (1945), the Inter-American Treaty of Reciprocal Assistance (1947), the North Atlantic Alliance (1949), and the pact among Australia, New Zealand, and the United States (1951).[4]

"RECIPROCAL ASSISTANCE AND COOPERATION FOR THE DEFENSE OF THE NATIONS OF THE AMERICAS

"The Second Meeting of the Ministers of Foreign Affairs of the American Republics

"DECLARES:

"That any attempt on the part of a non-American state against the integrity or inviolability of the territory, the sovereignty or the political independence of an American state shall be considered as an act of aggression against the states which sign this declaration.

"In case acts of aggression are committed or should there be reason to believe that an act of aggression is being prepared by a non-American nation against the integrity or inviolability of the territory, the sovereignty or the political independence of an American nation, the nations signatory to the present declaration will consult among themselves in order to agree upon the measure it may be advisable to take.

"All the signatory nations, or two or more of them, according to circumstances, shall proceed to negotiate the necessary complementary agreements so as to organize cooperation for defense and the assistance that they shall lend each other in the event of aggressions such as those referred to in this declaration."

5. Blue Book on Argentina

The United States made almost every possible effort from 1933 to 1942, to develop a genuine spirit of continental solidarity among all the American nations. The ready response of all the Latin-American countries, except Argentina and Chile, to support the United States after the Pearl Harbor attack was an indication of the success of the policy throughout most of the Hemisphere. Although Chile lined up with the other nations in 1943, Argentina, despite its break with the Axis in 1944, not only remained aloof but gave aid and comfort to the enemy—probably more comfort than aid.

The United States tried threats, economic pressure—even a mild form of appeasement for a short time—without success.

[4] Second Meeting of the Ministers of Foreign Affairs of the American Republics, Dept. of State, Conf. Ser., 48, (Washington, 1941), pp. 71-72.

After the surrender of Germany the documents of the German Foreign Office were captured and Assistant Secretary of State Spruille Braden was chiefly instrumental in having the State Department comb the documents for evidences of collaboration between the Nazis and the Argentines during the war. A large booklet commonly called the "Blue Book" was issued by the United States Government in February, 1946, which contained a summary of the evidence found in those documents. The plan of the United States was to have a consultation among the American nations to discuss a common policy toward Argentina. The timing of this action may have backfired, as Juan D. Perón, who was then campaigning for the Presidency of Argentina, won the election. It did not appear that there was very much that could be done with Perón or Argentina after that event, and no consultation was ever held.[5]

"On October 3, 1945, the Department of State initiated consultation among the American republics with respect to the Argentine situation. All of the other American republics agreed to participate in this consultation.

"During the intervening period, this Government has made a careful study and evaluation of all the information in its possession with regard to Argentina. An enormous volume of documents of the defeated enemy, in many cases found only with much difficulty and after prolonged search, have now been studied and verified. German and Italian officials charged with responsibility for activities in and with Argentina have been interrogated. Although this work of investigation continues, the Government of the United States at present has information which establishes that:

"1. Members of the military government collaborated with enemy agents for important espionage and other purposes damaging to the war effort of the United Nations.

"2. Nazi leaders, groups and organizations have combined with Argentine totalitarian groups to create a Nazi-Fascist state.

"3. Members of the military regime who have controlled the government since June, 1943, conspired with the enemy to undermine governments in neighboring countries in order to destroy their collaboration with the Allies and in an effort to align them in a pro-Axis bloc.

"4. Successive Argentine governments protected the enemy in economic matters in order to preserve Axis industrial and commercial power in Argentina.

"5. Successive Argentine governments conspired with the enemy to obtain arms from Germany.

[5] *Consultation Among the American Republics With Respect to the Argentine Situation,* Dept. of State, Inter-Am. Ser., 29, (Washington, 1946), pp. 1-2; 86.

"This information warrants the following conclusions:

"1. The Castillo Government and still more the present military regime pursued a policy of positive aid to the enemy.

"2. Solemn pledges to cooperate with the other American republics were completely breached and are proved to have been designed to protect and maintain Axis interests in Argentina.

"3. The policies and actions of the recent regimes in Argentina were aimed at undermining the Inter-American System.

"4. The totalitarian individuals and groups, both military and civilian, who control the present government in Argentina, have, with their Nazi collaborators, pursued a common aim: The creation in this Hemisphere of a totalitarian state. This aim has already been partly accomplished.

"5. Increasingly since the invasion of Normandy, and most obviously since the failure of the last German counteroffensive in January, 1945, the military regime has had to resort to a defensive strategy of camouflage. The assumption of the obligations of the Inter-American Conference on Problems of War and Peace[6] to wipe out Nazi influence and the repeated avowals of pro-democratic intentions proceeded from this strategy of deception.

"6. By its brutal use of force and terrorist methods to strike down all opposition from the Argentine people the military regime has made a mockery of its pledge to the United Nations 'to reaffirm faith in human rights, in the dignity and worth of the human person.' . . . .

"In October 1945, when consultation concerning the Argentine situation was requested by the United States, it had substantial reason to believe from the evidence then at its disposal that the present Argentine Government and many of its high officials were so seriously compromised in their relations with the enemy that trust and confidence could not be reposed in that government.

"Now the Government of the United States possesses a wealth of incontrovertible evidence. This document, based on that evidence, speaks for itself.

"The Government of the United States looks forward to receiving from the governments of the other American republics the benefit of their views in the premises."

6. Inter-American Treaty of Reciprocal Assistance

At the Mexico City Conference in 1945, the American nations (excluding Argentina) drafted the Act of Chapultepec, but it was merely a wartime agreement. Unquestionably, the United

[6] Mexico City Conference which adopted the Act of Chapultepec to prevent aggression from within or from without the Hemisphere.

States and certain other nations looked upon Argentina as the possible aggressor at the time of the conference in Mexico. Following the conclusion of that meeting, however, Argentina signed the final act of the conference, including the Act of Chapultepec, and was welcomed back into the family of American nations, for a while at least.

Whereas Argentina, in 1945, was considered a menace to Hemispheric security, by 1947 the United States had turned its attention to the growing threat presented by the Soviet Union. Consequently in pressing for the conclusion of a permanent military alliance among the nations of the Western World along the lines of the Act of Chapultepec, the United States was thinking mainly of the menace from overseas rather than one from within the New World.

The treaty signed at Rio de Janeiro in 1947, however, was designed to prevent aggression from any quarter, within or without the Americas. The importance of the Rio Conference lay in the fact that it was the first military alliance entered into by the United States since our agreement with France in 1778 during the American Revolution.[7]

"ARTICLE 1

"The High Contracting Parties formally condemn war and undertake in their international relations not to resort to the threat or the use of force in any manner inconsistent with the provisions of the Charter of the United Nations or of this Treaty.

"ARTICLE 2

"As a consequence of the principle set forth in the preceding Article, the High Contracting Parties undertake to submit every controversy which may arise between them to methods of peaceful settlement and to endeavor to settle any such controversy among themselves by means of the procedures in force in the Inter-American System before referring it to the General Assembly or the Security Council of the United Nations.

"ARTICLE 3

"1. The High Contracting Parties agree that an armed attack by any State against an American State shall be considered as an attack against all the American States and, consequently, each one of the said Contracting Parties undertakes to assist in meeting the attack in the exercise of the inherent right of individual or collective self-defense recognized by Article 51 of the Charter of the United Nations.

"2. On the request of the State or States directly attacked and until

[7] *Inter-American Treaty of Reciprocal Assistance*, Dept. of State, Treat. and other Int. Act Ser., 1838, (Washington, 1949), pp. 23-29.

the decision of the Organ of Consultation of the Inter-American System, each one of the Contracting Parties may determine the immediate measures which it may individually take in fulfillment of the obligation contained in the preceding paragraph and in accordance with the principle of continental solidarity. The Organ of Consultation shall meet without delay for the purpose of examining those measures and agreeing upon the measures of a collective character that should be taken.

"3. The provisions of this Article shall be applied in case of any armed attack which takes place within the region described in Article 4 or within the territory of an American State. When the attack takes place outside of the said areas, the provisions of Article 6 shall be applied.

"4. Measures of self-defense provided for under this Article may be taken until the Security Council of the United Nations has taken the measures necessary to maintain international peace and security. . . .

"ARTICLE 5

"The High Contracting Parties shall immediately send to the Security Council of the United Nations, in conformity with Articles 51 and 54 of the Charter of the United Nations, complete information concerning the activities undertaken or in contemplation in the exercise of the right of self-defense or for the purpose of maintaining inter-American peace and security.

"ARTICLE 6

"If the inviolability or the integrity of the territory or the sovereignty or political independence of any American State should be affected by an aggression which is not an armed attack or by an extra-continental or intra-continental conflict, or by any other fact or situation that might endanger the peace of America, the Organ of Consultation shall meet immediately in order to agree on the measures which must be taken in case of aggression to assist the victim of the aggression or, in any case, the measures which should be taken for the common defense and for the maintenance of the peace and security of the Continent.

"ARTICLE 7

"In the case of a conflict between two or more American States, without prejudice to the right of self-defense in conformity with Article 51 of the Charter of the United Nations, the High Contracting Parties, meeting in consultation shall call upon the contending States to suspend hostilities and restore matters to the *statu quo ante bellum*, and shall take in addition all other necessary measures to reestablish or maintain inter-American peace and security and for the solution of the conflict by peaceful means. The rejection of the pacifying action will be considered in the determination of the aggressor and in the application of the measures which the consultative meeting may agree upon.

"ARTICLE 8

"For the purposes of this Treaty, the measures on which the Organ of Consultation may agree will comprise one or more of the following: recall of chiefs of diplomatic missions; breaking of diplomatic relations; breaking of consular relations; partial or complete interruption of economic relations or of rail, sea, air, postal, telegraphic, telephonic, and radiotelephonic or radiotelegraphic communications; and use of armed force.

"ARTICLE 9

"In addition to other acts which the Organ of Consultation may characterize as aggression, the following shall be considered as such:

"a. Unprovoked armed attack by a State against the territory, the people, or the land, sea or air forces of another State;

"b. Invasion, by the armed forces of a State, of the territory of an American State, through the trespassing of boundaries demarcated in accordance with a treaty, judicial decision, or arbitral award, or, in the absence of frontiers thus demarcated, invasion affecting a region which is under the effective jurisdiction of another State. . . .

"ARTICLE 11

"The consultations to which this treaty refers shall be carried out by means of the Meetings of Ministers of Foreign Affairs of the American Republics which have ratified the Treaty, or in the manner or by the organ which in the future may be agreed upon.

"ARTICLE 12

"The Governing Board of the Pan American Union may act provisionally as an organ of consultation until the meeting of the Organ of Consultation referred to in the preceding Article takes place.

"ARTICLE 13

"The consultations shall be initiated at the request addressed to the Governing Board of the Pan American Union by any of the Signatory States which has ratified the Treaty. . . .

"ARTICLE 17

"The Organ of Consultation shall take its decisions by a vote of two-thirds of the Signatory States which have ratified the Treaty.

"ARTICLE 18

"In the case of a situation or dispute between American States, the parties directly interested shall be excluded from the voting referred to in two preceding Articles. . . .

"ARTICLE 20

"Decisions which require the application of the measures specified in Article 8 shall be binding upon all the Signatory States which have ratified this Treaty, with the sole exception that no State shall be required to use armed force without its consent. . . .

"ARTICLE 26

". . . Done in the city of Rio de Janeiro, in four texts respectively in the English, French, Portuguese and Spanish languages, on the second of September nineteen hundred forty-seven."

7. Bogotá Conference

The Ninth International Conference of American States which met in Bogotá, Colombia, from March 30 to May 2, 1948, had the unique distinction of having its proceedings interrupted for several days by a violent revolution. Despite these difficulties, however, the delegates at Bogotá completed their tasks. The major accomplishments of this Conference were in adopting the Charter of the Organization of American States and the Pact of Bogotá. The Charter reorganized the entire structure of the Inter-American system, which had developed piecemeal for over half a century. The Pact of Bogotá was designed as a supplement to the Rio Treaty of 1947. Whereas the 1947 instrument provided for the disposition of disputes that had not been settled, even to the point of using armed force, the Pact of Bogotá was drawn up with the proper machinery to prevent disputes from reaching the point where the Inter-American Treaty of Reciprocal Assistance might have to be used.

The quotation below is taken from the report of the delegation of the United States, explaining the essential features of the Organization of American States as agreed upon at Bogotá.[8]

"The Complex of agencies and institutions originally known as the 'Union of the American Republics' and, more recently, as the 'Inter-American System' has developed gradually and pragmatically over the past 60 years through treaties, resolutions, declarations, and practices among the American republics. The rate of growth and the creation of new Inter-American agencies were particularly stimulated by the necessities of World War II. In the light of this and with the proposed establishment of a new world organization, the American republics early in 1945 undertook a broad program to reorganize, consolidate, and strengthen the system. In resolution IX of the Inter-American Conference on Problems of War and Peace certain broad outlines of this reorganization were agreed upon, and, pursuant to a directive contained in the resolution, the Governing Board of the Pan American Union worked out over a period of months a comprehensive draft of an 'Organic Pact of the Inter-American System' which, in revised form, was submitted to the Ninth Conference and used as the basis of discussion. . . .

"This program of reorganization culminated in the adoption by the Ninth Conference of the charter of the Organization of American States,

[8] *Ninth International Conference of American States*, Dept. of State, Pub. 3263, (Washington, 1948), pp. 10-12.

together with a series of complementary and implementing resolutions. A brief summary of the principal organizational aspects of the Organization and a discussion of the major problems which faced the Conference in the preparation of the charter are set forth below.

"The Organization consists principally of three sets of institutions: the conferences, the Council and the Pan American Union, and the specialized organizations.

"The conferences are of three categories:

"1. The Inter-American Conferences, formerly the International Conference of American States, which normally convenes every five years and which, as 'the supreme organ of the Organization . . . decides the general action and policy of the Organization and determines the structure and functions of its organs, and has the authority to consider any matter relating to friendly relations among the American States';

"2. The Meeting of Consultation of the Ministers of Foreign Affairs, held whenever necessary 'to consider problems of an urgent nature and of common interest to the American States, and to serve as the Organ of Consultation' under the Rio mutual-assistance treaty in cases of attack or threats or other dangers to continental peace, together with its military adjunct, the Advisory Defense Committee;

"3. The specialized conferences, held in a majority of cases under the sponsorship of various specialized organizations and convened 'to deal with special technical matters or to develop specific aspects of inter-American cooperation'.

"The second set of institutions is the Council, the three organs of the Council, and the Pan American Union. These are the principal continuing executive bodies of the Organization.

"The Council, composed of one representative from each member state, has previously been known as the Governing Board of the Pan American Union. Partially in recognition of the expanding nature of its work, it has been separated from the Union and made the Council of the Organization of American States, with a number of important political, advisory, and coordinating functions. It takes cognizance of any matter referred to it by the two major types of conferences, and it acts provisionally, under the Rio treaty, as the organ of consultation in security matters. It supervises the work of the Pan American Union, which is the general secretariat of the Organization. The Council coordinates the work of its three organs in the economic and social, juridical, and cultural fields and, to a lesser extent, the work of the various specialized organizations by virtue of agreements with them. The Council is in continuous session.

"The charter also sets up three organs of the Council: the Inter-American Economic and Social Council, the Inter-American Council of Jurists, and the Inter-American Cultural Council. These are likewise composed of representatives of all the member states. Although enjoying technical autonomy, the organs function under the general surveillance of the Council. The Pan American Union is the secretariat of these organs, and the heads of the appropriate departments of the Union are the executive secretaries. In addition, the Council of Jurists and the Cultural Council each have a small permanent body in continuous session to carry on the technical work, particularly between the meetings of the organs themselves.

"The Advisory Defense Committee, originally conceived as the fourth organ of the Council, occupies a somewhat special status. Its principal function is the special one of advising the organ of consultation (the Meeting of Foreign Ministers or provisionally the Council) on military problems in connection with defense measures to be taken under the Rio treaty. It is, therefore, made directly dependent upon the organ of consultation and will normally meet only when the latter meets to consider security action under the Rio treaty. The Inter-American Defense Board will remain in existence as, in effect, the continuing body to undertake technical work of inter-American military cooperation between meetings of the Advisory Defense Committee.

"The name, 'Pan American Union,' which until now has been used to indicate the entity composed of the Governing Board and the various administrative, promotional, and informational offices in Washington under the direction of a Director General, will henceforth be applied only to the latter. Under the charter, the Pan American Union is officially designated as 'the General Secretariat of the Organization' and its 'central and permanent organ.' The Director General of the Union will be known as the 'Secretary General of the Organization.'

"The Union has a double function. As 'general secretariat' it is to serve the other organs of the Organization in much the same way as the United Nations secretariat serves the other organs of the United Nations. As 'central organ' it will also be a focal point for the promotion of relations among the member states in the economic, social, juridical, and cultural fields.

"The third principal set of institutions comprising the Organization is the specialized organizations. These are separate, autonomous, technical agencies, defined in the charter (article 95) as those 'inter-governmental organizations established by multilateral agreements and having specific functions with respect to technical matters of common interest to the American States.' They are to be registered with the Council (article 96) and are to enter into agreements with the latter to determine their relationships with it (article 53c). Although the specialized organizations will, with some possible exceptions, continue to maintain their own secretariats, the agreements with the Council may provide that the Pan American Union shall act in effect as fiscal agent for them (article 99).

"Because of the special circumstances attending the Conference, it was not possible to make as much progress as had been hoped in the direction of eliminating and amalgamating various specialized organizations. However, the Council was requested to make a complete survey of them 'in order to adopt, with the authorization of the Governments, the necessary measures for' their discontinuance, strengthening, adoption, or merger (resolution III)."

8. The Good Neighbor Policy Reaffirmed in 1952

Immediately after the death of Franklin D. Roosevelt, President Harry S. Truman stated that he would carry forward the foreign policies of his great predecessor; and there were other statements during 1945 by various high-ranking government officials to the effect that the Good Neighbor Policy would be continued.

Despite these reassurances, however, the United States became so involved with the problems of the 'Cold War,' and later with the actual outbreak of hostilities in Korea, that Latin America received less and less attention. Consequently, a feeling developed among many Latin Americans that we had abandoned the Good Neighbor Policy.

Certainly that sentiment was not justified in view of the fact that the United States still adhered firmly to nonintervention and continued to cooperate with the Latin American governments inside and outside the Organization of American States. However, the phrase—Good Neighbor Policy—had overtones and meant a great many things to a great many people. From 1933 to 1945, the United States had spent a great deal of money and time in cultivating the goodwill of the Latin Americans, and to many, this close attentiveness to the desires and sentiments of our neighbors to the south was the Good Neighbor Policy. When events in other parts of the world after 1945 diverted the attention of the United States to those areas, the Latin Americans felt like a fiancee who had been suddenly neglected by her suitor.

Secretary of State Dean Acheson recognized this fact rather belatedly in 1952 when he decided to go to Brazil in an attempt to convince not only the Brazilians but all the Latin Americans that we had in fact never abandoned the Good Neighbor Policy.

The following are excerpts from a speech made by Acheson at a banquet given by the Brazilian Foreign Minister at Itamaraty Palace, Rio de Janeiro, on July 3, 1952.[9]

"I am deeply gratified and greatly honored to be with you here. More than once I have envied my predecessors whose official duties brought them to Brazil: Elihu Root, Charles Evans Hughes, Cordell Hull, Edward Stettinius, George Marshall. . . .

"President Truman's message of good will is extended from the people of the United States to the Brazilian people, who as peoples have an unbroken—I speak from the heart when I say, an unbreakable and very special—record of friendship.

"It has been a friendship never passive, but always actively coopera-tive. . . .

"Since the end of World War II, my Government has necessarily devoted much attention in the field of foreign relations to organizing the defense of the free world against the immediate threat of aggression in Europe and in the East. We have had to face up to difficult and complex problems. This has required months and, in some cases, years of painstaking negotiation. All this has been done under the threat of one of the most terrible menaces to the freedom of mankind that the world has ever known.

"We live in an era of grave danger and we have had to address our-selves to that danger. But the fact that we have been involved in these difficult problems in Europe and in the East does not mean any lessening of our interest in this part of the world. Although the United States has become, out of necessity, involved in many ways, against our natural incli-nation, in other parts of the world, our cooperative programs in this hemi-sphere are being carried out more intensively than at any time in our history. And we have continued meanwhile to weave the fabric of our inter-American relations.

"The problem of our security is indivisible. We cannot have categories or priorities in this regard. My country has been called upon to work simultaneously on all fronts, but these problems are not ours alone. For Western Europe or Indo-china or Iran or Turkey to fall into the hands of the Soviet Union would be just as catastrophic as for a citizen of Belo Horizonte or Recife or a citizen of Boston or San Francisco. Likewise, though we are involved very deeply in Europe and the East, our interest in the welfare of Canada or Brazil or Chile must necessarily be greater today than at any time in the past. We should not mistake new commit-ments in other parts of the world for a slackening of interest in this part of the world. . . .

[9] Dean Acheson, "A Review of U.S.-Brazilian Relations," *Department of State Bulletin*, Vol. XXVII, (July 14, 1952), pp. 47-51.

"This month we are having two political conventions in our country, and from now until November we shall be hearing the sound and fury of our Presidential election campaign. But it is certain that no one in either party will challenge the sanctity and the validity of the Good Neighbor Policy. And whichever candidate of whichever party comes into office next year, will, I am certain, adhere firmly to the principles of our inter-American policy which have been worked out by both Democrats and Republicans in our country over the last 25 years. . . ."

CHAPTER XVI.

WORLD WAR II

AMERICAN diplomacy during World War II aimed at securing a closer degree of collaboration among our allies in the war effort, toward preventing the Axis nations from utilizing the neutral nations for their own purposes, and, during the later years, the formulation of plans to govern our relations with the peoples of Germany, Italy, and Japan after their defeat.

The great decision which faced the United States after the Pearl Harbor attack was whether our efforts should be concentrated in the Pacific against Japan, or whether they should be directed against Hitler's forces in Europe. Roosevelt and Churchill, at a meeting held in Washington late in December, 1941, made the decision to combine their forces first against Germany and Italy and later against Japan. This decision raised certain diplomatic problems. The British and Russians obviously were pleased over the outcome of this Washington conference, but the Chinese, who had been engaged in a life and death struggle with the Japanese since 1937, were very unhappy over this decision.

Because of the initial Japanese gains as a result of their surprise attack at Pearl Harbor and other Pacific bases, plus the decision made in Washington to concentrate British and American strength in Europe, the tide of war swung against the United Nations in the Pacific area. The Japanese occupied in quick succession Thailand, the Malay Peninsula, the Philippine Islands, the Netherlands East Indies, and other areas in the vast reaches of the Pacific. At the time, the British were battling the Nazis in North Africa to keep them from the Near East, and when the Russians were taking a heavy toll of German troops as they marched deeper into Soviet territory, the United States turned its full energies into creating a military force and the weapons to be used by that force. For the people of the United States, the year 1942 was one of defeat and disappointment.

An important problem confronting the United States during that year was how to sustain and placate Chiang Kai-shek until such time as the full strength of the United States could be brought to bear against Japan. General Joseph W. Stilwell was sent to China as Chiang's chief of staff and commander of the United Nations forces in the China-Burma-India theater. China was allotted all the lend-lease material which the United States could spare for that area. American air forces started an airlift over the Himalaya Mountains in order to deliver this trickle of aid to the beleaguered Chinese. The voluntary relinquishment of the right of extraterritoriality by the United States in 1943 did not aid China in a material way, but it was an indication of good-will and confidence in the Chinese Government and people. These actions by the United States, however, did not satisfy Chiang Kai-shek.

The Nationalists who had been engaged in war with the Japanese for more than four years before December 7, 1941, appeared to be dragging their feet now that the United States and Great Britain had entered the war against Japan. Stilwell, who became more and more convinced that the Chinese Government was not doing its part, discovered that he was in a position where it was virtually impossible to achieve anything. He had responsibility without authority. Our Government did not have adequate supplies for him, and Roosevelt never gave him the enthusiastic backing which other commanders received. Chiang, the head of the Chinese Government, would not support Stilwell's decisions— and lacking Chiang's backing, Stilwell was unable to control the Chinese armies which were ostensibly under his command.

Another obstacle to successful operations in the Orient was the existence of the Chinese Communists. Chiang, who had been struggling against the Communists since 1928, was reluctant to use them against the Japanese, even if it could have been arranged. The Generalissimo apparently preferred to withhold some of his forces to meet any Communist threat which might develop after the defeat of Japan. General Stilwell and the United States Government, intent on the primary objective of destroying the Japanese, made repeated attempts—especially in 1944 and 1945—to achieve some degree of cooperation between the Nationalists and the Communists in order to bring the maximum pressure on Japan. This basic difference in the policies of the United States and China was never resolved during the war.

America's diplomatic difficulties were by no means confined to the Far East. Following the surrender of the French Republic in June, 1940, the United States decided to establish diplomatic relations with the Vichy regime headed by Marshal Pétain. Despite the fact that Pétain had been one of the major heroes of the first World War, the men of Vichy existed only at the sufferance of the Nazis. Many persons in the United States criticized our Government for adopting a policy of appeasement in dealing with Vichy while ignoring General Charles de Gaulle, who was attempting to maintain the struggle against Germany outside of France.

After the landing of British and American troops in North Africa in November, 1942, and following the occupation of all of France by the Germans, the United States explained that its Vichy policy had been chosen for the following reasons: (1) to prevent, if possible, the transfer of French naval vessels and overseas bases to the Nazis, (2) to gain information about German plans by maintaining a diplomatic post within an area partially controlled by our adversaries, and (3) to further American plans for the invasion of North Africa.

Our relations with the Franco government in Spain were in some respects similar to those with Vichy. General Francisco Franco was undoubtedly more pro-Nazi than was Marshal Pétain. In deciding to maintain relations with Franco during the war, the United States did so in order to exert all its influence to keep Spain neutral, to secure certain strategic supplies, and at the same time prevent the Nazis from acquiring them.

While China, France, and Spain were important areas in the global diplomacy of the United States as described above, the greatest emphasis was placed on our relationship with Great Britain and the Soviet Union. This was true, not only because of the great war potential of these two countries, but also because of their geographic location relative to the main theater of war.

Britain never posed any critical problems for American diplomacy. Long before the United States was at war, Roosevelt had clearly indicated his desire to aid the British. The repeal of the arms embargo in 1939, the transfer of the fifty destroyers in 1940, the Lend-Lease Act and the Atlantic Charter in 1941, proved beyond any doubt that the United States was willing to use all its resources except armed force to bolster Britain in its time of need. It is true that there were many areas of disagreement between the two nations during the war. There were arguments about command, supply, tactics, and occasionally over-all strategy, but in the main the degree of cooperation was remarkable.

The same statement could hardly be made about our relations with the Soviet Union, although there was a higher degree of cooperation during the war than was the case either before or after the conflict. The Russians appeared no better than the Nazis in American eyes in 1939 and 1940, when they occupied the eastern half of Poland and the Baltic States and struck at Finland when they refused to sign a "friendship pact." The German invasion of Russia in June, 1941, brought a rapid reversal of policy and opinion in the United States.

Americans applauded the stubborn defense put up by the Russians, and our Government extended lend-lease aid even before we were at war. From 1941 to 1945, the Soviets received over eleven billion dollars in lend-lease aid. This aid in itself indicated no particular friendship for the Soviet Union. Since Germany was a common enemy, it was to our advantage as it was to theirs, to crush the Nazis.

As the war progressed, however, and as the admiration of the American people increased for the fighting qualities of the Russian armies which were wreaking havoc with Hitler's finest divisions, the United States made a decided effort to improve relations with the Soviet Union. This appeared feasible, not only because of the common war effort, but also because it became obvious that the great nations of the world would be responsible for making and keeping the peace in the postwar world.

The Soviet Union adopted certain policies which made it appear that they, too, were willing to establish closer relations with the United States and the other Western powers. In May, 1943, the Comintern, which had been instituted to spread revolutionary propaganda throughout the world, was abolished. And from that date until shortly after the surrender of Japan, Soviet propaganda stressed the importance of the common fight against Fascism and the possibility of their cooperation with the non-Communist nations. This change in Soviet policy unquestionably led many persons in the United States, both inside as well as outside the government, to hope or believe that a genuine understanding with Russia was possible.

Most of the major policy decisions affecting the United States, Great Britain, and the Soviet Union, were made at high level conferences held during the war.

At Moscow in October, 1943, the foreign ministers met and agreed to the following: (1) that war criminals would be punished; (2) that a European Advisory Commission would be set up in London to make joint recommendations to the three governments; (3) that a democratic regime would be instituted in Italy following the war; and (4) that these powers would sponsor and support an international organization to be created for the purpose of guaranteeing world peace after the war.

In November-December, 1943, Roosevelt, Churchill, and Stalin met for the first time at Tehran. Stalin was primarily interested in the opening of a second front by the United States and Britain to relieve the pressure on his troops. Roosevelt and Churchill assured him that they had every intention of assaulting Nazi forces in the west; Stalin promised that with the defeat of Germany, Russian troops would be used against the Japanese. The Big Three also pledged themselves to respect the sovereignty, independence, and territorial integrity of Iran, the nation which was host to the meeting.

Shortly before the surrender of Germany, the Big Three and their top advisers met again, this time at Yalta on the Crimean Peninsula, in February, 1945. This conference was unquestionably the most important held during the war, because of its scope and influence on the postwar period. When Roosevelt, Churchill, and Stalin met at Yalta, it was obvious that the German armies could not long withstand the hammer blows being dealt them from the east and west. Consequently, it was necessary for these leaders to make decisions as to a course of action for the immediate future.

The three men announced at the conclusion of the conference that they had agreed to the occupation of Germany upon its defeat by the United States, Great Britain, the Soviet Union and France; that a conference of the United Nations would be held in San Francisco in April, 1945; that a broadly based and democratic provisional government would be established in Poland; and that they would support a Tito-Subasic regime in Yugoslavia. The three powers also agreed that the provisional governments to be established in "liberated" Europe would be based on democratic principles, but the failure to define the word "democratic" led to many postwar difficulties.

Among the most important secret clauses of the Yalta agreement were the provisions concerning the Far East. In return for a promise by Russia to enter the war against Japan sixty or ninety days after the surrender of Germany, Churchill and Roosevelt assured the Russians valuable concessions in that area. The Kurile Islands and the southern half of Sakhalin, which belonged to Japan, were to be handed over to the Soviet Union. The *status quo* in Outer Mongolia was to be preserved, which guaranteed the Soviets their control over that area; Russia was to have its "rights" as of 1904 in Manchuria restored, which included the use of a naval base at Port Arthur and commercial rights in Dairen, and the re-establishment of Sino-Russian control over the South Manchurian and Chinese Eastern railroads. The concessions in Outer Mongolia and Manchuria were to have the approval of Chiang Kai-shek before they were to be fully operative, but the Generalissimo actually had little choice in the matter and he gave his approval in August, 1945.

Since the end of the war, the Yalta agreement has been the subject of bitter partisan debate in the United States. It may be years before scholars with access to all the documents will come to any agreement concerning the significance of Yalta.

It seems fairly clear at this date, however, that Roosevelt and most of his advisers believed in the possibility of agreement with the Russians, which has proved to be a false hope. It is also a fact that Soviet influence in the Far East has increased tremendously since the war, whereas that of the United States has declined. Whether this is due to the Yalta agreement, or whether the Russians would have been able to have achieved that result without the agreement, is still subject to debate. One fact should be considered when the Far Eastern provisions of Yalta are discussed: the concessions made by the United States and Britain to the Soviet Union in February, 1945, were based on the belief that the end of the war with Japan was not yet in sight. The first atomic bomb had not yet been exploded, and Roosevelt's military advisers told him that in all probability an invasion of the mainland of Japan would be necessary to end the war. The moral question is: Were Roosevelt and Churchill justified in making concessions in areas beyond their own jurisdiction for the purpose of sparing American and British lives?

The last major wartime conference was held at Potsdam, Germany in July, 1945. Truman and Stalin met with Churchill, and later with Atlee, after Churchill's defeat in the British elections. The Big Three called for Japan's unconditional surrender and reached a number of other vital decisions concerning the fate of the defeated nations.

1. *Roosevelt's Address to Congress, 1942*

On January 6, 1942, President Roosevelt delivered his annual message to Congress, in which he reviewed in broad detail our national goals at the beginning of the war.[1]

"In fulfilling my duty to report upon the State of the Union, I am proud to say to you that the spirit of the American people was never higher than it is today—the Union was never more closely knit together—this country was never more deeply determined to face the solemn tasks before it.

"The response of the American people has been instantaneous, and it will be sustained until our security is assured.

"Exactly one year ago today I said to this Congress: 'When the dictators . . . are ready to make war upon us, they will not wait for an act of war on our part. . . . They—not we—will choose the time and the place and the method of their attack.'

"We know their choice of the time: a peaceful Sunday morning—December 7, 1941.

"We know their choice of the place: an American outpost in the Pacific.

"We know their choice of the methods: the method of Hitler himself.

"Japan's scheme of conquest goes back half a century. It was not merely a policy of seeking living room: it was a plan which included the subjugation of all the peoples in the Far East and in the islands of the Pacific, and the domination of that ocean by Japanese military and naval control of the western coasts of North, Central, and South America.

"The development of this ambitious conspiracy was marked by war against China in 1894; the subsequent occupation of Korea; the war against Russia in 1904; the illegal fortification of the mandated Pacific islands following 1920; the seizure of Manchuria in 1931; and the invasion of China in 1937.

"A similar policy of criminal conquest was adopted by Italy. The Fascists first revealed their imperial designs in Libya and Tripoli. In 1935

[1] *Congressional Record,* 77th Cong., 2nd Sess., Vol. 88, Pt. 1, pp. 32-35.

they seized Abyssinia. Their goal was the domination of all North Africa, Egypt, parts of France, and the entire Mediterranean world.

"But the dreams of empire of the Japanese and Fascist leaders were modest in comparison with the gargantuan aspirations of Hitler and his Nazis. Even before they came to power in 1933, their plans for that conquest had been drawn. Those plans provided for ultimate domination, not of any one section of the world, but of the whole world and all the oceans on it.

"When Hitler organized his Berlin-Rome-Tokyo alliance, all these plans of conquest became a single plan. Under this, in addition to her own schemes of conquest, Japan's role was obviously to cut off our supply of weapons of war to Britain and Russia and China—weapons which increasingly were speeding the day of Hitler's doom. The act of Japan at Pearl Harbor was intended to stun us—to terrify us to such an extent that we would divert our industrial and military strength to the Pacific area, or even to our own continental defense.

"The plan has failed in its purpose. We have not been stunned. We have not been terrified or confused. This very reassembling of the Seventy-seventh Congress today is proof of that; for the mood of quiet, grim resolution which here prevails bodes ill for those who conspired and collaborated to murder world peace.

"That mood is stronger than any mere desire for revenge. It expresses the will of the American people to make very certain that the world will never so suffer again.

"Admittedly, we have been faced with hard choices. It was bitter, for example, not to be able to relieve the heroic and historic defenders of Wake Island. It was bitter for us not to be able to land a million men in a thousand ships in the Philippine Islands.

"But this adds only to our determination to see to it that the Stars and Stripes will fly again over Wake and Guam. Yes, see to it that the brave people of the Philippines will be rid of Japanese imperialism; and will live in freedom, security, and independence.

"Powerful and offensive actions must and will be taken in proper time. The consolidation of the United Nations' total war effort against our common enemies is being achieved.

"That was and is the purpose of conferences which have been held during the past two weeks in Washington, Moscow and Chungking. That is the primary objective of the declaration of solidarity signed in Washington on January 1, 1942, by 26 Nations united against the Axis powers. . . .

"For the first time since the Japanese and the Fascists and the Nazis started along their blood-stained course of conquest they now face the fact that superior forces are assembling against them. Gone forever are the days when the aggressors could attack and destroy their victims one by one without unity of resistance. We of the United Nations will so dispose our forces that we can strike at the common enemy wherever the greatest damage can be done him. . . .

"Destruction of the material and spiritual centers of civilization—this has been and still is the purpose of Hitler and his Italian and Japanese chessmen. They would wreck the power of the British Commonwealth and Russia and China and the Netherlands—and then combine all their forces to achieve their ultimate goal, the conquest of the United States. . . .

"Our own objectives are clear; the objective of smashing the militarism imposed by war lords upon their enslaved peoples—the objective of liberating the subjugated Nations—the objective of establishing and securing freedom of speech, freedom of religion, freedom from want, and freedom from fear everywhere in the world.

"We shall not stop short of these objectives—nor shall we be satisfied merely to gain them and call it a day. I know that I speak for the American people—and I have good reason to believe that I speak also for all the other peoples who fight with us—when I say that this time we are determined not only to win the war, but also to maintain the security of the peace that will follow. . . .

"We are fighting today for security, for progress, and for peace, not only for ourselves but for all men, not only for one generation but for all generations. We are fighting to cleanse the world of ancient evils, ancient ills.

"Our enemies are guided by brutal cynicism, by unholy contempt for the human race. We are inspired by a faith that goes back through all the years to the first chapter of the Book of Genesis: 'God created man in His own image.'

"We on our side are striving to be true to that divine heritage. We are fighting, as our fathers have fought, to uphold the doctrine that all men are equal in the sight of God. Those on the other side are striving to destroy this deep belief and to create a world in their own image—a world of tyranny and cruelty and serfdom.

"That is the conflict that day and night now pervades our lives. No compromise can end that conflict. There never has been—there never can be—successful compromise between good and evil. Only total victory can reward the champions of tolerance, and decency, and freedom, and faith."

2. *War Plans for 1942*

With the United States at war, the first question to be decided was the over-all strategy. On December 7, 1941, Winston Churchill called the White House by transatlantic telephone and made arrangements for a conference with Roosevelt in Washington. At this meeting, termed the Arcadia Conference, held the latter part of December and the first part of January, 1942, the

Americans and the British worked out their war plans. The following is an excerpt from the suggestions of General George C. Marshall and Admiral Harold R. Stark, as presented to Roosevelt and Churchill and accepted by them:[2]

"1. At the A-B [abbreviation for American-British] Staff Conversations in February, 1941, it was agreed that Germany was the predominant member of the Axis Powers, and consequently the Atlantic and European area was considered to be the decisive theatre.

"2. Much has happened since February last, but nothwithstanding the entry of Japan in the War, our view remains that Germany is still the prime enemy and her defeat is the key to victory. Once Germany is defeated, the collapse of Italy and the defeat of Japan must follow."

After this plan had been accepted, the participants at the Arcadia Conference decided on the following measures to be taken against Germany in 1942:[3]

"15. In 1942 the main methods of wearing down Germany's resistance will be:—

"a. Ever-increasing air bombardment by British and American Forces.

"b. Assistance to Russia's offensive by all available means.

"c. The blockade.

"d. The maintenance of the spirit of revolt in the occupied countries, and the organization of subversive movements.

"16. It does not seem likely that in 1942 any large scale land offensive against Germany except on the Russian front will be possible. We must, however, be ready to take advantage of any opening that may result from the wearing down process referred to in paragraph 15 to conduct limited land offensives.

"17. In 1943 the way may be clear for a return to the Continent, across the Mediterranean, from Turkey into the Balkans, or by landings in Western Europe. Such operations will be the prelude to the final assault on Germany itself, and the scope of the victory program should be such as to provide means by which they can be carried out."

3. *The North African Invasion*

The only large-scale offensive action by American forces in 1942 was the invasion of North Africa, which started on November 8. This action, referred to by the code name TORCH, was

[2] Robert E. Sherwood, *Roosevelt and Hopkins*, p. 445.
[3] *Ibid.*, p. 459.

decided upon after long and sometimes acrimonious debate between American and British authorities. Roosevelt overruled
Secretary of War Henry L. Stimson, Chief of Staff General
George C. Marshall, and General Dwight D. Eisenhower in
deciding in favor of TORCH instead of operation BOLERO,
which was designed to build up a large force in Britain in antici-
pation of a limited transchannel invasion of France in 1942, called
operation SLEDGEHAMMER. Operation TORCH was fur-
ther complicated by the fact that the United States decided to
seek the cooperation of persons in the Vichy French regime,
whereas the British, and probably the majority of American
citizens, were much more sympathetic to the Free French regime
headed by General Charles de Gaulle.

The following is an account of the North African invasion
by Samuel I. Rosenman, the compiler of the papers of Franklin D.
Roosevelt:[4]

". . . During Prime Minister Churchill's conferences with the President in Washington in June, 1942 . . . the news of Rommel's capture
of Tobruk and the German threat to Egypt caused a revival of the plan
for a North African invasion. In July, the final decision was made to
proceed with the invasion of Northwest Africa concurrently with a British
drive westward from El Alamein. This decision was made only after
spirited discussions throughout the early months of 1942 among American
and British military and naval staffs. . . .

"The objectives of the North African operation were: to open up the
Mediterranean as an Allied supply line; to bolster Allied security by removing the threat of German activities in Western Morocco and Dakar; to
draw off German troops from the Russian front; and to stimulate French
morale and the morale of all free peoples. Convinced that the French in
North Africa would offer less resistance to the Americans than to the British,[5] the President insisted in two cables to Prime Minister Churchill on
August 30 and September 2, 1942, that the North African operation be
primarily an American one. Although General de Gaulle had built up a
large following among patriotic Frenchmen, the President and the Prime
Minister agreed that it was strategically wise not to include him in the
invasion negotiations. This decision was based on the hope that without the
active participation of General de Gaulle, there was more likelihood of
greater cooperation from the Vichy-appointed French leaders in Algiers.

[4] Samuel I. Rosenman, (comp.), *The Public Papers and Addresses of Franklin
D. Roosevelt,* 1942, pp. 452-54.
[5] After the surrender of France and the establishment of the Vichy regime,
British and French forces had come into armed conflict with each other at various
places.

"Initially, it was hoped that task forces could strike early in the fall simultaneously at Algiers, Oran, and Casablanca; but the operation was postponed until November because of the shortage of landing craft and the need for training of the crews. Under the direction of General Dwight D. Eisenhower, planning for the operation proceeded in London during the summer of 1942. Elaborate and skillful psychological warfare was conducted by the Office of Strategic Services and by the Department of State representatives among the French peoples on the African continent. Robert D. Murphy was appointed Adviser on Civil Affairs to General Eisenhower and assisted in the difficult diplomatic and political negotiations which preceded the military operations.

"Some compromise had to be made on the question of inclusion of British forces, and one of the three task forces—that which landed at Algiers—was a combined British-American ground force escorted by the British Navy; the other two task forces consisted almost wholly of American ground troops. Two of the task forces sailed from the British Isles on October 25, 1942, while the third was organized in the United States and assembled at sea on October 24. While the convoys were at sea, General Eisenhower opened his command post at Gibraltar, where he completed final arrangements with General Henri Giraud, who was subsequently made commander of all French forces in North Africa and Governor of the French North African provinces.

"On November 8, landings began. Within 48 hours of the landings, the major airfields and ports of North Africa had been secured. Only token resistance was encountered at Algiers. At Oran, bitter opposition, particularly from French naval units, was met for two days. Along the Moroccan coast, the French military resistance was far more serious."

4. *Problem of the Second Front, 1943*

From the time of the Arcadia Conference in January, 1942, until the decision to assault the Normandy beaches was finally reached, the question of a second front was almost constantly discussed by British and American officials. Roosevelt, Stimson, and Marshall were convinced that Hitler could not be defeated unless a massive attack were made across the English Channel, which would allow a drive into the heart of Germany itself. It soon became obvious to American leaders that neither Churchill nor his military advisers had any real enthusiasm for such a venture, and without their wholehearted support such an operation, which would have to start from England, could hardly be successful.

Not until Roosevelt, Churchill, and Stalin met at Tehran in November, 1943, was there any firm agreement among the three powers that there would be a large-scale invasion of France. Shortly after the Tehran conference, Roosevelt named Dwight D. Eisenhower to the supreme command of this operation, which was called OVERLORD.

The following is a letter Secretary of War Stimson wrote to Roosevelt on August 10, 1943, urging the President to use all his influence on the British to agree to the opening of a second front in France.[6]

"Dear Mr. President:

"In my memorandum of last week, which was intended to be as factual as possible, I did not include certain conclusions to which I was driven by experiences of my trip. For a year and a half they have been looming more and more clearly through the fog of our successive conferences with the British. The personal contacts, talks, and observations of my visit made them very distinct.

"First: We cannot now rationally hope to be able to cross the Channel and come to grips with our German enemy under a British commander. His Prime Minister and his Chief of the Imperial Staff are frankly at variance with such a proposal. The shadows of Passchendaele and Dunkerque still hang too heavily upon the imagination of these leaders of his government. Though they have rendered lip service to the operation, their hearts are not in it and it will require more independence, more faith, and more vigor than it is reasonable to expect we can find in any British commander to overcome the natural difficulties of such an operation carried on in such an atmosphere of his government. There are too many natural obstacles to be overcome, too many possible side avenues of diversion which are capable of stalling and thus thwarting such an operation.

"Second: The difference between us is a vital difference of faith. The American staff believes that only by massing the immense vigor and power of the American and British nations under the overwhelming mastery of the air, which they already exercise far into the north of France and which can be made to cover our subsequent advance in France just as it has in Tunis and Sicily, can Germany be really defeated and the war brought to a real victory.

"On the other side, the British theory (which cropped out again and again in unguarded sentences of the British leaders with whom I have just been talking) is that Germany can be beaten by a series of attritions in northern Italy, in the eastern Mediterranean, in Greece, in the Balkans, in Rumania and other satellite countries. . . .

[6] Henry L. Stimson and McGeorge Bundy, *On Active Service in Peace and War,* pp. 436-38.

"To me, in the light of the postwar problems which we shall face, that attitude . . . seems terribly dangerous. We are pledged quite as clearly as Great Britain to the opening of a real second front. None of these methods of pinprick warfare can be counted on by us to fool Stalin into believing that we have kept that pledge.

"Third: I believe therefore that the time has come for you to decide that your government must assume the responsibility of leadership in this great final movement on the European war which is now confronting us. We cannot afford to confer again and close with a lip tribute to BOLERO which we have tried twice and failed to carry out. We cannot afford to begin the most dangerous operation of the war under halfhearted leadership which will invite failure or at least disappointing results. Nearly two years ago the British offered us this command. I think that now it should be accepted—if necessary, insisted on. . . .

"Faithfully yours,

HENRY L. STIMSON
Secretary of War"

5. Stilwell's Analysis of China, 1944

General Joseph W. Stilwell, who was sent to China in 1942 to lead the Allied forces in that area, remained there until he was recalled by Roosevelt the latter part of 1944 at the insistence of Chiang Kai-shek. Most of the entries in Stilwell's diary during his tour of duty in China relate his day-to-day experiences in the most frustrating command given any American general during the war. Shortly before his recall, he made certain entries concerning the nature of the Chinese Government and commented about prospects for the future. The excerpts quoted below are taken from his papers:[7]

"In time of war you have to take your allies as you find them. We were fighting Germany to tear down the Nazi system—one-party government, supported by the Gestapo and headed by an unbalanced man with little education. We had plenty to say against such a system. China, our ally, was being run by a one-party government (the Kuomintang), supported by a Gestapo (Tai Li's organization) and headed by an unbalanced man with little education [Chiang Kai-shek]. This government, however, had the prestige of the possession of power—it was opposing Japan, and its titular head had been built up by propaganda in America out of all proportion to

[7] Joseph W. Stilwell and Theodore H. White, (ed.), *The Stilwell Papers*, pp. 320-22.

his deserts and accomplishments.[8] We had to back the existing regime in order to have any chance of getting China to pull her weight. To change the structure during the emergency would have been next to impossible. All through the Chinese machinery of government there are interlocking ties of interest . . . family, financial, political, etc. No man, no matter how efficient, can hope for a position of authority on account of being the man best qualified for the job: he simply must have other backing. To reform such a system, it must be torn to pieces. You build a framework to grow grapevines on: in the course of time, the vines grow all over it, twisting in and out and around and pretty soon the frame is so tightly held by the vines that if you start pulling them out, you will tear the frames to pieces. We could not risk it, we had to take the instrument as we found it and do the best we could. But because it was expedient to back this government to get action against Japan, it was not necessarily advisable to endorse its methods and policies. We could have required some return for our help.

"Chiang K'ai-shek made a great point of how badly the U.S.A. had neglected China, who had been fighting desperately for so long, while Lend-Lease materials had been poured into Great Britain and Russia by the billion. His case was that we owed him a great debt and that it was a crying shame that we didn't do more to discharge it. This attitude met with sympathy in the U.S. It was true that large quantities of Lend-Lease materials were going to Russia and Great Britain. It was also true that Russia and Great Britain, particularly Russia, were making good use of this material against Germany. It was also true that there was no possible way of delivering the goods to Chiang K'ai-shek unless he made an effort on his part to help break the blockade. It seemed reasonable to expect Great Britain to use the huge Indian Army for the purpose. The U.S. was fighting Germany in Europe, and Japan in the Pacific. She was supplying enormous quantities of munitions and food to all the Allies. Under the circumstances it seemed reasonable for somebody else to display a little energy in Burma.

"To keep the show going, I had to overlook some of these incongruities and pretend, like the other players. If not, the critics would say it was a bum show, and we are very much afraid of the critics in our show.

"[This paper was never finished]

"SOLUTION IN CHINA [Probably July, 1944]

"The cure for China's troubles is the elimination of Chiang K'ai-shek. The only thing that keeps the country split is his fear of losing control. He hates the Reds and will not take any chances on giving them a toehold in the government. The result is that each side watches the other and neither gives a damn about the war [against Japan]. If this condition persists, China will have civil war immediately after Japan is out. If Russia enters the war before a united front is formed in China, the Reds, being immediately accessible,

[8] Stilwell undoubtedly was referring to the work of the China Lobby in the United States.

will naturally gravitate to Russia's influence and control. The condition will directly affect relations between Russia and China, and therefore indirectly those between Russia and the U.S.

If we do not take action, our prestige in China will suffer seriously. China will contribute nothing to our effort against Japan, and the seeds will be planted for chaos in China after the war."

6. Hurley Mission to China, 1944-1945

By the summer of 1944 the military, political, and economic situation in China took a decided turn for the worse. The relationship between Chiang Kai-shek and General Stilwell, which had never been cordial, reached a stage of open hostility. Japanese advances in China posed the most serious military threat to the Chungking regime since the fall of Burma. Inflation threatened the already tottering economy of the nation. Both Chiang and the Communists seemed to be far more interested in saving their forces than in using them against the Japanese.

At this critical juncture, Roosevelt decided to send General Patrick J. Hurley to China as his personal representative to assist in improving a situation which had been serious during the early days of the war, but was worse in 1944 than at any time in the past. As will be noted in the following selection, an excerpt from the State Department "White Paper," American policy at that time was to unify the forces of the Communists and the Kuomintang for the purpose of speeding the defeat of Japan. This necessitated some type of political agreement which was the objective of the United States.[9]

"According to General Hurley's report to the Department of State his instructions from the White House dated August 18 were (1) to serve as personal representative of the President to Generalissimo Chiang Kai-shek; (2) to promote harmonious relations between Chiang and General Joseph Stilwell and to facilitate the latter's exercise of command over the Chinese armies placed under his direction; (3) to perform certain additional duties respecting military supplies; and (4) to maintain intimate contact with Ambassador Gauss. A few months later, after his appointment as Ambassador, General Hurley outlined his understanding of his mission and of United States policy in China in the following terms: '(1) To prevent the collapse of the National Government, (2) to sustain Chiang Kai-shek as President of the Republic and Generalissimo of

[9] *United States Relations With China,* Dept. of State, Far East. Ser. 30, (Washington, 1949), pp. 71-75.

the Armies, (3) to harmonize relations between the Generalissimo and the American Commander, (4) to promote production of war supplies in China and prevent economic collapse, and (5) to unify all the military forces in China for the purpose of defeating Japan.'. . .

"Upon arriving at Chungking in September, General Hurley came to the conclusion that the success of his mission to 'unify all the military forces in China for the purpose of defeating Japan' was dependent on the negotiations already under way for the unification of the Chinese military forces. Accordingly, shortly after his arrival he undertook active measures of mediation between the Chinese National Government and the Chinese Communist Party.

"In December 1944 General Hurley commented as follows regarding his early efforts at reconciliation:

" 'At the time I came here Chiang Kai-shek believed that the Communist Party in China was an instrument of the Soviet Government in Russia. He is now convinced that the Russian Government does not recognize the Chinese Communist Party as Communist at all and that (1) Russia is not supporting the Communist Party in China, (2) Russia does not want dissensions or civil war in China, and (3) Russia desires more harmonious relations with China.

" 'These facts have gone far toward convincing Chiang Kai-shek that the Communist Party in China is not an agent of the Soviet Government. He now feels that he can reach a settlement with the Communist Party as a Chinese political party without foreign entanglements. When I first arrived, it was thought that civil war after the close of the present war or perhaps before that time was inevitable. Chiang Kai-shek is now convinced that by agreement with the Communist Party of China he can (1) unite the military forces of China against Japan, and (2) avoid civil strife in China.'

"With respect to specific steps taken by him, General Hurley reported in December 1944 that with the consent, advice and direction of the Generalissimo and members of his Cabinet and on the invitation of leaders of the Communist Party, he had begun discussions with the Communist Party and Communist military leaders for the purpose of effecting an agreement to regroup, coordinate and unite the military forces of China for the defeat of Japan. He continued: 'The defeat of Japan is, of course, the primary objective, but we should all understand that if an agreement is not reached between the two great military establishments of China, civil war will in all probability ensue.'

"Following discussions with Chinese Government and Chinese Communist representatives in Chungking, General Hurley on November 7, 1944, flew to Yenan for a two-day conference with Mao Tse-tung, the Chairman of the Central Executive Committee of the Chinese Communist Party. The Communist leaders were impressed by the fact that General

Hurley had taken the initiative in making this flight and cordial relations were established at once. As a result of these discussions there was evolved at Yenan a five-point draft, entitled 'Agreement Between the National Government of China, the Kuomintang of China and the Communist Party of China,' which was signed by Mao Tse-tung as Chairman of the Central Executive Committee of the Communist Party on November 10, 1944, and by General Hurley as witness. This important agreement read as follows:

" '(1) The Government of China, the Kuomintang of China and the Communist Party of China will work together for the unification of all military forces in China for the immediate defeat of Japan and the reconstruction of China.

" '(2) The present National Government is to be reorganized into a coalition National Government embracing representatives of all anti-Japanese parties and non-partisan political bodies. A new democratic policy providing for reform in military, political, economic and cultural affairs shall be promulgated and made effective. At the same time the National Military Council is to be reorganized into the United National Military Council consisting of representatives of all anti-Japanese armies.

" '(3) The coalition National Government will support the principles of Sun Yat-sen for the establishment in China of a government of the people, for the people and by the people. The coalition National Government will pursue policies designed to promote progress and democracy and to establish justice, freedom of conscience, freedom of press, freedom of speech, freedom of assembly and association, the right to petition the government for the redress of grievances, the right of writ of habeas corpus and the right of residence. The coalition National Government will also pursue policies intended to make effective the two rights defined as freedom from fear and freedom from want.

" '(4) All anti-Japanese forces will observe and carry out the orders of the coalition National Government and its United National Military Council and will be recognized by the Government and the Military Council. The supplies acquired from foreign powers will be equitably distributed.

" '(5) The coalition National Government of China recognizes the legality of the Kuomintang of China, the Chinese Communist Party and all anti-Japanese parties.'

"General Hurley felt that this Five-Point Draft Agreement, which he promptly submitted to the National Government, offered a practical plan for settlement with the Communists. National Government leaders, however, said that the Communist plan was not acceptable. The National Government submitted as counter-proposal a Three-Point Agreement reading as follows:

" '(1) The National Government, desirous of securing effective unification and concentration of all military forces in China for the purpose of accomplishing the speedy defeat of Japan, and looking forward to the post-war reconstruction of China, agrees to incorporate, after reorganization,

the Chinese Communist forces in the National Army who will then receive
equal treatment as the other units in respect to pay, allowance, munitions
and other supplies, and to give recognition to the Chinese Communist Party
as a legal party.

" '(2) The Communist Party undertakes to give their full support to
the National Government in the prosecution of the war of resistance, and
in the post-war reconstruction, and give over control of all their troops to
the National Government through the National Military Council. The
National Government will designate some high ranking officers from among
the Communist forces to membership in the National Military Council.

" '(3) The aim of the National Government to which the Communist
Party subscribes is to carry out the Three People's Principles of Dr. Sun
Yat-sen for the establishment in China of a government of the people, for
the people and by the people and it will pursue policies designed to promote
the progress and development of democratic processes in government.

" 'In accordance with the provisions of the *Program of Armed Resistance and National Reconstruction,* freedom of speech, freedom of the press,
freedom of assembly and association and other civil liberties are hereby guaranteed, subject only to the specific needs of security in the effective prosecution of the war against Japan.' "

7. *The Yalta Agreement*

Roosevelt, Churchill, and Stalin met for the last time at Yalta
and reached agreements for the postwar world which contributed
to the hope in the Western World that the major allies in World
War II were more united in their purposes than had been the
case following World War I.

Even before Roosevelt died, two months after Yalta, his
faith in the sincerity of the Russians to abide by their pledged
word was shaken, in view of their failure to set up a truly representative government in Poland. Since Roosevelt's death, the
Yalta agreement has been subject to almost constant attack
within the United States as an act of stupidity on the part of
President Roosevelt and his advisers, in view of the fact that
since the end of the war the Russians have expanded their control
over wide areas in eastern Europe and the Communists have
seized control of China. It should be pointed out, however, that
the Eisenhower resolution in 1953 did not criticize the Yalta
agreement but the Russian violations of it.

The following are excerpts from the Yalta agreement.[10]

[10] *A Decade of American Foreign Policy, Basic Documents, 1941-49,* 81st Cong.,
1st Sess., Senate Document No. 123, (Washington, 1950), pp. 27-34.

"THE CRIMEAN (YALTA) CONFERENCE, FEBRUARY 4-11, 1945

"I. WORLD ORGANIZATION

"It was decided:

"(1) that a United Nations Conference on the proposed world organisations should be summoned for Wednesday, 25th April, 1945, and should be held in the United States of America.

"(2) the Nations to be invited to this Conference should be:

(a) the United Nations as they existed on the 8th February, 1945; and

(b) such of the Associated Nations as have declared war on the common enemy by 1st March, 1945. (For this purpose by the term 'Associated Nation' was meant the eight Association Nations and Turkey.) When the Conference on World Organization is held, the delegates of the United Kingdom and United States of America will support a proposal to admit to original membership two Soviet Socialist Republics, i.e. the Ukraine and White Russia.

"(3) that the United States Government on behalf of the Three Powers should consult the Government of China and the French Provisional Government in regard to decisions taken at the present Conference concerning the proposed World Organisation. . . .

" 'C' VOTING

"1. Each member of the Security Council should have one vote.

"2. Decisions of the Security Council on procedural matters should be made by an affirmative vote of seven members.

"3. Decisions of the Security Council on all other matters should be made by an affirmative vote of seven members including the concurring votes of the permanent members; provided that, in decisions under Chapter VIII, Section A and under the second sentence of paragraph 1 of Chapter VIII, Section C, a party to a dispute should abstain from voting.

"Further information as to arrangements will be transmitted subsequently. . . .

"TERRITORIAL TRUSTEESHIP

"It was agreed that the five Nations which will have permanent seats on the Security Council should consult each other prior to the United Nations Conference on the question of territorial trusteeship.

"The acceptance of this recommendation is subject to its being made clear that territorial trusteeship will only apply to (a) existing mandates of the League of Nations; (b) territories detached from the enemy as a result of the present war; (c) any other territory which might voluntarily be placed under trusteeship; and (d) no discussion of actual territories is contemplated at the forthcoming United Nations Conference or in the preliminary consultations, and it will be a matter for subsequent agreement which territories within the above categories will be placed under trusteeship.

"II. DECLARATION ON LIBERATED EUROPE

"The following declaration has been approved:

" 'The Premier of the Union of Soviet Socialist Republics, the Prime Minister of the United Kingdom and the President of the United States of America have consulted with each other in the common interests of the peoples of their countries and those of liberated Europe. They jointly declare their mutual agreement to concert during the temporary period of instability in liberated Europe the policies of their three governments in assisting the peoples liberated from the domination of Nazi Germany and the peoples of the former Axis satellite states of Europe to solve by democratic means their pressing political and economic problems.

" 'The establishment of order in Europe and the re-building of national economic life must be achieved by processes which will enable the liberated peoples to destroy the last vestiges of Nazism and Fascism and to create democratic institutions of their own choice. This is a principle of the Atlantic Charter—the right of all peoples to choose the form of government under which they will live—the restoration of sovereign rights and self-government to those peoples who have been forcibly deprived of them by the aggressor nations.

" 'To foster the conditions in which the liberated peoples may exercise these rights, the three governments will jointly assist the people in any European liberated state or former Axis satellite state in Europe where in their judgment conditions require (a) to establish conditions of internal peace; (b) to carry out emergency measures for the relief of distressed peoples; (c) to form interim governmental authorities broadly representative of all democratic elements in the population and pledged to the earliest possible establishment through free elections of governments responsive to the will of the people; and (d) to facilitate where necessary the holding of such elections.

" 'The three governments will consult the other United Nations and provisional authorities or other governments in Europe when matters of direct interest to them are under consideration.

" 'When, in the opinion of the three governments, conditions in any European liberated state or any former Axis satellite state in Europe make such action necessary, they will immediately consult together on the measures necessary to discharge the joint responsibilities set forth in this declaration.

" 'By this declaration we reaffirm our faith in the principles of the Atlantic Charter, our pledge in the Declaration by the United Nations, and our determination to build in cooperation with other peace-loving nations world order under law, dedicated to peace, security, freedom and general well-being of all mankind.

" 'In issuing this declaration, the Three Powers express the hope that the Provisional Government of the French Republic may be associated with them in the procedure suggested.'

"III. DISMEMBERMENT OF GERMANY

"It was agreed that Article 12 (a) of the Surrender Terms for Germany should be amended to read as follows:

'The United Kingdom, the United States of America and the Union of Soviet Socialist Republics shall possess supreme authority with respect to Germany. In the exercise of such authority they will take such steps, including the complete disarmament, demilitarisation and dismemberment of Germany as they deem requisite for future peace and security.'

"The study of the procedure for the dismemberment of Germany was referred to a Committee, consisting of Mr. Eden (Chairman), Mr. Winant and Mr. Gousev. This body would consider the desirability of associating with it a French representative.

"IV. ZONE OF OCCUPATION FOR THE FRENCH
CONTROL COUNCIL FOR GERMANY

"It was agreed that a zone in Germany, to be occupied by the French Forces, should be allocated to France. This zone would be formed out of the British and American zones and its extent would be settled by the British and Americans in consultation with the French Provisional Government.

"It was also agreed that the French Provisional Government should be invited to become a member of the Allied Control Council for Germany. . . .

"VI. MAJOR WAR CRIMINALS

"The Conference agreed that the question of the major war criminals should be subject of enquiry by the three Foreign Secretaries for report in due course after the close of the Conference.

"VII. POLAND

"The following declaration on Poland was agreed by the Conference:

" 'A new situation has been created in Poland as a result of her complete liberation by the Red Army. This calls for the establishment of a Polish Provisional Government which can be more broadly based than was possible before the recent liberation of Western Poland. The Provisional Government which is now functioning in Poland should therefore be reorganised on a broader democratic basis with the inclusion of democratic leaders from Poland itself and from Poles abroad. This new Government should then be called the Polish Provisional Government of National Unity.

" 'M. Molotov, Mr. Harriman and Sir A. Clark Kerr are authorized as a commission to consult in the first instance in Moscow with members of the present Provisional Government and with other Polish democratic leaders from within Poland and from abroad, with a view to the reorganisation of the present Government along the above lines. This Polish Provisional Government of National Unity shall be pledged to the holding of free and unfettered elections as soon as possible on the basis of universal suffrage and secret ballot. In these elections all democratic and anti-Nazi parties shall have the right to take part and to put forward candidates.

" 'When a Polish Provisional Government of National Unity has been properly formed in conformity with the above, the Government of the U.S.S.R., which now maintains diplomatic relations with the present Provisional Government of Poland, and the Government of the United Kingdom and the Government of the United States of America will establish diplomatic relations with the new Polish Provisional Government of National Unity, and will exchange Ambassadors by whose reports the respective Governments will be kept informed about the situation in Poland.

" 'The three Heads of Government consider that the Eastern frontier of Poland should follow the Curzon Line with digressions from it in some regions of five to eight kilometers in favour of Poland. They recognise that Poland must receive substantial accessions of territory in the North and West. They feel that the opinion of the new Polish Provisional Government of National Unity should be sought in due course on the extent of these accessions and that the final delimitation of the Western frontier of Poland should thereafter await the Peace Conference.'

"VIII. YUGOSLAVIA

"It was agreed to recommend to Marshal Tito and to Dr. Subasic:

"(a) that the Tito-Subasic Agreement should immediately be put into effect and a new Government formed on the basis of the Agreement.

"(b) that as soon as the new Government has been formed it should declare:

(i) that the Anti-Fascist Assembly of National Liberation (AVNOJ) will be extended to include members of the last Yugoslav Skupstina who have not compromised themselves by collaboration with the enemy, thus forming a body to be known as a temporary Parliament and

(ii) that the legislative acts passed by the Anti-Fascist Assembly of National Liberation (AVNOJ) will be subject to subsequent ratification by a Constituent Assembly; and that this statement should be published in the Communique of the Conference. . . .

"X. YUGOSLAV-BULGARIAN RELATIONS

"There was an exchange of views between the Foreign Secretaries on the question of the desirability of a Yugoslav-Bulgarian pact of alliance. The question at issue was whether a state still under an armistice regime could be allowed to enter into a treaty with another state. Mr. Eden suggested that the Bulgarian and Yugoslav Governments should be informed that this could not be approved. Mr. Stettinius suggested that the British and American Ambassadors should discuss the matter further with Mr.

Molotov in Moscow. M. Molotov agreed with the proposal of Mr. Stettinius.

"XI. SOUTH EASTERN EUROPE

"The British Delegation put in notes for the consideration of their colleagues on the following subjects:

"(a) the Control Commission in Bulgaria.

"(b) Greek claims upon Bulgaria, more particularly with reference to reparations.

"(c) Oil equipment in Rumania.

"XII. IRAN

"Mr. Eden, Mr. Stettinius and M. Molotov exchanged views on the situation in Iran. It was agreed that this matter should be pursued through the diplomatic channel.

"XIII. MEETINGS OF THE THREE FOREIGN SECRETARIES

"The Conference agreed that permanent machinery should be set up for consultation between the three Foreign Secretaries; they should meet as often as necessary, probably about every three or four months.

"These meetings will be held in rotation in the three capitals, the first meeting to be held in London.

"XIV. THE MONTREUX CONVENTION AND THE STRAITS

"It was agreed that at the next meeting of the three Foreign Secretaries to be held in London, they should consider proposals which it was understood the Soviet Government would put forward in relation to the Montreux Convention and report to their Governments. The Turkish Government should be informed at the appropriate moment. . . .

"(b) *Protocol on German Reparations*

"The Heads of the three governments agreed as follows:

"1. Germany must pay in kind for the losses caused by her to the Allied nations in the course of the war. Reparation are to be received in the first instance by those countries which have borne the main burden of the war, have suffered the heaviest losses and have organized victory over the enemy.

"2. Reparation in kind are to be exacted from Germany in three following forms:

   (a) Removals within 2 years from the surrender of Germany or the cessation of organised resistance from the national wealth of Germany located on the territory of Germany herself as well as outside her territory (equipment, machine-tools, ships, rolling stock, German investments abroad, shares of industrial, transport and other enterprises in Germany, etc.), these removals to be carried out chiefly for purpose of destroying the war potential of Germany.

   (b) Annual deliveries of goods from current production for a period to be fixed.

(c) Use of German labour.

"3. For the working out on the above principles of a detailed plan for exaction of reparation from Germany an Allied Reparation Commission will be set up in Moscow. It will consist of three representatives—one from the Union of Soviet Socialist Republics, one from the United Kingdom and one from the United States of America.

"4. With regard to the fixing of the total sum of the reparation as well as the distribution of it among the countries which suffered from the German aggression the Soviet and American delegations agreed as follows:

" 'The Moscow Reparation Commission should take in its initial studies as a basis for discussion the suggestion of the Soviet Government that the total sum of the reparation in accordance with the points (a) and (b) of the paragraph 2 should be 20 billion dollars and that 50% of it should go to the Union of the Soviet Socialist Republics.'

"The British delegation was of the opinion that pending consideration of the reparation question by the Moscow Reparation Commission no figures of reparation should be mentioned.

"The above Soviet-American proposal has been passed to the Moscow Reparation Commission as one of the proposals to be considered by the Commission. . . .

"(c) *Agreement Regarding Japan*

"The leaders of the three Great Powers—the Soviet Union, the United States of America and Great Britain—have agreed that in two or three months after Germany has surrendered and the war in Europe has terminated the Soviet Union shall enter into the war against Japan on the side of the Allies on condition that:

"1. The status quo in Outer-Mongolia (The Mongolian People's Republic) shall be preserved;

"2. The former rights of Russia violated by the treacherous attack of Japan in 1904 shall be restored, viz:

(a) the southern part of Sakhalin as well as all the islands adjacent to it shall be returned to the Soviet Union,

(b) the commercial port of Dairen shall be internationalized, the preeminent interests of the Soviet Union in this port being safeguarded and the lease of Port Arthur as a naval base of the U.S.S.R. restored,

(c) the Chinese-Eastern Railroad and the South-Manchurian Railroad which provides an outlet to Dairen shall be jointly operated by the establishment of a joint Soviet-Chinese Company it being understood that the preeminent interests of the Soviet Union shall be safeguarded and that China shall retain full sovereignty in Manchuria;

"3. The Kuril islands shall be handed over to the Soviet Union.

"It is understood, that the agreement concerning Outer-Mongolia and the ports and the railroads referred to above will require concurrence of

Generalissimo Chiang Kai-shek. The President will take measures in order to obtain this concurrence on advice from Marshal Stalin.

"The Heads of the three Great Powers have agreed that these claims of the Soviet Union shall be unquestionably fulfilled after Japan has been defeated.

"For its part the Soviet Union expresses its readiness to conclude with the National Government of China a pact of friendship and alliance between the U.S.S.R. and China in order to render assistance to China with its armed forces for the purpose of liberating China from the Japanese yoke.

JOSEPH V. STALIN

FRANKLIN D. ROOSEVELT

WINSTON S. CHURCHILL

"February 11, 1945"

8. *American—Soviet Relations, 1945*

Despite the rift in United States-Soviet relations, which appeared almost immediately after Yalta over the failure of the Russians to live up to the Yalta agreement with reference to the Provisional Government of Poland, American official statements all pointed to the prospects of a rosy future. Unquestionably the most hopeful declaration as to future relations between the two nations made by a responsible official was that given in a radio address on May 26, 1945, by Assistant Secretary of State Archibald MacLeish.[11]

". . . Specifically—and there is every reason to be specific—some observers see a striking contrast between our fortunate collaboration with the Russians in San Francisco and what they consider the failure of our collaboration with the Russians in Poland, and elsewhere in eastern Europe.

"It is now generally recognized, in spite of differences which have of course occurred, and in spite of the sensational headlines which introduced certain San Francisco stories earlier in the Conference, that the real news of San Francisco is not the alleged crises, clashes, and collisions, but the fact that what might have been crises, and what might have been collisions, turned out, for the most part, to be cordial and understanding agreements.

"The so-called regional issue is an excellent example. We and the Russians were described as being completely at loggerheads on that question.

[11] Archibald MacLeish, "United States-Soviet Relations," *Department of State Bulletin,* May 27, 1945, pp. 950-52.

When the whole story was in, it became clear, even to those who make a business of discovering differences of opinion, that there had never been a serious difference between the Russian Delegation and our own. . . .[12]

"All this is as disturbing as it is confusing to the sensible citizens of this country. It would be serious also—tragically serious—if it were not for one thing: that the facts speak for themselves and that what the facts speak of is profoundly reassuring to any man who will open his ears and listen. The facts are these.

"First, the Soviet Union and the United States have proved, in the most difficult geographic, economic, and psychological circumstances under which allies have ever attempted to act as allies, that they can work together in the difficult and trying prosecution of a total war.

"Second, the United States and the Soviet Union have proved in the laborious conversations at Dumbarton Oaks, and in the delicate negotiations at Yalta, and in the difficult four-power stage at San Francisco, that they can reconcile their views and arrive at common understandings on problems which have resisted, hitherto, the best efforts of the best diplomatic minds of many generations, and which have never yet been solved.

"These, however, are only the more obvious facts. There are also certain underlying facts which speak with equal eloquence.

"The first is this:

the vital interests of the United States and the Soviet Union conflict at no point on the earth's surface.

"The second is this:

the United States and the Soviet Union are countries independently rich in their own resources, needing little from the world outside.

"And there is a third:

the United States and the Soviet Union are both young, strong, self-confident countries, with their own business to attend to; countries which, however they may differ in philosophy, and however they may differ in practice, aim in their several and dissimilar ways at what they believe to be the betterment of the lot of their own people and not at the conquest of the earth.

"There is no necessary reason, in other words, in the logic of geography, or in the logic of economics, or in the logic of national objectives, why the United States and the Soviet Union should ever find themselves in conflict with each other, let alone in the kind of conflict reckless and irresponsible men have now begun to suggest.

"There are differences between us: real differences. Poland is one. It will take will and time and effort—Russian will and time and effort as well

[12] This statement is hardly borne out by the diaries of Senator Arthur H. Vandenberg, a delegate to the Conference, as published in the *Papers of Senator Vandenberg.*

as American will and time and effort—to find an answer to Poland. But there is no necessary or logical reason why an answer to Poland or to any other difference should not be found. Indeed the answers must be found.

"What underlies the current talk of inevitable conflict between the two nations, in other words, is nothing real: nothing logical. The basis of fear is only fear. The basis of the suspicion is nothing more substantial than suspicion. . . ."

CHAPTER XVII.

POSTWAR PLANNING

ITLER had hardly completed the conquest of Poland in the fall of 1939 before officials in the Department of State began thinking about the type of world which would emerge from the European conflict. During the latter part of 1939 and the first months of 1940, the United States was officially neutral although openly sympathetic to the British, French and Chinese, and at that date most Americans believed that this nation would not become actively engaged in the war. State Department officials, however, aware of the potential influence of the United States in world affairs, began to draft plans which they hoped would aid in the creation of a more peaceful postwar world.

In January, 1940, the Department of State announced the creation of a special committee to study postwar problems. The plans compiled by this committee were tentative and had to be modified by the course of events during the war.

The first high-level announcement of American postwar policy came on August 14, 1941, when Roosevelt and Churchill released the text of the Atlantic Charter. It is important to realize that this joint American-British declaration came *before* the United States was at war, and that it was not a treaty. It was no more than a manifesto of the hopes of the leaders of the two great democracies as to the kind of world they would like to see emerge from the war. Nevertheless, it was an important declaration because it did represent the over-all desires of the United States, and many of its principles were incorporated later into the Charter of the United Nations.

The next important step in postwar planning came on January 1, 1942, when representatives of the twenty-six nations then at war with the Axis powers signed the Declaration of the United Nations. According to Robert E. Sherwood, who had access to Harry Hopkins' notes, the phrase "United Nations" was conceived by Roosevelt; and the Declaration was a short statement which committed the signatories to the principles expressed in the Atlantic Charter and to the prosecution of the war with every resource at their command. The Declaration also contained a pledge that no nation would make a separate peace with the Axis.

While State Department officials continued to formulate plans for the postwar period, the Congress of the United States adopted the Fulbright Resolution in the late fall of 1943, expressing its approval of the creation of an international organization designed to keep the peace and to which the United States should belong.

At almost the same time, in November, 1943, the Governments of the United States, the United Kingdom, the Soviet Union, and China issued a declaration from Moscow following a foreign ministers' conference pledging themselves to the creation of such an international organization based upon the principles expressed in the Declaration of the United Nations.

In the late summer and early fall of 1944, the same nations which had issued the Moscow declaration sent representatives to Washington to meet at the Dumbarton Oaks Conference for the purpose of drawing up the plans for an international organization which would be submitted for the approval of all the United Nations at a later date. In many respects, the Charter of the United Nations is quite similar to the plans drawn up at Dumbarton Oaks, but several problems—including the veto power— were left undecided in 1944.

At Yalta, the Big Three agreed to have the conference held in San Francisco in April, 1945, for the purpose of drawing up a world organization based on the plans adopted at Dumbarton Oaks. They also agreed that China and the Provisional French Government should be included among the powers sponsoring the conference, and that all permanent members of the Security Council, which included the Big Five powers, must concur on all non-procedural matters before action could be taken. By virtue of this Yalta provision the veto power was established, which meant that all of the Big Five powers would have to agree before the Security Council could act.

Roosevelt died before the San Francisco Conference had started, but President Harry S. Truman announced that the conference would proceed as planned. Representatives from forty-six nations opened the conference in San Francisco on April 25, and four additional nations were admitted later. Precisely two months after the opening date, the conference adjourned with the Charter of the United Nations as the product of its handiwork.

In drastic contrast with the situation in 1919 when the Senate prevented the United States from joining the League of Nations, the Senate quickly ratified the Charter of the United Nations, and the United States, on August 8, 1945, became the first nation to become a member of the world organization.

There were a few voices raised against this newly-created body, but sentiment for an international organization pledged to keep the peace was overwhelming; and for better or for worse, the United States took the leadership in throwing its full weight behind what seemed to be the world's best hope for a lasting peace.

1. Moscow Conference, 1943

Secretary Cordell Hull explained the achievements of this foreign ministers' conference to a joint session of the Congress of the United States on November 18, 1943.[1]

"The attention of the Conference was centered upon the task of making sure that the nations upon whose armed forces and civilian efforts rests the main responsibility for defeating the enemy will, along with other peacefully minded nations, continue to perform their full part in solving the numerous and vexatious problems of the future. From the outset, the dominant thought at the Conference was that, after the attainment of victory, cooperation among peace-loving nations in support of certain paramount mutual interests will be almost as compelling in importance and necessity as it is today in support of the war effort.

"At the end of the war, each of the United Nations and of the nations associated with them will have the same common interest in national security, in world order under law, in peace, in the full promotion of the political, economic, and social welfare of their respective peoples—in the principles and spirit of the Atlantic Charter and the Declaration by United Nations. The future of these indispensable common interests depends absolutely upon international cooperation. Hence, each nation's own primary interest requires it to cooperate with the others.

"These considerations led the Moscow Conference to adopt the four-nation declaration with which you are all familiar. I should like to comment briefly on its main provisions.

[1] Cordell Hull, "The Moscow Conference," Dept. of State, Pub. 2027, (Washington, 1943).

"In that document, it was jointly declared by the United States, Great Britain, the Soviet Union, and China 'That their united action, pledged for the prosecution of the war against their respective enemies, will be continued for the organization and maintenance of peace and security.'

"To this end, the four Governments declared that they 'recognize the necessity of establishing at the earliest practicable date a general international organization, based on the principle of the sovereign equality of all peace-loving states, and open to membership by all such states, large and small.' I should like to lay particular stress on this provision of the declaration. The principle of sovereign equality of all peace-loving states, irrespective of size and strength, as partners in a future system of general security will be the foundation stone upon which the future international organization will be constructed.

"The adoption of this principle was particularly welcome to us. Nowhere has the conception of sovereign equality been applied more widely in recent years than in the American family of nations, whose contribution to the common effort in wartime will now be followed by representation in building the institutions of peace.

"The four Governments further agreed that, pending the inauguration in this manner of a permanent system of general security, 'they will consult with one another and as occasion requires with other members of the United Nations with a view to joint action on behalf of the community of nations' whenever such action may be necessary for the purpose of maintaining international peace and security.

"Finally, as an important self-denying ordinance, they declared 'That after the termination of hostilities they will not employ their military forces within the territories of other states except for the purposes envisaged in this declaration and after joint consultation.'

"Through this declaration, the Soviet Union, Great Britain, the United States, and China have laid the foundation for cooperative effort in the post-war world toward enabling all peace-loving nations, large and small, to live in peace and security, to preserve the liberties and rights of civilized existence, and to enjoy expanded opportunities and facilities for economic, social, and spiritual progress. No other important nations anywhere have more in common in the present war or in the peace that is to follow victory over the Axis powers. No one, no two of them can be most effective without the others, in war or in peace. . . ."

2. Charter of the United Nations

The culmination of all postwar planning was the Charter of the United Nations drawn up by the delegates of the fifty nations which met in San Francisco from April 25 to June 26, 1945. Excerpts are quoted below:[2]

"We the peoples of the United Nations determined
to save succeeding generations from the scourge of war, which twice in our lifetime has brought untold sorrow to mankind, and
to reaffirm faith in fundamental human rights, in the dignity and worth of the human person, in the equal rights of men and women and of nations large and small, and
to establish conditions under which justice and respect for the obligations arising from treaties and other sources of international law can be maintained, and
to promote social progress and better standards of life in larger freedom,
and for these ends
to practice tolerance and live together in peace with one another as good neighbors, and
to unite our strength to maintain international peace and security, and
to ensure, by the acceptance of principles and the institution of methods, that armed force shall not be used, save in the common interest, and
to employ international machinery for the promotion of the economic and social advancement of all peoples,
have resolved to combine our efforts to accomplish these aims.

"Accordingly, our respective Governments, through representatives assembled in the city of San Francisco, who have exhibited their full powers found to be in good and due form, have agreed to the present Charter of the United Nations and do hereby establish an international organization to be known as the United Nations.

"Chapter I
"PURPOSES AND PRINCIPLES
"*Article 1*
"The Purposes of the United Nations are:
"1. To maintain international peace and security, and to that end: to take effective collective measures for the prevention and removal of threats to the peace, and for the suppression of acts of aggression or other breaches of the peace, and to bring about by peaceful means, and in conformity with the principles of justice and international law, adjustment or settlement of international disputes or situations which might lead to a breach of the peace;
"2. To develop friendly relations among nations based on respect for

[2] *Charter of the United Nations,* Dept. of State, Pub. 2353, Int. Org. and Conf. Ser., III, pp. 1-85.

the principle of equal rights and self-determination of peoples, and to take other appropriate measures to strengthen universal peace;

"3. To achieve international cooperation in solving international problems of an economic, social, cultural, or humanitarian character, and in promoting and encouraging respect for human rights and for fundamental freedoms for all without distinction as to race, sex, language, or religion; and

"4. To be a center for harmonizing the actions of nations in the attainment of these common ends.

"Article 2

"The Organization and its Members, in pursuit of the Purposes stated in Article 1, shall act in accordance with the following Principles.

"1. The Organization is based on the principle of the sovereign equality of all its Members.

"2. All Members, in order to ensure to all of them the rights and benefits resulting from membership, shall fulfill in good faith the obligations assumed by them in accordance with the present Charter.

"3. All Members shall settle their international disputes by peaceful means in such a manner that international peace and security, and justice, are not endangered.

"4. All Members shall refrain in their international relations from the threat or use of force against the territorial integrity or political independence of any state, or in any other manner inconsistent with the Purposes of the United Nations.

"5. All Members shall give the United Nations every assistance in any action it takes in accordance with the present Charter, and shall refrain from giving assistance to any state against which the United Nations is taking preventive or enforcement action.

"6. The Organization shall ensure that states which are not Members of the United Nations act in accordance with these Principles so far as may be necessary for the maintenance of international peace and security.

"7. Nothing contained in the present Charter shall authorize the United Nations to intervene in matters which are essentially within the domestic jurisdiction of any state or shall require the Members to submit such matters to settlement under the present Charter; but this principle shall not prejudice the application of enforcement measures under Chapter VII.

"Chapter II

"MEMBERSHIP

"<i>Article 3</i></div>

"The original Members of the United Nations shall be the states which, having participated in the United Nations Conference on International Organization at San Francisco, or having previously signed the Declaration by United Nations of January 1, 1942, sign the present Charter and ratify it in accordance with Article 110.

"*Article 4*

"1. Membership in the United Nations is open to all other peace-loving states which accept the obligations contained in the present Charter and, in the judgment of the Organization, are able and willing to carry out these obligations.

"2. The admission of any such state to membership in the United Nations will be effected by a decision of the General Assembly upon the recommendation of the Security Council. . . .

"*Article 6*

"A Member of the United Nations which has persistently violated the Principles contained in the present Charter may be expelled from the Organization by the General Assembly upon the recommendation of the Security Council.

"Chapter III

"ORGANS

"*Article 7*

"1. There are established as the principal organs of the United Nations: a General Assembly, a Security Council, an Economic and Social Council, a Trusteeship Council, an International Court of Justice, and a Secretariat.

"2. Such subsidiary organs as may be found necessary may be established in accordance with the present Charter. . . .

"Chapter IV

"THE GENERAL ASSEMBLY

"COMPOSITION

"*Article 9*

"1. The General Assembly shall consist of all the Members of the United Nations.

"2. Each Member shall have not more than five representatives in the General Assembly.

"FUNCTIONS AND POWERS

"*Article 10*

"The General Assembly may discuss any questions or any matters within the scope of the present Charter or relating to the powers and functions of any organs provided for in the present Charter, and except as provided in Article 12, may make recommendations to the Members of the United Nations or to the Security Council or to both on any such questions or matters. . . .

"*Article 12*

"1. While the Security Council is exercising in respect of any dispute or situation the functions assigned to it in the present Charter, the General Assembly shall not make any recommendation with regard to that dispute or situation unless the Security Council so requests. . . .

"voting
"*Article 18*
"1. Each member of the General Assembly shall have one vote.

"2. Decisions of the General Assembly on important questions shall be made by a two-thirds majority of the members present and voting. These questions shall include: recommendations with respect to the maintenance of international peace and security, the election of the non-permanent members of the Security Council, the election of the members of the Economic and Social Council, the election of the members of the Trusteeship Council. . . , the admission of new Members. . . , the suspension of the rights and privileges of membership, the expulsion of Members, questions relating to the operation of the trusteeship system, and budgetary questions. . . .

"procedure
"*Article 20*
"The General Assembly shall meet in regular annual sessions and in such special sessions as occasion may require. Special sessions shall be convoked by the Secretary-General at the request of the Security Council or of a majority of the Members of the United Nations. . . .

"*Article 22*
"The General Assembly may establish such subsidiary organs as it deems necessary for the performance of its functions.

"Chapter V
"THE SECURITY COUNCIL
"composition
"*Article 23*
"1. The Security Council shall consist of eleven Members of the United Nations. The Republic of China, France, the Union of Soviet Socialist Republics, the United Kingdom of Great Britain and Northern Ireland, and the United States of America shall be permanent members of the Security Council. The General Assembly shall elect six other Members of the United Nations to be non-permanent members of the Security Council, due regard being specially paid, in the first instance to the contribution of Members of the United Nations to the maintenance of international peace and security and to the other purposes of the Organization, and also to equitable geographical distribution.

"2. The non-permanent members of the Security Council shall be elected for a term of two years. . . .

"3. Each member of the Security Council shall have one representative.
"functions and powers
"*Article 24*
"1. In order to ensure prompt and effective action by the United Nations, its Members confer on the Security Council primary responsibility

for the maintenance of international peace and security, and agree that in carrying out its duties under this responsibility the Security Council acts on their behalf. . . .

"Article 25

"The Members of the United Nations agree to accept and carry out the decisions of the Security Council in accordance with the present Charter. . . .

*"*VOTING

"Article 27

"1. Each member of the Security Council shall have one vote.

"2. Decisions of the Security Council on procedural matters shall be made by an affirmative vote of seven members.

"3. Decisions of the Security Council of all other matters shall be made by an affirmative vote of seven members including the concurring votes of the permanent members. . . .

*"*PROCEDURE

"Article 28

"1. The Security Council shall be so organized as to be able to function continuously. Each member of the Security Council shall for this purpose be represented at all times at the seat of the Organization. . . .

"Chapter VI
"PACIFIC SETTLEMENT OF DISPUTES

"Article 33

"1. The parties to any dispute, the continuance of which is likely to endanger the maintenance of international peace and security, shall, first of all, seek a solution by negotiation, enquiry, mediation, conciliation, arbitration, judicial settlement, resort to regional agencies or arrangements, or other peaceful means of their own choice.

"2. The Security Council shall, when it deems necessary, call upon the parties to settle their dispute by such means.

"Article 34

"The Security Council may investigate any dispute, or any situation which might lead to international friction or give rise to a dispute, in order to determine whether the continuance of the dispute or situation is likely to endanger the maintenance of international peace and security. . . .

"Chapter VII
"ACTION WITH RESPECT TO THREATS TO THE PEACE, BREACHES OF THE PEACE, AND ACTS OF AGGRESSION

"Article 39

"The Security Council shall determine the existence of any threat to the peace, breach of the peace, or act of aggression and shall make recommendations, or decide what measures shall be taken in accordance with Articles 41 and 42, to maintain or restore international peace and security. . . .

"Article 41

"The Security Council may decide what measures not involving the use of armed force are to be employed to give effect to its decisions, and it may call upon the Members of the United Nations to apply such measures. These may include complete or partial interruption of economic relations and of rail, sea, air, postal, telegraphic, radio, and other means of communication, and the severance of diplomatic relations.

"Article 42

"Should the Security Council consider that measures provided for in Article 41 would be inadequate or have proved to be inadequate, it may take such action by air, sea, or land forces as may be necessary to maintain or restore international peace and security. Such action may include demonstrations, blockade, and other operations by air, sea, or land forces of Members of the United Nations. . . .

"Article 48

"1. The action required to carry out the decisions of the Security Council for the maintenance of international peace and security shall be taken by all the Members of the United Nations or by some of them, as the Security Council may determine. . . .

"Article 51

"Nothing in the present Charter shall impair the inherent right of individual or collective self-defense if an armed attack occurs against a Member of the United Nations, until the Security Council has taken the measures necessary to maintain international peace and security. Measures taken by Members in the exercise of this right of self-defense shall be immediately reported to the Security Council and shall not in any way affect the authority and responsibility of the Security Council under the present Charter to take at any time such action as it deems necessary in order to maintain or restore international peace and security.

"Chapter VIII
"REGIONAL ARRANGEMENTS

"Article 52

"1. Nothing in the present Charter precludes the existence of regional arrangements or agencies for dealing with such matters relating to the maintenance of international peace and security as are appropriate for regional action, provided that such arrangements or agencies and their activities are consistent with the Purposes and Principles of the United Nations. . . .

"Chapter X
"THE ECONOMIC AND SOCIAL COUNCIL
"COMPOSITION
"*Article 61*
"1. The Economic and Social Council shall consist of eighteen Members of the United Nations elected by the General Assembly. . . .

"FUNCTIONS AND POWERS
"*Article 62*
"1. The Economic and Social Council may make or initiate studies and reports with respect to international economic, social, and cultural, educational, health, and related matters and may make recommendations with respect to any such matters to the General Assembly, to the Members of the United Nations, and to the specialized agencies concerned.

"2. It may make recommendations for the purpose of promoting respect for, and observance of, human rights and fundamental freedoms for all. . . .

"Chapter XII
"INTERNATIONAL TRUSTEESHIP SYSTEM
"*Article 75*
"The United Nations shall establish under its authority an international trusteeship system for the administration and supervision of such territories as may be placed thereunder by subsequent individual agreements. These territories are hereinafter referred to as trust territories.

"*Article 76*
"The basic objectives of the trusteeship system, . . . shall be:

a. to further international peace and security;

b. to promote the political, economic, social, and educational advancement of the inhabitants of the trust territories, and their progressive development towards self-government or independence as may be appropriate to the particular circumstances of each territory and its peoples and the freely expressed wishes of the peoples concerned, and as may be provided by the terms of each trusteeship agreement;

c. to encourage respect for human rights and for fundamental freedoms for all without distinction as to race, sex, language, or religion, and to encourage recognition of the interdependence of the peoples of the world; and

d. to ensure equal treatment in social, economic, and commercial matters for all Members of the United Nations and their nationals, and also equal treatment for the latter in the administration of justice, without prejudice to the attainment of the foregoing objectives and subject to the provisions of Article 80.

"*Article 77*
"1. The trusteeship system shall apply to such territories in the follow-

ing categories as may be placed thereunder by means of trusteeship agreements:

    a. territories now held under mandate;

    b. territories which may be detached from enemy states as a result of the Second World War; and

    c. territories voluntarily placed under the system by states responsible for their administration. . . .

"Chapter XIII
"THE TRUSTEESHIP COUNCIL

"COMPOSITION
"*Article 86*

"1. The Trusteeship Council shall consist of the following Members of the United Nations:

    a. those Members administering trust territories;

    b. such of those Members mentioned by name in Article 23 as are not administering trust territories; and

    c. as many other Members elected for three-year terms by the General Assembly as may be necessary to ensure that the total number of members of the Trusteeship Council is equally divided between those Members of the United Nations which administer trust territories and those which do not. . . .

"FUNCTIONS AND POWERS
"*Article 87*

"The General Assembly and, under its authority, the Trusteeship Council, in carrying out their functions, may:

    a. consider reports submitted by the administering authority;

    b. accept petitions and examine them in consultation with the administering authority;

    c. provide for periodic visits to the respective trust territories at times agreed upon with the administering authority; and

    d. take these and other actions in conformity with the terms of the trusteeship agreements.

"*Article 88*

"The Trusteeship Council shall formulate a questionnaire on the political, economic, social, and educational advancement of the inhabitants of each trust territory, and the administering authority for each trust territory within the competence of the General Assembly shall make an annual report to the General Assembly upon the basis of such questionnaire. . . .

"Chapter XIV
"THE INTERNATIONAL COURT OF JUSTICE

"*Article 92*

"The International Court of Justice shall be the principal judicial organ of the United Nations. It shall function in accordance with the annexed Statute, which is based upon the Statute of the Permanent Court of International Justice and forms an integral part of the present Charter.

"Article 93

"1. All Members of the United Nations are *ipso facto* parties to the Statute of the International Court of Justice. . . .

"Article 94

"1. Each Member of the United Nations undertakes to comply with the decision of the International Court of Justice in any case to which it is a party.

"2. If any party to a case fails to perform the obligations incumbent upon it under a judgment rendered by the Court, the other party may have recourse to the Security Council, which may, if it deems necessary, make recommendations or decide upon measures to be taken to give effect to the judgment. . . .

"Article 96

"1. The General Assembly or the Security Council may request the International Court of Justice to give an advisory opinion on any legal question.

"2. Other organs of the United Nations and specialized agencies, which may at any time be so authorized by the General Assembly, may also request advisory opinions of the Court on legal questions arising within the scope of their activities.

"Chapter XV

"THE SECRETARIAT

"Article 97

"The Secretariat shall comprise a Secretary-General and such staff as the Organization may require. The Secretary-General shall be appointed by the General Assembly upon the recommendation of the Security Council. He shall be the chief administrative officer of the Organization.

"Article 98

"The Secretary-General shall act in that capacity in all meetings of the General Assembly, of the Security Council, of the Economic and Social Council, and of the Trusteeship Council, and shall perform such other functions as are entrusted to him by these organs. The Secretary-General shall make an annual report to the General Assembly on the work of the Organization.

"Article 99

"The Secretary-General may bring to the attention of the Security Council any matter which in his opinion may threaten the maintenance of international peace and security.

"Article 100

"1. In the performance of their duties the Secretary-General and the staff shall not seek or receive instructions from any government or from any other authority external to the Organization. They shall refrain from any action which might reflect on their position as international officials responsible only to the Organization.

"2. Each Member of the United Nations undertakes to respect the exclusive international character of the responsibilities of the Secretary-General and the staff and not to seek to influence them in the discharge of their responsibilities. . . .

"Chapter XVIII
"AMENDMENTS

"Article 108

"Amendments to the present Charter shall come into force for all Members of the United Nations when they have been adopted by a vote of two thirds of the Members of the General Assembly and ratified in accordance with their respective constitutional processes by two thirds of the Members of the United Nations, including all the permanent members of the Security Council.

"Article 109

"1. A General Conference of the Members of the United Nations for the purpose of reviewing the present Charter may be held at a date and place to be fixed by a two-thirds vote of the members of the General Assembly and by a vote of any seven members of the Security Council. Each Member of the United Nations shall have one vote in the conference.

"2. Any alteration of the present Charter recommended by a two-thirds vote of the conference shall take effect when ratified in accordance with their respective constitutional processes by two-thirds of the Members of the United Nations including all the permanent members of the Security Council.

"3. If such a conference has not been held before the tenth annual session of the General Assembly following the coming into force of the present Charter, the proposal to call such a conference shall be placed on the agenda of that session of the General Assembly, and the conference shall be held if so decided by a majority vote of the members of the General Assembly and by a vote of any seven members of the Security Council. . . ."

POSTWAR POLICY:
COOPERATION AND THE "COLD WAR"

THE postwar world began on August 14, 1945, amid noisy and jubilant celebrations throughout the length and breadth of the land. No one at that moment of relief thought about the really serious problems which would confront the nation and the world during the following days and months. However, even to the more sober-minded, the prospects for the future seemed encouraging. Germany, Italy, and Japan lay prostrate. No more would the Fascist dictators, who had plunged the entire world into turmoil, threaten civilization. Chiang Kai-shek, who had been battling the Japanese for over eight years, was still the ruler of most of China. Stalin had signed the Yalta and Potsdam agreements, and Soviet leaders had often spoken of the possibility of a genuine cooperation between the East and the West. The Charter of the United Nations was being presented for ratification to the legislatures of the various nations which had attended the San Francisco Conference, and the people of a war-torn world hoped that this time the efforts of statesmen to form an international organization to keep the peace would succeed better than the League of Nations. That these hopes have not been realized has been due chiefly to the Soviet policy of expansion and to a revival of the old Communist line that the non-Communist world must destroy itself or be destroyed.

American foreign policy from the Japanese surrender to the time of this writing falls into four phases: a) attempted cooperation with the Soviet Union, from the end of the war against Japan to the announcement of the Truman Doctrine in the spring of 1947; b) containment of Soviet aggression in Europe, from 1947 to the end of the Truman Administration; c) conflict in the Far East, from 1945 to the end of the Truman Administration; and d) the Eisenhower administration, which has promised a more

vigorous policy toward the Soviet Union than the mere containment of Communist aggression.

During the first period, the United States made every attempt
at cooperation with the Soviet Union. Although there were many
points of friction between the two nations, as revealed in the
various foreign ministers' meetings, in their interpretation of
the provisions of the Yalta and Potsdam agreements, in attempting to set up a workable trusteeship in Korea, and in the United
Nations, the relationship between the U.S. and the U.S.S.R.
appeared to be rather friendly on the surface. Highly-placed
American officials did not proclaim the fact that there were really
serious differences between the two countries.

The second phase—the beginning of the containment policy—
was ushered in on March 12, 1947, when President Truman
asked Congress to authorize the sending of aid to Greece and
Turkey to assist those peoples who were "resisting attempted
subjugation by armed minorities or by outside countries." The
President did not then refer to Communism or the Soviet Union
by name, but no one mistook his meaning. The British had given
notice that they could no longer afford to retain their troops in
Greece, and the task of containing the forcible expansion of
Communism fell by default to the United States.

Congress appropriated $400,000,000 for this purpose and in
July, American troops and supplies were sent to Greece and
Turkey. The Truman Doctrine did not signify that the United
States had abandoned the possibility of settling differences with
the Soviet Union and its satellites by negotiation, but it was a
clear indication that this nation was willing to meet force with
force after it had become apparent that words alone were useless.

Several months following Truman's request for aid to Greece
and Turkey, Secretary of State George C. Marshall, in addressing
a commencement audience at Harvard University, put forward
an idea for tendering economic aid to Europe which, when implemented, became known as the Marshall Plan. The Communist
nations in Europe refused to accept the plan as outlined by
Marshall and formed the Cominform to combat it, but the
United States created the Economic Cooperation Administration
which furnished more than twelve billion dollars of aid to the
eighteen Western European nations which comprised the Organization for European Economic Cooperation. Military and economic aid, not only to Europe but to other areas of the world,

were continued after the ending of the ECA in January, 1952, by the Mutual Security Agency. American ECA and MSA aid not only strengthened the economy of the Western European nations, but it stimulated the forces of democracy against the rising tide of Communism, especially in France and Italy in the winter of 1947-48.

Even before the Marshall Plan had been enacted into law in April, 1948, the "Cold War" between the East and the West had increased in intensity. In February, 1948, Communist forces seized Czechoslovakia in a *coup d'état* which shocked the Western World. Although the Communists had used similar tactics in gaining control of Poland and the Balkan nations, the fate of those countries did not arouse the West as did the fall of Czechoslovakia. Eduard Beneš and Jan Masaryk, the Czech leaders, were widely known throughout the Western World; and the free nations remembered all too well that the rape of Czechoslovakia by the Nazis in 1939 preceded the outbreak of World War II by only a few months.

One reaction to this Communist coup in Czechoslovakia was the conclusion of the Brussels Pact in March, 1948, which bound Britain, France, and the Benelux powers[1] in a common defense agreement. The Soviet response to the actions taken by the Western nations in protecting themselves against the spread of Communism was to proclaim a blockade of Berlin in June, 1948. The Western powers were able to retain their foothold in Berlin as a result of the establishment of an airlift by the American and British air forces, which maintained a steady flow of supplies into the former German capital. Not until May, 1949, did the Russians finally lift the blockade.

The growing concern over Soviet aims stimulated the United States to form a defensive military alliance with the Atlantic community of nations to curb the spread of Soviet influence. In April, 1949, the North Atlantic Treaty was signed in Washington by Belgium, Canada, Denmark, France, Iceland, Italy, Luxembourg, the Netherlands, Norway, Portugal, the United Kingdom, and the United States. Greece and Turkey joined the North Atlantic Treaty Organization in 1952. This agreement, which was patterned after the Rio de Janeiro treaty of 1947 and which did not violate the Charter of the United Nations, bound the

[1] Belgium, the Netherlands, and Luxembourg.

signatory powers to consider an attack against any one nation an attack against all. Following the conclusion of the North Atlantic Pact, the United States implemented it by sending arms to its allies. It also sent General Dwight D. Eisenhower, in 1951, to head the military organization instituted by the North Atlantic Powers. After Eisenhower's resignation in the early summer of 1952 to return to the United States to become a candidate for the Presidency, General Matthew B. Ridgway went to Paris as his successor. In view of American tradition against entangling alliances, the conclusion of this treaty and subsequent actions by the United States indicated not only the gravity of the international situation but also the degree to which the American people had matured in accepting world-wide responsibilities.

One of the major objectives of American postwar policy has been to strengthen the United Nations as a safeguard to world peace. To those who expected miracles of this organization, the record of the last several years has been a vast disappointment. It should be pointed out, however, that this international organization has been confronted with problems which its founders did not anticipate. It was designed as a postwar, which meant post-treaty, organization. No one thought that it would or should have to cope with the problems that have arisen as a result of the disagreement among the major powers as to the terms of the peace treaties.

The major task of preventing aggression and keeping the peace was assigned to the Security Council by the Charter of the United Nations. It has failed to live up to expectations because of the rule that the five major powers, the permanent members of the Security Council, must concur before any action can be taken. The cleavage between the East and the West has resulted in the Soviet Union using its veto power to prevent the Security Council from exercising the authority intended for it by the founders of the United Nations.

No one in 1945 could have predicted that the veto power of any major nation would have kept the Security Council deadlocked most of the time. And no one realized that the General Assembly would, in some respects, become the most important organ of the U.N. It was intended to be mainly a debating body with powers only to recommend. Although the Charter has not been amended, the General Assembly has assumed more importance than had been anticipated.[2] In November, 1947, the General Assembly decided to create an Interim Committee to remain in session at times when the main body was in recess. Then, in November, 1950, the General Assembly adopted the Uniting for Peace resolution which provided that if the Security Council failed to act in preventing aggression, the General Assembly should consider the matter immediately and recommend action, including the use of force. This resolution by the General Assembly might well be considered the most important action taken by any organ of the United Nations since its inception. The Uniting for Peace resolution is important because no nation has a veto power and a two-thirds vote of the General Assembly could result in the same type of action which formerly had been reserved for the Security Council.

American foreign policy since 1945 has of necessity been directed toward easing the tensions that have developed since the war and in combatting the growing strength of Communism throughout the world. However, a very significant aspect of American policy and one that has great promise for the future has been the Point Four Program. As announced by President Truman in June, 1947, it is designed as a long-term policy to create better relations among the nations of the world by improving the health and economic status of peoples everywhere. The philosophy behind this program is that poverty, ignorance, and ill health breed wars. The United States has embarked on a plan to improve conditions in those parts of the world that have been willing to accept technical and scientific aid from us in order to raise their general standard of living. Although this program is small in terms of dollars appropriated, it may become one of the most important contributions that the United States could make toward world peace.

If American policy toward Europe appeared to follow a logical pattern, especially after the announcement of the Truman Doctrine, our Far Eastern policy was as confusing and contradictory as a Chinese puzzle.

When the war ended in August, 1945, there appeared to be no good reason why the Nationalists, who had withstood eight years of Japanese assault and almost twenty years of intermittent strife with the Chinese Communists, could not continue to govern

[2] John Foster Dulles pointed out the necessity for the revision of the Charter in a speech given before the American Bar Association in August, 1953.

China. Despite the surface appearance of the situation, however, the Nationalists lost territory, supplies, and troops to the Communist forces until Chiang Kai-shek was forced to resign from the Presidency of China in January, 1949. In December the Nationalists, having been driven from the Chinese mainland, moved to the Island of Formosa. In March, 1950, Chiang resumed his position as President of Nationalist China, and he and his forces were still on Formosa when this was written.

American policy toward China since 1945 has been 1) to maintain diplomatic relations with the Nationalists; 2) to attempt to bring about an understanding between Chiang Kai-shek and the Chinese Communists until 1947; 3) to send the Nationalists a limited amount of economic and military aid; and 4) with the other members of the United Nations, to wage an undeclared war against the Chinese Communists in Korea from the fall of 1950 until the truce was signed in the summer of 1953.

The numerous critics of American Far Eastern policy pointed out the inconsistency of attempting to contain Communism in Europe while making the effort to persuade Chiang to cooperate with Mao Tse-tung in China. These same critics have also wondered why, if we were supporting Chiang, we sent *some* aid, but obviously not enough to defeat the Communists. They argued that it would have been more logical to have sent no aid at all or to have sent enough to have accomplished whatever purposes we may have had in sending anything.

The State Department explanation as contained in its "White Paper" published in July, 1949, disclaimed responsibility for the fiasco in China. This volume pointed out that the Kuomintang was so corrupt and inefficient that it could not command the respect or the support of the Chinese masses. Dean Acheson stated that nothing short of an all out military effort by the United States could have stopped the Chinese Communists.

Our policy in China undoubtedly will be discussed by the man on the street and studied by scholars for many years. Until all the documentary material is available, no one will have a definitive answer as to the reasons for our policy toward China, or whether this nation could have prevented the Communists from seizing that vast area. However, on the basis of such evidence as was available when this was written, certain conclusions seem warranted: 1) American policy toward the Far East, and particularly toward China, was influenced to some degree by pro-Communist sympathizers;[3] 2) our policy of attempting to achieve a coalition government composed of the Nationalists and the Communists, of placing an arms embargo against Chiang Kai-shek's forces in 1946, and of giving only a limited amount of economic aid to the Nationalists strengthened the position of Mao Tse-tung; and 3) American policy coupled with the ineptness of the Nationalists to solve their own problems were major factors contributing to the ultimate success of the Communists in their ultimate victory in China.

The loss of China to the Communists was a severe blow to the West, but the full significance of that event did not become apparent until the early summer of 1950, when the forces of the North Koreans launched an attack against the Republic of Korea.

On June 25, 1950, the day of the attack, the Security Council of the United Nations (with the Soviet member temporarily absent) passed a resolution condemning this act of Communist aggression and requested the North Koreans to withdraw to the 38th Parallel. On the same day, the United States announced that it would furnish military supplies to Korea in compliance with the U.N. resolution. On June 27 the President ordered American air and sea forces in the area to aid the South Koreans. That night, the Security Council adopted a U.S. sponsored resolution requesting all U.N. members to use armed force in repelling the aggressor.[4] Within a short time it became evident that land forces would also be needed, and Truman committed our full strength then available to the defense of the victims of this first act of armed Communist aggression since the end of the war. For the first year, the undeclared war by the North Koreans and later the Chinese Communists against the forces of the United Nations raged up and down the peninsula. During the last two years of the conflict, from 1951 to 1953, truce talks were carried out intermittently while the fighting continued on a reduced scale along a battle line roughly along the 38th Parallel.

The fall of China, and the Korean War, led the United States to strengthen its Pacific defenses against the possibility of further Communist aggression. A peace treaty with Japan was signed in September, 1951, which allowed the United States to maintain a garrison in that important island nation off the coast of

[3] See *Institute of Pacific Relations,* 82d Cong., 2d Sess., Senate Report No. 2050, (Washington, 1952).

[4] Sixteen members of the U.N., including the United States, sent forces to Korea.

Asia; and at almost the same time the United States signed a mutual defense pact with Australia and New Zealand patterned somewhat along the lines of the North Atlantic Pact. These agreements, along with a similar pact with the Philippine Republic, strengthened the defenses of the United States and its allies in the Pacific. However, American diplomats still had the task of attempting to cope with the problem of preventing Communist expansion into the densely-populated and vast regions of southern Asia extending all the way from Indochina to Turkey, composed of a number of nations not tied to the United States or its allies by mutual security agreements.

The inauguration of President Dwight D. Eisenhower, on January 20, 1953, marked the beginning of the most recent phase in American foreign policy. The conduct of the Korean War, which had been a major issue during the presidential election campaign in 1952, had first priority of all the foreign problems confronting the newly-elected President. Although Eisenhower issued an order, shortly after his inauguration, withdrawing the Seventh Fleet from the waters between Formosa and China, which some persons interpreted as the beginning of a more aggressive Far Eastern policy, the United States took no further action in that area. In continuing to support the concept of a limited war in Korea, the American President rejected the MacArthur thesis that the United Nations could win the war by extending it. After many stormy sessions with the Communist negotiators in Korea, the United Nations signed a truce on July 27, 1953. A conference in Geneva to draft a Korean peace treaty was being held in May, 1954, when this was written.

The Eisenhower Administration continued to give economic aid to the French fighting Communism in Indochina. However, the fall of the French fortress Dien Bien Phu in May, 1954, spurred the United States to try to conclude some type of security pact to prevent the further spread of Communism in Southeast Asia.

Eisenhower's policy toward Europe was quite similar to that which the United States had followed since 1947. Having been a former commander of the North Atlantic Treaty Organization forces in Europe, the American President urged continued American economic and military aid throughout the world, most of which, however, was destined for Western Europe. Congress responded by increasing the amount of our foreign aid program in 1953 over that appropriated in 1952. The Eisenhower Administration acted to bolster the defenses of Western Europe by signing a pact with Spain, in the fall of 1953, which allowed the United States to build and maintain military bases in that strategically-located nation protected by the Pyrenees Mountains, in return for economic aid to be furnished to Generalissimo Franco's government. The United States continued to urge the unification of Germany by democratic processes and the conclusion of a peace treaty with Austria.

The major preoccupation of the American Government and the people in 1954 was still the Cold War. Despite the death of Stalin in March, 1953, the Soviet Union continued as the greatest menace to the peace and security of the entire free world. Although the United States and its allies have taken great strides toward building up their economic and military strength, every sign pointed to a long period of tension between the West and the East.

1. *Baruch Atomic Energy Proposal*

The atomic bombs dropped on Hiroshima and Nagasaki not only served to bring the war against Japan to a sudden halt, but they were also an ominous warning that man now had the power to destroy himself in a very literal sense, unless he possessed enough intelligence and good will to avoid this catastrophe.

The United States, which alone possessed the bomb at the end of the war, took the lead in attempting to persuade the United Nations to agree to a plan which would forever outlaw the use of this dreadful weapon. The American proposal—presented to the United Nations on June 14, 1946, by Bernard Baruch—called for the creation of an international agency which would have exclusive control over the manufacture and use of atomic energy, as well as the power to inspect plants throughout the world engaged in the processing of fissionable material. This proposal was not accepted. The Soviet Union suggested a treaty outlawing the use of atomic weapons, but they rejected the principle of international inspection which was at the heart of the American proposal.[5]

[5] *The International Control of Atomic Energy,* Dept. of State, Pub. 2702, (Washington), pp. 138-47.

"MY FELLOW MEMBERS of the UNITED NATIONS ATOMIC ENERGY COMMISSION,

and

"MY FELLOW CITIZENS of the WORLD:

"We are here to make a choice between the quick and the dead.

"That is our business.

"Behind the black portent of the new atomic age lies a hope which, seized upon with faith, can work our salvation. If we fail, then we have damned every man to be the slave of Fear. Let us not deceive ourselves: We must elect World Peace or World Destruction.

"Science has torn from nature a secret so vast in its potentialities that our minds cower from the terror it creates. Yet terror is not enough to inhibit the use of the atomic bomb. The terror created by weapons has never stopped man from employing them. For each new weapon a defense has been produced, in time. But now we face a condition in which adequate defense does not exist.

"Science, which gave us this dread power, shows that it *can* be made a giant help to humanity, but science does *not* show us how to prevent its baleful use. So we have been appointed to obviate that peril by finding a meeting of the minds and the hearts of our peoples. Only in the will of mankind lies the answer.

"It is to express this will and make it effective that we have been assembled. We must provide the mechanism to assure that atomic energy is used for peaceful purposes and preclude its use in war. . . .

"In that desire the United States shares ardently and hopefully. The search of science for the absolute weapon has reached fruition in this country. But she stands ready to proscribe and destroy this instrument—to lift its use from death to life—if the world will join in a pact to that end. . . .

"The United States proposes the creation of an International Atomic Development Authority, to which should be entrusted all phases of the development and use of atomic energy, starting with the raw material and including—

"1. Managerial control or ownership of all atomic-energy activities potentially dangerous to world security.

"2. Power to control, inspect, and license all other atomic activities.

"3. The duty of fostering the beneficial uses of atomic energy.

"4. Research and development responsibilities of an affirmative character intended to put the Authority in the forefront of atomic knowledge and thus to enable it to comprehend, and therefore to detect, misuse of atomic energy. To be affective, the Authority must itself be the world's leader in the field of atomic knowledge and development and thus supplement its legal authority with the great power inherent in possession of leadership in knowledge.

"I offer this as a basis for beginning our discussion.

"But I think the peoples we serve would not believe—and without faith nothing counts—that a treaty, merely outlawing possession or use of the atomic bomb, constitutes effective fulfillment of the instructions to this Commission. Previous failures have been recorded in trying the method of simple renunciation, unsupported by effective guaranties of security and armament limitation. No one would have faith in that approach alone. . . .

"When an adequate system for control of atomic energy, including the renunciation of the bomb as a weapon, has been agreed upon and put into effective operation and condign punishments set up for violations of the rules of control which are to be stigmatized as international crimes, we propose that—

"1. Manufacture of atomic bombs shall stop;

"2. Existing bombs shall be disposed of pursuant to the terms of the treaty, and

"3. The Authority shall be in possession of full information as to the know-how for the production of atomic energy.

"Let me repeat, so as to avoid misunderstanding: my country is ready to make its full contribution toward the end we seek, subject, of course, to our constitutional processes, and to an adequate system of control becoming fully effective, as we finally work it out.

"Now as to violations: in the agreement, penalties of as serious a nature as the nations may wish and as immediate and certain in their execution as possible, should be fixed for:

"1. Illegal possession or use of an atomic bomb;

"2. Illegal possession, or separation, of atomic material suitable for use in an atomic bomb;

"3. Seizure of any plant or other property belonging to or licensed by the Authority;

"4. Wilful interference with the activities of the Authority;

"5. Creation or operation of dangerous projects in a manner contrary to, or in the absence of, a license granted by the international control body.

"It would be a deception, to which I am unwilling to lend myself, were I not to say to you and to our peoples, that the matter of punishment lies at the very heart of our present security system. It might as well be admitted, here and now, that the subject goes straight to the veto power contained in the Charter of the United Nations so far as it relates to the field of atomic energy. The Charter permits penalization only by concurrence of each of the five great powers—Union of Soviet Socialist Republics, the United Kingdom, China, France and the United States.

"I want to make very plain that I am concerned here with the veto power only as it affects this particular problem. There must be no veto to protect those who violate their solemn agreements not to develop or use atomic energy for destructive purposes.

"The bomb does not wait upon debate. To delay may be to die. The time between violation and preventive action or punishment would be all too short for extended discussion as to the course to be followed. . . ."

2. *United States' Policy toward Germany, 1946*

On September 6, 1946, Secretary of State James F. Byrnes delivered an address to the German people in Stuttgart, in which he outlined the plans and policies of the United States toward the German peoples.[6]

"I have come to Germany to learn at first hand the problems involved in the reconstruction of Germany and to discuss with our representatives the views of the United States Government as to some of the problems confronting us.

"We in the United States have given considerable time and attention to these problems because upon their proper solution will depend not only the future well-being of Germany but the future well-being of Europe.

"We have learned, whether we like it or not, that we live in one world, from which world we cannot isolate ourselves. We have learned that peace and well-being are indivisible and that our peace and well-being cannot be purchased at the price of the peace or the well-being of any other country.

"I hope that the German people will never again make the mistake of believing that because the American people are peace-loving they will sit back hoping for peace if any nation uses force or the threat of force to acquire dominion over other peoples and other governments.

"In 1917 the United States was forced into the first World War. After that war we refused to join the League of Nations. We thought we could stay out of Europe's wars, and we lost interest in the affairs of Europe. That did not keep us from being forced into a second world war.

"We will not again make that mistake. We intend to continue our interests in the affairs of Europe and of the world. . . .

"The American people want peace. They have long since ceased to talk of a hard or a soft peace for Germany. This never has been the real issue. What we want is a lasting peace. We will oppose soft measures which invite the breaking of the peace.

"In agreeing at Potsdam that Germany should be disarmed and demilitarized and in proposing that the four major powers should by treaty jointly undertake to see that Germany is kept disarmed and demilitarized for a generation, the United States was not unmindful of the responsibility resting upon it and its major Allies to maintain and enforce peace under the law.

[6] *Restatement of U.S. Policy on Germany,* Dept. of State, Eur. Ser., 13, (Washington, 1946).

"Freedom from militarism will give the German people the opportunity, if they will but seize it, to apply their great energies and abilities to the works of peace. It will give them the opportunity to show themselves worthy of the respect and friendship of peace-loving nations, and in time, to take an honorable place among the members of the United Nations.

"It is not in the interest of the German people or in the interest of world peace that Germany should become a pawn or a partner in a military struggle for power between the East and the West.

"German militarism and Nazism have devastated twice in our generation the lands of Germany's neighbors. It is fair and just that Germany should do her part to repair that devastation. Most of the victims of Nazi aggression were before the war less well off than Germany. They should not be expected by Germany to bear, unaided, the major costs of Nazi aggression. . . .

"The basis of the Potsdam Agreement was that, as part of a combined program of demilitarization and reparations, Germany's war potential should be reduced by elimination and removal of her war industries and the reduction and removal of heavy industrial plants. It was contemplated this should be done to the point that Germany would be left with levels of industry capable of maintaining in Germany average European living standards without assistance from other countries. . . .

". . . The levels of industry fixed are only sufficient to enable the German people to become self-supporting and to maintain living standards approximating the average European living conditions.

"That principle involves serious hardships for the German people, but it only requires them to share the hardships which Nazi aggression imposed on the average European.

"The German people were not denied, however, the possibility of improving their lot by hard work over the years. . . .

"That was the principle of reparations to which President Truman agreed at Potsdam. And the United States will not agree to the taking from Germany of greater reparations than was provided by the Potsdam Agreement.

"The carrying out of the Potsdam Agreement has, however, been obstructed by the failure of the Allied Control Council to take the necessary steps to enable the German economy to function as an economic unit. Essential central German administrative departments have not been established, although they are expressly required by the Potsdam Agreement.

"The equitable distribution of essential commodities between the several zones so as to produce a balanced economy throughout Germany and reduce the need for imports has not been arranged, although that too is expressly required by the Potsdam Agreement. . . .

"The time has come when the zonal boundaries should be regarded as defining only the areas to be occupied for security purposes by the armed forces of the occupying powers and not as self-contained economic or political units. . . .

"So far only the British Government has agreed to let its zone participate. We deeply appreciate their cooperation. Of course, this policy of unification is not intended to exclude the governments not now willing to join. The unification will be open to them at any time they wish to join. . . .

"So far as many vital questions are concerned, the Control Council is neither governing Germany nor allowing Germany to govern itself. . . .

"The Potsdam Agreement, concluded only a few months after the surrender, bound the occupying powers to restore local self-government and to introduce elective and representative principles into the regional, provincial, and state administration as rapidly as was consistent with military security and the purposes of the military occupation.

"The principal purposes of the military occupation were and are to demilitarize and de-Nazify Germany but not to raise artificial barriers to the efforts of the German people to resume their peace-time economic life. . . .

"It is the view of the American Government that the German people throughout Germany, under proper safeguards, should now be given the primary responsibility for the running of their own affairs.

"More than a year has passed since hostilities ceased. The millions of German people should not be forced to live in doubt as to their fate. It is the view of the American Government that the Allies should, without delay, make clear to the German people the essential terms of the peace settlement which they expect the German people to accept and observe. . . .

". . . Unfortunately our proposal for a treaty was not agreed to.

"Security forces will probably have to remain in Germany for a long period. I want no misunderstanding. We will not shirk our duty. We are not withdrawing. We are staying here. As long as there is an occupation army in Germany, American armed forces will be part of that occupation army. . . .

"While we shall insist that Germany observe the principles of peace, good-neighborliness, and humanity, we do not want Germany to become the satellite of any other power or powers or to live under a dictatorship, foreign or domestic. The American people hope to see peaceful, democratic Germans become and remain free and independent. . . .

"The Soviets and the Poles suffered greatly at the hands of Hitler's invading armies. As a result of the agreement at Yalta, Poland ceded to the Soviet Union territory east of the Curzon Line. Because of this, Poland asked for revision of her northern and western frontiers. The United States will support a revision of these frontiers in Poland's favor. However, the extent of the area to be ceded to Poland must be determined when the final settlement is agreed upon.

"The United States does not feel that it can deny to France, which has been invaded three times by Germany in 70 years, its claim to the Saar territory, whose economy has long been closely linked with France. Of course, if the Saar territory is integrated with France she should readjust her reparation claims against Germany.

"Except as here indicated, the United States will not support any encroachment on territory which is indisputably German or any division of Germany which is not genuinely desired by the people concerned. So far as the United States is aware the people of the Ruhr and the Rhineland desire to remain united with the rest of Germany. And the United States is not going to oppose their desire. . . .

"The United States cannot relieve Germany from the hardships inflicted upon her by the war her leaders started. But the United States has no desire to increase those hardships or to deny the German people an opportunity to work their way out of those hardships so long as they respect human freedom and follow the paths of peace.

"The American people want to return the government of Germany to the German people. The American people want to help the German people to win their way back to an honorable place among the free and peace-loving nations of the world."

3. United States Trusteeship of Former Japanese Mandated Islands

The only territories which the United States desired to control at the end of the war were the Pacific Islands formerly held by Japan under a mandate from the League of Nations. These island groups, the Marshalls, the Marianas, and the Carolines, had been the scene of many bloody battles during the war, and the American people, for security reasons, were reluctant to relinquish these islands which had cost them so much in blood and treasure.

On April 2, 1947, the Security Council of the United Nations agreed to designate the United States as the power to hold these islands in trust for the United Nations. The following is part of a statement presented to the Security Council by the United States representative on February 26, 1947, pointing out our reasons for desiring that particular trust.[7]

"Mr. President, the United States, like other nations adhering to the United Nations Declaration of January 1, 1942, subscribed to the Atlantic Charter principle that 'their countries seek no aggrandizement, territorial or other.'

"It was for the purpose of making clear that the United States adheres

[7] *Draft Trusteeship Agreement for the Japanese Mandated Islands,* Dept. of State, Far East. Ser., 20, (Washington, 1947).

unswervingly to this principle that the President of the United States on November 6, 1946, declared our intentions regarding Pacific islands whose control by Japan enabled her to attack the United States. The President said:

" 'The United States is prepared to place under trusteeship, with the United States as the administering authority, the Japanese Mandated Islands and any Japanese islands for which it assumes responsibility as a result of the second World War. In so far as the Japanese Mandated Islands are concerned, this Government is transmitting for information to the other members of the Security Council (Australia, Brazil, China, Egypt, France, Mexico, the Netherlands, Poland, the Union of Soviet Socialist Republics, and the United Kingdom) and to New Zealand and the Philippines a draft of a strategic area trusteeship agreement which sets forth the terms upon which this Government is prepared to place those islands under trusteeship. At an early date we plan to submit this draft agreement formally to the Security Council for its approval.'

"Final disposition of islands belonging to Japan must, of course, await the peace settlement with Japan. The draft trusteeship agreement submitted to the Security Council for its approval relates only to the former Japanese Mandated Islands, which never belonged to Japan but were a part of the League of Nations mandate system. . . .

"The Japanese Mandated Islands—the Marshalls, Marianas, and Carolines—consist of some 98 islands and island clusters with a total land mass of only 846 square miles, a total population of only about 48,000 native inhabitants, and negligible indigenous economic resources.

"The tremendous strategic value of the Mandated Islands to Japan is evident, however, in the way these islands were used in carrying out its basic plan of aggression. Before Japan entered the war on December 7, 1941, she had established fortified positions, naval bases, and air bases in the islands of the Japanese Mandates. As a whole, the islands formed a deep, well-defended barrier between the United States and Guam, the Philippines, and its British and Dutch Allies in the Far East. . . .

"Tens of thousands of American lives, vast expeditures of treasure, and years of bitter fighting were necessary to drive the Japanese aggressors back from these islands. These islands constitute an integrated strategic physical complex vital to the security of the United States.

"The American people are firmly resolved that this area shall never again be used as a springboard for aggression against the United States or any other member of the United Nations.

"Most of the strategically important areas of the world, including those in the Pacific, are at present under the exclusive sovereignty of various of the larger nations. The United States, however, is proposing trusteeship rather than annexation as the basis for its administration of these highly strategic islands.

"In undertaking to place under trusteeship a territory of such strategic importance to the United States as these islands, the United States is expressing its faith in the United Nations. . . .

"In conformity with the provisions of the Charter for strategic areas the trust territory will contain bases. Many atolls in the territory have potential value as base sites or as anchorages. Few such sites, however, are being developed and maintained at present.

"The United States will administer this strategic trust territory in accordance with the provisions of the Charter. In particular, the United States will administer the territory in accordance with the obligations contained in article 2, paragraph 4, to 'refrain . . . from the threat or use of force against the territorial integrity or political independence of any state, or in any other manner inconsistent with the Purposes of the United Nations.' . . .

"The United States draft agreement provides that the administering authority may from time to time specify certain areas as closed for security reasons. This provision will not, of course, prejudice the full application to the entire trust territory of all international control and inspection measures that become part of a system of international control of atomic energy, other weapons of mass destruction, and conventional armaments.

"The United States is willing to submit to international supervision as provided in the agreement, the political, economic, social, and educational development of the inhabitants of the trust territory. It is equally willing to submit military and naval installations to whatever degree of supervision and control may be provided by agreements for the international control of armaments and armed forces.

"In preparing this draft trusteeship agreement the Government of the United States bore constantly in mind article 73 of the Charter:

" 'Members of the United Nations which have or assume responsibilities for the administration of territories whose peoples have not yet attained a full measure of self-government recognize the principle that the interests of the inhabitants of these territories are paramount, and accept as a sacred trust the obligation to promote to the utmost, within the system of international peace and security established by the present Charter, the well-being of the inhabitants.'

"The United States Government believes that the draft trusteeship agreement now before you conforms fully with this principle in its provisions for the political, economic, social, and educational advancement of the inhabitants of the trust territory. . . ."

4. *Treaty of Peace with Rumania, 1947*

Much of the tension which has developed between the United States and the Soviet Union during the last few years, has arisen because of their different interpretation of the war and postwar agreements. The Treaty of peace with Rumania, concluded in 1947, was a case in point. This agreement, which was quite similar to those signed with the other Balkan states, stipulated that Rumania would guarantee the fundamental human rights to its inhabitants. The treaty also stated that Rumania would abolish Fascist-type organizations hostile to the Soviet Union.

Rumania, like the other Communist-dominated nations behind the Iron Curtain, has suppressed human rights and freedom in much the same way that the Soviet Union has acted against its own citizens. The United States, as a signatory to the treaty, has lodged repeated protests to the effect that Rumania has violated the treaty in this respect. The Communist regime has claimed that it is abiding by the terms of the treaty in moving only to stamp out Fascist-type groups hostile to the Soviet Union, which, according to its interpretation, includes all non-Communist groups. The following are excerpts from the Treaty with Rumania.[8]

"SECTION I
"*Article 3*
"1. Roumania shall take all measures necessary to secure to all persons under Roumanian jurisdiction, without distinction as to race, sex, language or religion, the enjoyment of human rights and of the fundamental freedoms, including freedom of expression, of press and publication, of religious worship, of political opinion and of public meeting.

"2. Roumania further undertakes that the laws in force in Roumania shall not, either in their content or in their application, discriminate or entail any discrimination between persons of Roumanian nationality on the ground of their race, sex, language or religion, whether in reference to their persons, property, business, professional or financial interests, status, political or civil rights or any other matter.

"*Article 4*
"Roumania, which in accordance with the Armistice Agreement has taken measures to set free, irrespective of citizenship and nationality, all persons held in confinement on account of their activities in favour of, or because of their sympathies with, the United Nations or because of their racial origin, and to repeal discriminatory legislation and restrictions imposed thereunder, shall complete these measures and shall in future not take any measures or enact any laws which would be incompatible with the purposes set forth in this Article.

[8] *Treaty of Peace With Roumania,* Dept. of State, Treat. and other Inter. Acts Ser., 1649, (Washington, 1947).

"Article 5

"Roumania, which in accordance with the Armistice Agreement has taken measures for dissolving all organizations of a Fascist type on Roumanian territory, whether political, military or para-military, as well as other organizations conducting propaganda hostile to the Soviet Union or to any of the other United Nations, shall not permit in future the existence and activities of organizations of that nature which have as their aim denial to the people of their democratic rights. . . ."

5. *The Containment Policy, 1947—1953*

From VJ Day until the announcement of the Truman Doctrine, American policy toward the Soviet Union was based on the assumption that a genuine meeting of the minds between the Communists and non-Communists was possible. It had become increasingly clear to Secretaries Stettinius, Byrnes, and Marshall, during that period in their dealings with the Russians relative to Poland, the Balkan states, Iran, and in the United Nations, that Soviet objectives were very different from what we had hoped and thought they were when the major wartime agreements were signed. The realization came slowly to American statesmen that even the words used in the Yalta and Potsdam agreements meant one thing to the Russians and another thing to us. For instance, the words "friendly," "democratic," and "representative," as used in the Yalta and Potsdam accords, meant "Communist" to the Russians judging by their policies toward Poland, and the Balkan states. It is hardly necessary to suggest that those words were not so defined by the Americans who signed those agreements.

In view of the growing realization of the true nature of Soviet policy, the United States, in sending aid to Greece and Turkey, in bolstering the economy of Western Europe, in signing the North Atlantic Pact, adopted what has become known as the Containment Policy.

The individual who in a very real sense was the architect of the Containment Policy was George F. Kennan. Kennan, a long-time career diplomat and an acknowledged expert on Soviet affairs, has in recent years held such responsible positions as Counselor of our Embassy in Moscow, head of the Policy Planning Committee of the Department of State, and American Ambassador to the Soviet Union.

His concept of the nature of Soviet foreign policy, as well as his suggestions as to our policy in order to meet the Soviet threat, appeared in an article in *Foreign Affairs* in July, 1947, signed "X." Not until later was it revealed that Kennan was the author of that article, from which excerpts are quoted below.[9]

"The political personality of Soviet power as we know it today is the product of ideology and circumstances: ideology inherited by the present Soviet leaders from the movement in which they had their political origin, and circumstances of the power which they now have exercised for nearly three decades in Russia. There can be few tasks of psychological analysis more difficult than to try to trace the interaction of these two forces and the relative rôle of each in the determination of official Soviet conduct. Yet the attempt must be made if that conduct is to be understood and effectively countered.

"It is difficult to summarize the set of ideological concepts with which the Soviet leaders came into power. Marxian ideology, in its Russian-Communist projection, has always been in process of subtle evolution. The materials on which it bases itself are extensive and complex. But the outstanding features of Communist thought as it existed in 1916 may perhaps be summarized as follows: (a) that the central factor in the life of man, the factor which determines the character of public life and the 'physiognomy of society,' is the system by which material goods are produced and exchanged; (b) that the capitalist system of production is a nefarious one which inevitably leads to the exploitation of the working class by the capital-owning class and is incapable of developing adequately the economic resources of society or of distributing fairly the material goods produced by human labor; (c) that capitalism contains the seeds of its own destruction and must, in view of the inability of the capital-owning class to adjust itself to economic change, result eventually and inescapably in a revolutionary transfer of power to the working class; and (d) that imperialism, the final phase of capitalism, leads directly to war and revolution.

"The rest may be outlined in Lenin's own words: 'Unevenness of economic and political development is the inflexible law of capitalism. It follows from this that the victory of Socialism must come originally in a few capitalist countries or even in a single capitalist country. The victorious proletariat of that country, having expropriated the capitalists and having organized Socialist production at home, would rise against the remaining capitalist world, drawing to itself in the process the oppressed classes of other countries.' It must be noted that there was no assumption that capitalism would

[9] X, "The Sources of Soviet Conduct," *Foreign Affairs,* Vol. 25, (July, 1947) pp. 566-82. Possibly because of the intense criticism of the Containment policy, Kennan was permitted to resign from the government during the early months of the Eisenhower Administration.

perish without proletarian revolution. A final push was needed from a revolutionary proletariat movement in order to tip over the tottering structure. But it was regarded as inevitable that sooner or later that push be given. . . .

"The circumstances of the immediate post-revolutionary period—the existence in Russia of civil war and foreign intervention, together with the obvious fact that the Communists represented only a tiny minority of the Russian people—made the establishment of dictatorial power a necessity. The experiment with 'war Communism' and the abrupt attempt to eliminate private production and trade had unfortunate economic consequences and caused further bitterness against the new revolutionary régime. While the temporary relaxation of the effort to communize Russia, represented by the New Economic Policy, alleviated some of this economic distress and thereby served its purpose, it also made it evident that the 'capitalistic sector of society' was still prepared to profit at once from any relaxation of governmental pressure, and would, if permitted to continue to exist, always constitute a powerful opposing element to the Soviet régime and a serious rival for influence in the country. Somewhat the same situation prevailed with respect to the individual peasant who, in his own small way, was also a private producer.

"Lenin, had he lived, might have proved a great enough man to reconcile these conflicting forces to the ultimate benefit of Russian society, though this is questionable. But be that as it may, Stalin, and those whom he led in the struggle for succession to Lenin's position of leadership, were not the men to tolerate rival political forces in the sphere of power which they coveted. Their sense of insecurity was too great. Their particular brand of fanaticism, unmodified by any of the Anglo-Saxon traditions of compromise, was too fierce and too jealous to envisage any permanent sharing of power. From the Russian-Asiatic world out of which they had emerged they carried with them a skepticism as to the possibilities of permanent and peaceful coexistence of rival forces. Easily persuaded of their own doctrinaire 'rightness' they insisted on the submission or destruction of all competing power. Outside of the Communist Party, Russian society was to have no rigidity. There were to be no forms of collective human activity or association which would not be dominated by the Party. No other force in Russian society was to be permitted to achieve vitality or integrity. Only the Party was to have structure. All else was to be an amorphous mass.

"And within the Party the same principle was to apply. The mass of Party members might go through the motions of election, deliberation, decision and action; but in these motions they were to be animated not by their own individual wills but by the awesome breath of the Party leadership and the overbrooding presence of 'the word.' . . .

"Now the outstanding circumstance concerning the Soviet régime is that down to the present day this process of political consolidation has never been completed and the men in the Kremlin have continued to be predominantly absorbed with the struggle to secure and make absolute the power which they seized in November, 1917. They have endeavored to secure it primarily against forces at home, within Soviet society itself. But they have also endeavored to secure it against the outside world. For ideology, as we have seen, taught them that the ouside world was hostile and that it was their duty eventually to overthrow the political forces beyond their borders. The powerful hands of Russian history and tradition reached up to sustain them in this feeling. Finally, their own aggressive intransigence with respect to the outside world began to find its own reaction; and they were soon forced, to use another Gibbonesque phrase, 'to chastise the contumacy' which they themselves had provoked. It is an undeniable privilege of every man to prove himself right in the thesis that the world is his enemy; for if he reiterates it frequently enough and makes it the background of his conduct he is bound eventually to be right. . . .

"Now the maintenance of this pattern of Soviet power, namely, the pursuit of unlimited authority domestically, accompanied by the cultivation of the semi-myth of implacable foreign hostility, has gone far to shape the actual machinery of Soviet power as we know it today. Internal organs of administration which did not serve this purpose withered on the vine. Organs which did serve this purpose became vastly swollen. The security of Soviet power came to rest on the iron discipline of the Party, on the severity and ubiquity of the secret police, and on the uncompromising economic monopolism of the state. The 'organs of suppression,' in which the Soviet leaders had sought security from rival forces, became in large measure the masters of those whom they were designed to serve. Today the major part of the structure of Soviet power is committed to the perfection of the dictatorship and to the maintenance of the concept of Russia as in a state of siege, with the enemy lowering beyond the walls. And the millions of human beings who form that part of the structure of power must defend at all costs this concept of Russia's position, for without it they are themselves superfluous.

"As things stand today, the rulers can no longer dream of parting with these organs of suppression. The quest for absolute power, pursued now for nearly three decades with a ruthlessness unparalleled (in scope at least) in modern times, has again produced internally, as it did externally, its own reaction. The excesses of the police apparatus have fanned the potential opposition to the régime into something far greater and more dangerous than it could have been before those excesses began.

"But least of all can the rulers dispense with the fiction by which the maintenance of dictatorial power has been defended. For this fiction has been canonized in Soviet philosophy by the excesses already committed in its name; and it is now anchored in the Soviet structure of thought by bonds far greater than those of mere ideology.

"II

"So much for the historical background. What does it spell in terms of the political personality of Soviet power as we know it today?

"Of the original ideology, nothing has been officially junked. Belief is maintained in the basic badness of capitalism, in the inevitability of its destruction, in the obligation of the proletariat to assist in that destruction and to take power into its own hands. But stress has come to be laid primarily on those concepts which relate most specifically to the Soviet régime itself: to its position as the sole truly Socialist régime in a dark and misguided world, and to the relationships of power within it.

"The first of these concepts is that of the innate antagonism between capitalism and Socialism. We have seen how deeply that concept has become imbedded in foundations of Soviet power. It has profound implications for Russia's conduct as a member of international society. It means that there can never be on Moscow's side any sincere assumption of a community of aims between the Soviet Union and powers which are regarded as capitalist. It must invariably be assumed in Moscow that the aims of the capitalist world are antagonistic to the Soviet régime, and therefore to the interests of the peoples it controls. If the Soviet Government occasionally sets its signature to documents which would indicate the contrary, this is to be regarded as a tactical manoeuvre permissible in dealing with the enemy (who is without honor) and should be taken in the spirit of *caveat emptor*. Basically, the antagonism remains. It is postulated. And from it flow many of the phenomena which we find disturbing in the Kremlin's conduct of foreign policy: the secretiveness, the lack of frankness, the duplicity, the wary suspiciousness, and the basic unfriendliness of purpose. These phenomena are there to stay, for the foreseeable future. There can be variations of degree and of emphasis. When there is something the Russians want from us, one or the other of these features of their policy may be thrust temporarily into the background; and when that happens there will always be Americans who will leap forward with gleeful announcements that 'the Russians have changed,' and some who will even try to take credit for having brought about such 'changes.' But we should not be misled by tactical manoeuvres. These characteristics of Soviet policy, like the postulate from which they flow, are basic to the internal nature of Soviet power, and will be with us, whether in the foreground or the background, until the internal nature of Soviet power is changed.

"This means that we are going to continue for a long time to find the Russians difficult to deal with. It does not mean that they should be considered as embarked upon a do-or-die program to overthrow our society by a given date. The theory of the inevitability of the eventual fall of capitalism has the fortunate connotation that there is no hurry about it. The forces of progress can take their time in preparing the final *coup de grâce*. Meanwhile, what is vital is that the 'Socialist fatherland'—that oasis of power which has been already won for Socialism in the person of the Soviet Union—should be cherished and defended by all good Communists at home and abroad, its fortunes promoted, its enemies badgered and confounded. The promotion of premature, 'adventuristic' revolutionary projects abroad which might embarrass Soviet power in any way would be inexcusable, even a counter-revolutionary act. The cause of Socialism is the support and promotion of Soviet power, as defined in Moscow.

"This brings us to the second of the concepts important to contemporary Soviet outlook. That is the infallibility of the Kremlin. The Soviet concept of power, which permits no focal points of organization outside the Party itself, requires that the Party leadership remain in theory the sole repository of truth. For if truth were to be found elsewhere, there would be justification for its expression in organized activity. But it is precisely that which the Kremlin cannot and will not permit.

"The leadership of the Communist Party is therefore always right, and has been always right ever since in 1929 Stalin formalized his personal power by announcing that decisions of the Politburo were being taken unanimously.

"On the principle of infallibility there rests the iron discipline of the Communist Party. In fact, the two concepts are mutually self-supporting. Perfect discipline requires recognition of infallibility. Infallibility requires the observance of discipline. And the two together go far to determine the behaviorism of the entire Soviet apparatus of power. But their effect cannot be understood unless a third factor be taken into account: namely, the fact that the leadership is at liberty to put forward for tactical purposes any particular thesis which it finds useful to the cause at any particular moment and to require the faithful and unquestioning acceptance of that thesis by the members of the movement as a whole. This means that truth is not a constant but is actually created, for all intents and purposes, by the Soviet leaders themselves. It may vary from week to week, from month to month. It is nothing absolute and immutable—nothing which flows from objective reality. It is only the most recent manifestation of the wisdom of those in whom the ultimate wisdom is supposed to reside, because they represent the logic of history. The accumulative effect of these factors is to give to the whole subordinate apparatus of Soviet power an unshakeable stubbornness and steadfastness in its orientation. This orientation can be changed at will by the Kremlin but by no other power. Once a given party line has been laid down on a given issue of current policy, the whole Soviet governmental machine, including the mechanism of diplomacy, moves inexorably along the prescribed path, like a persistent toy automobile wound up and headed in a given direction, stopping only when it meets some unanswerable force. The individuals who are the components of this machine are unamenable to argument or reason which comes to them from outside sources. Their whole training has taught them to mistrust and discount the glib persuaveness of the outside world. Like the white dog before the phonograph, they hear only the 'master's voice.' And if they are to be called off from the purposes last dictated to them, it is the master who must call them off. Thus the foreign representative cannot hope that his words will make any impression on them. The most that he can hope is that they will be transmitted to those at the top, who are capable of changing the party line. But even those are not likely to be swayed by any normal logic in the words of the bourgeois representative. Since there can be no appeal to common purposes, there can be no appeal to common mental approaches. For this reason, facts speak louder than words to the ears of the Kremlin; and words carry the greatest weight when they have the ring of reflecting, or being backed up by, facts of unchallengeable validity.

"But we have seen that the Kremlin is under no ideological compulsion to accomplish its purposes in a hurry. Like the Church, it is dealing in ideological concepts which are of long-term validity, and it can afford to be patient. It has no right to risk the existing achievements of the revolution for the sake of vain baubles of the future. The very teachings of Lenin himself require great caution and flexibility in the pursuit of Communist purposes. Again, these precepts are fortified by the lessons of Russian history: of centuries of obscure battles between nomadic forces over the stretches of a vast unfortified plain. Here caution, circumspection, flexibility and deception are the valuable qualities; and their value finds natural appreciation in the Russian or the oriental mind. Thus the Kremlin has no compunction about retreating in the face of superior force. And being under the compulsion of no timetable, it does not get panicky under the necessity for such retreat. Its political action is a fluid stream which moves constantly, wherever it is permitted to move, toward a given goal. Its main concern is to make sure that it has filled every nook and cranny available to it in the basin of world power. But if it finds unassailable barriers in its path, it accepts these philosophically and accommodates itself to them. The main thing is that there should always be pressure, unceasing constant pressure, toward the desired goal. There is no trace of any feeling in Soviet psychology that the goal must be reached at any given time.

"These considerations make Soviet diplomacy at once easier and more difficult to deal with than the diplomacy of individual aggressive leaders like Napoleon and Hitler. On the one hand it is more sensitive to contrary force, more ready to yield on individual sectors of the diplomatic front when that force is felt to be too strong, and thus more rational in the logic and rhetoric of power. On the other hand it cannot be easily defeated or discouraged by a single victory on the part of its opponents. And the patient persistence by which it is animated means that it can be effectively countered not by sporadic acts which represent the momentary whims of democratic opinion but only by intelligent long-range policies on the part of Russia's adversaries— policies no less steady in their purpose, and no less variegated and resourceful in their application, that those of the Soviet itself.

"In these circumstances it is clear that the main element of any United States policy toward the Soviet Union must be that of long-term, patient but firm and vigilant containment of Russian expansive tendencies. It is important to note, however, that such a policy has nothing to do with outward histrionics: with threats or blustering or superfluous gestures of outward 'toughness.' While the Kremlin is basically flexible in its reaction to political realities, it is by no means unamenable to considerations of prestige. Like almost any other government, it can be placed by tactless and threatening gestures in a position where it cannot afford to yield even though this might be dictated by its sense of realism. The Russian leaders are keen judges of human psychology, and as such they are highly conscious that loss of temper and of self-control is never a source of strength in political affairs. They are quick to exploit such evidences of weakness. For these reasons, it is a *sine qua non* of successful dealing with Russia that the foreign government in question should remain at all times cool and collected and that its demands on Russian policy should be put forward in such a manner as to leave the way open for a compliance not too detrimental to Russian prestige.

"III

"In the light of the above, it will be clearly seen that the Soviet pressure against the free institutions of the western world is something that can be contained by the adroit and vigilant application of counter-force at a series of constantly shifting geographical and political points, but which cannot be charmed or talked out of existence. The Russians look forward to a duel of infinite duration, and they see that already they have scored great successes. . . .

"But if ideology convinces the rulers of Russia that truth is on their side and that they can therefore afford to wait, those of us on whom that ideology has no claim are free to examine objectively the validity of that premise. The Soviet thesis not only implies complete lack of control by the west over its own economic destiny, it likewise assumes Russian unity, discipline and patience over an infinite period of time. Let us bring this apocalyptic vision down to earth, and suppose that the western world finds the strength and resourcefulness to contain Soviet power over a period of ten to fifteen years. What does that spell for Russia itself? . . .

"It is difficult to see how these deficiencies[10] can be corrected at an early date by a tired and dispirited population working largely under the shadow of fear and compulsion. And as long as they are not overcome, Russia will remain economically a vulnerable, and in a certain sense an impotent, nation, capable of exporting its enthusiasms and of radiating the strange charm of its primitive political vitality but unable to back up those articles of export by the real evidences of material power and prosperity.

[10] Spiritual, economic, physical exhaustion which followed the end of World War II plus the fact that there is no real social cohesion in Russia.

"Meanwhile, a great uncertainty hangs over the political life of the Soviet Union. That is the uncertainty involved in the transfer of power from one individual or group of individuals to others.

"This is, of course, outstandingly the problem of the personal position of Stalin. We must remember that his succession to Lenin's pinnacle of preëminence in the Communist movement was the only such transfer of individual authority which the Soviet Union has experienced. That transfer took 12 years to consolidate. It cost the lives of millions of people and shook the state to its foundations. The attendant tremors were felt all through the international revolutionary movement, to the disadvanage of the Kremlin itself.

"It is always possible that another transfer of preëminent power may take place quietly and inconspicuously, with no repercussions anywhere. But again, it is possible that the questions involved may unleash, to use some of Lenin's words, one of those 'incredibly swift transitions' from 'delicate deceit' to 'wild violence' which characterizes Russian history, and may shake Soviet power to its foundations. . . .

"And if disunity were ever to seize and paralyze the Party, the chaos and weakness of Russian society would be revealed in forms beyond description. For we have seen that Soviet power is only a crust concealing an amorphous mass of human beings among whom no independent organizational structure is tolerated. In Russia there is not even such a thing as local government. The present generation of Russians have never known spontaneity of collective action. If, consequently, anything were ever to occur to disrupt the unity and efficacy of the Party as a political instrument, Soviet Russia might be changed overnight from one of the strongest to one of the weakest and most pitiable of national societies. . . .

"It is clear that the United States cannot expect in the foreseeable future to enjoy politically intimacy with the Soviet régime. It must continue to regard the Soviet Union as a rival, not a partner, in the political arena. It must continue to expect that Soviet politics will reflect no abstract love of peace and stability, no real faith in the possibility of a permanent happy coexistence of the Socialist and capitalist worlds, but rather a cautious, persistent pressure toward the disruption and weakening of all rival influence and rival power.

"Balanced against this are the facts that Russia, as opposed to the western world in general, is still by far the weaker party, that Soviet policy is highly flexible, and that Soviet society may well contain certain deficiencies which will eventually weaken its own total potential. This would of itself warrant the United States entering with reasonable confidence upon a policy of firm containment, designed to confront the Russians with unalterable counter-force at every point where they show signs of encroaching upon the interests of a peaceful and stable world.

"But in actuality the possibilities for American policy are by no means limited to holding the line and hoping for the best. It is entirely possible for the United States to influence by its actions the internal developments, both within Russia and throughout the international Communist movement, by which Russian policy is largely determined. This is not only a question of the modest measure of informational activity which this government can conduct in the Soviet Union and elsewhere, although that, too, is important. It is rather a question of the degree to which the United States can create among the peoples of the world generally the impression of a country which knows what it wants, which is coping successfully with the problems of its internal life and with the responsibilities of a World Power, and which has a spiritual vitality capable of holding its own among the major ideological currents of the time. To the extent that such an impression can be created and maintained, the aims of Russian Communism must appear sterile and quixotic, the hopes and enthusiasm of Moscow's supporters must wane, and added strain must be imposed on the Kremlin's foreign policies. For the palsied decrepitude of the capitalist world is the keystone of Communist philosophy. Even the failure of the United States to experience the early economic depression which the ravens of the Red Square have been predicting with such complacent confidence since hostilities ceased would have deep and important repercussions throughout the Communist world.

"By the same token, exhibitions of indecision, disunity and internal disintegration within this country have an exhilarating effect on the whole Communist movement. At each evidence of these tendencies, a thrill of hope and excitement goes through the Communist world; a new jauntiness can be noted in the Moscow tread; new groups of foreign supporters climb on to what they can only view as the band wagon of international politics; and Russian pressure increases all along the line in international affairs.

"It would be an exaggeration to say that American behaviour unassisted and alone could exercise a power of life and death over the Communist movement and bring about the early fall of Soviet power in Russia. But the United States has in its power to increase enormously the strains under which Soviet policy must operate, to force upon the Kremlin a far greater degree of moderation and circumspection than it has had to observe in recent years, and in this way to promote tendencies which must eventually find their outlet in either the break-up or the gradual mellowing of Soviet power. For no mystical, Messianic movement—and particularly not that of the Kremlin— can face frustration indefinitely without eventually adjusting itself in one way or another to the logic of that state of affairs.

"Thus the decision will really fall in large measure in this country itself. The issue of Soviet-American relations is in essence a test of the over-all worth of the United States as a nation among nations. To avoid destruction the United States need only measure up to its own best traditions and prove itself worthy of preservation as a great nation.

"Surely, there was never a fairer test of national quality than this. In the light of these circumstances, the thoughtful observer of Russian-American relations will find no cause for complaint in the Kremlin's challenge to American society. He will rather experience a certain gratitude to a Providence which by providing the American people with this implacable challenge, has made their entire security as a nation dependent on their pulling themselves together and accepting the responsibilities of moral and political leadership that history plainly intended them to bear."

6. *The North Atlantic Treaty, 1949*

Twelve nations signed the North Atlantic Treaty in Washington on April 4, 1949. This instrument, along with the Rio pact of 1947, was another link in the chain forged by the non-Communist nations to contain the ever-increasing menace of the Soviet union.[11]

"PREAMBLE

"The Parties to this Treaty reaffirm their faith in the purposes and principles of the Charter of the United Nations and their desire to live in peace with all peoples and all governments.

"They are determined to safeguard the freedom, common heritage and civilization of their peoples, founded on the principles of democracy, individual liberty and the rule of law.

"They seek to promote stability and well-being in the North Atlantic area.

"They are resolved to unite their efforts for collective defense and for the preservation of peace and security.

"They therefore agree to this North Atlantic Treaty: . . . .

"Article 3

"In order more effectively to achieve the objectives of this Treaty, the Parties, separately and jointly, by means of continuous and effective self-help and mutual aid, will maintain and develop their individual and collective capacity to resist armed attack.

"Article 4

"The Parties will consult together whenever, in the opinion of any of them, the territorial integrity, political independence or security of any of the Parties is threatened.

"Article 5

"The Parties agree that an armed attack against one or more of them in Europe or North America shall be considered an attack against them all; and consequently they agree that, if such an armed attack occurs, each of them, in exercise of the right of individual or collective self-defense recog-

[11] *North Atlantic Treaty,* Dept. of State, Gen. For. Pol. Ser., 8, (Washington, 1949).

nized by Article 51 of the Charter of the United Nations, will assist the Party or Parties so attacked by taking forthwith, individually and in concert with the other Parties, such action as it deems necessary, including the use of armed force, to restore and maintain the security of the North Atlantic area.

"Any such armed attack and all measures taken as a result thereof shall immediately be reported to the Security Council. Such measures shall be terminated when the Security Council has taken the measures necessary to restore and maintain international peace and security.

"Article 6

"For the purpose of Article 5 an armed attack on one or more of the Parties is deemed to include an armed attack on the territory of any of the Parties in Europe or North America, on the Algerian departments of France, on the occupation forces of any Party in Europe, on the islands under the jurisdiction of any Party in the North Atlantic area north of the Tropic of Cancer or on the vessels or aircraft in this area of any of the Parties.

"Article 7

"This Treaty does not affect, and shall not be interpreted as affecting, in any way the rights and obligations under the Charter of the Parties which are members of the United Nations, or the primary responsibility of the Security Council for the maintenance of international peace and security. . . .

"Article 9

"The Parties hereby establish a council, on which each of them shall be represented, to consider matters concerning the implementation of this Treaty. The council shall be so organized as to be able to meet promptly at any time. The council shall set up such subsidiary bodies as may be necessary; in particular it shall establish immediately a defense committee which shall recommend measures for the implementation of Articles 3 and 5.

"Article 10

"The Parties may, by unanimous agreement, invite any other European state in a position to further the principles of this Treaty and to contribute to the security of the North Atlantic area to accede to this Treaty. Any state so invited may become a party to the Treaty by depositing its instrument of accession with the Government of the United States of America. The Government of the United States of America will inform each of the Parties of the deposit of each such instrument of accession. . . .

"Article 12

"After the Treaty has been in force for ten years, or at any time thereafter, the Parties shall, if any of them so requests, consult together for the purpose of reviewing the Treaty, having regard for the factors then affecting peace and security in the North Atlantic area, including the development of universal as well as regional arrangements under the Charter of the United Nations for the maintenance of international peace and security.

"Article 13

"After the Treaty has been in force for twenty years, any Party may cease to be a party one year after its notice of denunciation has been given to the Government of the United States of America, which will inform the Governments of the other Parties of the deposit of each notice of denunciation. . . ."

7. *Issues in Dispute with the Soviet Union, 1949*

One of the most concise statements made by any responsible American official as to the basic issues in dispute between the Soviet Union and the rest of the non-Communist world, was contained in an address given by Deputy Undersecretary of State Dean Rusk, on October 10, 1949.[12]

". . . If we are concerned about the Soviet Union, it is not because they wish to organize themselves along Communist lines—if they wish to waste their energies and resources that is their business. But we are concerned because the Soviet Union is pursuing a course of Russian imperialism incompatible with the minimum conduct required by the international community of nations. In Yugoslavia we have, if we ever needed it, a clear demonstration that being Communist is not enough for the Kremlin. Communists in other lands are expected to yoke themselves to the national interests of the Russian state. While western Communists are stirring with resentment at this compulsion, we can wonder how long it will take those Chinese who have fallen under Communist domination to begin to feel the impact of the same bitter truth.

"There has been considerable talk of the need for an 'agreement' with the Soviet Union. If by 'agreement' is meant a settlement of the particular points at issue between us at any one time, we are ready to do what we can to reach such a settlement in the proper forum. But if it is supposed that our problem would be met by a new over-all pact with the Soviet Union, then the nature of the problem is not fully understood. Basically, what we need is not a new 'agreement' but performance on the agreements we already have; not an additional piece of parchment to sign, but execution of the promises already made. The United Nations Charter is our peace pact, the greatest in the history of man, and United Nations machinery is available to help in the settlement of disputes. Compliance with the Charter and support for United Nations machinery would bring us a long way down the road toward a stable peace.

"I said a moment ago that we are ready to do what we can to reach a settlement of specific issues in the proper forum. Why the 'proper forum'?

[12] Dean Rusk, "The Stake of Business in American Foreign Policy," *Dept. of State Bulletin,* Vol. XXI, (October 24, 1949), pp. 630-33.

There are very few strictly bilateral issues between the United States and the Soviet Union. The lend-lease settlement, Madame Kasenkina, Mr. Gubitchev, the treatment of American citizens by Soviet authorities are a few examples. These matters are troublesome, but I believe they can be negotiated out. But these are not the causes of the deep anxiety which has marked the post war period. Greece, Iran, Korea, China, Germany, Austria, Japan, Yugoslavia, Palestine, Kashmir, Indonesia—these have been the scenes where issues have arisen to threaten the peace. But these are not matters which concern only the Soviet Union and ourselves. In fact, they involve the vital interests of other government and peoples—in some instances the very disposition of large populations. Others are, in fact, more deeply interested than are we ourselves. We are able in many cases, as comparatively disinterested parties, to lend a hand in an effort to find a solution—an effort which itself has imposed great burdens upon the conduct of our foreign relations. It is not always comfortable to have the task of finding a point of agreement between Dutch and Indonesian, Pakistani and Indian, Jew and Arab. But these and other such issues are not to be settled by the United States and the Soviet Union in a bilateral trading-out of the basic interests of others in exchange for an endurable *modus-vivendi* between the two of us —for a result which would have to be imposed upon the unhappy victims of big-power politics. President Truman said at Berkeley, California, in June 1948:

" 'I have said before and I repeat now: The door is always open for honest negotiations looking for genuine settlements.

" 'The door is not open, however, for deals between great powers to the detriment of other nations or at the expense of principle.'

"The main issue of peace is the issue of aggression—direct aggression by armed forces across national frontiers as well as indirect aggression by subversion, infiltration, intimidation, and sabotage. This is in no sense an issue between the United States and the Soviet Union—it is an issue between the Soviet Union and the rest of the world. . . ."

8. Far Eastern Policy, 1950

On January 12, 1950, Secretary Acheson made an address before the National Press Club in Washington, entitled, "Crisis in Asia—An Examination of U.S. Policy." This speech, which was made after the Nationalists had been driven to Formosa from the Chinese mainland by the Communists and approximately five months before the North Koreans launched their attack against the South Koreans, has often been cited by Acheson's critics as a diplomatic blunder because he did not include Korea within the "defensive perimeter" to be held by the United States. Excerpts are quoted below.[13]

"The attitude and interest of the Russians in north China, and in these other areas as well, long antedates communism. This is not something that has come out of communism at all. It long antedates it. But the Communist regime has added new methods, new skills, and new concepts to the thrust of Russian imperialism. Thus Communistic concept and techniques have armed Russian imperialism with a new and most insidious weapon of penetration. Armed with these new powers, what is happening in China is that the Soviet Union is detaching the northern provinces [areas] of China from China and is attaching them to the Soviet Union. This process is complete in outer Mongolia. It is nearly complete in Manchuria, and I am sure that in inner Mongolia and in Sinkiang there are very happy reports coming from Soviet agents to Moscow. This is what is going on. It is the detachment of these whole areas, vast areas—populated by Chinese—the detachment of these areas from China and their attachment to the Soviet Union. . . .

"The consequences of this Russian attitude and this Russian action in China are perfectly enormous. They are saddling all those in China who are proclaiming their loyalty to Moscow, and who are allowing themselves to be used as puppets of Moscow, with the most awful responsibility which they must pay for. Furthermore, these actions of the Russians are making plainer than any speech, or any utterance, or any legislation can make throughout all of Asia, what the true purposes of the Soviet Union are and what the true function of communism as an agent of Russian imperialism is. These I suggest to you are the fundamental factors, fundamental realities of attitude out of which our relations and policies must grow.

"Now, let's in the light of that consider some of these policies. First of all, let's deal with the question of military security. I deal with it first because it is important and because, having stated our policy in that regard, we must clearly understand that the military menace is not the most immediate.

"What is the situation in regard to the military security of the Pacific area, and what is our policy in regard to it?

"In the first place, the defeat and the disarmament of Japan has placed upon the United States the necessity of assuming the military defense of Japan so long as that is required, both in the interest of our security and in the interests of the security of the entire Pacific area and, in all honor, in the interests of Japanese security. . . . I am not in a position to speak for the Australians, but I can assure you that there is no intention of any sort of abandoning or weakening the defenses of Japan and that whatever arrangements are to be made either through permanent settlement or otherwise, that defense must and shall be maintained.

[13] Dean Acheson, "Crisis in Asia—An Examination of U.S. Policy," *Department of State Bulletin,* Vol. XXII, (January 23, 1950), pp. 111-18.

"This defensive perimeter runs along the Aleutians to Japan and then goes to the Ryukyus. We hold important defense positions in the Ryukyu Islands, and those we will continue to hold. In the interest of the population of the Ryukyu Islands, we will at an appropriate time offer to hold these islands under trusteeship of the United Nations. But they are essential parts of the defensive perimeter of the Pacific, and they must and will be held.

"The defensive perimeter runs from the Ryukus to the Philippine Islands. Our relations, our defensive relations with the Philippines are contained in agreements between us. Those agreements are being loyally carried out. Both peoples have learned by bitter experience the vital connections between our mutual defense requirements. We are in no doubt about that, and it is hardly necessary for me to say an attack on the Philippines could not and would not be tolerated by the United States. But I hasten to add that no one perceives the imminence of any such attack.

"So far as the military security of other areas in the Pacific is concerned, it must be clear that no person can guarantee these areas against military attack. But it must also be clear that such a guarantee is hardly sensible or necessary within the realm of practical relationship.

"Should such an attack occur—one hesitates to say where such an armed attack could come from—the initial reliance must be on the people attacked to resist it and then upon the commitments of the entire civilized world under the Charter of the United Nations which so far has not proved a weak reed to lean on by any people who are determined to protect their independence against outside aggression. . . ."

9. Mutual Defense of the West, 1950

Following the signing of the North Atlantic pact the next step in the containment of Communism was the passage of the Mutual Defense Assistance Act by Congress in October, 1949, for the purpose of implementing the pact. In June, 1950, the Department of State issued a pamphlet explaining the relationship between the North Atlantic Treaty and the Mutual Defense Assistance Program relative to American Foreign Policy.[14]

"The North Atlantic Treaty and the Mutual Defense Assistance Program share an identical objective. They aim to maintain and develop the individual and collective capacity of Western Europe and other countries under the act to resist aggression through self-help and mutual aid. In practical terms, they are designed to buttress the frontiers of the North Atlantic community and, in the event of aggression, to provide a common defense by free nations with the will and the means to resist.

[14] *A Background Summary Mutual Defense of the West,* Dept. of State, June, 1950, p. 5.

"Secretary Acheson offers the explanation of the need for the Mutual Defense Assistance Program:

'One of the facts we must face is that the free nations of Western Europe, with whose security own own security is bound up, are incapable today of defending themselves against a major armed attack. Another fact is that the Soviet Union today maintains the largest peacetime military force in the history of the world, while exerting iron-fisted con-trol over its neighbors and pursuing a policy of exploiting any evidence of weakness in others.

'The combination of these two facts—a huge aggressive force on one side and admittedly inadequate defense forces on the other—has created a morbid and pervasive sense of insecurity in Western Europe. The fear is justified. The danger is real, however much some may try to argue it out of existence.'

"Chief of Staff General Omar N. Bradley offers the following analysis of the military significance of NAT and MDAP:

'Not only does it [NAT] unite free nations whose common interests and common frontiers are imperiled by aggression but it frees us and our partners from the fear that a nation which would bravely resist aggression might find itself fighting friendless and alone. The North Atlantic Pact would deny to any aggressor the deadly opportunity to pick off single nations one by one.

'This reassurance is especially vital to those Western European nations whose boundaries lie within striking distance of instant land attack. In the final analysis, Western Europe can be saved only by the Western Europeans. But to save themselves they must have the will and the means to resist. This will to resist is developed partly by possession of the means and partly by the assurance they would be adequately helped in sufficient time.

'Without these means and without these specific assurances of aid, any nation of Western Europe, if threatened by aggression, might fall victim of despair. And that despair is worth a hundred divisions to an aggressor on the march. The North Atlantic Pact and some military assistance will provide both an assurance of aid and the means to resist. Together they can produce a will resolute enough to fight and firm enough to forewarn aggressors.' "

10. *Background of Korean War, 1945–1950*

In July, 1950, shortly after the North Korean attack against the Republic of Korea, the Department of State issued a pamphlet entitled *United States Policy in the Korean Crisis*. The Introduction to this pamphlet, quoted below, not only gives a brief sketch of events in Korea from the end of World War II until the outbreak of the Korean War, but it is also an official statement of American policy.[15]

"During World War II the United States, the United Kingdom, and China pledged their determination, in the Cairo Declaration of December 1943, that Korea would 'in due course' become free and independent. This pledge was reaffirmed in the Potsdam Declaration of July 26, 1945, and was subscribed to by the Soviet Union when it declared war against Japan on August 8, 1945. The defeat of Japan made it possible for Korea to look forward to the realization of its desire for independence.

"Korea was never formally divided into zones of occupation by agreement between the United States and the Soviet Union at any of the high-level wartime conferences. After receipt of the Japanese offer of surrender, with the nearest American troops at Okinawa and with Soviet troops already in Korea, the United States Government, in providing for the surrender of Japanese troops, proposed that Soviet troops accept the surrender of Japanese troops in Korea north of the 38th parallel and that Japanese troops in Korea south of that line surrender to American forces. After this arrangement had been accepted by Generalissimo Stalin, it was incorporated in the first General Order which General MacArthur, as Supreme Commander for the Allied Powers, caused to be issued on September 2, 1945. The United States did not contemplate a lasting division of Korea along this line, which was a fortuitous line resulting from the exigencies of the war.

"Soviet forces first entered Korea on August 12, 1945, and proceeded to occupy the northern half of Korea. American troops landed on September 8 and accepted the surrender of Japanese troops in the southern part of the peninsula on the following day. It soon became apparent that the division of Korea for surrender purposes was to be arbitrarily interpreted by the Soviet occupation authorities as creating a permanent delineation between two military zones, passage between which was possible only by permission of the military commanders. This situation continued despite persistent efforts of the United States Commander to negotiate arrangements with his Soviet counterpart with a view to reestablishing the essential unity of the country.

"At Moscow in December 1945 the Foreign Ministers of the United States, the United Kingdom, and the Soviet Union agreed that a provisional Korean democratic government should be set up for all Korea. the Moscow Agreement, to which the Chinese Government subsequently adhered, provided that the United States and Soviet commands in Korea were to form a Joint Commission which, in consultation with Korean democratic parties and social organizations, was to make recommendations to the Four Powers

---

[15] *United States Policy in the Korean Crisis*, Dept. of State, Far East. Ser., 34, (Washington, 1950), pp. ix-xi.

for the organization of a provisional Korean democratic government. Every effort to give effect to this agreement, however, was blocked by Soviet intransigence.

"The United States, unwilling to permit this situation to delay further the realization of Korean independence, then laid the question of Korean independence before the United Nations. The General Assembly of the United Nations in November 1947 called for an election, under the observation of the United Nations Temporary Commission on Korea, to choose representatives, not mere appointees of military authorities in Korea, who might be invited to participate in the discussion of the question by the United Nations and who, constituting a National Assembly, should draft a democratic constitution and establish a National Government.

"The Soviet Union held that the Korean question, like others connected with the conclusion of peace treaties, did not fall within the jurisdiction of the United Nations. It adopted a 'negative attitude' toward the Temporary Commission and refused to allow it even to enter the northern part of Korea. Consequently, the right of the Korean people to participate in a free election and to establish a free government was confined to southern Korea. The election was held on May 10, 1948, under the supervision of the United Nations Temporary Commission on Korea, and the Government of the Republic of Korea was established on August 15, 1948.

"The Government of the Republic of Korea was accepted by the United Nations in December 1948 as the validly elected, lawful Government of the area in which elections were permitted—and the only such government in Korea. The General Assembly established a reconstituted Commission to continue to work for unification and a representative government for the entire country. The United States recognized the new Government on January 1, 1949, and 31 other nations have done likewise. The Soviet Union and its satellites have not recognized the Republic of Korea, whose membership in the United Nations has been blocked by the Soviet use of the veto in the Security Council.

"Meanwhile, north of the 38th parallel, which had become a part of the 'Iron Curtain', the Soviet Union established a Communist regime. The formal creation of this regime, the so-called 'Democratic People's Republic of Korea,' claiming jurisdiction over the entire country, was proclaimed on September 9, 1948. This regime has lived, as it was created, in complete defiance of the United Nations.

"In pursuance of the recommendation contained in the General Assembly's resolution of December 12, 1948, to the effect that the occupying Powers should 'withdraw their occupation forces from Korea as early as practicable,' the United States completed the withdrawal of its occupation forces on June 29, 1949. This withdrawal was observed and verified by the United Nations Commission on Korea as recorded in its report dated at Seoul, July 28, 1949. The Soviet Union announced that it had completed withdrawal of its troops in December 1948, but the United Nations Commission has not been permitted to verify this action.

"It has been the aim of the United States to provide the people of the Republic of Korea with sufficient assistance and support to enable them to progress through their own efforts toward freedom and independence. The transfer of functions from the United States Military Government to Korean agencies was carried out progressively from the establishment of the Republic. The United States continued to give assistance and support to the Republic both within the framework of the United Nations and directly. The United States has extended economic aid and technical advice and, in general, has assisted the people of Korea in establishing a democratic political and economic structure responsive to their needs."

11. The Great Debate of 1951— General Douglas MacArthur

The recall of General Douglas MacArthur by President Truman in the spring of 1951, touched off the most heated debate on foreign policy since the period before the Pearl Harbor attack. Every circumstance connected with the event tended to provoke bitter discussion. MacArthur himself, a kind of demigod in the minds of many Americans, was considered to be almost sacrosanct, even by many of the ranking officers in the Pentagon. The war in Korea had lasted longer than Americans thought it should, and seemingly there was no end to it. There always had been a division of opinion in the United States as to whether Europe or the Far East was more important to our security. The loss of China to the Communists had been a tremendous shock to Americans. The dismissal of MacArthur was just the spark needed to unloose an avalanche of criticism against Truman, Marshall, Acheson and almost everyone remotely connected with the formulation of the Far Eastern policy of the United States since the end of the war.

On April 19, 1951, MacArthur delivered an address to a joint session of the Congress of the United States in which he presented his side of the case to the American people.[16]

"Mr. President, Mr. Speaker and distinguished members of the Congress: I stand on this rostrum with a sense of deep humility and great pride—humility in the wake of those great American architects of our history who have stood here before me, pride in the reflection that this home of

[16] *Congressional Record,* 82nd Cong., 1st Sess., Vol. 97, Pt. 3, pp. 4123-25.

legislative debate represents human liberty in the purest form yet devised.

"Here are centered the hopes and aspirations and faith of the entire human race.

"I do not stand here as advocate for any partisan cause, for the issues are fundamental and reach quite beyond the realm of partisan considerations. They must be resolved on the highest plane of national interest if our course is to prove sound and our future protected.

"I trust, therefore, that you will do me the justice of receiving that which I have to say as solely expressing the considered viewpoint of a fellow American.

"I address you with neither rancor nor bitterness in the fading twilight of life, with but one purpose in mind: To serve my country.

"The issues are global, and so interlocked that to consider the problem of one sector oblivious to those of another is to court disaster for the whole. While Asia is commonly referred to as the gateway to Europe, it is no less true that Europe is the gateway to Asia, and the broad influence of the one cannot fail to have its impact upon the other.

"There are those who claim our strength is inadequate to protect on both fronts, that we cannot divide our effort. I can think of no greater expression of defeatism.

"If a potential enemy can divide his strength on two fronts, it is for us to counter his efforts. The Communist threat is a global one. . . .

"Of more direct and immediate bearing upon our national security are the changes wrought in the strategic potential of the Pacifis Ocean in the course of the past war.

"Prior thereto, the western strategic frontier of the United States lay on the littoral line of the Americas, with an exposed island salient extending through Hawaii, Midway and Guam to the Philippines. That salient proved not an outpost of strength but an avenue of weakness along which that enemy could, and did, attack. The Pacific was a potential area of advance for any predatory force intent upon striking at the bordering land areas.

"All this was changed by our Pacific victory. Our strategic frontier then shifted to embrace the entire Pacific Ocean, which became a vast moat to protect us as long as we held it. Indeed, it acts as a protective shield for all of the Americas and for all free lands of the Pacific Ocean area. We control it to the shores of Asia by a chain of islands extending in an arc from the Aleutians to the Marianas, held by us and our free Allies.

"From this island chain we can dominate with sea and air power every Asiatic port from Vladivostok to Singapore—with sea and air power, every port, as I said, from Vladivostok to Singapore—and prevent any hostile movements into the Pacific.

"Any predatory attack from Asia must be an amphibious effort. No amphibious force can be successful without control of the sea lanes and air power over those lanes in its avenue of advance. With naval and air supremacy and modest ground elements to defend bases, any major attack from continental Asia toward us or our friends in the Pacific would be doomed to failure.

"Under such conditions, the Pacific no longer represents menacing avenues of approach for a prospective invader. It assumes, instead, the friendly aspect of a peaceful lake.

"Our line of defense is a natural one and can be maintained with a minimum of military effort and expense. It envisions no attack against anyone, nor does it provide the bastions essential for offensive operations, but properly maintained, would be an invincible defense against aggression.

"The holding of this littoral defense line in the western Pacific is entirely dependent upon holding all segments thereof, for any major breach of that line by an unfriendly power would render vulnerable to attack every other major segment. This is a military estimate as to which I have yet to find a military leader who will take exception.

"For that reason, I have strongly recommended in the past, as a matter of military urgency, that under no circumstances must Formosa fall under Communist control. Such an eventuality would at once threaten the freedom of the Philippines and the loss of Japan and might well force our western frontier back to the coast of California, Oregon and Washington. . . .

"With this brief insight into the surrounding areas, I now turn to the Korean conflict.

"While I was not consulted prior to the President's decision to intervene in support of the Republic of Korea, that decision, from a military standpoint, proved a sound one. As I say, it proved a sound one, as we hurled back the invader and decimated his forces. Our victory was complete, and our objective within reach, when Red China intervened with numerically superior ground forces.

"This created a new war and an entirely new situation, a situation not contemplated when our forces were committed against the North Korean invaders; a situation which called for new decisions in the diplomatic sphere to permit the realistic readjustment of military strategy. Such decisions have not been forthcoming.

"While no man in his right mind would advocate sending our ground forces into continental China, and such was never given a thought, the new situation did urgently demand a drastic revision of strategic planning if our political aim was to defeat this new enemy as we had defeated the old.

"Apart from the military need, as I saw it, to neutralize the sanctuary protection given the enemy north of the Yalu, I felt that military necessity in the conduct of the war made necessary—

"(1) The intensification of our economic blockade against China.

"(2) The imposition of a naval blockade against the China coast.

"(3) Removal of restrictions on air reconnaissance of China's coastal area and of Manchuria.

"(4) Removal of restrictions on the forces of the Republic of China on Formosa, with logistical support to contribute to their effective operations against the Chinese mainland.

"For entertaining these views, all professionally designed to support our forces committed to Korea and bring hostilities to an end with the least possible delay and at a saving of countless American and Allied lives, I have been severely criticized in lay circles, principally abroad, despite my understanding that from a military standpoint the above views have been fully shared in the past by practically every military leader concerned with the Korean campaign, including our own Joint Chiefs of Staff.

"I called for reinforcements, but was informed that reinforcements were not available. I made clear that if not permitted to destroy the enemy built-up bases north of the Yalu, if not permitted to utilize the friendly Chinese forces of some 600,000 men on Formosa, if not permitted to blockade the China coast to prevent the Chinese Reds from getting succor from without, and if there were to be no hope of major reinforcements, the position of the command from the military viewpoint forbade victory. . . .

"I know war as few other men now living know it, and nothing to me is more revolting. I have long advocated its complete abolition, as its very destructiveness on both friend and foe has rendered it useless as a means of settling international disputes. . . .

"But once war is forced upon us, there is no other alternative than to apply every available means to bring it to a swift end. War's very object is victory not prolonged indecision.

"In war there is no substitute for victory.

"There are some who for varying reasons would appease Red China. They are blind to history's clear lesson, for history teaches with unmistakable emphasis that appeasement begets new and bloodier war. It points to no single instance where this end has justified that means, where appeasement has led to more than a sham peace.

"Like blackmail, it lays the basis for new and successively greater demands until, as in blackmail, violence becomes the only other alternative. Why, my soldiers asked of me, surrender military advantages to an enemy in the field? I could not answer.

"Some may say to avoid spread of the conflict into an all-out war with China. Others, to avoid Soviet intervention. Neither explanation seems valid, for China is already engaged with the maximum power it can commit, and the Soviet will not necessarily mesh its actions with our moves. Like a cobra, any new enemy will more likely strike whenever it feels that the relativity in military or other potential is in its favor on a world-wide basis. . . ."

12. *Acheson's Defense of America's Far Eastern Policy, 1951*

The MacArthur speech, in addition to stimulating sharp debate throughout the nation, led the Senate to make a thorough investigation of the entire Far Eastern policy of the United States since the end of the war. MacArthur, Acheson, the Joint Chiefs of Staff, and other high-ranking officials, testified at great length before Senate Committees as to their views on the question.

The following quotation, which was a defense of American policy toward China, was part of a statement made by Acheson on June 4, 1951, before a Joint Senate Committee composed of the Senate Committee on Armed Forces and the Senate Committee on Foreign Relations.[17]

"Now, in that situation the United States Government had three choices open to it.

"One choice was to pull out of China and say, 'We have defeated the Japanese. The Chinese from now on must paddle their own canoe, and we have to wash our hands of it.' That was an impossible choice to take because with the presence of a million two hundred thirty-five thousand armed Japanese troops in China, exclusive of Manchuria, and of another million seven hundred thousand Japanese civilians—government officials, economic people, clerks, and businessmen, one thing or another—there was a Japanese force and a Japanese influence so great in China that by throwing its weight to either side in this civil war it could have taken over the administration of the country, and Japan in defeat would have found itself in actual control of China, a result which we could not, of course, help to bring about.

"The second choice was that the United States Government might have put into China unlimited resources and all the necessary military power to try and defeat the Communists, remove the Japanese, and remove the Russians from Manchuria.

"That was a task so great and so repugnant to the American people that the Government could not undertake it, and it was one which was not in accord with American interests.

"The third choice, and the one which was chosen, was to give important assistance of all sorts to the Chinese Government and to assist in every way in the preservation of peace in China and the working out of the agreements which were so necessary to enable the Chinese Government

[17] *American Policy Toward China,* Dept. of State, Far East. Ser., 43, (Washington, 1951), pp. 11-12, 48-49.

to reestablish itself in those parts of China where it had been before and to get, for the first time, into areas of China where it never had been. . . .

"Apart from this, the United States Government, in the period from VJ-Day until early 1949, authorized grants and credits to China totaling approximately two billion dollars, of which approximately a billion, six, were grants; and four hundred million were on credit terms.

"This total is divided almost equally between military and economic aid. The amounts do not include United States surplus property, except where the sales were on credit terms.

"Surplus property, with a total estimated procurement cost of over a billion dollars, has been sold to China for the agreed realization to the United States of 230 million dollars, of which 95 million were on credit terms.

"By the spring of 1949, the military position of the Chinese Government collapsed to the point where the Chinese Communists controlled the major centers of population, and railways from Manchuria south to the Yangtze.

"The military collapse of the Chinese Government had, for the most part, been the consequence of inept political and military leadership, and a lack of the will to fight on the part of its armies, rather than inadequate military supplies.

"It was at that time the considered judgment of responsible United States Government observers in China that only the extension of unlimited American economic and military aid involving the use of our own troops and operations which might require the extensive control of the Chinese Government operations would enable the Nationalist Government to maintain a foothold in South China.

"It was believed that United States involvement in Chinese civil war under the existing conditions would be clearly contrary to American interests.

"As the last note of this tragic story, I should like to read you the message of the Acting President of China, General Li Tsung-jen.

"*Senator Wiley.* What is the date?

"*Secretary Acheson.* May 5, 1949, in a letter which he addressed to President Truman. He says: 'This policy'—he had described our help to China during the war, and then he had discussed our aid to China after the war as I have described it to you. He says:

" 'This policy of friendly assistance was continued when some years ago General Marshall under instructions from your good self took up the difficult task of mediation in our conflict with the Chinese Communists to which he devoted painstaking effort. All this work was unfortunately rendered fruitless by the lack of sincerity on the part of both the then government[18] and the Chinese Communists.

18 Chiang Kai-shek's government.

" 'In spite of this your country continued to extend its aid to our Government. It is regrettable that owing to the failure of our then government to make judicious use of this aid and to bring about appropriate political, economic and military reforms, your assistance has not produced the desired effect. To this failure is attributable the present predicament in which our country finds itself.' "

13. America's Future

In 1947, after he had resigned as Secretary of War, Henry L. Stimson wrote an article—"The Challenge to Americans"—in which he surveyed in broad, philosophic terms the nature of the threat posed by the Soviet Union to the United States. This article by Stimson, that brilliant statesman who served in the cabinets of three Presidents—two Republicans and one a Democrat, was written about a specific situation then confronting the nation. However, it may well rank with those rare bits of wisdom which will be considered as timely a half-century from now as it is today.[19]

"We have been very patient with the Soviet Government, and very hopeful of its good intentions. I have been among those who shared these hopes and counseled this patience. The magnificent and loyal war effort of the Russian people, and the great successful efforts at friendliness made during the war by President Roosevelt, gave us reason for hope. I have believed—and I still believe—that we must show good faith in all our dealings with the Russians, and that only by so doing can we leave the door open for Russian good faith toward us. I cannot too strongly express my regret that since the early spring of 1945—even before the death of Mr. Roosevelt—the Soviet Government has steadily pursued an obstructive and unfriendly course. It has been our hope that the Russians would choose to be our friends; it was and is our conviction that such a choice would be to their advantage. But, for the time being, at least, those who determine Russian policy have chosen otherwise, and their choice has been slavishly followed by Communists everywhere.

"No sensible American can now ignore this fact, that those who now choose to travel in company with American Communists are very clearly either knaves or fools. This is a judgment which I make reluctantly, but there is no help for it. I have often said that the surest way to make man trustworthy is to trust him. But I must add that this does not always apply to a man who is determined to make you his dupe. Before we can make friends

[19] Henry L. Stimson, "The Challenge to Americans," *Foreign Affairs,* Vol. 26, (October, 1947), pp. 5-14.

with the Russians, their leaders will have to be convinced that they have nothing to gain, and everything to lose, by acting on the assumption that our society is dying and that our principles are outworn. Americans who think they can make common cause with present-day Communism are living in a world that does not exist. . . .

"But I see no reason for any man to face the American future with any other feeling than one of confident hope. However grave our problems, and however difficult their solution, I do not believe that this country is ready to acknowledge that failure is foreordained. It is our task to disprove and render laughable that utterly insulting theory. Our future does not depend on the tattered forecasts of Karl Marx. It depends on us. . . .

"We need not suppose that the task we face is easy, or that all our undertakings will be quickly successful. The construction of a stable peace is a longer, more complex and greater task than the relatively simple work of war-making. But the nature of the challenge is the same. The issue before us today is at least as significant as the one which we finally faced in 1941. By a long series of mistakes and failures, dating back over a span of more than 20 years, we had in 1941 let it become too late to save ourselves by peaceful methods; in the end we had to fight. This is not true today. If we act now, with vigor and understanding, with steadiness and without fear, we can peacefully safeguard our freedom. It is only if we turn our backs, in mistaken complacence or mistrusting timidity, that war may again become inevitable.

"How soon this nation will fully understand the size and nature of its present mission, I do not dare to say. But I venture to assert that in a very large degree the future of mankind depends on the answer to this question. And I am confident that if the issues are clearly presented, the American people will give the right answer. Surely there is here a fair and tempting challenge to all Americans, and especially to the nation's leaders, in and out of office."

14. President Eisenhower's Foreign Policy

The first detailed statement on foreign policy made by President Dwight D. Eisenhower after he entered the White House, was delivered at a luncheon in Washington to the American Society of Newspaper Editors on April 16, 1953. It came more than a month after the death of Stalin and at a time when the new Soviet regime headed by Premier Malenkov appeared to be launching a new "peace" offensive. The Chinese Communists had agreed to the exchange of sick and wounded prisoners of war, and the prospects of a truce in Korea appeared brighter than they had been since talks were broken off in October, 1952. The

Russians had made a number of seemingly conciliatory moves;
and the Eisenhower address was reportedly designed to achieve
two objectives: 1) to offset the advantages which the Soviet
Union may have gained in having sponsored occasional "peace offensives"; and 2) to present to the world an embracing statement
of American foreign policy.[20]

"In this spring of 1953, the free world weighs one question above all
others: the chances for a just peace for all peoples.

"To weigh this chance is to summon instantly to mind another recent
moment of great decision. It came with that yet more hopeful spring of
1945, bright with the promise of victory and of freedom. The hope of all
just men in that moment, too, was a just and lasting peace.

"The eight years that have passed have seen that hope waver, grow
dim, and almost die. And the shadow of fear again has darkly lengthened
across the world.

"Today the hope of free men remains stubborn and brave, but it is
sternly disciplined by experience.

"It shuns not only all crude counsel of despair, but also the self-deceit
of easy illusion.

"It weighs the chances of peace with sure, clear knowledge of what
happened to the vain hopes of 1945.

"In the spring of victory, the soldiers of the Western Allies met the
soldiers of Russia in the center of Europe. They were triumphant comrades
in arms. Their peoples shared the joyous prospect of building, in honor of
their dead, the only fitting monument—an age of just peace.

"All these war-weary peoples shared, too, this concrete, decent purpose:
to guard vigilantly against the domination ever again of any part of the
world by a single, unbridled aggressive power.

"This common purpose lasted an instant—and perished. The nations
of the world divided to follow two distinct roads.

"The United States and our valued friends, the other free nations,
chose one road.

"The leaders of the Soviet Union chose another.

"The way chosen by the United States was plainly marked by a few
clear precepts which govern its conduct in world affairs.

"First: No people on earth can be held—as a people—to be an enemy,
for all humanity shares the common hunger for peace and fellowship and
justice.

"Second: No nation's security and well-being can be lastingly achieved
in isolation, but only in effective cooperation with fellow-nations.

"Third: Any nation's right to form a government and an economic
system of its own choosing in inalienable.

[20] *Washington Post,* April 17, 1953.

"Fourth: Every nation's attempt to dictate to other nations their form of government is indefensible.

"And fifth: A nation's hope of lasting peace cannot be firmly based upon any race in armaments, but rather upon just relations and honest understanding with all other nations.

"In the light of these principles, the citizens of the United States defined the way they proposed to follow, through the aftermath of war, toward true peace.

"This way was faithful to the spirit that inspires the United Nations: to prohibit strife, to relieve tensions, to banish fears. This way was to control and to reduce armaments. This way was to allow all nations to devote their energies and resources to the great and good tasks of healing the war's wounds, of clothing and feeding and housing the needy, of perfecting a just political life, of enjoying the fruits of their own toil.

"The Soviet Government held a vastly different vision of the future.

"In the world of its design, security was to be found—not in mutual trust and mutual aid—but in force: huge armies, subversion, rule of neighbor nations. The goal was power superiority—at all costs. Security was to be sought by denying it to all others.

"The result has been tragic for the world and, for the Soviet Union, it has also been ironic.

"The amassing of Soviet power alerted free nations to a new danger of aggression. It compelled them in self-defense to spend unprecedented money and energy for armaments. It forced them to develop weapons of war now capable of inflicting instant and terrible punishment upon any aggressor.

"It instilled in the free nations—and let none doubt this—the unshakable conviction that, as long as there persists a threat to freedom, they must, at any cost, remain armed, strong and ready for the risk of war.

"It inspired them—and let none doubt this—to attain a unity of purpose and will beyond the power of propaganda or pressure to break, now or ever.

"There remained, however, one thing essentially unchanged and unaffected by Soviet conduct: this unchanged thing was the readiness of the free world to welcome sincerely any genuine evidence of peaceful purpose enabling all peoples again to resume their common quest for peace. And the free world still holds to that purpose.

"The free nations, most solemnly and repeatedly, have assured the Soviet Union that their firm association has never had any aggressive purpose whatsoever.

"Soviet leaders, however, have seemed to persuade themselves—or tried to persuade their people—otherwise.

"And so it has come to pass that the Soviet Union itself has shared and suffered the very fears it has fostered in the rest of the world.

"This has been the way of life forged by eight years of fear and force.

"What can the world—any nation in it—hope for if no turning is found on this dread road?

"The worst to be feared and the best to be expected can be simply stated.

"The worst is atomic war.

"The best would be this: A life of perpetual fear and tension; a burden of arms draining the wealth and the labor of all peoples; a wasting of strength that defies the American system or the Soviet system or any system to achieve true abundance and happiness for the peoples of this earth.

"Every gun that is made, every warship launched, every rocket fired signifies—in the final sense—a theft from those who hunger and are not fed, those who are cold and are not clothed.

"This world in arms is not spending money alone.

"It is spending the sweat of its laborers, the genius of its scientists, the hopes of its children.

"The cost of one modern heavy bomber is this: A modern brick school in more than 30 cities.

"It is: Two electric power plants, each serving a town of 60,000 population.

"It is: Two fine, fully equipped hospitals.

"It is some 50 miles of concrete pavement.

"We pay for a single fighter plane with a half million bushels of wheat.

"We pay for a single destroyer with new homes that could have housed more than 8000 people.

"This—I repeat—is the best way of life to be found on the road the world has been taking.

"This is not a way of life at all, in any true sense. Under the cloud of threatening war, it is humanity hanging from a cross of iron.

"These plain and cruel truths define the peril and point the hope that come with this spring of 1953.

"This is one of those times in the affairs of nations when the gravest choices must be made—if there is to be a turning toward a just and lasting peace.

"It is a moment that calls upon the governments of the world to speak their intentions with simplicity and with honesty.

"It calls upon them to answer the question that stirs the hearts of all sane men: Is there no other way the world may live?

"The world knows that an era ended with the death of Josef Stalin. The extraordinary 30-year span of his rule saw the Soviet empire expand to reach from the Baltic Sea to the Sea of Japan, finally to dominate 800 million souls.

"The Soviet system shaped by Stalin and his predecessors was born of one world war. It survived with stubborn and often amazing courage a second world war. It has lived to threaten a third.

"Now a new leadership has assumed power in the Soviet Union. Its links to the past, however strong, cannot bind it completely. Its future is, in great part, its own to make.

"This new leadership confronts a free world aroused, as rarely in its history, by the will to stay free.

"The free world knows—out of the bitter wisdom of experience—that vigilance and sacrifice are the price of liberty.

"It knows that the peace and defense of western Europe imperatively demands the unity of purpose and action made possible by the North Atlantic Treaty Organization, embracing a European Defense Community.

"It knows that Western Germany deserves to be a free and equal partner in this community; and that this, for Germany, is the only safe way to full, final unity.

"It knows that aggression in Korea and in southeast Asia are threats to the whole free community to be met only through united action.

"This is the kind of free world which the new Soviet leadership confronts. It is a world that demands and expects the fullest respect of its rights and interests. It is a world that will always accord the same respect to all others.

"So the new Soviet leadership now has a precious opportunity to awaken, with the rest of the world, to a point of peril reached, and to help turn the tide of history.

"Will it do this?

"We do not yet know. Recent statements and gestures of Soviet leaders give some evidence that they may recognize this critical moment.

"We welcome every honest act of peace.

"We care nothing for mere rhetoric.

"We care only for sincerity of peaceful purpose—attested by deeds. The opportunities for such deeds are many. The performance of a great number of them waits upon no complex protocol, but only upon the simple will to do them. Even a few such clear and specific acts—such as the Soviet Union's signature upon an Austrian treaty, or its release of thousands of prisoners still held from World War II—would be impressive signs of sincere intent. They would carry a power of persuasion not to be matched by any amount of oratory.

"This we do know: a world that begins to witness the rebirth of trust among nations can find its way to a peace that is neither partial nor punitive.

"With all who will work in good faith toward such a peace, we are ready—with renewed resolve—to strive to redeem the near-lost hopes of our day.

"The first great step long this way must be the conclusion of an honorable armistice in Korea.

"This means the immediate cessation of hostilities and the prompt initiation of political discussions leading to the holding of free elections in a united Korea.

"It should mean—no less importantly—an end to the direct and indirect attacks upon the security of Indo-China and Malaya. For any armistice in Korea that merely released aggressive armies to attack elsewhere would be a fraud.

"We seek, throughout Asia as throughout the world, a peace that is true and total.

"Out of this can grow a still wider task—the achieving of just political settlements for the other serious and specific issues between the free world and the Soviet Union.

"None of these issues, great or small, is insoluble—given only the will to respect the rights of all nations.

"Again we say: The United States is ready to assume its just part.

"We have already done all within our power to speed conclusion of a treaty with Austria which will free that country from economic exploitation and from occupation by foreign troops.

"We are ready not only to press forward with the present plans for closer unity to the nations of Western Europe but also, upon that foundation, to strive to foster a broader European community, conducive to the free movement of persons, of trade, and of ideas.

"This community would include a free and united Germany, with a government based upon free and secret ballot.

"This free community and the full independence of the East European nations could mean the end of the present unnatural division of Europe.

"As progress in all these areas strengthens world trust, we could proceed concurrently with the next great work—the reduction of the burden of armaments now weighing upon the world. To this end, we would welcome and enter into the most solemn agreements. These could properly include:

"1. The limitation, by absolute numbers or by an agreed international ratio, of the sizes of the military and security forces of all nations;

"2. A commitment by all nations to set an agreed limit upon that proportion or total production of certain strategic materials to be devoted to military purposes;

"3. International control of atomic energy to promote its use for peaceful purposes only, and to insure the prohibition of atomic weapons;

"4. A limitation or prohibition of other categories of weapons of great destructiveness;

"5. The enforcement of all these agreed limitations and prohibitions by adequate safeguards, including a practical system of inspection under the United Nations.

"The details of such disarmament programs are manifestly critical and complex. Neither the United States nor any other nation can properly claim to possess a perfect, immutable formula. But the formula matters less than the faith—the good faith without which no formula can work justly and effectively.

"The fruit of success in all these tasks would present the world with the greatest task—and the greatest opportunity—of all. It is this: The dedication of the energies, the resources, and the imaginations of all peaceful nations to a kind of war. This would be a declared, total war, not upon any human enemy, but upon the brute forces of poverty and need.

"The peace we seek, founded upon a decent trust and cooperative effort among nations, can be fortified—not by weapons of war but by wheat and by cotton; by milk and by wool; by meat and timber and rice.

"These are words that translate into every language on earth.

"These are needs that challenge this world in arms.

"This idea of a just and peaceful world is not new or strange to us. It inspired the people of the United States to initiate the European Recovery Program in 1947. That program was prepared to treat, with equal concern, the needs of eastern and western Europe.

"We are prepared to reaffirm, with the most concrete evidence, our readiness to help build a world in which all peoples can be productive and prosperous.

"This Government is ready to ask its people to join with all nations in devoting a substantial percentage of the savings achieved by disarmament to a fund for world aid and reconstruction. The purposes of this great work would be to help other peoples to develop the undeveloped areas of the world, to stimulate profitable and fair world trade, to assist all peoples to know the blessings of productive freedom.

"The monuments to this new war would be these: Roads and schools, hospitals and homes, food and health.

"We are ready, in short, to dedicate our strength to serving the needs, rather than the fears, of the world.

"I know of nothing I can add to make plainer the sincere purpose of the United States.

"I know of no course, other than that marked by these and similar actions, that can be called a highway of peace.

"I know of only one question upon which progress waits. It is this:

"What is the Soviet Union ready to do?

"Whatever the answer is, let it be plainly spoken.

"Again we say: The hunger for peace is too great, the hour in history too late, for any government to mock men's hopes with mere words and promises and gestures.

"Is the new leadership of the Soviet Union prepared to use its decisive influence in the Communist world—including control of the flow of arms—to bring not merely an expedient truce in Korea but genuine peace in Asia?

"Is it prepared to allow other nations, including those in Eastern Europe, the free choice of their own form of government?

"Is it prepared to act in concert with others upon serious disarmament proposals?

"If not—where then is the concrete evidence of the Soviet Union's concern for peace?

"There is, before all peoples, a precious chance to turn the black tide of events.

"If we failed to strive to seize this chance, the judgment of future ages will be harsh and just.

"If we strive, but fail, and the world remains armed against itself, it at least would need be divided no longer in its clear knowledge of who has condemned human kind to this fate.

"The purpose of the United States, in stating these proposals, is simple.

"These proposals spring—without ulterior motive or political passion—from our calm conviction that the hunger for just peace is in the hearts of all peoples—those of Russia and of China no less than of our own country.

"They conform to our firm faith that God created men to enjoy, not destroy, the fruits of the earth and of their own toil.

"They aspire to this: The lifting, from the backs and from the hearts of men, of their burden of arms and of fears, so that they may find before them a golden age of freedom and of peace.

"Thank you."

SUGGESTED READINGS

I N selecting the titles included in the lists of suggested readings, my sole purpose was to aid the student who might be
interested in learning more about American foreign policy.
The books indicated below include only a small portion of those
which pertain to the period covered by this documentary text;
but it is my opinion that an extensive list probably would dis-
courage rather than furnish the student with an incentive for
further study.

In addition to the volumes listed below, there are several
series, sets, and special works with which the student of American
foreign policy should be familiar. The major government publications are found in the Bibliography, but I would like to emphasize the importance of the *Papers Relating to the Foreign
Relations of the United States,* and the *Department of State
Bulletin.* The former, published annually, contains significant
documents from the files of the State Department. The most
recent volumes published in 1953 cover the year 1935. The
Department of State Bulletin, published weekly, is invaluable
for anyone who desires to keep abreast of current official policy
statements.

Possibly the most useful United Nations publications are
the *Annual Review of United Nations Affairs;* the *United Nations Bulletin,* published twice a month; and the *United Nations
Reporter,* published monthly.

The *Survey of International Affairs,* published for the Royal
Institute of International Affairs, is a set of twenty-seven volumes
which covers the years from 1920 to 1952. Written by Arnold J.
Toynbee, and in more recent years by several other writers, it
is an excellent continuing work. Many of the most important
documents are to be found in the thirteen-volume work, *Documents on American Foreign Relations,* covering the years 1939
to 1951 and published by the World Peace Foundation. The set

is being continued, and the 1952 volume was published by Harper and Bros. for the Council on Foreign Relations. The thirteen volume set of *The Public Papers and Addresses of Franklin D. Roosevelt,* compiled by Samuel I. Rosenman, is invaluable for the student interested in that era.

The *Congressional Record* is indispensable for anyone interested in the influence of the legislative branch of government on foreign policy. The laws enacted by Congress and other materials are found in the *United States Statutes at Large.* Texts of treaties can be found in the various collections listed in the Bibliography of this volume.

Two continuing surveys of recent policy are the Brookings Institution's *Major Problems of United States Foreign Policy,* which began in 1947, and the *United States in World Affairs,* published by Harper and Bros. for the Council on Foreign Relations, and edited by J. C. Campbell and others.

The American Foreign Policy Library series, edited by Sumner Welles and Donald C. McKay, and published by the Harvard University Press, is a useful collection for those interested in the relations between the United States and certain other nations or areas.

Among the most useful textbooks are Thomas A. Bailey's *A Diplomatic History of the American People,* Samuel Flagg Bemis' *A Diplomatic History of the United States,* and Richard W. Van Alstyne's *American Diplomacy in Action.*

CHAPTER I.   *American Expansionism*

CHADWICK, FRENCH E. *The Relations of the United States and Spain: Diplomacy.* New York: Charles Scribner's Sons, 1909.

DENNETT, TYLER. *John Hay: From Poetry to Politics.* New York: Dodd, Mead and Co., 1933.

DENNIS, A. L. P. *Adventures in American Diplomacy, 1896-1906.* New York: E. P. Dutton and Co., 1928.

HOFSTADTER, RICHARD. *Social Darwinism in American Thought, 1860-1915.* Philadelphia: University of Pennsylvania Press, 1945.

LANGER, WILLIAM L. *The Diplomacy of Imperialism, 1890-1902.* New York: Alfred A. Knopf, 1935.

MILLIS, WALTER. *The Martial Spirit.* Boston: Houghton Mifflin Co., 1931.

PRATT, JULIUS. *Expansionists of 1898.* Baltimore: Johns Hopkins Press, 1936.

————. *America's Colonial Experiment.* New York: Prentice-Hall, 1950.

PRINGLE, H. F. *Theodore Roosevelt: A Biography.* New York: Harcourt, Brace and Co., 1931.

THAYER, WILLIAM H. *The Life and Letters of John Hay.* 2 vols. Boston: Houghton Mifflin Co., 1915.

WILKERSON, MARCUS M. *Public Opinion and the Spanish-American War.* Baton Rouge: Louisiana State University Press, 1932.

WISAN, JOSEPH E. *The Cuban Crisis as Reflected in the New York Press, 1895-1898.* New York: Columbia University Press, 1934.

CHAPTER II.   The Far East, 1898-1914

CROLY, HERBERT. *Willard Straight.* New York: The Macmillan Co., 1924.

DENNETT, TYLER. *John Hay: From Poetry to Politics.* New York: Dodd, Mead and Co., 1933.

————. *Roosevelt and the Russo-Japanese War.* Garden City: Doubleday, Doran and Co., 1925.

GRISWOLD, A. WHITNEY. *The Far Eastern Policy of the United States.* New York: Harcourt, Brace and Co., 1938.

JESSUP, PHILIP. *Elihu Root.* New York: Dodd, Mead and Co., 1938.

NEARING, SCOTT, AND FREEMAN, JOSEPH. *Dollar Diplomacy.* New York: B. W. Huebsch and the Viking Press, 1925.

PRINGLE, H. F. *Theodore Roosevelt: A Biography.* New York: Harcourt, Brace and Co., 1931.

TREAT, PAYSON J. *Diplomatic Relations Between the United States and Japan, 1895-1905.* Stanford: Stanford University Press, 1938.

VARG, PAUL. *Open Door Diplomat: The Life of W. W. Rockhill.* Urbana: University of Illinois Press, 1952.

CHAPTER III.   Latin-American Policy, 1898-1914

BEMIS, SAMUEL F. *The Latin American Policy of the United States.* New York: Harcourt, Brace and Co., 1943.

CALLCOTT, WILFRID H. *The Caribbean Policy of the United States, 1890-1920.* Baltimore: The Johns Hopkins Press, 1942.

EISTER, ALLAN W. *The United States and the A.B.C. Powers, 1889-1906.* Dallas: Southern Methodist University Press, 1953.

FITZGIBBON, RUSSELL H. *Cuba and the United States, 1900-1935.* Menasha, Wisc.: George Banta Publishing Co., 1935.

GUGGENHEIM, HARRY F. *The United States and Cuba: A Study in International Relations.* New York: The Macmillan Co., 1934.

HILL, HOWARD C. *Roosevelt and the Caribbean.* Chicago: University of Chicago Press, 1927.

JONES, CHESTER LLOYD. *The Caribbean Since 1900.* New York: Prentice-Hall, 1936.

McCAIN, W. D. *The United States and the Republic of Panama.* Durham: Duke University Press, 1937.

MUNRO, DANA G. *The Five Republics of Central America.* New York: Oxford University Press, 1918.

PERKINS, DEXTER. *Hands Off: A History of the Monroe Doctrine.* Boston: Little, Brown and Co., 1942.

———. *The United States and the Caribbean. (The American Foreign Policy Library,* ed. SUMNER WELLES) Cambridge: Harvard University Press, 1947.

RIPPY, J. FRED. *Latin America in World Affairs.* New York: F. S. Crofts and Co., 1938.

———. *The Caribbean Danger Zone.* New York: G. P. Putnam's Sons, 1940.

STUART, GRAHAM. *Latin America and the United States.* New York: The Century Co., 1922.

CHAPTER IV. Wilson's Far Eastern Policy

BAKER, RAY S. *Woodrow Wilson and World Settlement.* 3 vols. Garden City: Doubleday, Page and Co., 1922.

BEMIS, SAMUEL F. (ed.). *American Secretaries of State and their Diplomacy.* 10 vols. New York: Alfred A. Knopf, 1927-29.

FIFIELD, RUSSELL H. *Woodrow Wilson and the Far East.* New York: Thomas Y. Crowell Co., 1953.

GRISWOLD, A. WHITNEY. *The Far Eastern Policy of the United States.* New York: Harcourt, Brace and Co., 1938.

LANSING, ROBERT. *War Memoirs of Robert Lansing, Secretary of State.* Indianapolis: Bobbs, Merrill Co., 1935.

MACNAIR, HARLEY F., AND LACH, DONALD F. *Modern Far Eastern International Relations.* New York: D. Van Nostrand Co., 1950.

REINSCH, PAUL S. *An American Diplomat in China.* Garden City, N. Y.: Doubleday, Page and Co., 1922.

TAKEUCHI, TATSUJI. *War and Diplomacy in the Japanese Empire.* Garden City, N. Y.: Doubleday, Doran and Co., 1935.

WHEELER, WILLIAM R. *China and the World War.* New York: The Macmillan Co., 1919.

CHAPTER V. Latin-American Policy of Woodrow Wilson

See readings for Chapter III in addition to following:

CALLAHAN, JAMES M. *American Foreign Policy in Mexican Relations.* New York: The Macmillan Co., 1932.

CUMBERLAND, C. C. *Mexican Revolution.* Austin: University of Texas Press, 1952.

MILLSPAUGH, A. C. *Haiti under American Control, 1915-1930.* Boston: World Peace Foundation, 1931.

RIPPY, J. FRED. *The United States and Mexico.* New York: F. S. Crofts and Co., 1931.

STIMSON, HENRY L. *American Policy in Nicaragua.* New York: Charles Scribner's Sons, 1927.

WELLES, SUMNER. *Naboth's Vineyard: The Dominican Republic, 1844-1924.* 2 vols. New York: Harcourt, Brace and Co., 1928.
WILLIAMS, BENJAMIN H. *Economic Foreign Policy of the United States.* New York: McGraw-Hill Book Co., 1929.

CHAPTER VI.   *Neutrality, 1914-1917*

BRYAN, WILLIAM JENNINGS, AND BRYAN, M. E. *The Memoirs of William Jennings Bryan.* Philadelphia: John C. Winston Co., 1925.
GUICHARD, LOUIS. *The Naval Blockade, 1914-1918.* Edited and translated by Christopher R. Turner. New York: D. Appleton-Century Co., 1930.
MILLIS, WALTER. *Road to War: America, 1914-1917.* Boston: Houghton Mifflin Co., 1935.
MORRISSEY, ALICE M. *The American Defense of Neutral Rights, 1914-1917.* Cambridge: Harvard University Press, 1939.
NOTTER, HARLEY. *The Origins of the Foreign Policy of Woodrow Wilson.* Baltimore: The Johns Hopkins Press, 1937.
PAXSON, FREDERIC L. *American Democracy and the World War: Pre-War Years, 1913-1917.* Boston: Houghton Mifflin Co., 1936.
PETERSON, HORACE C. *Propaganda for War.* Norman: University of Oklahoma Press, 1939.
SEYMOUR, CHARLES. *American Neutrality, 1914-1917.* New Haven: Yale University Press, 1935.
SPENCER, SAMUEL R. *Decision for War, 1917.* Rindge, N. H.: Richard R. Smith Publisher, 1953.
TANSILL, CHARLES C. *America Goes to War.* Boston: Little, Brown and Co., 1938.

CHAPTER VII.   *The First World War*

See readings for Chapter VI in addition to following:
GERARD, JAMES W. *My Four Years in Germany.* New York: Grossett and Dunlap, 1918.
GRAVES, WILLIAM S. *America's Siberian Adventure, 1918-1920.* New York: Peter Smith, 1931.
HENDRICK, BURTON J. *The Life and Letters of Walter Hines Page.* 3 vols. Boston: Houghton Mifflin Co., 1925.
LANSING, ROBERT. *War Memoirs.* Indianapolis: Bobbs-Merrill Co., 1935.
PAXSON, FREDERIC L. *America at War, 1917-1918.* Boston: Houghton Mifflin Co., 1939.
SCHUMAN, FREDERICK L. *American Policy Toward Russia Since 1917.* New York: International Publishers Co., 1928.
SEYMOUR, CHARLES (arr.). *Intimate Papers of Colonel House.* 4 vols. Boston: Houghton Mifflin Co., 1926-28.
————. *American Diplomacy during the World War.* Baltimore: The Johns Hopkins Press, 1934.

SULLIVAN, MARK. *Our Times, 1900-1925.* 6 vols. New York: Charles Scribner's Sons, 1936.

STRAKHOVSKY, L. I. *The Origins of American Intervention in North Russia, 1918.* Princeton: Princeton University Press, 1937.

CHAPTER VIII. Liquidation of World War I

BAILEY, THOMAS A. *Woodrow Wilson and the Great Betrayal.* New York: The Macmillan Co., 1945.

————. *Woodrow Wilson and the Lost Peace.* New York: The Macmillan Co., 1944.

BAKER, RAY S. *Woodrow Wilson and World Settlement.* 3 vols. Garden City: Doubleday, Page and Co., 1922.

BIRDSALL, PAUL. *Versailles Twenty Years After.* New York: Reynal and Hitchcock, 1941.

BUELL, RAYMOND L. *The Washington Conference.* New York: D. Appleton and Co., 1922.

FLEMING, D. F. *The United States and the League of Nations, 1918-1920.* New York: G. P. Putnam's Sons, 1932.

HOAG, C. L. *Preface to Preparedness: The Washington Disarmament Conference and Public Opinion.* Washington: American Council on Public Affairs, 1941.

HOLT, W. STULL. *Treaties Defeated by the Senate.* Baltimore: The Johns Hopkins Press, 1933.

HOUSE, E. M., AND SEYMOUR, CHARLES. *What Really Happened at Paris—The Story of the Peace Conference, 1918-1919.* New York: Charles Scribner's Sons, 1921.

ICHIHASHI, YAMATO. *The Washington Conference and After.* Stanford: Stanford University Press, 1928.

LANSING, ROBERT. *The Peace Negotiations: A Personal Narrative.* Boston: Houghton Mifflin Co., 1921.

LLOYD GEORGE, DAVID. *Memoirs of the Peace Conference.* 2 vols. New Haven: Yale University Press, 1939.

LODGE, HENRY CABOT. *The Senate and the League of Nations.* New York: Charles Scribner's Sons, 1925.

SHOTWELL, JAMES T. *At the Paris Peace Conference.* New York: The Macmillan Co., 1938.

CHAPTER IX. Postwar Diplomacy

FLEMING, D. F. *The United States and World Organization, 1920-1933.* New York: Columbia University Press, 1938.

FUESS, C. M. *Calvin Coolidge: the Man from Vermont.* Boston: Little, Brown and Co., 1940.

HOOVER, HERBERT. *The Memoirs of Herbert Hoover.* 2 vols. New York: The Macmillan Co., 1951-52.

JOHNSON, C. O. *Borah of Idaho*. New York: Longmans, Green and Co., 1936.

MILLER, DAVID HUNTER. *The Peace Pact of Paris*. New York: G. P. Putnam's Sons, 1928.

MOULTON, HAROLD G., AND PASVOLSKY, LEO. *War Debts and World Prosperity*. New York: Century Co., 1932.

MYERS, WILLIAM S., AND NEWTON, W. H. *The Hoover Administration: A Documented Narrative*. New York: Charles Scribner's Sons, 1936.

SHOTWELL, JAMES T. *War as an Instrument of National Policy and its Renunciation in the Pact of Paris*. New York: Harcourt, Brace and Co., 1929.

SIMONDS, FRANK H. *American Foreign Policy in the Post-War Years*. Baltimore: The Johns Hopkins Press, 1935.

WILBUR, RAY L., AND HYDE, A. M. *The Hoover Policies*. New York: Charles Scribner's Sons, 1937.

WILLIAMS, BENJAMIN H. *Economic Foreign Policy of the United States*. New York: McGraw-Hill Book Co., 1929.

CHAPTER X. America's Hegemony in the Western World

See readings for Chapters III and V in addition to following:

DE CONDE, ALEXANDER. *Herbert Hoover's Latin American Policy*. Stanford: Stanford University Press, 1951.

DUNN, FREDERICK S. *The Diplomatic Protection of Americans in Mexico*. New York: Columbia University Press, 1933.

FITZGIBBON, RUSSELL H. *Cuba and the United States, 1900-1935*. Menasha, Wisc.: George Banta Publishing Co., 1935.

HILL, ROSCOE R. *Fiscal Intervention in Nicaragua*. Washington: The Author, 1933.

STIMSON, HENRY L. *American Policy in Nicaragua*. New York: Charles Scribner's Sons, 1927.

STUART, GRAHAM. *Latin America and the United States*. New York: D. Appleton-Century Co., 1938.

CHAPTER XI. Isolationism

BEARD, CHARLES A. *American Foreign Policy in the Making, 1932-1940*. New Haven: Yale University Press, 1946.

BEARD, CHARLES A., AND MARY R. *America in Midpassage*. New York: The Macmillan Co., 1939.

BORCHARD, EDWIN M., AND LAGE, W. P. *Neutrality for the United States* New Haven: Yale University Press, 1940.

COLE, WAYNE S. *America First: The Battle Against Intervention*. Madison: University of Wisconsin Press, 1953.

FENWICK, CHARLES G. *American Neutrality: Trial and Failure*. New York: New York University Press, 1940.

CHAPTER XII. *"The Gathering Storm"*

DAVIES, JOSEPH E. *Mission to Moscow.* New York: Simon and Schuster, 1941.

EARLE, EDWARD MEAD. *Against This Torrent.* Princeton: Princeton University Press, 1941.

HENDERSON, SIR NEVILE M. *Failure of a Mission: Berlin, 1937-1939.* New York: G. P. Putnam's Sons, 1940.

LANGER, WILLIAM L., AND GLEASON, S. EVERETT. *The Challenge to Isolation, 1937-1940.* New York: Harper and Bros., 1952.

RAUCH, BASIL. *Roosevelt: From Munich to Pearl Harbor.* New York: Creative Age Press, 1950.

SPYKMAN, NICHOLAS J. *America's Strategy in World Politics.* New York: Harcourt, Brace and Co., 1942.

TOYNBEE, ARNOLD J., AND ASHTON-GWATKIN, FRANK I. *Survey of International Affairs, 1939-1946, The World in March 1939.* London: Oxford University Press, 1952.

VAN ALSTYNE, RICHARD W. *American Crisis Diplomacy.* Stanford: Stanford University Press, 1952.

WHEELER-BENNETT, JOHN W. *Munich: Prologue to Tragedy.* New York: Duell, Sloan and Pearce, 1948.

CHAPTER XIII. *Poland to Pearl Harbor*

BEARD, CHARLES A. *President Roosevelt and the Coming of the War, 1941.* New Haven: Yale University Press, 1941.

BELOFF, MAX. *The Foreign Policy of Soviet Russia from 1929 to 1941.* 2 vols. New York: Oxford University Press, 1947-1949.

CARR, EDWARD HALLETT. *German-Soviet Relations Between the Two World Wars, 1919-1939.* Baltimore: The Johns Hopkins Press, 1951.

HULL, CORDELL. *The Memoirs of Cordell Hull.* 2 vols. New York: The Macmillan Co., 1948.

LANGER, WILLIAM L. *Our Vichy Gamble.* New York: Alfred A. Knopf, 1947.

LANGER, WILLIAM L., AND GLEASON, S. EVERETT. *The Undeclared War, 1940-1941.* New York: Harper and Bros., 1953.

RAUCH, BASIL. *Roosevelt: From Munich to Pearl Harbor.* New York: Creative Age Press, 1950.

SHERWOOD, ROBERT E. *Roosevelt and Hopkins: An Intimate History.* New York: Harper and Bros., 1948.

SONTAG, RAYMOND J., AND BEDDIE, JAMES S. (eds.). *Nazi-Soviet Relations 1939-1941.* ("Publications of the United States Department of State," No. 3023.) Washington: Government Printing Office, 1948.

WILLIAMS, WILLIAM A. *American Russian Relations: 1781-1947.* New York: Rinehart and Co., 1952.

CHAPTER XIV. *The United States and the Far East, 1931-1941*

BISSON, T. A. *America's Far Eastern Policy*. New York: The Macmillan Co., 1945.

FEIS, HERBERT. *The Road to Pearl Harbor*. Princeton: Princeton University Press, 1950.

GREW, JOSEPH. *Ten Years in Japan 1931-1941*. New York: Simon and Schuster, 1944.

——. *The Turbulent Era, A Diplomatic Record of Forty Years, 1904-1945*. 2 vols. Boston: Houghton Mifflin Co., 1952.

HORNBECK, STANLEY K. *The United States and the Far East*. Boston: World Peace Foundation, 1942.

JONES, F. C. *Manchuria Since 1931*. New York: Oxford University Press, 1949.

LEVI, WARNER. *Modern China's Foreign Policy*. Minneapolis: University of Minnesota Press, 1953.

MACNAIR, HARLEY F., AND LACH, DONALD F. *Modern Far Eastern International Relations*. New York: D. Van Nostrand Co., 1950.

MILLIS, WALTER. *This is Pearl! The United States and Japan—1941*. New York: William Morrow and Co., 1947.

MORGENSTERN, GEORGE. *Pearl Harbor: The Story of the Secret War*. New York: Devin-Adair Co., 1947.

MORISON, SAMUEL E. *The Rising Sun in the Pacific, 1931-April, 1942*. Boston: Little, Brown and Co., 1948.

QUIGLEY, HAROLD S. *Far Eastern War, 1937-1941*. Boston: World Peace Foundation, 1942.

TANSILL, CHARLES C. *Back Door to War*. Chicago: Henry Regnery Co., 1952.

TOMPKINS, PAULINE. *American-Russian Relations in the Far East*. New York: The Macmillan Co., 1949.

CHAPTER XV. *Latin-American Policy, 1933-1954*

BEALS, CARLTON, AND OTHERS. *What the South Americans Think of Us*. New York: Medill McBride Co., 1945.

BLANKSTEN, GEORGE I. *Peron's Argentina*. Chicago: University of Chicago Press, 1953.

DANIELS, JOSEPHUS. *Shirt Sleeve Diplomat*. Chapel Hill: University of North Carolina Press, 1947.

DUGGAN, LAURENCE. *The Americas: The Search for Hemispheric Security*. New York: Henry Holt and Co., 1949.

GUERRANT, EDWARD O. *Roosevelt's Good Neighbor Policy*. Albuquerque: University of New Mexico Press, 1950.

PERKINS, DEXTER. *The United States and the Caribbean. (The American Foreign Policy Library,* ed. SUMNER WELLES) Cambridge: Harvard University Press, 1947.

QUINTANILLA, LUIS. *A Latin American Speaks.* New York: The Macmillan Co., 1943.

RENNIE, YSABEL. *The Argentine Republic.* New York: The Macmillan Co., 1945.

RIPPY, J. FRED. *Latin America in World Politics.* New York: F. S. Crofts and Co., 1938.

SMITH, O. E. *Yankee Diplomacy: U. S. Intervention in Argentina.* Dallas: Southern Methodist University Press, 1953.

WELLES, SUMNER. *The Time for Decision.* New York: Harper and Bros., 1944.

WHITAKER, ARTHUR P. *The United States and South America: The Northern Republics. (The American Foreign Policy Library,* ed. SUMNER WELLES) Cambridge: Harvard University Press, 1948.

CHAPTER XVI. *World War II*

BARGHOORN, FREDERICK C. *The Soviet Image of the United States: A Study in Distortion.* New York: Harcourt, Brace and Co., 1950.

DALLIN, DAVID J. *The Big Three: The United States-Britain and Russia.* New Haven: Yale University Press, 1945.

DEANE, JOHN R. *The Strange Alliance.* New York: Viking Press, 1946.

DULLES, FOSTER R. *The Road to Tehran.* Princeton: Princeton University Press, 1944.

EISENHOWER, DWIGHT D. *Eisenhower's Own Story of the War.* New York: Arco Publishing Co., 1946.

FEIS, HERBERT. *The China Tangle.* Princeton: Princeton University Press, 1953.

————. *The Spanish Story.* New York: Alfred A. Knopf, 1948.

HAYES, CARLTON J. H. *Wartime Mission to Spain, 1942-1945.* New York: The Macmillan Co., 1945.

HULL, CORDELL. *The Memoirs of Cordell Hull.* 2 vols. New York: The Macmillan Co., 1948.

KENNAN, GEORGE F. *American Diplomacy, 1900-1950.* Chicago: University of Chicago Press, 1951.

KING, ERNEST J., AND WHITEHILL, WALTER MUIR. *Fleet Admiral King: A Naval Record.* New York: W. W. Norton and Co., 1952.

LEAHY, WILLIAM D. *I Was There.* New York: McGraw-Hill Book Co., 1950.

LOCHNER, LOUIS (ed.). *The Goebbels Diaries 1942-1943.* Garden City: Doubleday and Co., 1948.

MATLOFF, MAURICE, AND SNELL, EDWIN M. *Strategic Planning for Coalition Warfare.* Washington: Government Printing Office, 1953.

MILLIS, WALTER (ed.). *The Forrestal Diaries.* New York: Viking Press, 1951.

SHERWOOD, ROBERT E. *Roosevelt and Hopkins: An Intimate History.* New York: Harper and Bros., 1948.

STETTINIUS, EDWARD R., JR. *Roosevelt and the Russians: The Yalta Conference.* Garden City: Doubleday and Co., 1949.

STILWELL, JOSEPH W., AND WHITE, THEODORE H. (ed.). *The Stilwell Papers.* New York: William Sloane Associates, 1948.
STIMSON, HENRY L., AND BUNDY, McGEORGE. *On Active Service in Peace and War.* New York: Harper and Bros., 1948.
WELLES, SUMNER. *Where Are We Heading.* New York: Harper and Bros., 1946.

CHAPTER XVII. *Postwar Planning*

CHASE, EUGENE P. *The United Nations in Action.* New York: McGraw-Hill Book Co., 1950.
EAGLETON, CLYDE. *International Government.* New York: Ronald Press, 1948.
EVATT, HERBERT V. *The United Nations.* Cambridge: Harvard University Press, 1948.
GOODRICH, LELAND M., AND HAMBRO, EDVARD. *Charter of the United Nations: Commentary and Documents.* Boston: World Peace Foundation, 1949.
Postwar Foreign Policy Preparation, 1939-1945. ("Publications of the United States Department of State," No. 3580.) Washington: Government Printing Office, 1950.

CHAPTER XVIII. *Postwar Policy: Cooperation and the "Cold War"*

BAILEY, THOMAS A. *America Faces Russia: Russian-American Relations from Early Times to Our Day.* Ithaca, N. Y.: Cornell University Press, 1950.
BELOFF, MAX. *Soviet Policy in the Far East, 1944-1951.* New York: Oxford University Press, 1953.
BUNDY, McGEORGE (ed.). *The Pattern of Responsibility: From the Record of Dean Acheson.* Boston: Houghton Mifflin Co., 1952.
BYRNES, JAMES. *Speaking Frankly.* New York: Harper and Bros., 1947.
CLAY, LUCIUS D. *Decision in Germany.* Garden City: Doubleday and Co., 1950.
FAIRBANK, JOHN K. *The United States and China. (The American Foreign Policy Library,* ed. SUMNER WELLES) Cambridge: Harvard University Press, 1948.
FELLER, A. H. *United Nations and World Community.* Boston: Little, Brown and Co., 1952.
FRYE, RICHARD N. (ed.). *The Near East and the Great Powers.* Cambridge: Harvard University Press, 1951.
HARRIS, SEYMOUR E. *The European Recovery Program.* Cambridge: Harvard University Press, 1948.
KOUSOULAS, DIMITRIOS G. *The Prince of Freedom: Greece in World Affairs, 1939-1953.* Syracuse: Syracuse University Press, 1953.

LANE, ARTHUR BLISS. *I Saw Poland Betrayed.* Indianapolis: Bobbs-Merrill Co., 1948.

LATOURETTE, KENNETH SCOTT. *The American Record in the Far East, 1945-1951.* New York: The Macmillan Co., 1952.

LIPPMANN, WALTER. *The Cold War.* New York: Harper and Bros., 1947.

McCLOY, JOHN L. *The Challenge to American Foreign Policy.* Cambridge: Harvard University Press, 1953.

REISCHAUER, EDWIN O. *The United States and Japan. (The American Foreign Policy Library,* ed. SUMNER WELLES) Cambridge: Harvard University Press, 1950.

SCHWARTZ, BENJAMIN I. *Chinese Communism and the Rise of Mao.* Cambridge: Harvard University Press, 1951.

SETON-WATSON, HUGH. *From Lenin to Malenkov: The History of World Communism.* New York: Frederick A. Praeger, 1953.

SHARP, SAMUEL L. *Poland: White Eagle on a Red Field.* Cambridge: Harvard University Press, 1953.

SMITH, WALTER BEDELL. *My Three Years in Moscow.* Philadelphia: J. B. Lippincott Co., 1950.

United States Relations with China with Special Reference to the Period 1944-1949. ("Publications of the United States Department of State," Far Eastern Series 30) Washington: Government Printing Office, 1949.

VANDENBERG, ARTHUR H., JR. (ed.). *The Private Papers of Senator Vandenberg.* Boston: Houghton Mifflin Co., 1952.

VINACKE, HAROLD M. *The United States and the Far East, 1945-1951.* Stanford: Stanford University Press, 1952.

BIBLIOGRAPHY

Government Publications

(Washington, D.C.: U.S. Government Printing Office)

A Decade of American Foreign Policy, Basic Documents, 1941-49. 81st Congress, 1st Session, Senate Document No. 123. (1950).

Congressional Record. 1874—.

Compilation of Treaties in Force, 1904. (1904).

DEPARTMENT OF COMMERCE. Hal B. Lary: *The United States in the World Economy.* Economic Series No. 23. (1943).

DEPARTMENT OF STATE. *American Policy Toward China.* Far Eastern Series 43. (1951).

——. *A Background Summary, Mutual Defense of the West.* (June, 1950).

——. J. Rueben Clark: *Memorandum on the Monroe Doctrine.* Publication 37. (1930).

——. *Charter of the United Nations.* Publication 2353. International Organization and Conference Series III.

——. *Consultation Among the American Republics with Respect to the Argentine Situation.* Inter-American Series 29. (1946).

——. *Documents on German Foreign Policy, 1918-1945.* Series D (1937-1945). 2 vols. (1949).

——. *Draft Trusteeship Agreement for the Japanese Islands.* Far Eastern Series 20. (1947).

——. Cordell Hull: *The Moscow Conference.* Publication 2027. (1943).

——. *Inter-American Treaty of Reciprocal Assistance.* Treaty and other International Act Series 1838. (1949).

——. *The International Control of Atomic Energy.* Publication 2702.

——. *Ninth International Conference of American States.* Publication 3263. (1948).

——. *North Atlantic Treaty.* General Foreign Policy Series 8. (1949).

——. *Peace and War, United States Foreign Policy, 1931-1941.* (1943).

——. *Report of the Delegate of the United States of America to the Meeting of the Foreign Ministers of the American Republics.* Conference Series 44. (1940).

——. *Report of the Delegation of the United States of America to the Eighth International Conference of American States.* Conference Series No. 50. (1941).

———. *Restatement of U.S. Policy on Germany.* European Series 13.
(1946).

———. *Second Meeting of the Ministers of Foreign Affairs of the American Republics.* Conference Series 48. (1941).

———. *Treaty of Peace with Roumania.* Treaty and other International Act Series 1649. (1947).

———. *United States Policy in the Korean Crisis.* Far Eastern Series 34. (1950).

———. *United States Relations with China, with Special Reference to the Period 1944-1949.* (1949).

———. Sumner Welles: *The Accomplishments of the Inter-American Conference for the Maintenance of Peace.* Conference Series No. 26. (1937).

MALLOY, WILLIAM M. (comp.). *Treaties, Conventions, International Acts, Protocols and Agreements between the United States and other Powers, 1776-1909.* 2 vols. (1910).

Papers Relating to the Foreign Relations of the United States. (1862——). No volume issued in 1869.

Treaties, Conventions, International Acts, Protocols, and Agreements between the United States of America and other Powers, 1776-1937. 4 vols. (1910-1938).

United States Statutes at Large. (1875——).

Other Publications

BOWERS, CLAUDE G. *Beveridge and the Progressive Era.* Boston: Houghton Mifflin Co., 1932.

CROLY, HERBERT. *Willard Straight.* New York: The Macmillan Co., 1924.

JONES, S. SHEPARD, AND MYERS, DENYS P. (eds.). *Documents on American Foreign Relations.* 10 vols. to 1948. Boston: World Peace Foundation, 1939——.

ROSENMAN, SAMUEL I. (comp.). *The Public Papers and Addresses of Franklin D. Roosevelt.* 13 vols. New York: Random House, Vols. 1-5; The Macmillan Co., Vols. 6-9; Harper and Bros., Vols. 10-13, 1938-1950.

Selections from the Correspondence of Theodore Roosevelt and Henry Cabot Lodge, 1884-1918. 2 vols. New York: Charles Scribner's Sons, 1925.

SHERWOOD, ROBERT E. *Roosevelt and Hopkins: An Intimate History.* New York: Harper and Bros., 1948.

STILWELL, JOSEPH H., AND WHITE, THEODORE H. (ed.). *The Stilwell Papers.* New York: W. Sloane Associates, 1948.

STIMSON, HENRY L., AND BUNDY, McGEORGE. *On Active Service in Peace and War.* New York: Harper and Bros., 1948.

STRONG, JOSIAH. *The New Era or the Coming Kingdom.* New York: The Baker and Taylor Co., 1893.

Periodicals

ACHESON, DEAN. "Crisis in Asia, An Examination of U.S. Policy," *Department of State Bulletin,* XXII (January 23, 1950), pp. 111-18.
————. "A Review of U.S. Brazilian Relations," *Department of State Bulletin,* XXVII (July 14, 1952), pp. 47-51.
AN AMERICAN DIPLOMAT. "Our 'Dollar Diplomacy' and Secretary Knox," *Harper's Weekly,* LIV (April 23, 1910), p. 8.
LINDBERGH, CHARLES A. "An Appeal for Peace," *Vital Speeches,* VI (August 15, 1940), pp. 644-46.
LIPPMANN, WALTER. "Neutrality: The Immediate Problem," *Vital Speeches,* II (January 27, 1936), pp. 262-63.
MACLEISH, ARCHIBALD. "United States—Soviet Relations," *Department of State Bulletin,* XII (May 27, 1945), pp. 950-52.
MAHAN, A. T. "The Isthmus and Sea Power," *The Atlantic Monthly,* LXXII (October, 1893), pp. 459-72.
RUSK, DEAN. "The Stake of Business in American Foreign Policy," *Department of State Bulletin,* XXI (October 24, 1949), pp. 630-33.
STIMSON, HENRY L. "The Challenge to Americans," *Foreign Affairs,* 26 (October, 1947), pp. 5-14.
X. "The Sources of Soviet Conduct," *Foreign Affairs,* 25 (July, 1947), pp. 566-82.

INDEX

DATE DUE

DATE DUE			
DEC 1 2 '67			
MAY 3 0 7			
H 3			
OCT 22 '85			
OCT 22 '85			
GAYLORD			PRINTED IN U.S.A.